Marketplace Lending, Financial Analysis, and the Future of Credit

Marketplace Lending, Financial Analysis, and the Future of Credit

Integration, Profitability and Risk Management

IOANNIS AKKIZIDIS
MANUEL STAGARS

WILEY

To the innovators shaping the future of credit

Contents

Preface   xvii

Acknowledgments   xix

About the Authors   xxi

About the Website   xxiii

Introduction   1
    I.1   Who is This Book For?   2
    I.2   What is FinTech?   2
          I.2.1   Distinction between Financial Technology Innovation and
                 Financial Innovation   3
    I.3   Why Does This Book Focus on Online Lending?   4
    I.4   The Hybrid Financial Sector: The Opportunity to Build a Healthier
          Financial System   5

PART ONE

FinTech and the Online Lending Landscape—Where Are We Now?   11

CHAPTER 1

Introduction to the Business Models in Financial Technology   15
    1.1   Innovation Themes in FinTech   15
          1.1.1   Online lending   15
          1.1.2   Crowdfunding and crowdinvesting   17
          1.1.3   Transactions and payments   17
          1.1.4   Personal Financial Management   17
          1.1.5   Digital currency and cryptocurrency   18
          1.1.6   Mobile point of sale (mPOS)   18
          1.1.7   Online financial advisory   18
          1.1.8   Mobile-first banks   19
          1.1.9   A dynamic and fragmented space   19

1.2	The Promises and Pitfalls of FinTech Business Models	20
	1.2.1 Streamlining the user experience (UX) and digital integration	21
	1.2.2 Setting an industry standard that the financial industry failed to get off the ground	21
	1.2.3 Using someone else's network while only paying marginal cost	21
	1.2.4 Providing a worse service to customers at a lower price	21
1.3	The Pitfalls	22
	1.3.1 Overestimating the ability of data science to deal with concentration and adverse selection	22
	1.3.2 Overestimating the value of Big Data in transactions	23
	1.3.3 Overestimating people's willingness to trust a FinTech company instead of another middleman	23
	1.3.4 Overestimating the regulators' willingness to pardon a FinTech company flouting the rules	23
1.4	Why is Financial Technology Innovation Important?	23
1.5	Challenges and Roadblocks for FinTech Companies	24
	1.5.1 Lack of a human interface	24
	1.5.2 The need for banking licenses	25
	1.5.3 Concerns over privacy	26
1.6	FinTech is a Long-Term Play	26
1.7	Concluding Remarks	27

CHAPTER 2
How Does Online Lending Work? An Overview with a Focus on Marketplace Lending   **29**

2.1	Reliance on Technology and Data	29
2.2	How Do Online Lenders Differ From Banks?	30
2.3	Types of Online Lenders	31
	2.3.1 Marketplace lending platforms	31
	2.3.2 Online balance sheet lenders	34
	2.3.3 Lender-agnostic marketplaces	35
2.4	Some Background on Peer-to-Peer Networks	36
	2.4.1 Disintermediation or re-intermediation?	38
	2.4.2 Infomediaries, intermediary-oriented marketplaces, and the information value chain	39
2.5	The Business Model of Marketplace Lending Platforms	40
2.6	Onboarding Process	41
	2.6.1 Borrower onboarding	41
	2.6.2 Lender onboarding	43
2.7	Comparing Marketplace Loans with Bank Credit or Credit Card Debt	44
	2.7.1 How do marketplace loans differ from bank credit?	45
	2.7.2 How do marketplace loans differ from credit cards?	46
2.8	Who Are the Alternative Borrowers?	47
2.9	Who Are Investors in Marketplace Loans?	48
2.10	Underwriting and Credit Scoring	48
2.11	Regulation	49
	2.11.1 Transparency and disclosure	50
	2.11.2 Standardization of oversight and monitoring	50

2.12   The Response of Banks to Online Lending   51
2.13   Concluding Remarks   52

CHAPTER 3
What Made the Rise of Online Lending Possible?   **57**
3.1   Technological Factors   57
      3.1.1   Cheap and ubiquitous computing power, coupled with a revolution
              in Big Data and analytics   57
      3.1.2   Faster technology adoption   58
      3.1.3   Internet proliferation and network effects   58
      3.1.4   The boom in mobile screens   60
3.2   Social Factors   62
      3.2.1   Digital connectedness and friendships   62
      3.2.2   Impatience with the know-your-customer process   63
      3.2.3   Sentiment against the established financial sector   63
3.3   Structural Factors   63
      3.3.1   Stricter banking regulation   64
      3.3.2   Disappearance of smaller banks has decreased access to credit for
              consumers and SMEs   64
      3.3.3   Low interest rate environment   65
3.4   The Perfect Storm   65
      3.4.1   From unbundling to fragmentation and back   66
3.5   A Divergence of Trends   66
3.6   Concluding Remarks   67

CHAPTER 4
Why FinTech Lives Outside of Banks   **69**
4.1   The Technology Mudslide Hypothesis: Sustaining Innovation vs.
      Disruptive Innovation   70
      4.1.1   Small unproven markets with low-margin products   72
      4.1.2   The need for discovery-driven planning   73
4.2   Will Banks Notice the Next FinTech Breakthrough?   73
      4.2.1   Incentive misalignment between the short term and the long term 74
      4.2.2   Forcing banks to collaborate with online lenders   75
      4.2.3   Innovating in-house vs. buying innovation   75
4.3   Why Do Banks Have Difficulty in Innovating?   76
      4.3.1   Underinvestment in core competencies   77
      4.3.2   Imprisoned resources   77
      4.3.3   Bounded innovation   77
      4.3.4   Performers vs. producers   78
      4.3.5   Divergence between core competencies of banks with customer
              needs   78
4.4   Developing Core Competence in Financial Technology Innovation   79
      4.4.1   The trap of marginal thinking   80
      4.4.2   The way forward   80
4.5   Concluding Remarks   81

PART TWO

The Status Quo of Analytics in the Financial Industry—The Perspective of Banks   **83**
P2.1   Banking is Innovation   84
P2.2   Banking Goes Mobile   84
P2.3   Banks Are Far From Dead   85
P2.4   How to Read This Part of the Book   85
P2.5   What We Discuss in This Part   86

CHAPTER 5
Financial Contracts   **89**
5.1   Contract Elements   89
5.2   Time in Financial Contracts   90
5.3   Contract Mechanisms Producing Financial Events   92
       5.3.1   Principal patterns   94
       5.3.2   Interest patterns   99
       5.3.3   Accrual interest patterns   101
       5.3.4   Credit enhancements patterns   102
       5.3.5   Behavior patterns   103
       5.3.6   Other patterns   104
       5.3.7   Example of financial events   104
5.4   Concluding Remarks   106

CHAPTER 6
Markets   **107**
6.1   Real-world and Risk-neutral Expectations of Markets   108
6.2   Economic Scenarios Based on Real-world Probabilities   109
6.3   The Risk-neutral Expectations   110
       6.3.1   Yield curves   110
       6.3.2   Forward rates and prices   111
6.4   Beyond Market Risk-Free Rates   113
       6.4.1   Credit discount spreads based on risk-neutral default probabilities   114
       6.4.2   Liquidity spreads   115
6.5   Discounting Cash Flows   116
6.6   Considering Market Elements in P2P Finance   117
6.7   Concluding Remarks   118

CHAPTER 7
Counterparties   **121**
7.1   Types and Roles of Counterparties   121
7.2   Descriptive Characteristics   123
7.3   Default Probability   124
       7.3.1   Structural models   125
       7.3.2   Intensity models   127
       7.3.3   Real-world and risk-neutral default probabilities   128
7.4   Credit Ratings   129

7.5   Credit Spreads Based on Real-world Probabilities   130
7.6   Link of Counterparties via Markets   131
    7.6.1   Allocating obligor to its own specific risk   133
    7.6.2   Allocating obligor to specific market   134
    7.6.3   Apportioning obligors across several markets   134
    7.6.4   Allocating several obligors to a single market   135
    7.6.5   Allocating obligors to several correlated markets 135
7.7   Concluding Remarks   137

CHAPTER 8
Behavior Risk   **139**

8.1   Prepayments   140
8.2   Draw-downs/Remaining Principal/Facilities and Credit Lines 141
8.3   Withdrawals   143
8.4   Selling   143
8.5   Default and Downgrading   144
8.6   Use at Default   145
8.7   Recoveries   146
8.8   Concluding Remarks   147

CHAPTER 9
Credit Exposures   **151**

9.1   Gross Exposure   151
9.2   Net Exposure   152
9.3   Evolution of the Gross and Net Exposures   152
9.4   Exposure Distribution   155
9.5   Credit Losses   156
9.6   Link of Counterparties via Credit Exposures   157
9.7   Concluding Remarks   158

CHAPTER 10
Credit Enhancements   **161**

10.1   What Are Credit Enhancements? Types and Structure   162
10.2   Asset-based Credit Enhancements   162
    10.2.1   Allocating collateral to credit exposures   163
    10.2.2   Valuing and adjusting asset-based credit enhancements 164
10.3   Counterparty-based Credit Enhancements   165
    10.3.1   Guarantees   165
    10.3.2   Allocating guarantees to credit exposures   165
    10.3.3   Credit derivatives   166
    10.3.4   Lack of credit enhancements in marketplace lending exposures 167
10.4   Additional Elements Considered in Credit Enhancements   168
    10.4.1   Double default   168
    10.4.2   Wrong way risk   169
    10.4.3   Maturity mismatch and payment times   170
    10.4.4   Contracts and counterparties dependencies via credit
             enhancements   170

10.5	Extending Credit Enhancements in Marketplace Lending	170
	10.5.1 Real estate titles	172
	10.5.2 Phone contracts as stores of value	172
	10.5.3 Loyalty points	173
	10.5.4 Life insurance	174
	10.5.5 Guarantor systems	174
10.6	Concluding Remarks	175

CHAPTER 11
Systemic and Concentration Risks   **177**

11.1	Credit Exposure Systemic Risk	177
	11.1.1 Chain reactions after default credit event	178
	11.1.2 Chain reactions after credit downgrading	180
11.2	Counterparty Systemic Risk	180
11.3	Systemic Risk Exposures and Losses	183
11.4	Credit Exposure Concentration Risk	184
11.5	Counterparty Concentration Risk	185
11.6	Systemic Risk and Portfolio Diversification	187
11.7	Concluding Remarks	187

CHAPTER 12
Liquidity, Value, Income, Risk and New Production   **189**

12.1	Liquidity	190
	12.1.1 Financial contracts and liquidity	191
	12.1.2 The time factor and types of analysis in liquidity	191
	12.1.3 Market and funding liquidity risks	192
	12.1.4 Measuring and reporting liquidity and risk	195
12.2	Value and Income	197
	12.2.1 Estimating value	197
	12.2.2 Estimating income	198
	12.2.3 Profit and loss	199
	12.2.4 Valuation principles	199
	12.2.5 Risk on value and income	199
	12.2.6 Stress testing	200
	12.2.7 Designing dynamic and integrated stress testing	200
	12.2.8 Stochastic process	201
	12.2.9 Economic capital allocation and risk adjustments	202
	12.2.10 Some key points in applying risk management	203
12.3	New Production	203
12.4	Treasury and Funds Transfer Pricing (FTP)	205
	12.4.1 Funds transfer pricing (FTP) and transfer rates	207
	12.4.2 Treasury in P2P finance	209
12.5	Concluding Remarks	210

PART THREE

Toward the Future of the Hybrid Financial Sector   215
P3.1   Dangers of a Big Bang Approach to Catch Up with Technology Innovation   216
P3.2   The Need to Collaborate in a Hybrid Financial System   217

CHAPTER 13
Profitability and Risk of Marketplace Loans   219
13.1   Underlying Assumptions of the Analysis   220
    13.1.1   Getting the input data   220
    13.1.2   Time   220
    13.1.3   Risk factors   220
    13.1.4   Mapping the financial contract   220
    13.1.5   Calculating contractual financial events   220
    13.1.6   Constructing portfolios   221
    13.1.7   Analysis outputs   221
13.2   Risk Factors   222
    13.2.1   Market risk   222
    13.2.2   Counterparty credit risk   223
    13.2.3   Behavior   224
13.3   Portfolio Construction   224
    13.3.1   Portfolio exposure   225
13.4   Modeling Portfolio Performance   226
    13.4.1   Income performance   226
    13.4.2   Liquidity performance   227
    13.4.3   Stress testing   228
    13.4.4   Stress test scenarios   231
13.5   Risk Management   236
    13.5.1   Operational risk   239
    13.5.2   Likely overestimation of borrower quality in marketplace lending   240
    13.5.3   A note on portfolio restructuring and optimization   245
    13.5.4   A note on collateral and hedging exposure   246
13.6   The Road Forward   246
13.7   Concluding Remarks   247

CHAPTER 14
Digital Competencies and Digital Dilemmas   251
14.1   Digital Competencies   252
    14.1.1   Banks lag in some areas and lead in others: Analytics   252
14.2   Digital Dilemmas   255
    14.2.1   Dilemma 1: Disrupt or defend?   255
    14.2.2   Dilemma 2: Cooperate or compete?   256
    14.2.3   Dilemma 3: Diversify or concentrate?   258
    14.2.4   Dilemma 4: Keep digital businesses separate or integrate them?   259
    14.2.5   Dilemma 5: Buy or sell businesses in the portfolio?   259
14.3   Concluding Remarks   260

CHAPTER 15

Digital Strategy **263**

15.1 Who Needs Digital Strategy? 263
15.2 Frameworks to Analyze the Impact of Innovation 264
    15.2.1 The diffusion of innovations 264
    15.2.2 The hype cycle 265
    15.2.3 Big Bang Disruption 266
15.3 Spotting Signs of Trouble on the Horizon 267
15.4 How Banks Can Overcome the Innovator's Dilemma 269
    15.4.1 Develop disruptive innovation in a separate company 269
    15.4.2 Plan to fail cheaply 270
    15.4.3 Let those in charge of innovation formulate their own rules and processes 270
    15.4.4 Find new markets 271
15.5 From Producer to Supplier and Moving to a New Singularity 271
15.6 From Closed Innovation to Open Services Innovation 272
15.7 The Role of Leadership in Driving Emergent Strategy 273
15.8 Concluding Remarks 274

CHAPTER 16

The Hybrid Financial Sector **277**

16.1 Forces of Competition in the Digital Age 277
    16.1.1 New pressure on prices and margins 277
    16.1.2 Competitors emerging from unexpected places 278
    16.1.3 Winner-takes-all dynamics 278
    16.1.4 Plug-and-play business models 278
    16.1.5 Growing talent mismatches 278
    16.1.6 Converging global supply and demands 279
    16.1.7 Relentlessly evolving business models—at higher velocity 279
16.2 The Dangers of Knife Fights 279
16.3 Good Ideas in Marketplace Lending That Might Be Here to Stay 280
    16.3.1 Credit scoring with fringe alternative data 280
    16.3.2 Responsive, always-on banking and near-real-time credit 281
    16.3.3 Lending as a Service (LaaS) 282
    16.3.4 The ability to invest in fragments of loans 283
    16.3.5 Unbundled, streamlined financial services 284
    16.3.6 High standards for data and transparency 284
16.4 The Alternative to the Hybrid Financial Sector: A Doomsday Scenario for Established Banks? 286
16.5 Concluding Remarks 286

CHAPTER 17

Unified Analytics **289**

17.1 Why Do Marketplace Lending Platforms Need Unified Financial Analytics? 290
    17.1.1 Advantages for lenders 292
    17.1.2 Advantages for borrowers 293
    17.1.3 Advantages for marketplace lending platforms 294

17.1.4 Advantages for guarantors and protection sellers 295
17.1.5 Advantages for banks 295
17.2 An Overview of a Unified Analytics Platform 296
17.2.1 Standardizing financial data and analytics 299
17.3 Concluding Remarks 301

Bibliography **303**

Index **307**

Preface

In the aftermath of the financial crisis 2007/8, it seemed that the current banking model had failed. After supporting an unprecedented boom in financial markets for the last couple of hundred years, the traditional credit sector was now out of sync with the demands of customers. The system was ripe for a makeover, and online lending promised to step up to the plate. It was then that we began to think about the potential of FinTech, and marketplace lending in particular, ushering in the next era of banking. At that time, many marketplace lending platforms already existed and extended credit to borrowers whom banks turned down. We saw two additional needs in the market: resilience of marketplace loans so that online lending platforms could withstand a replay of the financial crisis of 2007/8, and empowerment of small communities to set up their own marketplace lending platforms with the ease of installing the blogging platform WordPress.

While one of us has a strong background in financial risk and profitability analysis (Akkizidis) and the other is an economist who founded several startups (Stagars), it seemed natural to join forces and take a magnifying glass to the brave new FinTech sector that was just emerging at the time. We analyzed the scene in much detail, with a focus on marketplace lending, by exploring its lending business model both structurally and analytically. Would FinTech introduce innovation in the established processes of credit underwriting? How could we apply risk and profitability analysis using financial analytics to the emerging asset class of marketplace loans?

Because we are in close contact with the financial sector that FinTech is trying to disrupt, drawing parallels between the two was a given. It became clear that both sides have much to learn from each other. FinTech companies have yet to catch up with the vast experience of banks in underwriting and managing credit. After a long hard look at the way banks cope with the emerging threat, it seems the financial sector might be in for a rude awakening unless they ramp up their capability to innovate in parallel with FinTech entrepreneurs. What can both sides do in this situation? In the quest to find answers to this question, this book came about. Thank you for reading it.

In the course of writing, we conducted many interviews with innovators in marketplace lending and those in charge of innovation in banks. Under our eyes, the peer-to-peer lending sector rebranded itself as marketplace lending. We watched the online credit sector mushroom into a multi-billion dollar behemoth with a confidence that would make the most brazen Wall Street honcho blush. At the same time, banks announced partnerships with marketplace lending platforms, institutional investors piled into the asset class, and the odd acquisition of a FinTech startup by a financial institution took place. The structural gap between the new entrant and the incumbent narrowed, but the alliance between the two is still uneasy and at risk of disintegrating should there be any economic turmoil ahead.

Marketplace lenders and banks can do better than that.

There exist clear benefits when the two join forces and evolve the future of credit together. The future is hardly an either/or proposition, and both parties have complementary roles in the emerging hybrid financial sector. No single tech company is likely to dominate, just as no conglomerate of banks will squash all marketplace lenders and prevail as the ringleader. The future of credit is hybrid, but how to get there is far from obvious. In this book, we have had much fun examining ways for innovators in marketplace lending and banks to co-create the future of credit together. When they succeed, the result is a stronger financial sector, one that is more transparent and more resilient.

Ioannis Akkizidis and Manuel Stagars
Zurich and Singapore

Acknowledgments

We are grateful to the FinTech entrepreneurs, financial professionals, and opinion leaders who have tested, challenged, and shaped the ideas in this book. Their stories and experience have helped us improve our analysis and recommendations. Special thanks to (in alphabetical order): Arjan Schuette, Brendan Dickinson, Brett King, Dan Ciporin, David Moss, David Snitkof, Dominic Chang, Frank Rotman, Gregg Schoenberg, Izabella Kaminska, Jon Moulton, Juerg Mueller, Matt Burton, Michael Chaille, Olivier Berthier, Patrick Goh, and Zoe Zhang. We appreciate you taking the time and giving us insights into your thinking regarding the future of credit.

We would also like to thank Vivianne Bouchereau for her outstanding review and corrections through the writing process of this manuscript. Ioannis would also like to thank his young son Filippos for his amazing smiles given during the dedicated work of writing this book.

At Wiley, an excellent team turned our ideas into the book you are reading. We would like to thank Werner Coetzee for believing in this project early on and the entire editorial board for supporting it. Many thanks to Jeremy Chia for contributing his knowledge and energy towards the development of this book.

Acknowledgments

About the Authors

Ioannis Akkizidis, BEng, MSc, PhD (Zurich, Switzerland) is the global product manager on financial risk management systems, in Wolters Kluwer Financial & Compliance Services, in Zürich, Switzerland. He has experience in designing and implementing advanced solutions in risk-management and profitability analysis fields for the financial industry all around the world. Turning theory into practice, he has been involved in many projects for implementing financial systems and models in the financial industry. Dr Akkizidis wrote his PhD thesis in modelling non-linear systems at the University of Wales, UK. He is a visiting Lecturer at the University of Zürich on the Master's Degree program Quantitative Finance, lecturing on a module based on the book *Unified Financial Analysis, the Missing Links of Finance*, published by Wiley, 2009, where he is the co-author. Dr Akkizidis is the author of several books, book chapters, handbooks and articles, in financial analysis and risk management. He is also a member of the Steering Committee of the Swiss Risk Association.

Manuel Stagars, CFA, CAIA, ERP (Zurich, Switzerland) is an economist and senior researcher at Singapore-ETH Centre with a focus on the technological and institutional aspects of data. He is also a serial entrepreneur who has founded companies in Switzerland, the United States, and Japan. Mr. Stagars has been supporting startups as an angel investor since 2007 and is a consultant to clients on entrepreneurship, business models and financial strategy. He is also the author of the books *Impact Investment Funds for Frontier Markets in Southeast Asia* (Palgrave Macmillan, 2015), and *University Startups and Spin-offs: Guide for Entrepreneurs in Academia* (Apress, 2014).

About the Website

Please visit this book's companion website at www.wiley.com/go/akkizidis to access the Annexes and Matlab Model.

The password for downloading the files is: credit123

The files available on the website are:

- **Annex A: Element of Time in Financial Events**
  This annex provides the list of the financial events in regards to:
  - Their appearance at Point in Time (PIT) and Through the Cycle (TTC) iterations.
  - The type of cash flow defined as Principal, Interest, Dividend, Recovery and Trading payments.
  - The resetting process at different times and cash flow types.

  These are aligned to the event patterns explained in Section 5.3 of Chapter 5 (Contract Mechanisms Producing Financial Mechanisms).

- **Annex B: Reduced Form Models Applied in Marketplace Lending Credit Portfolios**
  This annex provides a description of the intensity based credit risk models for estimating the default probability and the arrival time of the credit event. Such an intensity based model is applied for estimating and stressing, over time, the conditional default probabilities and default times for the marketplace lending portfolios. This model is fully explained and used in the case study described in Chapter 13 of this book.

- **Matlab Model**
  The provided Matlab model considers the information referring to market data, counterparty characteristics and behavior assumptions, mapping the standard contractual bilateral loan agreements between lenders and borrowers, calculating all expected and unexpected financial events, and reporting the liquidity, value and income together with their corresponding risk measurements. Stress scenarios, defined by the user, can also be applied in the credit portfolios. This model is used for performing the financial analysis of existing marketplace loans, as discussed extensively in Chapter 13. Note, however, that this model can also be used for any other loan portfolios provided by the user. Please read GettingStarted.pdf in the applications folder after installation for more instructions.

Introduction

Since the financial crisis in 2007/8, regulators and policy makers have focused most of their energy on strengthening the financial system. Massive amounts of capital and a tsunami of new regulation have swept banks and other financial institutions, causing many of them to complain about the exploding costs of doing businesses and extreme difficulty to comply with rules. Banks and the market have lost confidence in each other. Large financial losses, lack of transparency, bad reputation, and regulatory overheads are to blame, which rendered the financial industry ripe for a change. Meanwhile, a small community of renegades has been quietly chiseling away on new and different ways of "doing finance." FinTech promises advantages to customers, namely transparency, immediacy, and lower fees. From peer-to-peer lending (also called marketplace lending), to payments, to automated asset management, FinTech entrepreneurs in Silicon Valley, New York, and London have built small empires in recent years, worth billions of dollars in market capitalization. And they have no intention of stopping there: the ultimate goal is to encroach on the turf of the established financial sector and go for much larger profits.

Across the six lending segments in the U.S. (personal, small business, leveraged lending, commercial real estate, mortgages, and student loans), Goldman Sachs estimates $12 trillion of loans outstanding, with 59 percent held on bank balance sheets and the rest on the books of non-banks. If new entrants in the lending space mature, banks stand to lose tens of billions in profit annually in the U.S. alone.[1] Yet traditional credit institutions remain largely on the sidelines in the disruption of the financial sector even though they would have the most to gain from innovation. If they participated more actively in development, and integrated new ideas into their existing business model, they assured themselves leadership and new markets in the future. Otherwise, some critics warn, banks may suffer the fate of the music industry around the turn of the millennium, which technology turned upside down. For banking to stay relevant, the financial sector might ultimately become a hybrid financial sector, where established institutions and new entrants define the future of credit together.

At the same time, Wall Street and the venture capital community have a good track record of reporting about the success stories of sectors they heavily invested in. It is easy to get carried away by shiny new objects, especially in a bull market. Technology startups often fall short in delivering what they promise, and they come with challenges of their own: if FinTech continues on its growth trajectory, we may end up with a massive shadow banking system that is hard to regulate, a high potential for concentration risk, and yet increased financial instability. Because finance is a relatively complex field, things that sound too good to be true often are. Is this the case with FinTech also? We feel there is a need for a thorough analysis of financial technology innovation that takes into account the banking and analytics perspective, especially in the space that has been receiving the most attention and venture capital in recent years: marketplace lending. Hence, this book came about. To fully understand how marketplace lending works and how it differs from traditional bank credit, it is important to know how banks "do" credit, including profitability analysis and risk management. For this reason, we included an in-depth treatise on the mechanics of bank lending, which builds the foundation of our analysis and of understanding the complexity of credit in the financial system. We then apply a banking risk-management approach to address the financial management of marketplace lending platforms and portfolios of marketplace loans.

I.1   WHO IS THIS BOOK FOR?

Lending and deposits are the core business of financial credit institutions. Most people have heard about peer-to-peer lending in one form or another, especially if they live in one of the financial centers of the world. In light of increased interest by institutional investors in the peer-to-peer lending space, the sector has adopted an alternative name—marketplace lending—to better describe the asset class. Still, most literature about online lending is a glowing endorsement of the virtues of new entrants disrupting finance, without going into details of financial analytics and risk management. The exact mechanics, the technology, processes, people, and systems involved in the lifecycle of the credit are often a mystery to those outside of banks. There is no reference that is easy to understand for all stakeholders involved: traditional financial credit institutions, regulators, potential new entrants, and entrepreneurs. To improve the core functions of the financial system with innovative technology, they all need to be on the same level, with the same baseline of know-how.

If you work in the financial sector and are interested in innovation, this book is for you. If you are a FinTech entrepreneur interested in a broader perspective of credit and its analytics, this book is for you, too. Marketplace lending is still in a state of flux and in its infancy, and the business model of alternative credit must become more robust to become a serious contender for market share. Existing established credit institutions and newly emerging shadow lending institutions have complementary strengths and weaknesses. The current technological, social, and regulatory environment creates a confluence of opportunities, which could become the launch pad to build the next generation of credit institutions. If all stakeholders work together, they can reach this next step. We need to research and understand the main strengths and weaknesses of conventional institutions, the informal credit institutions, and new FinTech ventures for this purpose.

Figure I.1 shows how this book is organized. Part I gives the lay of the land in today's FinTech sector, with a focus on lending. Part II introduces how banks analyze and manage their credit portfolios. Finally, Part III brings both perspectives together in the hybrid financial sector.

I.2   WHAT IS FINTECH?

Even though the term *FinTech* describes applications beyond online lending, it makes sense to define the term. The acronym arrived on the tech scene sometime in early 2013. A combination of the words "financial" and "technology," the term broadly describes innovation in financial services through software and innovative uses of technology. It is used for a wide variety of firms including peer-to-peer lenders, cryptocurrencies such as Bitcoin, but even online payment

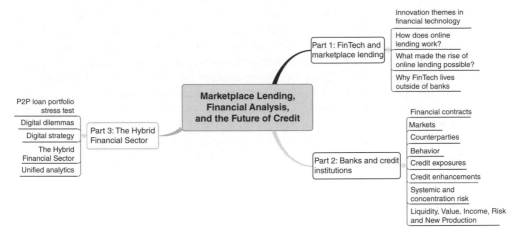

FIGURE I.1   Parts and chapters of this book

processors such as PayPal, which has been around since 1998. Even though established banks and credit institutions heavily push innovation through technology, FinTech often describes ideas that emerge outside the established financial sector. Services in this field are often called "alternative," as in "alternative to the established financial sector." For example, when we speak about online lending, this could mean loan origination via online channels by both established banks and new financial technology startups. Some authors therefore distinguish further by calling online lenders that are not banks *alternative* online lenders. In this book, we use online lenders to describe non-bank lenders. The kind of online lending we are interested in here is always an alternative to established channels of credit in the formal financial sector.

Silicon Valley is a hotbed for tech startups, and financial technology startups in particular. But in terms of FinTech, new additional innovation centers have emerged that attract entrepreneurs. Because of their proximity to the financial sector, New York and London have also become platforms for startups in this field. Established banks have begun to support FinTech accelerators and innovation labs, funding startups for a certain amount of time and giving them access to their networks. Their goal, of course, is to spot innovative solutions and talent before anybody else. As a consequence, the sale to a bank is a valid exit strategy for a FinTech startup, but only if their technology has proven worthwhile and profitable in the market in a relatively short amount of time. Unless banks can capitalize immediately on their investment, they are unlikely to nurture and develop disruptive ideas in their midst any time soon.

I.2.1   Distinction between Financial Technology Innovation and Financial Innovation

It is important to point out that this book is about something other than what financial professionals understand by the term "financial innovation." To be clear, *financial technology innovation (FinTech)* and *financial innovation* are different animals. Both are sometimes used interchangeably, and they certainly overlap. *Financial innovation* mostly describes innovation from *within* the established financial sector. Examples of financial innovation are structured products, such as credit default swaps (CDS) or collateralized debt obligations (CDOs). Credit cards and ATMs are also examples of financial innovation, as they grew out of banks that already existed. Products of financial innovation are rarely widely adopted at the very beginning, but they have a place somewhere in the established financial sector. *Financial technology innovation*, or *FinTech*, on the other hand, comes out of left field and aims to unseat the existing players in the financial sector. Even though ex-bankers and lawyers have founded some FinTech startups, many of them are venture-capital funded startups founded by entrepreneurs with good ideas but little experience in finance and investment. These ventures have technology at their core, and they have their roots outside of the established financial sector.

Software and technology is at the heart of almost everything in finance. So, on which areas of the financial system do FinTech startups focus? The most important ones are:

- Alternative online lending
- Crowdfunding and crowdinvesting
- Transactions and payments
- Personal finance management
- Digital currency and cryptocurrency
- Mobile point of sale (mPOS)
- Online financial advisory
- Mobile-first banks

All of these areas share the common requirements of data analytics, security, cloud computing, and customer relationship management (CRM) platforms. Those components are prerequisites for FinTech startups to make use of the technological possibilities that are available today.

I.3 WHY DOES THIS BOOK FOCUS ON ONLINE LENDING?

Non-bank online lending is an area that is complex and little understood. It has a large disruptive potential for the established financial sector, even though their market share is still small. Lending is still the bread and butter of commercial banks, so they should take their emerging competition seriously. It will be important for entrepreneurs, existing online lenders, and established credit institutions to understand how banks and FinTech entrepreneurs shape this dynamic sector. Both can learn from each other: bankers should learn from innovation in FinTech, while startup entrepreneurs can learn from established financial sector operators in terms of risk management, modeling, and analytics. It will be in the interest of all players to integrate ideas that originate in financial technology startups outside the established infrastructure and adapt to stay competitive in the future.

Network effects are crucial for the value proposition of technology firms. Their value lies in the number of their users and their activity on the system. When a financial technology startup builds a platform, it has to ensure that it puts up walls that prevent competitors from encroaching on their user base. Technology firms are effective at doing this. Platform and device dependency increases switching cost, and so does the inability to transfer profiles and connections from one social network to another. Making it difficult for users to switch is what banks have been doing for decades. The only novelty is that with the democratization of technology and connectivity, every startup can attack the established players now in their own territory. Because technology is at the core of the business model of the existing credit institutions, they are vulnerable. New startups are in effect playing a similar game like them, only with newer weapons. The investors are largely the same in banks and FinTech startups; large institutions or hedge funds provide the funds for many online lenders. Also, since online lenders are only loosely regulated, financial technology startups add to the already mushrooming shadow banking system. The larger and more fragmented these invisible pools of capital are, the less stable is the global financial system. If there were a failure of a well-known marketplace lending platform that resulted in total loss of capital for all investors, what would this do to the sector?

I.4 THE HYBRID FINANCIAL SECTOR: THE OPPORTUNITY TO BUILD A HEALTHIER FINANCIAL SYSTEM

The financial crisis of 2007/8 has been an undoubted shock in terms of credit, both for lenders and for borrowers. Despite the crisis, nominal amounts of credit outstanding to households and non-financial companies have mostly been going up, as the figures show for the United States, the United Kingdom, Australia, Germany and China (Figure I.2, Figure I.4, Figure I.6, Figure I.8, and Figure I.10). When we compare the amount of credit outstanding to the gross national income (GNI) of these countries, things look less promising: For all countries, with the exception of China, credit outstanding as a percentage of GNI has gone down across the board (Figure I.3, Figure I.5, Figure I.7, Figure I.9, and Figure I.11). It is certainly a good idea for countries to keep their debt in check, but at the same time, if firms and households cannot borrow, this will hamper growth in the longer term. Finding sources of credit for borrowers outside of the established channels therefore makes sense, as long as it will introduce no additional risk into the system.

At the same time as tech startups began to stake a claim in the financial sector and small business loans have decreased, more people have searched for "P2P lending" and "peer lending" on Google (Figure I.12). One trend need not be a cause for the other, but it is clear

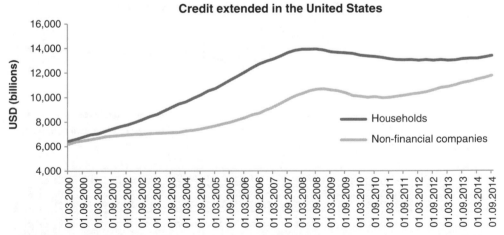

FIGURE I.2 Credit extended in the United States from all sectors to households and NPISHs and non-financial companies
Data source: Bank of International Settlements (BIS)

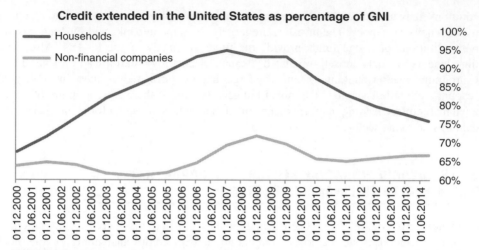

FIGURE I.3 Credit extended in the United States from all sectors to households and NPISHs and non-financial companies
Data sources: Bank of International Settlements (BIS) and World Bank for GDP and GNI data (GNI for 2014 is extrapolated with average growth rate of the previous three years)

that they have diverged in opposite directions in recent years, and online lenders have steadily increased the number of loans they underwrite.

While they are steadily increasing the numbers of loans they underwrite, financial technology startups ignore a large opportunity that exists in financial markets today: to use technology to make the financial system more resilient to external shocks. What the financial system needs is less a shuffling of the deck, with more unregulated new entrants, but more an evolved system that promises rewards to all stakeholders involved. Instead of building proprietary systems,

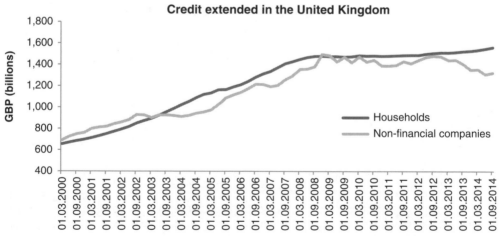

FIGURE I.4 Credit extended in the United Kingdom from all sectors to households and NPISHs and non-financial companies
Data source: Bank of International Settlements (BIS)

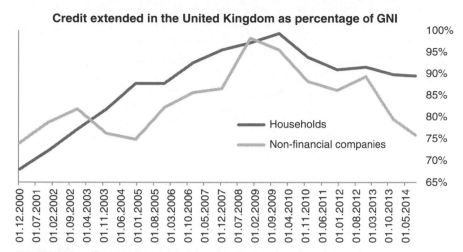

FIGURE I.5 Credit extended in the United Kingdom from all sectors to households and NPISHs and non-financial companies
Data sources: Bank of International Settlements (BIS) and World Bank for GDP and GNI data (GNI for 2014 is extrapolated with average growth rate of the previous three years)

financial technology innovators could reinvent how banking and lending are done at the core. This is hardly a question of building a better mousetrap, but of integrating systems to work together and address problems in a common language. As we saw in Figure I.10 and Figure I.11, which both show credit in China, households still hold far less credit than companies in emerging markets. This represents an enormous market potential. When FinTech startups find a new solution or a suite of new solutions that can serve the emerging middle classes of the world more efficiently than banks, the pie for all participants will expand. It is unlikely that

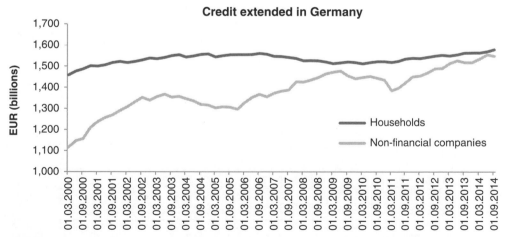

FIGURE I.6 Credit extended in Germany from all sectors to households and NPISHs and non-financial companies
Data source: Bank of International Settlements (BIS)

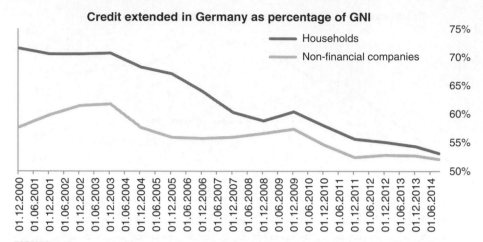

FIGURE I.7   Credit extended in Germany from all sectors to households and NPISHs and non-financial companies
Data sources: Bank of International Settlements (BIS) and World Bank for GDP and GNI data (GNI for 2014 is extrapolated with average growth rate of the previous three years)

market leadership in credit will be a question of a single bank or FinTech company cornering the market. Investors and borrowers will most likely use a suite of services that blend into each other seamlessly. Instead of wasting time in competing against each other, banks and FinTech innovators could build the hybrid financial sector of the future together, today.

An integrated view is only possible if innovation leaders understand how the financial system works. When they can integrate all existing parties and motivate them to evolve the

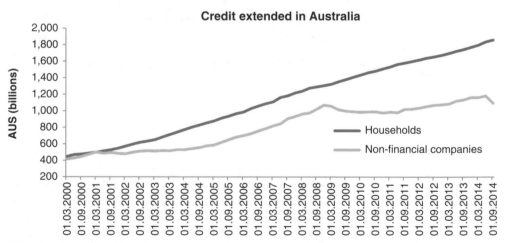

FIGURE I.8   Credit extended in Australia from all sectors to households and NPISHs and non-financial companies
Data source: Bank of International Settlements (BIS)

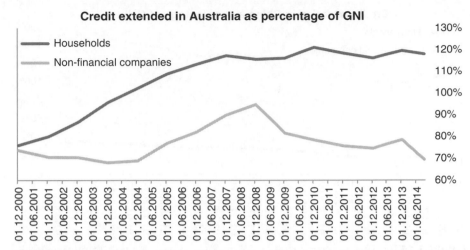

FIGURE I.9 Credit extended in Australia from all sectors to households and NPISHs and non-financial companies
Data sources: Bank of International Settlements (BIS) and World Bank for GDP and GNI data (GNI for 2014 is extrapolated with average growth rate of the previous three years)

system together, there will be radical change for the better. Without it, we see more walled gardens pop up that might confuse and cannibalize the existing system. Keeping in mind the evolution of the financial system and charting ways to design a more robust hybrid financial sector is the goal of this book. With this in mind, let's get started.

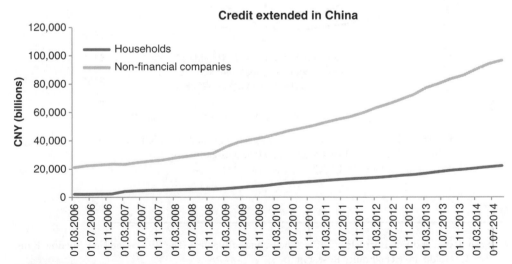

FIGURE I.10 Credit extended in China from all sectors to households and NPISHs and non-financial companies
Data source: Bank of International Settlements (BIS)

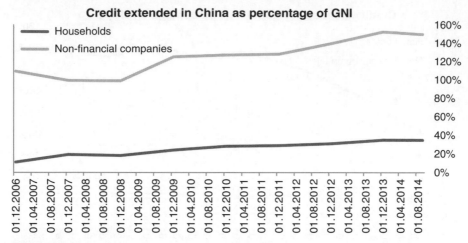

FIGURE I.11 Credit extended in China from all sectors to households and NPISHs and non-financial companies
Data sources: Bank of International Settlements (BIS) and World Bank for GDP and GNI data (GNI for 2014 is extrapolated with average growth rate of the previous three years)

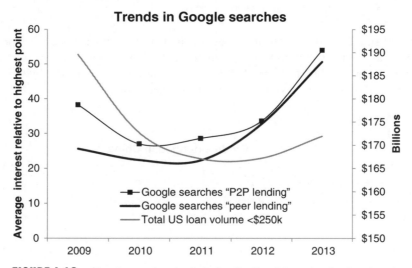

FIGURE I.12 Google searches for "p2p lending" and "peer lending" and total volume of U.S. small loans below $250,000 outstanding
Data sources: Google, FDIC

NOTE

1. Nash, Ryan, and Eric Beardsley (2015) "The Future of Finance: The Rise of the New Shadow Bank, Part 1," Goldman Sachs Equity Research.

One

FinTech and the Online Lending Landscape—Where Are We Now?

Online lending platforms have become a large part of the thriving FinTech sector, and startups in the space have become a mainstay in the financial press in recent years. Large amounts of venture capital are flowing into the sector. Many of the current initiatives in financial technology innovation promise great disruption to the status quo in finance. It has become popular to predict the demise of banking as we know it. In fact, the *Financial Times* even dedicated a series to the subject, aptly titled "Death of Banks."[1] But are recent FinTech innovations really a threat to the existing financial system? And if they are, who says that their solutions will be superior to those that exist today and consumers will be better off?

Even though banks are facing assaults on their hegemony on different fronts—payments, foreign exchange, wealth management, lending—we focus on *online lending* in this book. Let's first define what we mean with this broad term. Roughly speaking, online lending describes the emerging market outside of the established financial sector that is using technology to disrupt the lending market. There exist several business models in the online lending space, and different authors use different terminology to describe similar things. We realize this discussion can become confusing unless we agree on which terms we use for which approach. This is why we will describe several FinTech business models in more detail in Chapter 1, which will set out which terms describe which approaches in the rest of this book when we speak about marketplace lending.

Despite our focus on online lending, we also need an overview of the entire FinTech sector to understand the status quo and potential of the emerging hybrid financial sector. Many of the technologies are overlapping and building on each other. In their current form, most financial technology startups are still operating at small scale compared to the transaction volumes of established banks. In reality, FinTech startups in their current form are far from a threat. Nevertheless, the sector is attracting large amounts of venture capital, and this trend is set to continue, with global investment in FinTech on track to grow to up to $8 billion by 2018.[2] At

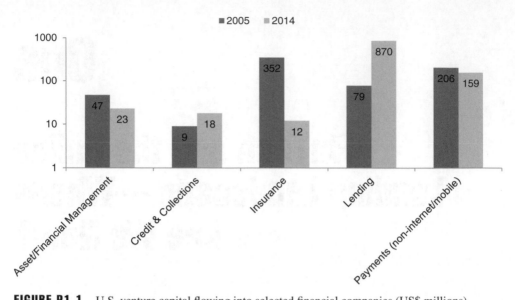

FIGURE P1.1   U.S. venture capital flowing into selected financial companies (US$ millions), excluding corporate venture capital
Data source: CB Insights

the same time, Gartner points out that banking and securities institutions are spending roughly $485 billion on information technology in 2014.[3] On a global scale, the United States attracts the lion's share of FinTech investment, about 83 percent of global investment in 2013. Several hubs for activity of financial technology startups have emerged in recent years. Silicon Valley is the biggest FinTech cluster in the world, New York ranks second. London and Hong Kong are evolving as hotspots for startups as well.

Out of the different focus areas of FinTech companies, lending has emerged as a winner in recent years. Especially in the United States, lending companies lead both in terms of the absolute amount of venture capital funding it attracts (Figure P1.1) and the share of total investment in financial companies (Figure P1.2). Figure P1.3 shows venture capital funding over time and the number of investments in lending companies between 2005 and 2014 in the United States. The data consider investments of venture capital firms in financial companies other than FinTech. Nevertheless, the growth trend of capital flows into the lending space is evident. Lending attracted US$ 870 million of venture capital in the United States in 2014, roughly 80 percent of the total investment amount for the year. In comparison, venture capital investors invested less than 10 percent of their funds in lending companies in 2005. Remember that these are equity investments in companies, not capital invested in loans originated by these companies. Another interesting observation is the relative draw of venture capital from the white-hot payments sector: even though mobile payments and digital wallets seem to occupy a prominent share of media attention, they were attracting less capital in 2014 than in 2005. The multiple of investment in payments over lending has changed from roughly 2.6 in 2005 (payments attracted 2.6 times the capital of lending) to under 0.2 in 2014.

The rise of online lending as a leader in the FinTech space is expected: current interest rates are at their lowest since the financial crisis of 2007/8. However, transaction volumes of online lending platforms still pale in comparison with those of the conventional financial

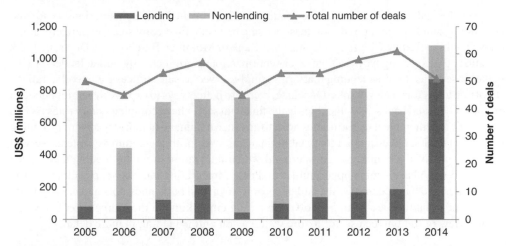

FIGURE P1.2   U.S. venture capital deal volume (US$), number of deals in financial companies, and proportion of investment in lending companies of total investment in financial companies, excluding investment banking and funds
Data source: CB Insights

sector. Nevertheless, author Charles Moldow predicts that by 2025, $1 trillion in loans will be originated on marketplace lending platforms globally.[4] Many technology experts predict that, in the near future, innovations in financial technology will pave the way for a massive paradigm shift that will unseat the existing players in financial markets. This is a possibility. No monopolist has been able to keep the walls up for over a hundred years. In essence, what financial technology startups promise is making transactions cheaper, faster, and more transparent, by replacing the current lending institutions with more effective platforms. They are "trying to eat the banks' lunch," as Jamie Dimon, chief executive of JPMorgan Chase, put it.[5] But can FinTech companies follow through on their promises?

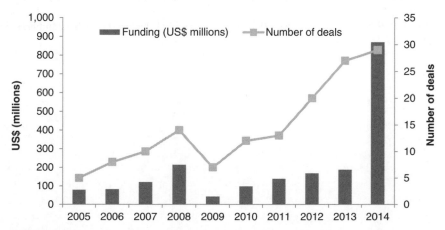

FIGURE P1.3   U.S. venture capital investment volume and number of deals in lending companies
Data source: CB Insights

The logical next step for online lenders and established credit institutions is to find common ground and join forces—at least in some respects. First baby steps are already taking place: banks including Citigroup, Capital One, Bank of Montreal, Barclays and Deutsche Bank are currently exploring ways to finance or securitize loans originated by online lenders.[6] This makes it seem as if online lending platforms simply served as sales offices for uncollateralized subprime loans for shadow banks. Of course, there are better ways to explore synergies between online lenders and banks, and all parties in the financial sector have complementary roles. When they work together, great opportunities arise to advance the financial industry toward providing better financial services and a more stable financial system. In the coming chapters, we will address some of the common themes around which innovation in online lending takes place today. We will also examine opportunities and risks. Integrating innovative, customer-centric approaches into banks comes with challenges of its own, and both innovators and banks should understand what they are getting involved in before embarking on the journey. Let's now get an overview of the FinTech sector before we focus on online lending in more detail.

NOTES

1. Kaminska, Izabella (2014a) "Death of Banks," *Financial Times*, http://ftalphaville.ft.com/tag/death-of-banks/, data accessed 9 December 2014.
2. Accenture (2014) "The Rise of FinTech: New York's Opportunity for Tech Leadership," http://www.accenture.com/us-en/Pages/insight-rise-fintech-new-york.aspx.
3. D'Orazio, Vittoria; Kandaswamy, Rajesh; Cournoyer, Susan; Narisawa, Rika (2014) "Forecast: Enterprise IT Spending for the Banking and Securities Market, Worldwide, 2011-2017, 4Q13 Update," (Gartner, 30 January 2014), https://www.gartner.com/doc/2659418/forecast-enterprise-it-spending-banking.
4. Moldow, Charles (2014) "A Trillion Dollar Market By the People, For the People" (Foundation Capital, 2014), http://www.foundationcapital.com/downloads/FoundationCap_MarketplaceLending Whitepaper.pdf.
5. Hall, Camilla; Braithwaite, Tom; Mishkin, Sarah (2014) "Apple looks to swipe the payments market" (*Financial Times*, 9 September 2014), http://www.ft.com/cms/s/0/85eb978a-3844-11e4-9fc2-00144feabdc0.html.
6. See *FT* http://www.ft.com/intl/cms/s/0/9a8e427e-2a07-11e3-9bc6-00144feab7de.html#axzz3HW byAH4w.

CHAPTER 1

Introduction to the Business Models in Financial Technology

M arketplace lending is but one of several approaches to online lending outside the established financial sector. To understand the position of marketplace lending in the FinTech space, it is helpful to get an overview of the scene in general. This chapter introduces different innovation themes and business models in FinTech, where many of the sectors and business models overlap and often inform each other or foreshadow what might happen in another segment. The FinTech landscape is changing fast, so it will make little sense to name and analyze each of the startups and companies in detail; several books and freely available reports are already doing that. Companies change their focus over time, so categorizing them by name would date this publication quickly.

Instead, we can classify financial technology innovation by sectors, themes, and their business models. This helps us to understand what these startups are trying to accomplish. Figure 1.1 and Table 1.1 list the innovation themes we will discuss in this chapter.

All these innovation themes rely on underlying technologies, such as data analytics, security, cloud computing, software-as-a-service (SaaS), or customer relationship management (CRM). These technologies are the prerequisites that allow FinTech startups to compete with established banks; they form a support layer on which all companies in the space rely in one form or another. Some companies in these support functions also qualify as FinTech, but discussing them here would go beyond the scope of this chapter. Figure 1.2 shows how the FinTech innovation themes function in relationship with each other and with their support layers.

1.1 INNOVATION THEMES IN FINTECH

The following paragraphs give an overview of the main innovation themes.

1.1.1 Online lending

Online lending is about creating a platform for borrowers to access loans outside the established credit system. Lenders are often individuals or professional investors such as funds and institutions. Authors Karen Gordon Mills and Brayden McCarthy identify three kinds of

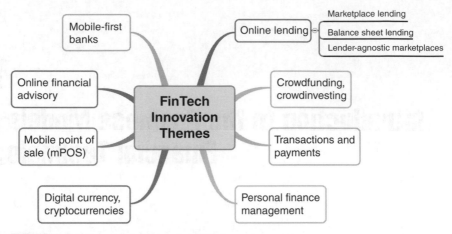

FIGURE 1.1   Innovation themes in FinTech

TABLE 1.1   The main innovation themes in financial technology

Sector	Description	Business model
Online lending	Lending to borrowers outside the established credit system, either for small businesses or consumers; Includes several approaches to lending, such as balance sheet lending, P2P/marketplace lending, or lender-agnostic marketplaces	Credit against interest, lead generation, fees and commissions
Crowdfunding and crowdinvesting	Raising funds from backers in exchange for rewards, debt, convertible debt or equity	Capital or debt against equity, fees and commissions
Transactions and payments	Cashless payment processing, involving credit cards or proprietary systems; Store of value on the cell phone or smartphone, either in official currency or credits (phone credits)	Credit against interest, service against fees
Personal finance management	Allows users to consolidate their financial statements, net worth, banking relationships, credit cards, and so on	Annual subscription fee, cross-selling
Digital currency and cryptocurrency	Alternative stores of value to established currencies, many of them encrypted, so transfers are without a trace and anonymous	Bitcoin mining, trading exchanges
Mobile point of sale (mPOS)	The ability to process payments with credit cards or contactless with a smartphone and a credit/debit card reader	Service against fees, credit against interest
Online financial advisory	Automated portfolio management and optimization according to a client mandate, also called "robo-advisory"	Service against fees
Mobile-first banks	Branchless banks that process all client interactions and services through a software storefront	Service against fees, credit against interest

online lenders: *online balance sheet lenders*, *peer-to-peer transactional marketplaces*, and *lender-agnostic marketplaces*.[1] Chapter 2 describes all three of them in detail. Online lending is one of the most promising segments of FinTech and potentially the most disruptive, with large amounts of venture capital pouring into existing and newly emerging platforms.

1.1.2   Crowdfunding and crowdinvesting

Crowdfunding describes raising capital for ventures or projects by collecting contributions from different individuals via the internet. Every crowdfunding project consists of at least three parties: the project initiator, backers who fund the project, and a platform that facilitates transactions. In 2013, the crowdfunding industry grew to be over $5.1 billion worldwide.[2] Different kinds of crowdfunding exist. In *reward-based crowdfunding*, entrepreneurs either pre-sell a product to customers without giving up equity or they are selling debt. *Equity-based crowdfunding* (also called *crowdinvesting*) describes the case where a backer receives unlisted shares of a startup in exchange for cash. Both terms are often used interchangeably, but they describe different approaches. Crowdinvesting can also entail funding with debt or convertible debt. In either case, crowdinvestors receive a residual financial claim of future cash flows in a startup, while crowdfunders don't.

1.1.3   Transactions and payments

Since its very beginning, the internet has facilitated commercial transactions. According to author John Markoff, the first e-commerce transaction took place when students at Stanford University and MIT used Arpanet accounts to quietly arrange the sale of an undetermined amount of marijuana in 1971 or 1972.[3] Likewise, e-commerce solutions that allowed credit card processing online are hardly a novelty. However, enabling online transactions and payments without needing a credit card, or making the service available to individuals and small businesses without the need of an expensive IT infrastructure, is relatively new. PayPal, one of the first providers of mainstream online payments, boasts 152 million user accounts at the time of this writing. Its total value of transactions in Q2 2014 was $55 billion.[4]

Mobile payments (also called *mobile money*, *mobile money transfers*, or *mobile wallets*) are payment services via a mobile phone. Although the concept of online payment has a long history, the technology to support such mobile payments and wallets has become widely available recently with the proliferation of smartphones. Online companies like PayPal, Amazon Payments, and Google Wallet also have mobile options. Large potential for mobile payments exists in the developing world. For example, Vodafone's M-Pesa, a mobile-phone based money transfer service, launched in 2007 in Kenya and Tanzania. It allows users with a national ID card to deposit, withdraw, and transfer money easily with a mobile device. M-Pesa has since expanded to Afghanistan, South Africa, India, and Eastern Europe.[5] People use such services often for micropayments. Mobile payments have a large potential to extend financial services to "unbanked" people, estimated at up to 50 percent of the world's adult population.[6]

1.1.4   Personal Financial Management

Personal Financial Management (PFM) describes software or online services that help people manage their finances. PFM lets users categorize their transactions and add different accounts from banks or credit card processors into a single view. Services often include data visualizations such as spending trends, budgets and net worth. One of the first pieces of PFM software available was Intuit's *Quicken*. Online startups entered the field in 2006, with Mint on the vanguard (acquired by Intuit in 2009). Several competitors offer comparable services free of charge, including the calculation of personal finance scores based on how well people manage their money. Some startups in the field also aim at helping users manage their debt.

1.1.5 Digital currency and cryptocurrency

Digital currency describes a medium of exchange that is electronically created and stored, as an alternative to physical currencies, which exist in the form of banknotes and coins. Digital currency can buy physical goods and services like traditional money, or the currency may be valid only inside an online game or a social network. Such restricted currencies are also called *virtual currencies*. Because they rely on the transmission of code across the internet, digital currencies promise a fast, secure, and inexpensive method of wealth transfer, independent of existing payment systems and banks. A subset of digital currencies are cryptocurrencies, where transactions are recorded, time-stamped, and displayed in a public ledger, called the "block chain." Public-key cryptography ensures that all computers in the network have a constantly updated and verified record of all transactions within the Bitcoin network, which prevents double-spending and fraud.[7] What irks governments about cryptocurrency is its decentralized control: the entire cryptocurrency system creates new currency in a "mining" process at a defined and publicly known rate. In centralized banking, such as the Federal Reserve System, governments control the supply of currency by printing units of fiat money or demanding additions to digital banking ledgers. Because governments cannot produce units of cryptocurrency they have no influence on its supply, which results in the loss of an important policy tool. Bitcoin emerged in 2008 as the first fully implemented cryptocurrency,[8] but several hundred other cryptocurrencies and digital currencies exist.

1.1.6 Mobile point of sale (mPOS)

A mobile point of sale is a smartphone, tablet or other wireless device that serves as a cash register to process payments. It allows individuals and small business owners to accept transactions without having to buy an electronic register or pay a traditional vendor such as Visa or Mastercard to supply a card reader and processing software. Any smartphone or tablet can become an mPOS with a downloadable mobile app. When installing the app, the user normally receives a card reader in the mail that plugs into the audio socket of the device. Some providers even offer additional devices that can print receipts. Every smartphone user can thus become a professional vendor with minimal fees and overhead.

1.1.7 Online financial advisory

Online financial advisors (also called robo-advisors) are financial advisory firms that provide automated portfolio management while relying on limited human intervention, which results in lower fees for account holders. Robo-advisors do not fully automate portfolio management: financial professionals make forecasts for investment performance of portfolio assets, so the investment strategies vary between different online advisors. However, for account management functions such as portfolio optimization, tax harvesting, or rebalancing, robo-advisors depend on similar algorithms. Among them are modern portfolio theory (MPT), or strategies to derive market assumptions such as the Black-Litterman model or the Gordon growth model.[9] Such algorithms have found wide application in conventional financial advisory firms for years. The novelty of robo-advisors is that they offer comparable financial services, rigorous mathematical models, and similar performance to established account managers but at a lower cost. In a robo-advisor, a small team with comparatively small overhead may compete with large wealth management divisions of established banks.

1.1.8 Mobile-first banks

Characteristics of mobile-first banks (also called mobile banks) are the absence of physical branches, transparent conditions, no minimum account balance requirements, and free service. Clients can open accounts quickly and securely, and they can manage their financial affairs online or on a mobile app without ever setting foot in a branch. Account balances are still held in a partnering bank that has conventional branches, but this partner bank exists entirely on the backend. Mobile-first banks may combine several FinTech services under one umbrella. The promise of mobile-first banks is that online services may gradually encroach on the business of traditional banks, to the point where mobile-first banks will challenge existing banks offline. An example of a mobile bank is Simple. Banco Bilbao Vizcaya Argentaria (BBVA), a Spanish banking group, acquired Simple in early 2014, when the startup had 100,000 customers. Users feared that the acquirer would shut down Simple's operation and merge its accounts into its existing business, but BBVA knew better. Instead of integrating Simple into its existing operations, BBVA states that its goal is to take advantage of a different way of thinking that the startup has achieved, namely how it has changed consumer behavior and engagement. Users of Simple conduct banking in a distinctly different way from traditional banking. About 25 percent of customers post pictures or tag transactions, like on a social network.[10] With Big Data and social network analysis (SNA) making forays into credit scoring, owning the platform could prove helpful for banks when assessing the quality of borrowers in the future.[11]

1.1.9 A dynamic and fragmented space

What becomes apparent is that the term FinTech is dynamic and evolving. Startups in the space offer a wide variety of services, from tools for retail customers to consolidate financial data to complex analytics for investment funds. Many of them blend several innovation themes, such as online transactions, mPOS, and mobile wallets. The approach to doing business varies widely between different FinTech companies: a startup producing a CRM system for banks may have a completely different culture and different customers than a disruptive cryptocurrency venture in Silicon Valley. Without trying to complicate the discussion, it is clear that FinTech is dynamic, fragmented and complex. At the same time, the classification by innovation theme from Table 1.1 and Figure 1.2 allows us to structure the discussion about the financial technology landscape. Because the focus of this book is marketplace lending, it is important to separate this segment from the others. Startups in the online lending space may still service several innovation themes at the same time and, if they do, we will recognize it by overlaying the classification we established.

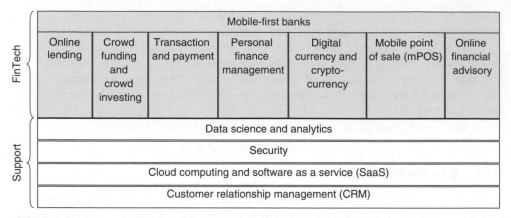

FinTech						
Mobile-first banks						
Online lending	Crowd funding and crowd investing	Transaction and payment	Personal finance management	Digital currency and crypto-currency	Mobile point of sale (mPOS)	Online financial advisory

Support			
Data science and analytics			
Security			
Cloud computing and software as a service (SaaS)			
Customer relationship management (CRM)			

FIGURE 1.2 The main financial technology innovation themes and their supporting technologies in relationship with each other

1.2 THE PROMISES AND PITFALLS OF FINTECH BUSINESS MODELS

Now that we know the main sectors and innovation themes in FinTech, we can group them by other attributes as well. FinTech companies take different approaches to disrupt the financial sector.[12] We may separate them into business models with a higher chance at disruption and those less likely to succeed. We begin by describing four business models with a better chance at disrupting the status quo. There are certainly more, but the ones we discuss here include streamlining the user experience (UX) and digital integration, setting an industry standard that the financial industry previously failed to get off the ground, using someone else's network while only paying marginal cost, and providing a worse service to customers at a lower price.[13] These business models overlap, as Figure 1.3 shows.

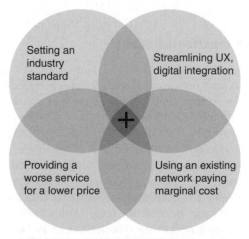

FIGURE 1.3 FinTech business models with high disruptive potential

1.2.1 Streamlining the user experience (UX) and digital integration

Banks have been notoriously slow to bring their services into the digital age. Even though most banks offer internet banking and mobile banking, loan application and decisioning are still miles apart from the ease of use and convenience that consumers appreciate in online services. Banks are hardly a cozy place to visit, and the mistrust between banks and the general public is hard to overcome. On the other hand, FinTech has the air of "new, cool and pure," and streamlining the user experience is one of the main selling points of FinTech services. Their interfaces are slick and clean, and they give users control of the experience at all times. Some mobile-first banks resemble more a social network or messaging service than a financial institution. Taking the pain and tedium out of banking is a huge niche that still has much room to grow, especially in payments and lending.

1.2.2 Setting an industry standard that the financial industry failed to get off the ground

Even though banks have global transaction networks, they often insert unnecessary steps in global transactions that reduce speed and ease of the customer experience at an additional cost. For instance, the reason an international bank transfer takes five business days is hardly that it takes money that long to travel around the globe. By holding money for several days before they transfer it into a recipient's bank account, banks get credit for free, which they can lend out for a fee. Customers have less and less tolerance for such shenanigans, and some FinTech companies have proven that money transfers can be instant. Whenever a startup manages to improve a financial service by orders of magnitude, this should be a wake-up call to banks. Much less because it is a new way of doing business, than because the established incumbents could have easily implemented it themselves had they made an honest effort at improving the service for their customers.

1.2.3 Using someone else's network while only paying marginal cost

Many FinTech companies depend on existing infrastructure that is often in the hands of incumbents in the financial sector. Online lending is an example, and so are payments. It seems surprising that the owners of the existing financial networks allow small companies to use them to offer competing services. The reason this is possible is that regulators seem to be keen on encouraging competition and entry in financial services markets. Several FinTech companies undercut incumbents for payment services. Even though they might compete in the short term, they actually stand a good chance for an acquisition later down the road. Customers love to pay less for a similar service, so paying only marginal cost plus a small fee can be a successful business model for new entrants in financial services.

1.2.4 Providing a worse service to customers at a lower price

Unbundling services that banks provide can be a viable business model for FinTech companies. Some customers may wish to pay for only a small segment of the bundled product offering that banks sell for a high price. The discount brokerage industry is an example for successful execution of this approach. Even though their service is more limited than that of a full-service broker, it is still good enough for many customers. This has allowed online brokerage to become the industry standard that has severely disrupted traditional brokers. Customers often have no need for up-market innovation that the incumbent provides. Instead, they want something new that gives them a similar experience for a lower price. In essence, this is the promise of disruptive innovation, and it seems to be one of the most promising approaches in FinTech.

1.3 THE PITFALLS

Some FinTech companies are prone to wrong assumptions about their chances for disruption, including overestimating data science to deal with concentration and adverse selection, overestimating the value of transaction data, overestimating people's willingness to trust technology companies, and overestimating the regulators' willingness to forgive small companies for flouting the rules.[14] Figure 1.4 shows how they overlap. The following paragraphs will briefly explain each of them.

1.3.1 Overestimating the ability of data science to deal with concentration and adverse selection

When technology companies segment the market into smaller and smaller fragments, which they service with niche offerings, their customer lists are often rife with concentration risk. When the fortunes of the financial markets change, customers with highly correlated behavior can bring abrupt failure to a company with an excellent track record. To be fair, some banks have been guilty of overestimating data science to deal with concentration risk and adverse selection as well. Why does data science fail to be the cure-all when selecting customers? Hardly because banks are smarter than we give them credit for, but because customer selection is more difficult than we think.

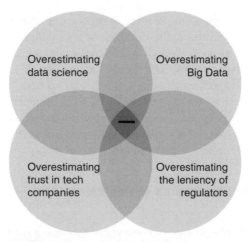

FIGURE 1.4   FinTech pitfalls

1.3.2 Overestimating the value of Big Data in transactions

Data science and Big Data are promising avenues. However, the dollar value of the data that individual users generate on a network is still open to debate. Even though it is interesting to know each and every step that users take on a network, transaction data in itself may be overvalued. Is combining social network analysis with neural net algorithms a billion dollar business idea? Extracting accurate predictions from Big Data still has several hurdles to overcome, and business models that depend on it are unproven. Those FinTech companies with transactions for the sake of generating data at their core might be in for a rough ride.

1.3.3 Overestimating people's willingness to trust a FinTech company instead of another middleman

Some FinTech companies build platforms that unite a fragmented market and make forex, bond trading and other financial transactions look similar to a stock exchange. In short, such platforms aim at disrupting the "middlemen." Companies with success in this game often involve a lot more "fin" and a lot less "tech" in their operations. A trading platform needs to convince all parties that transactions between them are safe and that the platform will function in a fair manner. Building trust and good relationships is far more important than cool technology alone. Those companies that manage to build trust make money whether or not they have good technology.

1.3.4 Overestimating the regulators' willingness to pardon a FinTech company flouting the rules

Financial regulation is strict for a reason: it aims to protect the consumer. The approach of startups to break the law and then send out a press release claiming regulators obstruct their innovative business model has little chance of success in FinTech. In the financial sector, small businesses come with severe diseconomies of scale in terms of regulation. When regulation comes to their doorstep, they will have to follow the same rules as everybody else, regardless of their size.

FinTech is still an immature space, and which business models will prevail is highly uncertain. Nevertheless, the financial industry is likely to profit from outside innovation.

1.4 WHY IS FINANCIAL TECHNOLOGY INNOVATION IMPORTANT?

Most of the services that FinTech startups provide already exist in one form or another. The only problem is that these existing services have been relatively expensive, inefficient, or exclusive. FinTech promises to democratize financial services by making them more efficient, transparent, fair, profitable, and robust. Consider, for example, payment processing. Shopkeepers have been able to accept cashless payments by credit cards for decades. However, this only makes sense for vendors of a certain size. Those who sell items at the flea market hardly have the scale to absorb the cost involved in processing credit cards. Several mPOS startups have sprung up in recent years that provide credit card readers that plug into a smartphone. Credit card processing is thus available for any merchant or private individual at low cost. The same goes for online financial advisors. A healthy industry of private wealth managers has prospered through the ages, but it existed only for a select group of high-net-worth individuals at considerable cost to the client. Robo-advisors slash this cost to a few basis points, while providing comparable services to almost anybody with a regular savings account or a retirement savings account, such as a 401(k).

Common themes in financial technology innovation are streamlining processes, reducing search costs, and minimizing transaction costs, which broadens access to financial services for new customers. FinTech startups thus serve two goals: they increase the market and re-segment it—at the expense of the incumbent players in the established financial sector. It is clear that most of the new services fulfill a need that customers have, mostly because the existing financial sector is not offering it, or is offering it at a price point that prohibits customers from using it. If banks offered a simple way to conduct financial transactions online, why would a payment processor like PayPal amass hundreds of millions of users?

In online lending, the existing gatekeepers are banks and other established lending institutions. How exactly banks operate will be the subject of Part Two of this book. For now, let's simplify and say that banks aggregate deposits from customers and then lend out these deposits to borrowers at a higher interest rate than they pay to those customers who deposited money in the accounts. To minimize the risk of default, they carefully select borrowers according to strict criteria. This often excludes individuals with a low credit score or SMEs with low revenues. Since the financial crisis of 2007/8, banks in the United States have issued on average 15 percent fewer loans to this customer group.[15] Online lenders therefore enjoy strong demand from borrowers starved for credit. Demand is hardly the problem for online lending platforms. The main challenge is making a credible case that those who invest in these platforms will receive healthy returns. Online lenders must therefore find the balance of carefully vetting their borrowers and improving on the lending process that established banks would provide. This is by no means a simple endeavor. It took banks hundreds of years to perfect their lending practices, so reinventing the sector at scale in a decade will be a gargantuan task.

1.5 CHALLENGES AND ROADBLOCKS FOR FINTECH COMPANIES

Next to business models relying on assumptions that might turn out to be wrong, FinTech companies have other roadblocks to overcome. Some of them are the lack of a human interface, the need for banking licenses, and the question whether data is in safe hands with technology companies.

1.5.1 Lack of a human interface

Most people are by nature risk-averse—as we will discuss later in more detail—and they dislike taking risks with their capital. At the same time, they want convenience and ubiquitous banking services, without understanding that the two are sometimes a trade-off. Banking might not have much in common with flying, but let us think about an analogy for a second: even though most airliners are mostly on autopilot nowadays, people feel safe when they know there are knowledgeable pilots in the cockpit and crew on board. They may never see them in person during the entire flight. Still, most passengers would be deeply troubled if there were no in-flight crew on the plane. Even though someone could remote-control a plane masterfully, flying without a pilot and crew on board *feels* unsafe. A similar approach still exists with financial services. Speaking with a trusted financial advisor or loan officer in person often beats interacting with robots and computers. The fact that the entire back office is fully automated is of little concern, as long as there exists a human somewhere in the process that customers can talk to.

When it comes to money, emotions play a vital part. Earning money with automated financial services that need little human interaction is only one part of the equation. The more important part is convincing mainstream customers that they are safe or even safer than the existing service that their banker or financial advisor provides. Sure, financial technology has already attracted much interest, to the point that banks should start to worry about it. Regardless, early adopters and tech-savvy Millennials are hardly enough for a service to achieve critical mass. To fully take off and rival established banks, they need to win over the minds and hearts of mainstream banking customers.

Imagining financial services as a hands-off affair still seems a long shot, and that is exactly what financial technology innovation is about: changing the way customers bank and transact in the next five to ten years, not immediately. Granted, few FinTech startups have mastered both their operations and their customer service to the point where they measure up to what customers expect from banks. However, this may change soon. The driverless car seemed like a science-fiction prophecy until Google announced a fully functional prototype in 2014.[16] Most major car companies are now working on similar technology, and most of them have an office in Silicon Valley to be close to the innovation.[17] Exactly when the first driverless car will become commercially available is in the stars. One thing we can be certain of is that when it hits the market and is successful, it will transform the way people think about driving. The same will happen in the financial sector: when one or several services together have solved our psychological attachment to speak with other humans about our financial affairs, they will take off. When they have achieved critical mass, people will have difficulty remembering how they could ever do without them. That is the moment that banks fear, not the spotty, early-stage innovation that only technology evangelists are interested in.

1.5.2 The need for banking licenses

How easy is it to get a new banking license in a major financial center nowadays? In most instances, it will be very expensive or even impossible because big banks firmly rule the scene. Getting the license is just the beginning; the tough part will be compliance with banking regulations. Banks have massive existing infrastructure to deal with regulation already set up. This is the trump card that established banks hold in their hands. As long as FinTech startups cannot legally accept deposits from anyone, banks feel they still own the last mile of retail banking. Technically, many FinTech services can operate well without a banking license— especially companies in marketplace lending, payments, or financial advisory. But their claim to unseat the established financial sector will only have merit when they actually play on the same level—regulation and all—with established players. It is in the interest of financial technology startups to seek dialogue with regulators, not avoid regulation by flying under the radar. In today's environment, an avoidance strategy will not be possible for long. Only if FinTech entrepreneurs are proactive will they have a chance to actively shape the regulation of their industry.

1.5.3 Concerns over privacy

Financial institutions have the reputation of being vaults for people's sensitive information. Even though this notion has softened slightly in the wake of high-profile data leaks and tax prosecution, most people expect banks to guard their information more safely than a social network would. Keeping secrets is actually at the core of the business model of banks. At the same time, this information can give banks insider knowledge. When information about investment opportunities is less accessible, markets become less efficient, and insiders increase their profits. By regulating the flow of information, banks may actively tilt the odds in their favor.[18] The opposite is true for technology companies. Their users' secrets are an asset they exploit as much as possible. As some believe, personal data will be the "new oil"—a new emerging asset class of the 21st century, that will touch all aspects of society.[19] Contrary to their reputation as secret keepers, banks are actually also selling information about their customers. Barclays Bank sold information about the spending habits of 13 million customers to other companies.[20] These data included images of customers, recordings of their voice, customers' comments in interactions with the bank on social media sites, and location data from mobile devices. At the same time, the bank assured customers that the data would be safely aggregated only to show trends and that individuals would remain anonymous. Banks and other companies have mined data on their customers internally for ages, but selling sensitive data to third parties is relatively new.

User data have become a resource in business beyond the realm of tech companies. Nevertheless, when a customer discusses details about her spending habits with a bank officer, she might share information more openly than on a social network. As an industry, banks still benefit from their reputation as guardians of secrets. The air of trust that a proper branch network radiates is hard to replicate for technology companies. Tech firms have to overcome the stigma that they exploit user data with little regard for privacy, even though they are hardly the only businesses doing so.

1.6 FINTECH IS A LONG-TERM PLAY

Technology will change the infrastructure of banking over time but it will not happen tomorrow. Sean Park, founder of the advisory firm Anthemis, believes that new companies in financial technology will encroach on the bank's turf over decades, not months or years. There is little danger that startups will replace the banking infrastructure overnight.[21] A bigger threat for banks arises when customers have learned that they can build—rebundle—their own bank out of several FinTech market leaders in individual niches. Such a modular arrangement could offer services to customers identical to those they receive from banks, only with more convenience, transparency, fairness, and at a fraction of the cost. As soon as customers can objectively compare such a new digital bank that thrives on bits with their existing bricks-and-mortar bank, the "old" style of banking will likely come across as clumsy and expensive—a bad deal for the customer.

Rebundling won't happen overnight, and FinTech companies will need several years to gain enough maturity and strength to become a serious threat. A short-term focus or even a medium-term view is hardly doing justice to the future of the hybrid financial sector. Nevertheless, banks should be aware that their business model will undergo massive change in the next five to ten years. To stay relevant with their customers, banks must take a more enlightened approach to working with FinTech entrepreneurs. This is in their own best interest. We will discuss the hybrid financial sector in more detail in Chapter 16 of the book. The next chapter homes in on online lending and how it works in particular.

1.7 CONCLUDING REMARKS

This chapter introduced nine different innovation themes in FinTech, including online lending, crowdfunding and crowdinvesting, transactions and payments, personal finance management, digital currency and cryptocurrency, mobile point of sale (mPOS), online financial advisory, and mobile-first banks. It then pointed out promises of FinTech business models, such as streamlining the user experience and digital integration, setting standards in which the financial industry previously failed, using existing networks at marginal cost, and providing a worse service to customers at a lower price. Pitfalls of FinTech are overestimating data science, overestimating the value of transaction data, overestimating people's trust in technology companies, and underestimating regulatory consequences of flouting the rules.

Even though they disrupt the financial sector in a big way, FinTech companies have several roadblocks to overcome before they are serious competition for banks. These roadblocks include the lack of a human interface, the need for banking licenses, and data safety. Nevertheless, focusing too narrowly on single niches in FinTech misses the larger picture. More dangerous for banks is the risk of several niche FinTechs rebundling their services on a plug-and-play banking platform that could offer services to customers identical to those they receive from banks—only with more convenience, transparency, fairness, and at a fraction of the cost.

NOTES

1. Gordon Mills, Karen and McCarthy, Brayden (2014) "The State of Small Business Lending: Credit Access during the Recovery and How Technology May Change the Game" (Harvard Business School Working Paper, 22 July 2014), http://www.hbs.edu/faculty/Publication%20Files/15-004_09b1bf8b-eb2a-4e63-9c4e-0374f770856f.pdf.
2. Broderick, Daniel (2014) "Crowdfunding's Untapped Potential In Emerging Markets" (*Forbes*, 8 May, 2014), http://www.forbes.com/sites/hsbc/2014/08/05/crowdfundings-untapped-potential-in-emerging-markets/.
3. Markoff, John (2005) *What the Dormouse Said: How the Sixties Counterculture Shaped the Personal Computer Industry* (New York: Penguin).
4. Paypal (2014) "Q2 2014 Fast Facts," https://www.paypal-media.com/assets/pdf/fact_sheet/PayPal_Q2_2014_FastFacts_Final.pdf.
5. M-Pesa (2014a) home page, https://www.mpesa.in, accessed 12 November 2014.
6. Demirguc-Kunt, Asli; Klapper, Leora (2012) "Measuring Financial Inclusion" (World Bank, Policy Research Working Paper 6025, April 2012), http://elibrary.worldbank.org/doi/pdf/10.1596/1813-9450-6025.
7. Brito, Jerry; Castilo, Andrea (2013) "Bitcoin, a Primer for Policy Makers" (George Mason University, 2013), mercatus.org/sites/default/files/Brito_BitcoinPrimer.pdf.
8. Ibid.
9. Wealthfront (2014a) "Wealthfront Investment Methodology White Paper," https://www.wealthfront.com/whitepapers/investment-methodology, date accessed 14 November 2014.

10. Groenfeldt, Tom (2014) "BBVA Makes Banking Simple," (*Forbes*, 7 March 2014), http://www .forbes.com/sites/tomgroenfeldt/2014/03/07/bbva-compass-makes-banking-simple/.
11. Knowledge@Wharton (2014a) "The 'Social' Credit Score: Separating the Data from the Noise," http://knowledge.wharton.upenn.edu/article/the-social-credit-score-separating-the-data-from-the-n oise, date accessed 5 June 2013.
12. Davies, Dan (2015) "A Cynic's Guide to FinTech: Several business models that are bound to fail— and a few that might have a chance," https://medium.com/bull-market/a-cynic-s-guide-to-fintech-3cd0995e0da3 (3 April 2015), date accessed 10 April 2015.
13. Some of these business models are inspired by Davies, Dan (2015) "A Cynic's Guide to Fintech: Several business models that are bound to fail—and a few that might have a chance," https://medium .com/bull-market/a-cynic-s-guide-to-fintech-3cd0995e0da3 (3 April 2015), date accessed 10 April 2015.
14. Davies, Dan (2015) "A Cynic's Guide to Fintech: Several business models that are bound to fail— and a few that might have a chance", https://medium.com/bull-market/a-cynic-s-guide-to-fintech-3cd0995e0da3 (3 April 2015), date accessed 10 April 2015.
15. FDIC (2014a) "Loans to Small businesses and Farms, FDIC-Insured Institutions 1995–2014," https://www2.fdic.gov/qbp/timeseries/SmallBusiness&FarmLoans.xls.
16. O'Brien, Matt (2014) "Google's 'goofy' new self-driving car a sign of things to come" (*San Jose Mercury*, 22 December 2014), http://www.mercurynews.com/business/ci_27190285/googles-goofy-new-self-driving-car-sign-things.
17. Gapper, John (2015) "Software is steering auto industry: This revolution makes it possible for a technology group to be a car company" (*Financial Times*, 18 February 2015), http://www.ft.com/cms/s/0/dce10162-b5f1-11e4-a577-00144feab7de.html.
18. Dang, Tri Vi and Gorton, Gary and Holstroem, Bengt and Ordonez, Guillermo (2014) "Banks as Secret Keepers", National Bureau of Economic Research (NBER), www.nber.org/papers/w20255, date accessed March 10, 2015.
19. World Economic Forum (2011) "Personal Data: The Emergence of a New Asset Class," http://www3. weforum.org/docs/WEF_ITTC_PersonalDataNewAsset_Report_2011.pdf, date accessed 10 April 2015.
20. Jones, Rupert (2013) "Barclays to sell customer data" (the *Guardian*, 24 June 2013), http:// www.theguardian.com/business/2013/jun/24/barclays-bank-sell-customer-data, date accessed 10 April 2015.
21. Gapper, John (2014) "Technology will hurt the banks, not kill them" (*Financial Times*, 10 October 2014), http://www.ft.com/cms/s/0/710445c4-52ed-11e4-b917-00144feab7de.html.

CHAPTER 2

How Does Online Lending Work?
An Overview with a Focus on
Marketplace Lending

Online lending has come a long way from its initially sketchy reputation. The first company in the space was London-based Zopa, which launched in 2005 and has since lent over £900 million.[1] It is still Europe's largest marketplace lending service. Two San Francisco based startups followed, Prosper and Lending Club. The former started in 2006 as the first peer-to-peer lending market place in the US. It now boasts over 2 million members and over $4 billion in funded loans.[2] Lending Club launched in 2007 and has since facilitated more than $9 billion in loans.[3] Authors Karen Gordon Mills and Brayden McCarthy point out that the outstanding portfolio balance of alternative online lenders is still comparatively small; the bank credit market is nearly 70 times its size. [4] Nevertheless, author Charles Moldow predicts a bright future for the sector: $1 trillion in loans originated globally by marketplace lending platforms by 2025.[5]

Despite their scale, online lenders and the technology they use is fundamentally changing the ways in which small businesses access capital. The new platforms create efficiencies, greater competition, and price transparency, and they make small business lending more profitable than established bank credit. Banks have been waiting on the sidelines while emerging online players are filling the technology gap between established financial services and market demands. Marketplace lenders are pushing innovation within the credit sector in the same ways in which other online platforms such as Amazon.com changed retail and the book trade and iTunes changed the music industry.

2.1 RELIANCE ON TECHNOLOGY AND DATA

Online lending companies create platforms that connect borrowers with lenders. The motivation to do this comes from the need for credit by consumers and SMEs that have no other access to capital at an affordable cost, which has opened up a lending gap. To bridge the gap, borrowers promise to pay above market-rate returns in exchange for renewed credit access. On the other hand, technology has evolved to the point where platforms are robust and secure enough to handle large datasets and the analytics necessary to connect borrowers directly with lenders. Cheap and ubiquitous computing power and storage have clearly enabled marketplace lending. By using technology and Big Data innovatively, online lenders fulfill two important functions: they lower search costs for borrowers and address the difficulties in assessing the creditworthiness of potential borrowers. Technology also improves ease of use and rapid turnaround of applications and capital disbursements.

Traditional lenders generally focus on the small business owners' personal credit history while the new alternative lenders also focus on the current performance of small businesses by analyzing non-traditional data sources. Most online lenders analyze data from social media interactions and reviews from online sources to assess the health of a borrower or business. For example, several online lenders create predictive indices based on access to current cash flow data from bank accounts and entries in accounting software. Most lenders have developed a proprietary end-to-end lending platform including a loan origination platform, a proprietary credit scoring model, and a collection platform that collects ACH payments from borrowers as frequently as each business day.[6]

Automation and smart analytics increase pressure on margins and fees. Other than technology leadership, the question is who can compete best on narrow margin in the credit sector of the future. Large financial institutions can absorb the big overhead necessary for regulatory compliance, but so can well-known online lending platforms with venture capital backing, should their regulatory overhead increase. Technology is a double-edged sword: it makes the sector attractive for new entrants, but runs the risk of undermining profitability in the long term.

2.2   HOW DO ONLINE LENDERS DIFFER FROM BANKS?

Despite the emergence of online lending, bank credit is still the main source of small business credit. But, since the financial crisis, alternative sources of capital have grown significantly. How do online lenders differ from established credit institutions? To answer this question, let's first examine how the lending process of established banks works in Figure 2.1.

In their lending operations, banks make capital available to borrowers, or—in banking parlance—obligors who have the obligation to pay back a loan with interest. They raise capital from two main sources: from depositors who keep a savings account with the bank and from capital markets. When banks lend depositors' funds out as loans, they keep the spread between the rate they pay to depositors and the rate that obligors need to pay. When the interest rate is low, then banks have a better chance of generating a spread in their lending operations. In this case, they might raise additional funds from the capital markets. For this to work, banks need to balance their liquidity carefully so they never run out of cash. This is the job of the treasury,

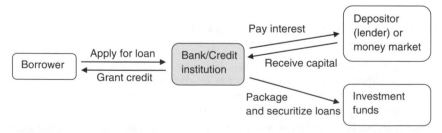

FIGURE 2.1   Lending process of a bank

which makes sure that the bank always has a good idea of the risks it has taken on and the obligations it needs to fulfill. We will discuss all this in more detail in the second part of the book, when we learn more about the operations of treasury in traditional bank lending. For now, let's acknowledge that banks are both lenders and borrowers at the same time, and that the loans they underwrite enter their balance sheet. This means they are liable if a borrower is unwilling or unable to pay back a loan. Obviously, it is in the interest of banks to take on as little risk as possible, but enough to still turn a profit. Some risk is necessary, but as long as banks understand this risk, they can manage it.

Some online lending platforms function in similar ways to banks: online balance sheet lenders raise money from private investors and lend it to borrowers. However, this is markedly different from the way in which marketplace lending platforms operate. At the same time, what all online lenders have in common is that they drive down their overhead by automating as many processes as they can. Let's look into the different types of online lenders and how they operate in more detail.

2.3 TYPES OF ONLINE LENDERS

Most people believe that all online lenders are peer-to-peer or marketplace lending platforms. This is incorrect. There are several different business models in online lending, and marketplace lending is just one of them. However, even though their business models differ, all online lending platforms have several attributes in common. Table 2.1 summarizes the most important of these attributes, their goals and challenges.

Authors Karen Gordon Mills and Brayden McCarthy identify three different kinds of alternative online lenders: *online balance sheet lenders*, *marketplace lending platforms*, and *lender-agnostic marketplaces*.[7]

Table 2.2 sums up the three types of online lenders, their business models, and challenges.

Let's now visit each of the three online lending business models in more detail.

2.3.1 Marketplace lending platforms

Marketplace lending or peer-to-peer lending means that individuals ("peers") lend directly to borrowers without going through a traditional financial intermediary. Other names for this type of online lending are "social lending" and "lend-to-save." Peer-to-peer lending underwent a rebranding as *marketplace lending* because many investors in loans are actually large investments funds and not the peers of borrowers. Marketplace lending is a more accurate term than peer-to-peer lending. In this book, we use the terms marketplace lending and peer-to-peer lending interchangeably to describe the same thing.

Marketplace lending platforms connect institutional and retail investors with prime and sub-prime quality borrowers, and many of the platforms use a proprietary credit model to assess borrowers. Revenue comes from origination fees and service fees. These lenders work by matching lenders and borrowers online. Their loans are short- to medium-term with a maximum term of 60 months, and their interest rates are fixed. The innovation in marketplace lending is that platforms are not raising capital by themselves to lend. Instead, they connect willing lenders with borrowers directly, which allows them to reduce operating costs while maintaining scalability compared to a consumer loan department within a traditional bank. Their value proposition lies mainly in lower interest rates for borrowers than credit cards

TABLE 2.1   Actions, characteristics, goals, and challenges of online lenders

Actions and characteristics	Goals	Challenges
Transactions take place online on a largely automated platform; Heavy use of technology and Big Data	Matching supply and demand without organizational overhead, lower search costs and due diligence cost	Intransparency when models are proprietary and undisclosed; Potential incongruency of data sources
Development of proprietary credit models for loan approvals and pricing	Superior credit scoring and default preemption	Intransparency when models are proprietary and undisclosed; Overreliance on Big Data analytics as the only form of risk management
Offering online and mobile loan applications (often done in under 30 minutes)	Simplicity of application, speed of capital delivery, greater focus on customer service; Verifying borrower identity, bank account, employment and income, performing credit checks and filtering out unqualified borrowers	Security; accuracy of customer information
Attractive to borrowers who have no other choice but seek alternative lenders	Tapping into a market with high demand, generating high fees for credit	Quality of counterparty, high correlation of borrowers, concentration risk
High loan approval rates, on average above 60 percent (vs. around 20 percent traditionally)[8]	Attracting borrowers with a high chance of approval; Attracting lenders with high funding liquidity	Credit quality; Avoiding the stigma of sub-prime
Platforms offer investors higher returns than conventional debt	Attracting lenders with high yields	Procyclical business model may disappoint under stress; Uncertain performance in times of economic downturn; High correlation of funding sources
Marketplace loans are uncollateralized; Loans are not protected by government guarantees	Rapid decisioning in the absence of hard assets; Tapping into a market with high demand, generating high fees for credit	High-risk investments; Uncertain performance under stress; Difficult risk management

or other alternative lenders, attractive returns for individual investors, and simple electronic interfaces for efficient transactions between lenders and borrowers. Figure 2.2 describes the marketplace lending process. This process has evolved over time, and it may change again in the future. Still, the overall mechanics will most likely remain.

In contrast to other online lending platforms, marketplace lending platforms cater to both borrowers and lenders at the same time. Most retail investors can invest in loans on these

TABLE 2.2   Online lenders, business models, challenges

	Marketplace lender	Online balance sheet lender	Lender-agnostic marketplace
Description	Connects institutional and retail investors with prime and sub-prime quality borrowers; Proprietary credit scoring models; Loans remain off the balance sheet of the lender	Raises funds and lends them through three main channels: direct, platform partnerships, and brokers; Operates similar to a bank, but is unregulated; May package and securitize loans; Loans are on the balance sheet of the lender	Lists lenders and borrowers similar to a registry or catalogue; Loans remain off the balance sheet of the lender
Business model	Commissions; Spread; Fees	Spread; Fees	Commissions
Challenges	Regulatory uncertainty; High correlation of capital sources; Potentially risky loans might underperform in economic downturn	Regulatory uncertainty; High correlation of capital sources; Potentially risky loans might underperform in economic downturn	Not a financial institution but an information resource; Will not enjoy returns of a lending platform

platforms, and they can diversify their investment across many loans. Because platforms have no banking license, they cannot accept deposits from investors directly. To collect and transfer payments from lenders to borrowers, the platform uses two accounts at an affiliated depository bank: a *funding account* and a *collections account*. The early peer-to-peer lending model launched as an auction marketplace where participants determined loan rates by bidding in a Dutch auction system. Lenders had the responsibility for setting rates, despite the fact that they had little understanding of credit risk. Nowadays, platforms set interest rates according to their own internal rating of borrowers. Most investors invest indirectly and partially in

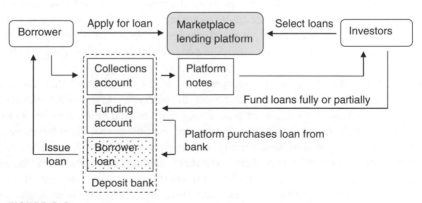

FIGURE 2.2   Origination process of a marketplace lending platform

loans. In most instances, investors simply determine which loan grades they wish to allocate capital to and the size of each investment, and the platform does the rest. Each loan has a funding account that gradually fills up according to the risk appetite of lenders. This account serves a similar function to an escrow account, to ensure investors have the capital available that they promise the borrower. Once the funding account reflects the amount the borrower specified, the depository bank will advance the loan to the borrower. At the same time, the marketplace lending platform operator purchases the borrower loan from the depository bank at nominal cost with the funds in the funding account. The marketplace lending platform then issues so-called *platform notes* to the investors. Each note is a small fraction of the full loan amount, and it reflects the amount a lender invested in the loan. Notes work like fixed income instruments with regular principal repayment and coupon payments. The platform operator collects loan repayments from the borrower in a collections account from which he draws the payments for the platform note. A diversified portfolio of platform notes on marketplace loans can easily exceed the returns available through investment vehicles such as money market funds and certificates of deposit, but it can also be volatile and risky.[9,10] Platform notes can be resold: Lenders can often auction off their notes on platform-specific marketplaces.

On some marketplace lending platforms, lenders pay a fee on the amount they lend to borrowers per year. Borrowers pay a borrowing fee if their loan application is approved. Marketplace lenders typically target mid-prime or near-prime borrowers and lend larger amounts for longer terms.

2.3.2 Online balance sheet lenders

Online balance sheet lenders originate small business loans through three main channels: *direct*, *platform partnerships* and *brokers*. They use their own balance sheet and are raising capital from private and institutional investors. This is similar to how existing banks operate, and some online balance sheet lenders also package and securitize their loans.

The direct channel allows companies to select and contact borrowers through a variety of marketing techniques including direct mail, online media, and email. In platform partnerships, companies connect with prospective borrowers through strategic relationships with third party partners that have access to the small business community. Some balance sheet lenders partner with established banks and credit institutions for small business lending, with the platforms serving as the banks' prospecting, distribution and performance-monitoring systems.[11] Through the broker channel, companies connect with prospective borrowers by entering into relationships with third-party independent brokers that typically offer a variety of financial services to small businesses including commission-based business loan brokerage services.

Balance sheet loans are typically short-term up to 24 months, and they fund working capital and inventory purchases for small and medium enterprises. Many of these loan products operate in a similar way to merchant cash advances, with a fixed amount or percent of sales deducted daily from the borrower's bank account over several months. Their business model is spread-based, as in conventional bank lending. Online balance sheet lenders use technology to automate their processes and to score their borrowers with data that banks rarely consider. For example, they might screen a borrower's social networking accounts and instant messaging channels, investigating her connections and analyzing her posts. The loan application and decision process often take minutes, which is much faster than in a bank. On the whole, online

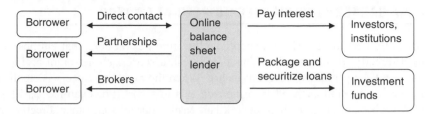

FIGURE 2.3   Lending process of an online balance sheet lender

balance sheet lenders function in similar ways to banks. Figure 2.3 describes the process of online balance sheet lenders.

Some online lenders are in essence just unregulated banks that issue uncollateralized loans. Online balance sheet lenders have no banking license. This prevents them from accepting deposits from retail investors. However, they invest capital from investment funds and other accredited investors. These platforms usually cater to borrowers only, and they secure funding for individual deals on the backend. To administer payments to investors, they rely on custodian accounts from licensed banks. Online balance sheet lenders charge origination fees on their loans as well as maintenance fees.

2.3.3   Lender-agnostic marketplaces

Another emerging online player in small business lending exists in the form of lender-agnostic marketplaces. This type of online lender creates a marketplace for borrowers to compare a range of loan products. On these platforms, term loans, lines of credit, merchant cash advances, and factoring products are on offer from alternative lenders to conventional banks, community banks, and regional banks. These online marketplaces reduce search costs, one of the biggest problems borrowers and lenders face. Figure 2.4 outlines the process of a lender-agnostic marketplace.

These marketplaces earn revenue by charging fees on top of the loan if a borrower gets funded and accepts the terms of a loan from the platform. Some of these lenders also sell business leads and contact details to loan officers. Such platforms are increasingly experimenting with ways to partner with banks, particularly community banks. Lender-agnostic marketplaces are encouraging banks to send small business borrowers they turned down to their online marketplace.

In this book, we focus on marketplace transactional marketplaces, which we will call marketplace lenders or peer-to-peer lenders from now on. Let's investigate the different meanings of the term peer-to-peer so we have clarity about the definition of the term.

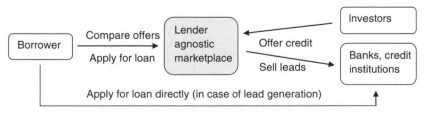

FIGURE 2.4   Lending process of a lender-agnostic marketplace

2.4 SOME BACKGROUND ON PEER-TO-PEER NETWORKS

At the heart of a peer-to-peer (P2P) network architecture lies the idea that entities or *peers* can connect directly with each other. This is trivial in a sense, as one might argue that all interactions between people are direct in nature. When the number of peers is small, this is true. They can easily find each other and match at a low cost. For example, as illustrated in Figure 2.5, all eight peers in the network can easily link to each other directly or indirectly. Assume that peer 6 would like to connect with peer 1: peer 6 can link to peer 1 either directly or via combination of peers, for example, $\{2\}, \{3, 2\}, \{4, 3, 2\}, \{5, 4, 3, 2\}, \{7\}$, and $\{7, 8\}$.

However, in a large set of peers, search costs are high. If many sellers and buyers exist in a market, it would take forever to meet every single person with whom they might want to enter into a transaction. In this case, a central authority may take on the burden of pooling all peers on one side of the transaction—such as the sell side—and represent itself as one peer that the other side can buy from. An example would be a supermarket; all producers sell directly to the supermarket, which becomes the convenient place to go for all buyers of produce. However, this convenience comes with several disadvantages. For instance, the central authority has a lot of power over buyers, as it is now the monopolist in the market with the power to set prices. If a supermarket has managed to lobby for laws that prevent individual sellers from selling directly to buyers, both sides are at the central authority's mercy. Sellers have only one party to sell to, and buyers have only one party to buy from (Figure 2.6). This form of interaction is no longer a peer-to-peer network.

Even though the central authority often argues that the convenience he provides to customers comes at a high cost which justifies a high price, a centralized system is rife with the

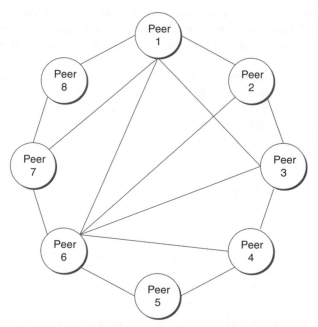

FIGURE 2.5   Peer-to-peer networking with direct and indirect connections

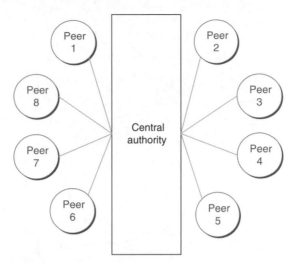

FIGURE 2.6   Centralized systems architecture, a supplier-oriented marketplace

potential for abuse. Is this really the best and most convenient system to transact? Clearly not. Enter peer-to-peer networks where many peers connect directly.

For direct connection to be economical, peers must have information about each other. When all peers already know each other, this is simple, but the burden of finding the right peer quickly increases with the number of peers in a network. At the same time, a system with many peers benefits strongly from network effects: the more individual peers exist, the more permutations for connections exist, which gives buyers more variety and sellers a bigger market. However, there must be a mechanism or platform for peers to gather information about each other, which will facilitate connections. As a trade-off, peer-to-peer platforms allow only bilateral connections among lenders and borrowers, not linkages via other peers. As you can see in Figure 2.7, peer 6 can have only bilateral links with all others in the system (peers 1, 2, 3, 4, 5 and 7).

The scale of centralized structures that we saw in Figure 2.6 had clear advantages for users who had no other way to access a market or gain information about potential trading partners. However, with the emergence of the biggest peer-to-peer network in history, the internet, it has become easier to collect, structure and make available searchable information about a large number of peers. In a sense, online peer-to-peer networks reintroduce the ancient way of direct interaction that humans used in trade hundreds of years ago.

Whenever we bring up the term peer-to-peer, most people first think of illegal file sharing services, such as Napster. In technical terms, Napster was a first-generation peer-to-peer system: it still relied on a centralized server structure that eventually proved its Achilles heel. The system could have detected illegal file sharing activity on its infrastructure but chose to ignore it. Subsequent protocols, such as Gnutella or BitTorrent, did away with a central directory. They completely distribute file searches and transfers among corresponding peers, with some systems, such as FreeNet, even providing client anonymity. The most advanced systems route requests indirectly through other clients and encrypt messages between peers. Illegal file sharing brought peer-to-peer applications into the mainstream. A few years later, the *voice over P2P* (VoP2P) application Skype proved that peer-to-peer technology had wider

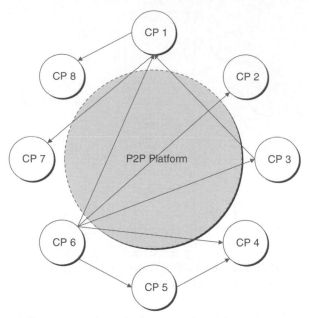

FIGURE 2.7   Peer-to-peer platforms allow only bilateral
linkage among peers

uses that also worked as a commercial business model. It expanded into other arenas, such as
television, with P2PTV.[12]

2.4.1   Disintermediation or re-intermediation?

By encroaching on the turf of the established financial sector, FinTech startups profess to
disintermediate the established players. Some platforms connect lenders and borrowers directly
in a marketplace, so they make the gatekeeper obsolete, they say. Providers of mobile wallets
and payment processors profess to abolish credit card companies. Cryptocurrencies aim to
unseat central banks. However, even though a platform may be neutral, it will reroute traffic
from elsewhere through its proprietary infrastructure. It is therefore more accurate to speak of
a *re-intermediation*, not a disintermediation. Even though some of the startups may disagree,
if their business models prove successful, there will simply be a new sheriff in town, in the
form of the platform, ruling over a particular niche. Over time, these new incumbents will
suffer a similar fate like the established players they unseated. They will have to be vigilant to
stay agile, continuing to innovate.

The same has happened in other sectors, where technology has upended established
companies. The book trade, for example, has seen widespread disruption, where traditional
retailers of books and their publishers gave up a large market share to online marketplaces. The
music industry suffered a similar fate: instead of major music labels, a computer company—
Apple—now dominates the online music space. While new entrants initially promised a flatter
system devoid of monopolies, they have become the new monopolists themselves. Instead of
watching for disintermediation, look out for re-intermediation and automated intermediation
in the FinTech space. Because financial services are at the heart of every business in the

economy, the issue might be more serious than the discussion about selling books or music online. Unless we understand the roles of new entrants clearly, we could end up with a gigantic shadow banking system that concentrates more risk on fewer unregulated intermediaries, which makes the system inherently unstable.

2.4.2 Infomediaries, intermediary-oriented marketplaces, and the information value chain

Information is a powerful enabler of peer-to-peer networks, and the spread of online transactions has given power to a new kind of intermediary: the *infomediary*. Authors John Hagel and Jeffrey Rayport coined the term to describe the function of a central negotiator who collects information about customers and helps them identify the best deals. Negotiations with consumers for information cost time and money, and the information is often messy and hard to compare. At the same time, many companies may collect information about customers, but they organize them poorly. When Hagel and Rayport wrote about infomediaries in 1997, they noted the process of collecting consumer information was already under way. However, they pointed out that it might take several years to play out across broad segments of customers and products.[13] Advances in online commerce and technology have pushed the necessity for information about counterparties into the mainstream. Consumers are also increasingly willing to share private information, such as their financial data, when they can benefit from it. When we look at the onboarding process of marketplace lending platforms, it becomes immediately obvious that information is at the core of this business. At every step, online lending platforms are trying to get the customer to give up information that platforms can use later to customize their services. With every interaction on their platform, online lenders are building an information supply chain.

When we compare the model of the infomediary to the supermarket we just discussed, we see how the supermarket could transform its business model to become an infomediary: instead of purchasing produce from sellers, it could simply collect information about their inventory in a database. When a buyer enters the store—offline or online—she could query that database and see which seller offers what she wants at this particular point in time. The buyer would then pay for the information and collect the products directly at the seller's location. Of course, markets have been infomediaries for quite a while. In parallel to the core business of selling produce, they have always collected information about buyers. Nevertheless, now that shopping increasingly shifts online, information has become more valuable and more important. Buyers search a database of products on a website where they complete the transaction. The seller receives a notification of a sale and the shipping address of the buyer to fulfill the purchase. This insight is by no means revolutionary because many marketplaces that operate this way exist, such as eBay, Amazon, or Alibaba. They are what author Dave Chaffey calls *intermediary-oriented marketplaces*, contrary to *supplier-oriented marketplaces* (which we saw in Figure 2.6) and *buyer-oriented marketplaces*. The organization that finances and runs the platform determines the orientation of a marketplace. In supplier-oriented marketplaces, the sellers of a good or service invest in information technology to attract buyers. In finance, this is what a bank would do by making available loan applications online, or by investing in online banking. When firms invest in setting up buyer-oriented marketplaces, they do this with the goal of reducing their procurement costs. Potential suppliers then compete for the business of the buyer. Only large corporations can afford to run such a marketplace, such as General Electric, or governments who request proposals for tenders. The advantage of an intermediary-oriented marketplace is that buyers and sellers incur no cost to run the marketplace and maintain the technology. Marketplaces are neutral and only help to match buyers and sellers in a virtual environment with lower transaction costs for all counterparties.[14]

Many network systems have developed with the idea of decentralization in mind. Even though they may not necessarily meet the technical definition of a peer-to-peer software application, distributing a resource across its users has many applications offline as well. Most commercial peer-to-peer systems benefit from using a central directory to organize the information about individual peers. This is a prerequisite for facilitating the exchange of value between individual peers. If enough users are connecting directly between each other, and are part of a network, the network itself becomes valuable. For example, think of the car-hailing service Uber: how useful would it be if there were only a handful of drivers connected to a large number of customers? Customers may have to wait a long time until drivers became available, and they might just as well use a taxi at a higher cost. However, when customers have ample choice between drivers, network effects kick in and customers ride faster and cheaper by using the service. Network effects bring down the search cost and transaction cost.

2.5   THE BUSINESS MODEL OF MARKETPLACE LENDING PLATFORMS

Let us examine how this logic relates to marketplace lending. If individual peers wish to borrow and lend between each other directly, they can always ask their friends and family to help them out. This comes with several challenges: Because borrowers have only one or a few counterparties, lenders have a high credit risk in case the borrower defaults. As we saw in Figure 2.7, if one borrower can connect with many lenders, their credit exposure decreases rapidly. However, most borrowers have only a limited number of direct links with potential lenders. For this reason, it makes sense for them to build a large network to increase the number of peers they can borrow from. This is what a marketplace lending platform does: it collects information about borrowers and lenders and makes it easily searchable. It then sells this information or takes a cut from the transaction costs to fund its operations and make a profit. As a result, both lenders and borrowers have lower search costs and transaction costs. The platform also rates borrowers and sets interest rates for loan contracts, which decreases the bargaining cost of counterparties. It has in place a reliable infrastructure that allows counterparties to make payments and collect interest, and it stays on top of borrowers' performance. Additional third-party infomediaries are part of this information supply chain: for example, the credit bureau that collects information about people's credit, or the data mining company that analyzes data from a social network to derive alternative information about users. It is also easy to see how existing intermediary-oriented marketplaces can upgrade their operations and offer credit to their customers. In some instances, this has already taken place: Alibaba, for example, offers payment and investment products,[15,16] Apple is offering a digital wallet.[17] Facilitating transactions between peers is primarily an exercise in leveraging information about users in a network. Companies that already own an information value chain can make the jump to become peer-to-peer lenders relatively quickly.

Some marketplace platforms started with the idea of replicating the corporate bond market for small borrowers, which is another reason we also call peer-to-peer lending *marketplace lending*. In a sense, the corporate bond market bears some similarities to marketplace lending. Companies can issue bonds in the market that interested investors can purchase. Rating agencies screen and rate these bonds, and a legal framework is in place that makes transactions and collections relatively straightforward. However, for lending between private parties and small enterprises, where the profits for facilitating transactions are much smaller, no bond market exists. No investment bank will go to the trouble of underwriting a corporate bond for a borrower who just needs a few thousand dollars. However, by using technology that drives down overhead, platforms can serve profitably as intermediaries between borrowers and lenders and facilitate even small loans.

All this may sound like the silver bullet for lenders, borrowers, and platforms: lenders can earn high interest rates by lending to counterparties that a central intelligence has rated. Instead of chasing after borrowers, the platform provides them with a dashboard that organizes their loans. Borrowers benefit as well: the platform gives them access to willing lenders who might provide lower interest rates than a bank, a credit card company, or a loan shark. Because platforms rely heavily on automation, their overhead is relatively modest. They can turn a profit by charging only a small fee or spread, so tiny that lenders and borrowers might not even notice it. Unfortunately, things are not so simple in the world of marketplace lending.

It might sound deceptively easy to build and maintain an information value chain, however, in borrowing and lending, organizing and making information accessible is hardly enough. Unique challenges exist for marketplace lending platforms. Table 2.3 lists some of them.

2.6   ONBOARDING PROCESS

Marketplace lending platforms cater to both lenders and borrowers. Therefore, usually the first thing they do is segment both target groups and provide each with the services they are looking for. Depending on the role visitors of a platform assign themselves—borrower or lender—they immediately enter a customized onboarding process. This process starts with getting users to sign up for accounts on the platform as they would on a social network. Additionally, and more importantly, it is also a mechanism for users to understand the risks and rewards of marketplace loans and the obligations of borrowers. In organizational psychology, onboarding describes the process through which new hires learn necessary skills and behaviors to become effective members in the organization.[18] Marketplace lending platforms use onboarding in a similar way. Rather than having subscribers with just a vague idea of how to use it, the platform only offers full functionality to verified users. This is done through a series of questions; the answers given by the users enter into an automated cross-check. User verification is instant, but if a check fails, the application will not be complete. There are also several disclaimers where users must confirm that they have read and understood how the platform will operate.

Because platforms distinguish between accounts for borrowers and lenders, if a visitor has signed up as either one, a second account will be necessary to become both a borrower and a lender.

2.6.1   Borrower onboarding

Figure 2.8 shows the onboarding process for borrowers, which most platforms follow in one form or another. Some might ask for certain kinds of information later in the process but, all in all, the process follows a similar logic.

Most platforms offer a quote for a loan by email on their landing page. Prospects will only receive this quote when their details have been verified. The level of detail at this step

TABLE 2.3   Challenges for marketplace lending platforms

Challenge	Description
Market risk	Market conditions hardly affect borrowers and lenders because of fixed rates. However, the fixed rate may be an unexpected disadvantage when it falls below the real interest rate when market conditions change.
Market conditions	Platforms thrive on the gap between normal and stress conditions after the financial crisis 2007/8. In markets with persistently low interest rates, can platforms compete with banks who make longer term loans at lower rates?
Credit risk and counterparty risk	Lenders are directly exposed to credit and counterparty risks of borrowers without a buffer in between.
Operational risk	There is additional operational risk such as fraud when dealing with platforms, due to lack of high security systems. This is especially important in less developed financial markets.
Concentration risk	Platforms do not assess or report concentration risk at the level of the counterparty or individual exposure.
Trust	Counterparties need to build trust in each other bilaterally in addition to trust between the counterparties and the platform.
Virtual presence	Operations of platforms are entirely web-based. Service providers of the back-end infrastructure play a secondary role.
Lack of collateral	In most instances, borrowers provide no collateral to secure credit exposures.
Intransparency and market fragmentation	Each platform has its own definitions, conventions, models, scoring algorithms, and analytics. This makes comparison between platforms difficult.
Counterparty rating	Rating process for identifying the credit worthiness of counterparties varies from platform to platform and is relatively intransparent. Banks, on the other hand, share the ratings provided by rating agencies; for retail portfolios, they disclose ratings via regulatory reports.
Design of contracts	The contracts defining the exchange of cash flows among the counterparties are relatively simple; they are short-term annuities with fixed interest rates.
Liquidity	The only assessment of liquidity is funding liquidity—the ease with which borrowers can obtain funding.
Loan valuation	Valuation rules applied to loan contracts during the term are intransparent.
Profit and loss analysis	Platforms do not conduct profit and loss analysis on the level of each counterparty; they do not estimate economic capital.
Speculation and securitization	Speculation by lenders against securitized exposure may undervalue risk on the platform.
Regulation	Currently, only limited regulation applies to marketplace lending platforms.

varies from platform to platform. Depending on the country in which they do business, there are different registers against which platforms can verify the identities of potential borrowers. Once the information has checked out, prospects will receive an email with a quote that they are free to reject or accept. At this point, they already have an account on the system, and they can log in and submit a formal loan application at any time. When they accept a loan, platforms undertake further verification of the ability and the willingness of borrowers to pay.

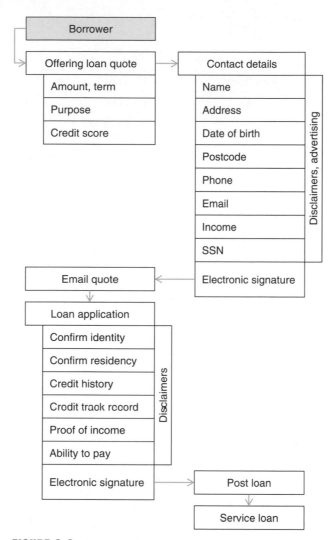

FIGURE 2.8   Borrower onboarding process of marketplace lending platforms

Finally, when borrowers have complied with this step, their loan request enters the system, and interested lenders can fund the loan fully or partially. The time from the first visit to receiving the decision about the loan via email also varies by platform. It normally takes about 48 hours, and several days more until the money arrives in the borrower's account. Overall, borrowers may receive credit within a week on marketplace lending platforms.

2.6.2   Lender onboarding

Signing up potential lenders follows a similar process, but it is generally much faster and requires less information. Figure 2.9 shows the onboarding process for lenders.

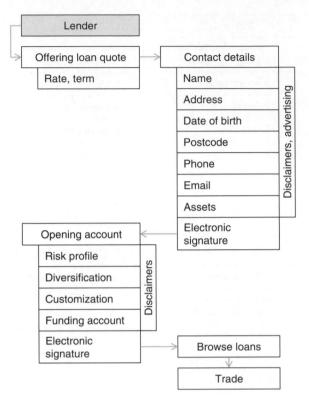

FIGURE 2.9   Lender onboarding process

When a visitor shows interest in becoming a lender, most platforms offer her a detailed quote of expected returns. To send the quote via email, they collect enough information to confirm her identity. By accepting a platform's terms and conditions, potential lenders automatically open an account. Platforms will then remind them periodically to fund their account and add details to become lenders on the system. As soon as lenders have linked a bank account to fund loans, they are ready to go. Many platforms offer the option of diversifying across several loans, sometimes with an investment of as little as $25 per loan. Highly diversified lenders often have no idea about the individual loans in their portfolio, nor do they care to know about the particulars. Because platforms classify loans by grades, lenders often construct their portfolio by selecting exposure to a certain grade, rather than to individual loans.

2.7   COMPARING MARKETPLACE LOANS WITH BANK CREDIT OR CREDIT CARD DEBT

From the perspective of borrowers, marketplace loans compare to credit card debt and short-term consumer loans in terms of interest rate. However, this comparison is less fitting that it might seem, as there exist important differences between these loan products and marketplace loans.

2.7.1   How do marketplace loans differ from bank credit?

Marketplace lending platforms have streamlined the process to get both borrowers and lenders to sign up. For example, all of the large marketplace lending platforms offer online and mobile loan applications that potential borrowers can complete in under 30 minutes. These are not just quotes and inquiries but actual loan applications. Compare this to an average of 26 hours that small businesses will spend on filling out paperwork at several conventional banks before securing some form of credit.[19]

Banks also offer ways for borrowers to apply for loans online. Their turnaround is usually slower but some banks, such as Wells Fargo in the U.S., offer same-day loans that allow the borrower to leave the branch with a check in their pocket. Still, bank loans usually cost more, and the chance that the application will be declined, especially for smaller loans, is high. When we compare the process of getting credit on a marketplace lending platform with getting a bank loan, both sides offer advantages and disadvantages. Table 2.4 compares a loan from popular marketplace lending platform Lending Club with a similar loan from Wells Fargo Bank.[20]

After banks have validated a borrower's credit history, the most important difference lies in how they mitigate their credit exposure. When banks underwrite a loan, they protect themselves from losses in two areas, as we will discuss later in Chapter 9 about credit exposures. First, banks calculate the *expected loss* under expected normal conditions and compute what they have to charge the borrower to hedge this loss. With collateralized loans, this step is very straightforward: the lender simply calculates the default probability as well as whether the value of the collateral is high enough to cover losses when they occur. When loans are uncollateralized or unsecured, such as in marketplace lending, the lender needs to compensate through the interest rate and spreads. Secondly, banks calculate the *unexpected loss* under stress conditions and ask themselves what they can do to minimize losses, survive, and remain profitable. This may include portfolio restructuring, optimizing collateral, hedging, increasing capital reserves, and other steps.

Conversely, does the interest rate of marketplace lending platforms cover loss from default under stress conditions? Should they charge more, or are they in fact destroying the market by undercutting prices? The interest rate in online lending is actually not market interest, but a counterparty spread. Under normal conditions, these spreads are fine because they cover credit losses. But under stress conditions, they fall short. This is markedly different to the way banks operate: banks hedge their exposure with higher interest and derivatives and optimize their portfolio with risk management techniques. When they are rolling over, they restructure and optimize their portfolios. Contrary to the practice of marketplace lenders, banks avoid

TABLE 2.4   Comparison of a personal loan for a borrower with perfect credit from Lending Club with a loan from Wells Fargo Bank in 2014

	P2P lending platform[21]	Wells Fargo Bank
Amount	Up to $35,000	Up to $100,000
Term	36 or 60 months	12 to 60 months
Interest rate	6.78%	7.23%
Turnaround time	Faster	Slower, except for *same-day* loans
Convenience	Higher, the entire process is online, with less paperwork involved	Lower, more paperwork involved

TABLE 2.5   Comparison of a personal loan from Lending Club with credit card debt

	P2P lending platform[22]	Credit card[23]
For excellent credit	6.7%	10.4%
For good credit	7–16%	14.91%
For fair credit	17–30%	23–30%
Interest rate	Fixed	Variable
Term	Fixed	—
Late fees	$15, no impact on interest rate	About $30, impacts interest rate

using their interest income as collateral to cover losses. They use actual collateral in the form of financial assets, hard assets, or guarantees. Then they hedge the remaining exposure with derivatives.

2.7.2   How do marketplace loans differ from credit cards?

Things look a little different when comparing a marketplace loan with credit card debt.[24] Table 2.5 shows some characteristics of each.

Credit card debt is not a loan but a credit line with a pre-approved limit. Credit lines are convenient to create and hard to pay down. Even though it is deceptively easy to max out a card, it takes much more discipline to pay down credit card debt than a loan with a designated term and a fixed interest rate. Most marketplace lending platforms are less expensive than credit cards, both in terms of the interest they charge and their fees. This is the reason why lenders use marketplace loans to refinance or consolidate credit card debt.

Credit cards provide free credit with no payments on interest for a certain term, for example for 45 days. A credit card owner may or may not use the agreed principal of the credit facility up to the credit line. Marketplace loans provide medium-term loans of 3 to 6 years. In bank credit, this hardly qualifies as a long-term loan, which would be a mortgage lasting 30 years or more. Regardless, marketplace loans are also not necessarily short-term loans in the classic sense, which might be a credit facility or short-term loans, such as payday loans.

Credit cards as short-term credit facilities have, under normal market conditions, insignificant market risk. The interest rate includes no market risk premium, with is the case also in marketplace loans. The interest rate is, in fact, a premium against counterparty credit risk, or in other words, the probability of default. Marketplace loans with a set amount of principal are exposed to both market and counterparty risks. Therefore, they should include a market risk premium and a counterparty risk premium. The rate should include the risk-free rate of the market and the risk-neutral probability of default. The expected loss drives the risk premium.

Most of the debate about marketplace lending platforms circles around the benefits for borrowers. However, banks currently offer no access to consumer credit or small business loans to lenders. There are some credit hedge funds that invest in this asset class, however, they are out of reach of retail investors. Marketplace lending offers them a chance to access credit and integrate it as a new asset class into their portfolio. Democratizing the investment in credit without securitization may be one of the most significant innovations that marketplace lending has brought about.

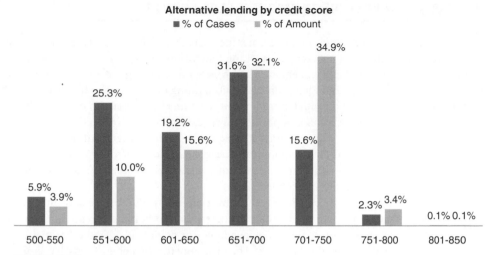

FIGURE 2.10 Alternative lending by credit score
Data source: Biz2Credit

2.8 WHO ARE THE ALTERNATIVE BORROWERS?

Companies with credit scores between 601 and 700 comprise about half of alternative lending deals arranged by online lending resource Biz2Credit in 2014.[25] As seen in Figure 2.10, companies ranging between 651 and 750 received most of the successfully funded loans by number: about 31 percent. Businesses with a credit score of between 701 and 750 received most funding, about 35 percent of the total amount. Those with higher credit scores had easier access to financing. Those with the highest credit scores are rarely using online lending platforms. They can get less expensive loans from established banks and credit institutions.

Figure 2.11 shows that most borrowers use their marketplace loans for loan refinancing and credit card payoff.[26]

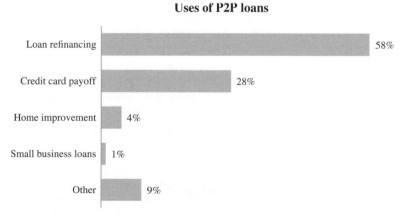

FIGURE 2.11 Uses of marketplace loans
Data source: Gartner Research

2.9 WHO ARE INVESTORS IN MARKETPLACE LOANS?

Most counterparties of marketplace loans are not individuals, but hedge funds and investment banks looking for yields in a sub-zero interest rate environment. Still, retail investors place 54 per cent of orders on marketplace lending platforms, with an average of $12,000 of indirect exposure, where they invest not in loans directly, but in rating classes.[27] The big investors are institutional investors and funds with tens of millions of *direct exposure* who pick and choose individual loans and fund them fully. Sophisticated investors, such as institutions and funds, allocate capital to marketplace loans with the prospect of earning high returns.[28] They are securitizing the loan portfolios they acquire from marketplace lenders to turn an unleveraged return of around 8 percent into a leveraged return of somewhere between 16 and 24 percent. Some funds exclusively invest in marketplace loans.

Professional money managers will run their own analytics before investing in a credit portfolio with the data that some marketplace lenders post on their site. Lending Club, for example, makes the raw data of its loan book available for download,[29] and other platforms have announced that they will do the same. The risk appetite of hedge funds has little in common with that of private individuals, who are 100 percent risk averse. Because hedge funds are by nature risk seekers, they can tolerate higher losses than retail investors. That raises the question about misalignment of interest: the originators and servicers of loans—the platforms—have little experience dealing with market cycles. Because their balance sheets never show the loans, they have very little skin in the game. Most online lenders do not align management compensation to performance of their loan portfolios, and they have no investment in the loans on their platform alongside other investors. This leads to the impression that they have less motivation to ensure their loan portfolio performs well.

Is an investment on a marketplace lending platform the new savings account? Definitely not. Not only do savings accounts allow depositors to withdraw money at any time, they also come with a deposit guarantee from the central bank. A portfolio of marketplace loans is more akin to a portfolio of uncollateralized bonds, which may yield returns when times are good, but could incur large losses when the underlying assets come under stress. Nevertheless, when one visits the websites of marketplace lending platforms, they seem to speak almost exclusively to retail investors. Even though platforms point out that well diversified investors rarely lose money, such loans have a higher risk than anything on offer at a conventional bank. Marketplace lenders demand no collateral from borrowers, and some of their income declarations are not even verified. Before retail investors invest, they should have a clear picture of what they're getting into. Investors may glean the expected performance of their investment, but when they wish to understand the underlying assets better, they are left to their own devices and Excel skills. The analytics provided by marketplace lenders are hardly adequate deciding factors for investors. Chapter 13 will discuss a detailed analysis and stress test of portfolios of marketplace loans under several scenarios. In the rest of this chapter, we look into more general characteristics of marketplace loans, such as borrower ratings and default rates.

2.10 UNDERWRITING AND CREDIT SCORING

Underwriting of many online lenders looks quirky at best to some traditionalists in the financial sector. Marketplace lending platforms often start with consumer credit risk scores, credit histories and debt-to-income ratios, and augment this to varying degrees with other data sources and analytics. In some cases, they use online search histories, social media and other web data. The algorithms that determine a borrower's creditworthiness are proprietary and closely guarded by the platforms.[30]

The marketplace lending platform Prosper, for example, uses credit scores and other standard consumer risk indicators as its basis for determining eligibility and credit spreads. They supplement these data with results from a proprietary loss-forecasting model called the Prosper Score. Proprietary modeling incorporates factors such as online referral channels as well; a borrower who arrives at Prosper via a debt education site may qualify for a cheaper rate. Prosper maintains that people coming from referral sites repay loans at a lower loss rate. For this reason, the platform uses the referral information in pricing. Prosper also employs data scientists who analyze other factors that inform pricing, among them credit availability and investor demand.

Lending Club's approach is a little more straightforward and focuses on Fico scores, debt-to-income ratios and credit histories to price loans.[31] Other marketplace lenders use Big Data explicitly to determine the risk of borrowers instead of relying on consumer credit scores. New York-based OnDeck, which specializes in small business loans, uses reviews on Yelp and Google Places as inputs in its underwriting model. One platform claims its machine-learning algorithm analyses 15,000 pieces of social media data to price loans, according to an investor in marketplace loans.[32]

Within the online lending industry, purely computer-driven models based on machine learning and Big Data have raised some eyebrows. Established underwriting methods have worked relatively well for decades, even though they lack algorithms and social media data. The loss of transparency that the proprietary algorithms of each online lending platform introduce is another cause for concern. As a result, some buyers of loans liken online lenders to "playing Wizard of Oz" with their black box underwriting methods.

Certain rules prohibit lending decisions based on information gathered from social media profiles. For example, the Equal Credit Opportunity Act (ECOA) prohibits lenders from making a lending decision on the basis of an applicant's race, color, sex, age, religion, national origin, marital status, or the fact that all or part of the applicant's income comes from a public assistance program.[33] As with any other emerging technology used in commerce, lenders should ensure their use of that technology is consistent with fair lending laws.

2.11 REGULATION

Disagreement exists about regulation of online lending. The space currently seems to fall between the cracks of financial regulators, such as the Federal Deposit Insurance Company (FDIC) in the U.S. or the Financial Services Authority (FSA) in the UK. Marketplace lending platforms essentially sell shares that are linked to the performance of their loan portfolios. This blurs the line between lending and securities registration. Fear exists that regulation could stifle growth and innovation, but it is obvious that regulation is necessary in any stable financial system. Another concern is how online lenders will perform in a downturn. Few data exist about their performance in the financial crisis of 2007/8, and they have yet to experience a full credit cycle.

However, some federal oversight of online lending exists. In 2008, the Securities and Exchange Commission (SEC) required that marketplace lending companies register their offerings as securities, according to the Securities Act of 1933. In the U.S., a marketplace lender must therefore register its platform notes with the SEC before selling securities to the public. However, as long as the operator offers platform notes privately to accredited investors, they can bypass registration. Additional requirements exist for the creation of a secondary market for platform notes, loan securitization, and other transactions. Then again, savvy platform operators can find a way to avoid most of these rules.[34]

Regulators should aim at the following main issues with online lending: transparency and disclosure, and standardization of oversight and monitoring. The following paragraphs describe each briefly.

2.11.1   Transparency and disclosure

Transparency is in the best interest of all stakeholders in marketplace lending. For borrowers, such protections would include measures against predatory or discriminatory practices, privacy protection and guidelines for debt collectors. Securities regulators have an interest in protecting lenders on marketplace lending platforms as they purchase platform notes. Those investor protections include disclosures required in any sale of securities, and remedies available to purchasers of securities harmed as a result of a failure of an issuer to adhere to securities laws. Lenders also benefit from the disclosure of profit and loss, the exposure to risks and ways to manage them. Online lending takes place mostly outside of the established financial sector, so the stability of the market should be of concern to regulators as well. Since borrowers and lenders have increasing exposure to the shadow banking system as a source of credit, they may be potentially vulnerable to shocks that are difficult to mitigate. In particular, credit volumes, and derivatives on these, should be transparent and reported in a straightforward manner. Of course, this is easier said than done. Because the online lending space is fragmented across many different private companies, it is impossible for regulators—and the platforms themselves—to gain a clear picture of the overall exposure of individual counterparties. How marketplace lending impacts the stability of the financial sector is therefore a topic on which more research is necessary. We will discuss some ideas along these lines in Chapter 16, in the third part of this book, where we map out the hybrid financial sector.

2.11.2   Standardization of oversight and monitoring

It is still unclear who exactly the regulator for newly emerging online financial services should be. Marketplace lending lingers in a grey zone between securities law and lending, and there is no capital adequacy. Regulatory agencies should take care to define responsibilities, standardize reporting requirements and monitoring practices. The online lending space has never experienced financial stress in its brief period of existence. As more lending platforms and their investors engage in securitization, being in the dark about effective risk could be dangerous. The funding sources of online lending platforms are highly correlated, with the bulk coming from institutional investors and other large investment funds. Financial transactions on platforms could be vulnerable to unforeseen volatility in the shadow banking sector, from which they draw capital.

2.12   THE RESPONSE OF BANKS TO ONLINE LENDING

Before we wrap up this overview of marketplace lending, it is important once more to put it into context with lending in the formal financial sector. Whenever the topic of online lending and marketplace lending in particular comes up, most bankers will contend that the sector is tiny compared to the total amount of credit to the private sector. Figure 2.12 shows the proportion of credit by the financial sector to both private and public parties, private parties only, and lending to private parties by banks only in relation to marketplace loans outstanding, as predicted by author Charles Moldow for 2025.[35] To extrapolate the amount of credit by banks in 2025, we have used nominal domestic credit provided by the financial sector, as reported by the World Bank,[36] and extrapolated this number to 2025 with a constant growth rate of 3 percent, which lies below the current growth rate predicted by the IMF World Economic Outlook.[37] Per definition by the World Bank, domestic credit provided by the aggregated global financial sector includes all gross credit to a variety of sectors, except credit to the central government, which is net. The financial sector includes monetary authorities and deposit money banks, finance and leasing companies, money lenders, insurance corporations, pension funds, and foreign exchange companies, where data is available.[38]

It sounds impressive, but one trillion of marketplace loans outstanding in 2025 is small fry compared to the total amount of credit in the financial system—a mere 1 percent of bank lending to the private sector. However, this fails to take into account that marketplace lending as we know it today is still in its first generation. There may be innovations that evolve the sector rapidly, innovations we have no chance of predicting at the current time. A similar example of a disruptive trend that started small is the rise of cell phones. Author Jon Agar found that in 1987, five years after launching the first mobile cell phones in Scandinavia, roughly 2 percent of the population in the region were subscribers. Truckers, engineers, and

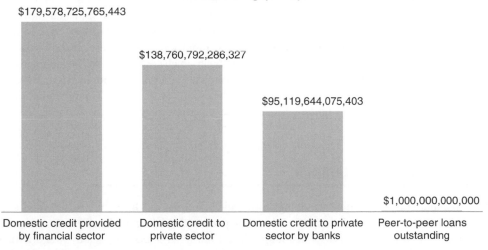

FIGURE 2.12   Domestic credit by the financial sector compared to marketplace loans outstanding in 2025
Data sources: World Bank, IMF and Foundation Capital

other professionals on the go used these devices, but only few found application in private use.[39] It took a lot of foresight to understand that these devices would proliferate like no other device before. The next generation of mobile phones—smartphones—are the latest outgrowth of a trend that started 20 years earlier with the first cell phone in the market. If banks are still on the sidelines when game-changing innovation takes place right under their nose, they may be up against a much bigger enemy than they can currently predict. They may be able to keep up for a while by simply buying up new ideas, but the knowledge gap between their in-house capabilities and the market will inevitably grow. This is dangerous and can be fatal: when misinformed incumbents make a desperate attempt to catch up with a market that they have missed, they often focus on technology that is precisely wrong. An example is Motorola's debacle with Iridium, where a short-sighted bet with the wrong underlying assumptions cost investors billions of dollars.[40] Dismissing a sector as too small and unimportant at the outset is hardly a good strategy in dealing with competition in the age of accelerating change.

Most importantly, the future of credit is unlikely to be an either/or proposition. Banks already have millions of small business customers and private customers. Without much effort, they could be important players in the emerging online lending market. In a sense, each new online lending platform tries to compete within a similar market segment by building its own financial network. How much more effective would it be if they could simply plug into the existing network of banks? Proprietary information that banks have could be valuable for platforms, and there are exciting opportunities for the formal financial sector and newly emerging alternative lenders to collaborate. Banks could easily position themselves as part of the solution in shaping the future of credit jointly with digital customers and entrepreneurs. Instead, when it comes to reinventing lending, they are being part of the problem. We will investigate this claim further in Chapter 5, where we examine why innovation in lending takes place outside of the established financial sector.

For the time being, banks have their own balance sheets to lend from and they hardly need to raise expensive capital from private parties in the current low-interest rate environment. However, financial services firms already make investments in potentially disruptive FinTech. Most likely, banks will hardly adapt the business model of marketplace lending by themselves in the near term, but they definitely want to be part of innovative startups when they take off. Banks have already acquired some promising FinTech startups when they fit into their operations. Mergers and acquisitions activity could rapidly pick up when FinTech business models mature. In marketplace lending, it is still unclear which companies and business models will be the game changers of the future. The reason that marketplace lending has emerged at this time in history is by no means a coincidence: the credit sector is ripe for innovation. In the next chapter, we look into the unique circumstances that have made the rise of online lending possible.

2.13 CONCLUDING REMARKS

This chapter explains how online lending works, and it outlines the different business models in online lending, namely marketplace lending, balance-sheet lending, and lender-agnostic marketplaces. Some FinTech services disintermediate traditional intermediaries by making them unnecessary. However, online lending re-intermediates banks and replaces them with a platform that organizes information about borrowers and lenders. Online lenders are infomediaries who turn data into value for their customers.

Individuals and companies who borrow on online lending platforms are by no means subprime borrowers only. However, platforms underwrite a large proportion of loans to borrowers with imperfect credit who use credit to refinance other loans or pay off credit card debt. Institutional investors firmly dominate investing in marketplace loans, which is the reason the sector has rebranded itself from peer-to-peer lending to marketplace lending.

Despite relatively loose regulation, online lenders have the potential to grab significant market share from traditional credit institutions. Their market share is still insignificant, yet banks need to respond to the emergence of new approaches to underwrite credit in the digital age. Banks may be able to keep up for a while by acquiring promising startups, but the knowledge gap between their in-house capabilities and market demands can be fatal. The established financial sector has much to gain from collaborating with innovators early on, and banks could co-create the future of credit jointly with customers and entrepreneurs.

NOTES

1. Zopa (2015a) home page, http://www.zopa.com/about, accessed 17 July 2015.
2. Prosper (2015a) home page, https://www.prosper.com/about, accessed 17 July, 2015.
3. Lending Club (2015a) home page, https://www.lendingclub.com, accessed 17 July 2015.
4. Gordon Mills, Karen and McCarthy, Brayden (2014) "The State of Small Business Lending: Credit Access during the Recovery and How Technology May Change the Game" (Harvard Business School Working Paper, 22 July 2014), http://www.hbs.edu/faculty/Publication%20Files/15-004_09b1bf8b-eb2a-4e63-9c4e-0374f770856f.pdf.
5. Moldow, Charles (2014) "A Trillion Dollar Market By the People, For the People" (Foundation Capital, 2014), http://www.foundationcapital.com/downloads/FoundationCap_MarketplaceLendingWhitepaper.pdf.
6. Gordon Mills, Karen and McCarthy, Brayden (2014) "The State of Small Business Lending: Credit Access during the Recovery and How Technology May Change the Game" (Harvard Business School Working Paper, 22 July 2014), http://www.hbs.edu/faculty/Publication%20Files/15-004_09b1bf8b-eb2a-4e63-9c4e-0374f770856f.pdf.
7. Ibid.
8. Biz2Credit (2014) "Lending Index October 2014," http://www.biz2credit.com/small-business-lending-index.
9. LendingClub (2014) "Prospectus for Member Payment Dependent Notes" (22 August 2014), https://www.lendingclub.com/fileDownload.action?file=Clean_As_Filed_20140822.pdf&type=docs
10. Manbeck, Peter; Hu, Samuel (2014) "The Regulation of Marketplace Lending: A Summary of the Principal Issues" (Chapman and Cutler LLP White Paper, April 2014), http://www.aba.com/Tools/Offers/Documents/Chapman_Regulation_of_Marketplace_Lending_0414.pdf.
11. Fink, Ronald (2014) "Online lenders and the evolution of banking," (Crain's New York Business, 27 April 2014) http://www.crainsnewyork.com/article/20140427/FINANCE/140429884/online-lenders-and-the-evolution-of-banking.
12. Buford, John and Yu, Heather and Lua, Eng Keong (2009) *P2P Networking and Applications* (Burlington: Elsevier).
13. Hagel, John III and Rayport, Jeffrey (1997) "The Coming Battle for Customer Information" (*Harvard Business Review*, January 1997 Issue), https://hbr.org/1997/01/the-coming-battle-for-customer-information, date accessed 28 March 2015.

14. Chaffey, Dave (2009) *E-Business and E-Commerce Management: Strategy, Implementation, and Practice* (Fourth Edition) (Essex: Pearson Education).
15. https://intl.alipay.com/index.htm.
16. Cheng, Allen (2014) "Yu'e Bao Wow! How Alibaba Is Reshaping Chinese Finance," Institutional Investor, 29 May 2014, http://www.institutionalinvestor.com/Article/3346365/Investors-Sovereign-Wealth-Funds/Yue-Bao-Wow-How-Alibaba-Is-Reshaping-Chinese-Finance.html, date accessed 29 March 2015.
17. https://www.apple.com/apple-pay/.
18. Chao, Georgia T. (2012) "Organizational Socialization: Background, Basics, and a Blueprint for Adjustment at Work," in Kozlowski, Steve (editor) *The Oxford Handbook of Organizational Psychology, Volume 1* (Oxford: Oxford University Press).
19. Federal Reserve Bank of New York (2014), "Key Findings of the Small Business Credit Survey, Q4/2013," http://www.newyorkfed.org/smallbusiness/Fall2013/pdf/summary-of-key-findings-2014.pdf.
20. Cunningham, Simon (2015a) "Wells Fargo Personal Loan? Lending Club Has Better Rates" (Lending Memo, 14 February 2014), http://www.lendingmemo.com/wells-fargo-personal-loan/, date accessed 27 March 2015.
21. Lending Club, adapted from Cunningham, Simon (2015a) "Wells Fargo Personal Loan? Lending Club Has Better Rates" (Lending Memo, 14 February 2014), http://www.lendingmemo.com/wells-fargo-personal-loan/, date accessed 27 March 2015.
22. Several P2P Platforms in the U.S., adapted from Cunningham, Simon (2015a) "Ditch the Credit Card and Get a Lending Club Loan: 5 Reasons" (Lending Memo, 13 January 2014), http://www.lendingmemo.com/credit-cards-vs-lending-club/, date accessed 27 March 2015.
23. Several credit cards in the U.S., adapted from Cunningham, Simon (2015a) "Ditch the Credit Card and Get a Lending Club Loan: 5 Reasons" (Lending Memo, 13 January 2014), http://www.lendingmemo.com/credit-cards-vs-lending-club/, date accessed 27 March 2015.
24. Cunningham, Simon (2015a) "Ditch the Credit Card and Get a Lending Club Loan: 5 Reasons" (Lending Memo, 13 January 2014), http://www.lendingmemo.com/credit-cards-vs-lending-club/, date accessed 27 March 2015.
25. Biz2Credit (2014a) "Biz2Credit's Analysis of Bank Failures from 2009 to 2014 Exposes a 'Credit Desert' in the South-Eastern U.S. and the Rise of Alternative Lending," http://www.biz2credit.com/research-reports/analysis-bank-failures-2009-2014-identifies-credit-desert, date accessed 15 November 2014.
26. Bradley, Anthony (2014) "Debt Crowdfunding Holds Much Promise," Gartner Research, http://blogs.gartner.com/anthony_bradley/2014/10/22/debt-crowdfunding-holds-much-promise/, date accessed 25 May 2015.
27. Cunningham, Simon (2014) "The State of Retail Investing in Peer to Peer Lending," http://www.lendingmemo.com/grow-p2p-lending-retail-investor-community/, date accessed 17 September 2015.
28. http://www.risk.net/risk-magazine/feature/2372612/hedge-funds-securitisation-and-leverage-change-p2p-game.
29. Lending Club (2015a) https://www.lendingclub.com/info/download-data.action.
30. Devasabai, Kris (2014) "Hedge funds, securitisation and leverage change P2P game" (Risk.net, 28 October 2014), http://www.risk.net/print_article/risk-magazine/feature/2372612/hedge-funds-securitisation-and-leverage-change-p2p-game.
31. Ibid.
32. Devasabai, Kris (2014) "Hedge funds, securitisation and leverage change P2P game" (Risk.net, 28 October 2014), http://www.risk.net/print_article/risk-magazine/feature/2372612/hedge-funds-securitisation-and-leverage-change-p2p-game.

33. Manbeck, Peter; Hu, Samuel (2014) "The Regulation of Marketplace Lending: A Summary of the Principal Issues" (Chapman and Cutler LLP White Paper, April 2014), http://www.aba.com/Tools/Offers/Documents/Chapman_Regulation_of_Marketplace_Lending_0414.pdf.

34. Ibid.

35. Moldow, Charles (2014) "A Trillion Dollar Market By the People, For the People" (Foundation Capital, 2014), http://www.foundationcapital.com/downloads/FoundationCap_Market placeLendingWhitepaper.pdf.

36. World Bank (2015a) "World Development Indicators," http://data.worldbank.org/data-catalog/world-development-indicators, date accessed 27 March 2015.

37. IMF (2015a) "World Economic Outlook Update January 2015," http://www.imf.org/external/pubs/ft/weo/2015/update/01/index.htm, date accessed 27 March 2015.

38. World Bank (2015a) "Domestic credit provided by financial sector (% of GDP)," http://data.worldbank.org/indicator/FS.AST.DOMS.GD.ZS, date accessed 27 March 2015.

39. Agar, Jon (2013) *Constant Touch: A Global History of the Mobile Phone* (London: Icon Books).

40. Ismail, Salim (2014) *Exponential Organizations: Why new organizations are ten times better, faster, and cheaper than yours (and what to do about it)* (New York: Diversion Books).

CHAPTER 3

What Made the Rise of Online Lending Possible?

There is a reason why financial technology startups are taking off now instead of 20 years ago. Still, it is important to remember that financial innovation is by no means a new phenomenon; one could argue that the revolution in financial technology started with the installation of the first ATM in 1967,[1] when banks began to automate away some of their traditional functions such as cash withdrawals and deposits. Banks themselves led this innovation to cut costs, and customers learned that visiting bank branches was less important for them than they thought. This realization laid the foundation for the proliferation of online banking. Because the first psychological barriers had disappeared to engage in financial transactions without a teller, new entrants in the online lending space had an easier pitch to attract lenders and borrowers. In a sense, banks themselves opened the door for FinTech entrepreneurs to compete with them head on.

Since the 1970s, much has changed in banking. The bulk of financial innovation happened behind the scenes in the form of faster computers, stronger analytics, and financial engineering. With the mainstream proliferation of the internet, financial technology innovation became more visible to retail banking customers. However, there is more to this story than the internet alone. The most noticeable factor that empowers technology startups to challenge the traditional monopoly function of banks is technology. However, social and structural factors are equally important. Table 3.1 summarizes these factors.

3.1 TECHNOLOGICAL FACTORS

Cheap and ubiquitous computing power, a revolution in Big Data and analytics, faster technology adoption, the rapid expansion of the internet, the boom in mobile screens, and software platforms that jump-started network effects, are the main technological factors that enable online lending. Let's examine each of them a little more closely.

3.1.1 Cheap and ubiquitous computing power, coupled with a revolution in Big Data and analytics

The oft-cited Moore's Law—the fact that the performance of computer chips doubles approximately every eighteen months, which decreases their relative cost[2]—is well documented, so

TABLE 3.1   Technological, social, and structural factors that empowered online lending

Technological factors	Social factors	Structural factors
■ Cheap and ubiquitous computing power, coupled with a revolution in Big Data and analytics ■ Faster technology adoption ■ Internet proliferation and acceptance, security and comparability of services ■ The boom in mobile screens, open architecture, tracking of mobile users ■ Network effects, intermediary platforms that connect lenders and borrowers	■ Digital connectedness and friendships ■ Impatience with the traditional know-your-customer process ■ Sentiment against the established financial sector	■ Stricter banking regulation ■ Mergers lead to disappearance of smaller banks, with decreased access to credit for consumers and SMEs ■ Low interest rate environment

we just touch it on the surface here. With teraflops of computing power available at bargain-basement prices, machines can do what seemed impossible a few decades ago. Author Ray Kurzweil extended the law of accelerating returns to any information technology. Kurzweil states that at the core of accelerating returns is information. Once information powers an industry, its price/performance doubles approximately annually without stopping.[3] We have already learned that peer-to-peer networks thrive on information. Additionally, computers have a long history in finance. It is only natural that exponential increases in cheap computing power have the potential to usher in a new era for financial services across the board.

3.1.2   Faster technology adoption

Concurrent with exponential growth, adoption rates of technology have accelerated. Author Michael DeGusta points out that electricity needed 30 years to reach 10 percent adoption. Telephones took 25 years for the same adoption rate. However, tablet devices achieved it in less than 5 years. It took another 54 years until telephones became widely adopted, with 40 percent penetration. Smartphones, on the other hand, accomplished a 40 percent penetration rate in just 10 years, assuming that the first smart phones were PDAs that could make phone calls, which emerged in 2002.[4] Networked devices in the hands of nearly everyone are new in the history of humankind. They are the great enablers of our time. Smartphones give users access to a portable computer anywhere they go. Better yet, the operating systems of smartphones have a plug-in architecture that allows anyone with coding skills to program apps that users can download onto their devices. Smartphones thereby create global open networks that allow their owners to interact with each other easily and inexpensively. They are ideal for painless interaction between peers. With faster adoption of technology, consumers unlock network effects faster.

3.1.3   Internet proliferation and network effects

The exponential growth in adoption rates of new technology has given rise to powerful network effects: the more people use a technology, the more benefits they derive from it. Instead of

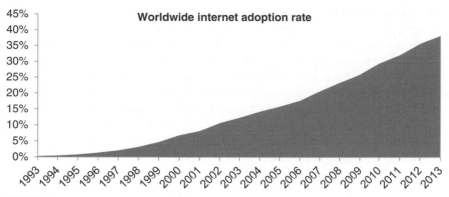

FIGURE 3.1 Worldwide internet adoption rate
Data source: World Bank

increasing linearly, the value of networks rises exponentially, as Metcalfe's law describes. The law is more a rule of thumb that states that the value of a telecommunications network is proportional to the square of the number of users of the system ($v \sim n^2$).[5] This rule describes the network effects of networks such as the internet and social networking. Just imagine there was a group of twenty people of whom only two owned a smart phone with a chat app. They were the only ones who could chat with each other. However, if all twenty people had the app on their phone, you have a marketplace in the making. The greater the number of connected users in the network, the more valuable the service becomes to the community.

This is especially true in social networks and similar platforms. Once everybody uses them, their utility mushrooms. The space of online payments and transactions is no exception. The more people use and accept such payments, the more useful the service. As a result, the sector signals high profitability, which attracts new entrants into the market and drives down costs for customers. This jump starts a virtuous cycle that speeds up change and adoption and improves services. Of course, a prerequisite for online services to take off is a high proliferation of stable and secure internet service. Figure 3.1 shows the worldwide internet adoption rate with close to 40 percent of the world population online—a market of around 2.6 billion people who are accessible with one inexpensive distribution channel.[6]

3.1.3.1 Online security and trust   Next to the proliferation of the internet and network effects, its acceptance as a secure communication channel is just as much a requirement for customers to use it for financial transactions. While security was an early concern with online banking, most banking platforms today use industrial-strength encryption and proprietary safety features. In the case of a security breach, they are relatively quick to respond. The risk to customers of using internet banking today is minimal. The same applies to financial services provided by (reputable) third parties. Sure, cybercrime is a serious concern, and some internet investment schemes or alternative currencies have turned out to be scams. But so have some reputable New York hedge funds that were beyond reproach until they unraveled. The technology to make an online service secure certainly exists today. And customers trust it all the same—whether a reputable bank, credit card company, or large brand name stands behind it.

3.1.3.2 Comparability and transparency Using the internet to look for banking services brings many advantages to customers. Search costs decline because services and rates are instantly comparable with free information. Transaction costs go down as technology automates processes in the back office. Banks today are in direct competition against each other and other players. When a bank offers the ability for online loan applications, customers of other banks will demand the same. Otherwise, they are free to vote with their feet and switch to the more accommodating bank. This has increased transparency, which is much to the disadvantage of the traditional financial sector. A significant factor in the banks' business model was the undisclosed fees, which appeared nowhere else than in the fine print of an application that the customer had to sign right there in the branch. Very few customers read the fine print in any contract they sign, but today they no longer have to take the word of their banker at face value. There is always a blogger or journalist who has compared different offers and has written about it for all to see. For those who know how to use information available online critically, research has become much easier, and financial products have gained in transparency.

3.1.4 The boom in mobile screens

The next liberating technology factor for the consumer was personal mobile computers. Tablets and smartphones are a boon in several ways for the consumer. Mobile computing has brought several advantages, mainly location independence, open software architecture, and the ability to generate user data. The first advantage of mobile screens is the ability of users to connect to information anywhere they may find themselves. While internet users of the past had to sit in front of a stationary desktop computer that connected to the internet through a cable, mobile devices can connect via wireless networks in public places or through a data plan. Internet surfing has become as convenient as phone calls. More and more people use the internet through mobile devices, and the number of shipments of mobile screens is forecast to surpass the number of desktops and laptops in 2015, as can be seen in Figure 3.2.[7]

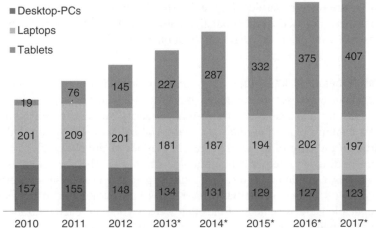

FIGURE 3.2 Forecast for global shipments of tablets, laptops and desktop PCs from 2010 to 2017 (in million units)
Data source: Statista

Share of smartphone users

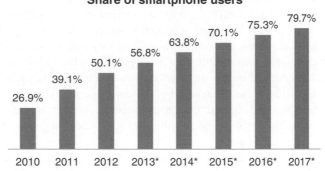

FIGURE 3.3   Smartphone users as a percentage of all mobile users in the U.S.
Data source: Statista

While a customer is sitting in a bank, looking over the loan documentation, she can compare the terms with other offers right there in the branch on her tablet. If there is a better loan on offer next door, she can get up and take her business elsewhere—a nightmare for every banker. There are more uses of smartphones we have not even imagined yet, and the adoption rate of smartphones is forecast to continue, as Figure 3.3 shows.[8]

3.1.4.1   Open architecture of mobile operating systems   A second advantage of mobile devices is their open architecture. Anybody can code an app that is instantly available for download on a variety of mobile devices. Whilst previously it was expensive and lengthy to develop software, app development has driven this cost down to a few thousand dollars. There are still backend costs to consider but, even so, mobile first startups can realistically launch competitive services that rival a large international bank for a few hundred thousand dollars. When the idea is strong and enough people are interested in using the service, the barriers to entry are lower than ever before.

3.1.4.2   Tracking of mobile users   The third advantage of mobile computing is that it generates a lot of personal data. Most devices have a GPS sensor embedded, which means every step its owners take can be recorded and tracked. The operating systems of mobile devices also transmit user data to the operator of an app. For example, some apps collect information about location, serial-number-like identifiers for the phone, and personal details such as gender and age. Marketing companies are collecting massive amounts of data on phone users, always teetering right at the brink of respecting the privacy of users. For financial service providers these data are extremely valuable. While it was difficult in the past to assess whether a borrower told the truth on a loan application, cross referencing between organically collected data may be helpful to verify such claims in a fraction of the time.

3.1.4.3   The next step: goodbye gatekeepers   When we discussed peer-to-peer networks, we learned that they need a central administrator or *infomediary* who organizes the information that peers need to transact. We then contrasted this with a supermarket that buys from sellers and sells to buyers, in the process marking up products and controlling access. The supermarket is an example of a network that is the opposite of peer-to-peer; a monopoly that controls interactions and is often the only way for people to trade in an economy. Of course, when an intermediary-oriented platform corners the market and pools information about most potential counterparties, it may become a monopolist just like the only supermarket in town. This has happened online, where powerful infomediaries are controlling the flow of information. Facebook, for example, makes little user data available to individual users, and Amazon will not disclose the identity of buyers to sellers on its marketplace. These are the monopolies of the digital age: their heavy use of technology and automation has driven transaction costs, but they still dictate terms and squeeze buyers and sellers to maximize their margins. While processes and data in online networks often still go through a central gatekeeper, the next step is to break down that barrier as well.

As soon as users connect directly to each other on a platform, with the data they are creating freely available to anyone, there is little need for a gatekeeper other than to keep the platform up and running. Marketplace lending platforms promise to be such intermediaries, and they might be the next generation of intermediary-oriented platforms. When we introduced peer-to-peer networks, we saw that it is in the nature of people to connect directly with each other in commerce. Platforms that facilitate this interaction globally have only become possible in recent years with all the technological factors in place at scale. In this sense, we are still in the early stages of business models that build on network effects and direct marketplace interaction. However, it is already clear that the peer-to-peer way of doing business is a course change from our current economic model. An omnipotent matchmaker who calls the shots and thrives on incomplete information between buyers and sellers will soon be a thing of the past. More and more challenges to the economic model of the gatekeeper at the center of transactions will arise in the near future. The disruption in financial services is just one of them.

3.2 SOCIAL FACTORS

Next to technological factors, social factors play an equally important role in the rise of FinTech and online lending in particular. The acceptance of digital connectedness and friendships, the impatience with the traditional know-your-customer (KYC) process, and an overall sentiment against the established financial sector are the social factors that empower online lending.

3.2.1 Digital connectedness and friendships

Author Sherry Turkle points out that today's young people have grown up with a digital network in a fully tethered life. They see robots and digital avatars no longer as inferior to real-world interaction as they take the power of online connectedness for granted. For today's digital natives, seeing the location of all their acquaintances within a ten-mile radius is a given.[9] With this strong sense of digital connectedness, introducing financial services into the relationship is a small step, especially when it promises direct interaction between online friends. Trusting someone you have never seen face to face would have seemed strange a few years ago, but today, it is perfectly acceptable. Most people, and millennials in particular, take online communication at face value. Figure 3.4 shows the proliferation of social networking across different age groups.[10] This is a strong enabler for online lending, where trust is essential.

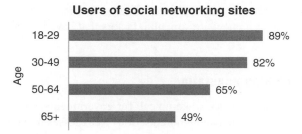

Users of social networking sites

FIGURE 3.4   Social networking site use by age group (January 2014)
Data source: Pew Research Center

3.2.2   Impatience with the know-your-customer process

As a counterpart to increased openness in online interactions, the know-your-customer process (KYC) of many banks has tightened in the years since the financial crisis of 2007/8. Standard protocol still demands a customer's presence in the bank branch when interviewing for a loan. Some banks offer online applications for potential borrowers to apply online. Regardless, at some point or other, the bank requires the borrower to step into a branch. Most banking documents require a handwritten signature. Many banks even record statements made by customers during the application process as digital audio files. Even opening a simple savings account can take hours this way, not counting the trip to and from the bank branch and time spent waiting for an account manager to be available. Such demands are in stark contrast to the way most people use the internet and their smart phones today, and they seem like relics from a time long gone. Author Brett King writes that banks fail to sell well online because of their onerous compliance and KYC processes. While banks always point toward regulations that require such practices, almost always the actual regulations around KYC require no physical distribution. Otherwise, online financial platforms such as Square and PayPal would simply not have been allowed to do what they did.[11]

3.2.3   Sentiment against the established financial sector

The perceived duplicity of banks galls many customers, young and old. Since the financial crisis of 2007/8, the sentiment against established large banks has soured even more. The ensuing global Occupy Movement against the 1 percent, including so-called "fat cat banks," has hardly helped the image of the financial sector, which has lost much goodwill in the process. It is therefore relatively easy for new entrants to play on the misgivings of customers towards banks. This has helped the popularity of online lenders, who often come across as the "better, fairer banks." Whether such claims are true is another question. Still, online lenders and marketplace lending platforms are careful to distance themselves from the established financial sector in their communications and corporate identity.

3.3   STRUCTURAL FACTORS

Finally, structural factors support both technological and social factors that have helped the popularity of online lending in recent years. Strict banking regulation, mergers that lead to the disappearance of smaller banks, which decreased access to credit for consumers and SMEs, and a low interest rate environment are structural factors that have helped online lending gain ground.

3.3.1 Stricter banking regulation

The financial crisis of 2007/8 was a wake-up call for governments and regulators. It became clear that they had underestimated and ignored serious weaknesses in the financial sector. The outcry about banks that were too big to fail prompted regulators to tighten the screws. As a result, banks needed to comply with higher capital requirements and higher loan-to-deposit (LTD) ratios. However, results of stricter regulation are mixed: rising compliance costs strain even large banks. For example, according to its CEO Stuart Gulliver, HSBC spent about US$800 million in 2014 on its compliance and risk program, an increase of roughly US$200 million from the previous year. The bank's chairman, Douglas Flint, sees unprecedented demands from regulators, and notes that the compliance workload diminishes resources that would otherwise benefit consumers.[12] Wells Fargo Bank added about 600 new employees to its risk management team to comply with increased regulation. Yet it is the smaller banks that suffer especially under the increased demands. Many of them claim that the current compliance reforms are unfairly applied, with the result that some of the smaller banks have had to double their compliance teams to keep up with regulations.[13]

Because most online lending platforms are non-banks, many regulations are of little concern to them, at least for the time being. While banks struggle to keep up with regulatory demands, non-banks can dedicate most of their resources to their core business: improving the simplicity of the loan application process, increasing the speed of delivery of capital, and improving the focus on customer service.

3.3.2 Disappearance of smaller banks has decreased access to credit for consumers and SMEs

As a result of regulatory overhead, smaller banks often see no other way out than to merge with larger ones to streamline their compliance departments. However, traditionally, it was often the small banks that underwrote smaller loans below $1 million to small and medium enterprises (SMEs). This has become less profitable for banks, as the cost for underwriting large loans is exactly the same as that for small loans. To cover their higher operating costs, banks focus on those transactions with higher profits. They have also become more risk averse, as loans to SMEs often involve higher risk and uncertainty than those to larger firms. The increased difficulty of accessing capital has driven up search costs and transaction costs for SMEs in need of credit. While most banks say they are lending without prejudice to company size, SMEs themselves have trouble getting loans. Figure 3.5 confirms this trend; it shows that loans below $1 million to small businesses and farms are about 15 percent down in the U.S. since the financial crisis of 2007/8.[14]

As authors Karen Gordon Mills and Brayden McCarthy point out, several banks have curtailed lending to firms with annual revenues below $2 million. This essentially cuts down on loans between $100,000 and $250,000 and opens up a lending gap, since over 50 percent of SMEs are seeking loans under $100,000. At the same time, however, high-growth segments like venture capital are at an all time high. Mills and McCarthy list a number of problems that exacerbate credit access of SMEs, many of them cyclical and structural. Since the financial

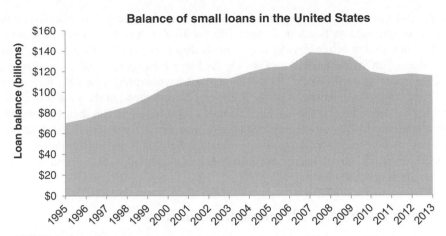

FIGURE 3.5 Loan balance in the U.S. of loans below $1 million to small businesses and farms. Shaded areas designate recessions.
Data source: FDIC

crisis of 2007/8, SME sales have largely been flat. This in turn has hurt their collateral, which often exists in the form of infrastructure and real estate of the founders.[15]

Another reason for banks to abandon small loans is that the market for securitized small business loans is relatively weak. When banks can easily package their loan portfolios and sell them to other banks or non-bank entities, they have a strong motivation to underwrite loans. However, several factors stand in the way of small business loan securitization; for instance, the lack of standardized lending terms and uniform underwriting guidelines, and the limited historical data on credit performance of small business loans. This further raises the costs of small business lending.[16]

3.3.3 Low interest rate environment

Finally, the low interest rates that banks offer on deposits are another enabler for online lenders. If depositors can get acceptable rates from their trusted bank, they might as well deposit their savings where they already have an existing relationship. Because interest rates hover around zero percent, savers and investors have started looking for alternatives. Online lenders promise comparatively high interest on deposits, which helps them attract capital. Traditional bank loans may yield a return of 5 to 7 percent while alternative lending platforms charge yields between 30 to 120 percent of the loan value, depending on the size, term and risk of the loan.[17]

3.4 THE PERFECT STORM

The spread-based business model has worked well for banks for centuries. Only in recent years have affordable computing power and connectivity allowed entrepreneurs outside of banks to offer similar services. Before the rise of social networking, it would have been difficult to imagine that people who only connected online would trust one another enough to underwrite a loan. At the same time, the proliferation of smartphones and the ease to access information on the go has raised the expectation of customers that everything has to be simple and immediate. This is somewhat at odds with the practices of established banks, who have gotten used to being in a monopoly position. When new companies can prove they offer cheaper and better services to customers than they get from their banks, customers will be more open than ever before to switch. As Steve Jobs said, "innovation distinguishes between a leader and a follower."[18] FinTech startups have written it on their flags to be the leaders, and banks have chosen to be the followers. Nevertheless, at the same time, FinTech companies are depending on the existing financial infrastructure to run their businesses: new mobile payments services use existing credit card infrastructure for security,[19] and marketplace lenders depend on banking infrastructure for funding their loans and collecting payments. To what degree FinTech entrepreneurs can afford to disrupt the providers of their enabling business infrastructure is another question.

3.4.1   From unbundling to fragmentation and back

At the core of the threat to banks is the fact that FinTech startups unbundle the services provided by the established banking sector. Startups compete with banks' payment infrastructure, mobile and social wallets, e-commerce and m-commerce solutions, lending, wealth management, stock brokerage, and more. We have already examined the question about what would happen if the new startups joined forces and merged into one platform, where they offered financial services in aggregate that customers would prefer to the services their bank provides. We are not proposing a single, large behemoth of a company comprising the marketleaders in FinTech, but a fluid infrastructure that offers users the experience of doing business on one platform, with several invisible service providers on the back end. If the disruptive entrants in the financial sector are rebundled in this way, we will witness the birth of a new kind of bank that has little in common with the banks we currently love and trust. All enablers of online lending would favor such a plug-and-play platform over the way banks conduct their business. There is little banks can do about this, other than brace themselves for the perfect storm.

Because much of the operation of a rebundled platform is technology enabled and automated, its overhead and footprint is much smaller than any bank with a branch network.[20] New players have zero legacy overhang, enabling them to take a fresh look at doing business, unafraid of regulators. Furthermore, because information flows freely on such a platform, all the data about its users' financial transactions history will be at its fingertips. This could usher in a new era of analytics and risk management. For instance, investors could get a measure of concentration risk, notoriously difficult to measure in today's financial sector. Investors could spot correlations between different borrowers, which would help them assess the impact of each loan on the stability of the financial system. Unified data would also result in one transparent interface that regulators could access. Instead of wading through arbitrary labels that change from bank to bank, regulators would be able to deal with harmonized data that is fully transparent.

3.5   A DIVERGENCE OF TRENDS

Looking at the statistics we discussed in this chapter shows an important point: the trends in internet use, mobile computing, and social networks diverge from the lending practices of established credit institutions. While a rise in the adoption of smartphones and tablets certainly makes traditional online banking easier, banks hardly seem to take full advantage of the newly emerging opportunities that technology brings. Instead of harnessing emergent consumer behavior, they seem to counteract it with a stubborn determination to build walls of procedures and bureaucracy between themselves and their customers. This has begun to erode the willingness of borrowers to comply with regulations that seem to benefit the banks but not the customer. The fact that customers now have somewhere else to take their business has opened up cracks in the monopoly position of traditional bank lending. Well-funded new entrants in online lending are ready and willing to exploit this opening. Online lending platforms have no burden of legacy processes and regulation, which aligns well with the demands of consumers. It is therefore hardly a surprise that online lending has taken the spotlight in popularity from traditional banks. But are the new entrants making the most of this opportunity, and are their services that much better than what traditional banking customers are used to? The next chapter will investigate this question.

3.6   CONCLUDING REMARKS

This chapter explains the enabling factors that have made the rise of online lending possible—technological factors, social factors, and structural factors. A confluence of cheap and ubiquitous computing power, the emergence of digital connectedness, customer dissatisfaction with current banking processes, and declining approval rates of loans for individuals and SMEs has led to a perfect storm that challenges banks head on. All factors that enabled online lending favor the plug-and-play banking platform (introduced in Chapter 1) that FinTech services could build collectively. FinTech companies still have massive opportunities ahead of them if they take advantage of the wind at their back.

NOTES

1. BBC (2007) "Enfield's cash gift to the world" (27 June 2007) http://www.bbc.co.uk/london/content/articles/2007/06/26/cash_machine_feature.shtml.
2. Intel (2015a) "50 Years of Moore's Law," http://www.intel.com/content/www/us/en/silicon-innovations/moores-law-technology.html, date accessed 17 September 2015.
3. Kurzweil, Ray (2005) *The Singularity Is Near: When Humans Transcend Biology* (London: Duckworth Overlook).
4. DeGusta, Michael (2012) "Are Smart Phones Spreading Faster than Any Technology in Human History?" (*MIT Technology Review*, 9 May 2012) http://www.technologyreview.com/news/427787/are-smart-phones-spreading-faster-than-any-technology-in-human-history/.
5. Shapiro, Carl and Varian, Hal (1999) *Information Rules* (Harvard: Harvard Business School Press).
6. World Bank (2014a) "Internet users per 100 people," http://data.worldbank.org/indicator/IT.NET.USER.P2.
7. Statista (2014a) Forecast for global shipments of tablets, laptops and desktop PCs from 2010 to 2017 (in million units), http://www.statista.com/statistics/272595/global-shipments-forecast-for-tablets-laptops-and-desktop-pcs/.
8. Statista (2014b) "Smartphone users as percentage of all mobile users in the U.S.," http://www.statista.com/statistics/201184/percentage-of-mobile-phone-users-who-use-a-smartphone-in-the-us/.
9. Turkle, Sherry (2011) *Alone Together: Why We Expect More from Technology and Less from Each Other* (New York: Basic Books).

10. PewResearch (2014a) "Social Networking Factsheet," http://www.pewinternet.org/fact-sheets/social-networking-fact-sheet/.

11. King, Brett (2013) *Bank 3.0: Why Banking is No Longer Somewhere You Go, But Something You Do* (Hoboken: Wiley).

12. Arnold, Martin (2014) "HSBC wrestles with soaring costs of compliance" (*Financial Times*, 4 August 2014) http://www.ft.com/intl/cms/s/0/0e3f0760-1bef-11e4-9666-00144feabdc0.html.

13. Allen, Mike (2014) "Cost of Compliance: Small Community Banks Say Dodd-Frank Reforms Are Unfairly Applied" (*San Diego Business Journal*, 5 September 2014), http://cbanews.sdsu.edu/ElySDBJ1.pdf.

14. FDIC (2014a) "Loans to Small businesses and Farms, FDIC-Insured Institutions 1995-2014," https://www2.fdic.gov/qbp/timeseries/SmallBusiness&FarmLoans.xls.

15. Gordon Mills, Karen and McCarthy, Brayden (2014) "The State of Small Business Lending: Credit Access during the Recovery and How Technology May Change the Game" (Harvard Business School Working Paper, 22 July 2014), http://www.hbs.edu/faculty/Publication%20Files/15-004_09b1bf8b-eb2a-4e63-9c4e-0374f770856f.pdf.

16. Ibid.

17. Ibid.

18. Gallo, Carmine (2010) *The Innovation Secrets of Steve Jobs: Insanely Different Principles for Breakthrough Success* (New York: McGraw-Hill).

19. Kar, Ian (2014) "Here's How the Security Behind Apple Pay Will Really Work" (Bank Innovation, 12 September 2014) http://bankinnovation.net/2014/09/heres-how-the-security-behind-apple-pay-will-really-work/, date accessed 21 March 2015.

20. Ismail, Salim (2015) *Exponential Organizations: Why new organizations are ten times better, faster, and cheaper than yours (and what to do about it)* (New York: Diversion Books).

CHAPTER 4

Why FinTech Lives Outside of Banks

Whenever a new FinTech service launches, the obvious first thing to do is to compare the new offering to those of the established financial sector. However, banks are already working closely with tech companies on the backend to provide services to customers. As much as FinTech entrepreneurs often distance themselves from the formal financial sector, they depend on each other more than they like to admit. For example, Apple Pay, the iOS app that turns the iPhone into a digital wallet, relies on deals with the three major credit and debit card providers: Visa, MasterCard, and American Express. In transactions, the credit card networks dynamically generate security tokens that are an essential part of the service and its security.[1] Major banks such as Bank of America, Capital One, Chase, Citi, and Wells Fargo have also signed up.[2] As a result of these commitments, Apple supports the cards that represent about 90 percent of the credit card purchase volume in the United States.[3] It is easy to see the benefit of using mobile payments, and even though banks are often reluctant to embrace change, it is in their interest to collaborate with a company like Apple. On the other hand, the tech company also needs the established financial firms; their technology is part of the security backbone on which the service operates. Without partners who control existing financial networks, Apple Pay would have to build its solution from zero. Labeling Apple Pay as a disruptive innovation that will usurp the existing financial sector is therefore missing the point. It is more an extension of similar transaction services that existed for a while, adapting them for the convenience of consumers in tune with their digital lifestyle.

Because they build on existing technology that is often in the hands of banks, FinTech services that improve existing solutions are less disruptive than they would like to appear. On the other hand, when advantages and market potential are less evident, entrepreneurs without a track record will have no chance convincing banks to give them a hand. The ideas that take off in the future often find few nods in the present and, because of that, the companies that will eventually shape the future of finance might be completely off the radar, far removed from the media spotlight and the public consciousness. This is a bigger issue than it seems: even though banks are aware of the necessity to change with the times, they underestimate the disruptive impact of a FinTech ecosystem that lives completely outside of banks.

Most banks have a digital strategy and their COOs are often knowledgeable about trends in FinTech. Many of them keep a close eye on developments in the financial technology innovation scene. In their view, whenever they see something interesting, they integrate it into their operations, with the goal of ensuring their long-term leadership in the financial sector. This might work while the FinTech ecosystem is still in its infancy and relatively immature.

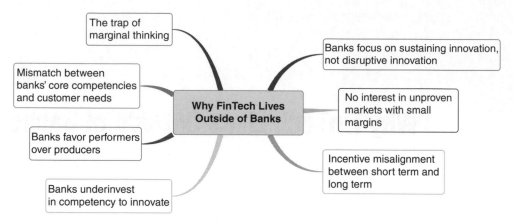

FIGURE 4.1   Reasons why FinTech lives outside of banks

However, for the acquisition strategy of banks to continue to work, FinTech entrepreneurs must be willing to play along. What will happen if an entrepreneur refuses to sell to a bank and prefers to challenge the financial sector head on? It may be possible to freeze out such insurgents for a while—by pointing towards the need for a banking license and compliance with regulation. In the end, a walled garden is only safe as long as someone has yet to find a way to scale that wall. This chapter examines why FinTech innovation is bound to happen on the periphery, and why banks and other market leaders in the financial sector will most likely overlook innovations with the most disruptive potential. Later in this book, in Part Three, we will chart ways for banks and FinTech companies to work together to build the hybrid financial sector of the future. Figure 4.1 gives an overview of the main points we discuss in this chapter.

4.1   THE TECHNOLOGY MUDSLIDE HYPOTHESIS: SUSTAINING INNOVATION VS. DISRUPTIVE INNOVATION

You may have heard of the "technology mudslide hypothesis": the struggle of established companies to keep up with technological change resembles an attempt to climb a mudslide that is accelerating down a hill.[4] Just as the red queen in Lewis Carroll's *Through the Looking Glass* is running just to keep in the same place,[5] companies need to keep up technologically with their competitors to avoid falling behind. The technology mudslide hypothesis is widely accepted, yet author Clayton Christensen has challenged this hypothesis. He found the difficulty of adapting to technological change had little to do with the failure of leading firms. Instead, market leaders are often aware of innovations, but they fail to pursue them because they are not profitable enough in the short term.

When refuting the technology mudslide hypothesis, Christensen introduced the distinction between *sustaining innovation* and *disruptive innovation*.[6] While sustaining innovation aims at improving existing product performance, disruptive innovation brings a new value proposition to the market. Think about the example of vacuum tubes: sustaining innovation provided a better and more efficient vacuum tube. Conversely, disruptive innovation led to the introduction of the transistor. This has made smaller, cheaper devices possible, which revolutionized the electronics industry. Disruptive innovation may underperform today, but it will outperform tomorrow. Because disruptive products are usually first commercialized in insignificant markets, these products are simpler and cheaper by design. In contrast, most established companies are looking upward in the market, not downward. Their goal is to increase the complexity of their products and services to move their existing customers toward premium pricing, not to simplify their product palette and lower the price.

The most profitable customers of incumbent market leaders often have no use for disruptive products at the beginning, which gives the established companies the illusion that they may safely ignore disruptive technology at the onset and focus on the higher margin products or services instead. Christensen calls this the *Innovator's Dilemma* in his eponymous book. It describes the inability of incumbent firms to recognize the significance of those technologies that eventually unseat them. It is called the *Innovator's Dilemma* because many market leaders actually come up with the innovations that ultimately prove their own downfall; but it is the competition that commercializes the innovation for lack of interest by the incumbent.

When you look at the actions of today's banks, is it possible that they are conforming to the mudslide hypothesis? Most likely. Are they suffering from the Innovator's Dilemma? Let's see. Even though it wasn't banks that invented peer-to-peer lending, it makes sense to liken their current challenges with new FinTech companies to the Innovator's Dilemma. The symptoms of the dilemma are certainly the same: could a large incumbent bank roll out a payment solution such as Apple Pay? Certainly. Nevertheless, an incumbent either sees no point in doing so because of the small market size or feels it might better capitalize on its old business model as long as possible. Banks could have been the ones to create many FinTech innovations, but according to the Innovator's Dilemma, established companies protect their own profitable businesses and eschew small emerging niches. Established companies naturally shy away from disintermediating their own products and services.

Theodore Levitt mentions the railroads as an example of an industry that failed to see market opportunities. American railroads have lost market share with personal travelers not because others—cars, trucks, airplanes—filled the need to travel but because the railroads failed to fill this need themselves. They let others siphon off their customers because they thought of themselves as being in the railroad business, not in the transportation business. They were "railroad-oriented," not "transportation-oriented," and their focus was on the product instead of the customer.[7] It is easy to rewrite this scenario so it matches the situation with the banks. While the financial sector was recovering from a global financial crisis and catching up with new regulations, FinTech entrepreneurs found better solutions to problems that people cared about.

When banks acquire FinTech companies or integrate their services, they do this to automate or streamline their existing operations, relative to those of their competitors. Especially in Big Data and analytics, banks enjoy an immediate payoff when deploying proven technology that external companies have developed. It is hard to identify the market potential of disruptive innovation. Large companies in need of big profits can rarely afford to take a long view. Online lending platforms, and marketplace lending in particular, show several characteristics of disruptive technology. For instance, they aim at small, unproven markets with low-margin products, and they require discovery-driven planning. The existence of this mismatch with the set of capabilities of established banks means that it's worth examining what this means in more detail.

4.1.1 Small unproven markets with low-margin products

Banks have phased out low-profit customers since the financial crisis and have focused on those operations with high profit margins. Multinational banks with hundreds of billions of dollars in assets can hardly afford to experiment with low-margin products in nascent markets that will cost a lot of money without foreseeable potential. Most new niche markets are too small to satisfy banks' requirements for growth. As a result, large companies adopt the strategy of waiting until new markets are "large enough to be interesting." When it comes to buying other companies that have developed technology that banks can use in their operations, they will only be interested in those innovations with an established track record so banks can monetize their acquisitions quickly. Nurturing technology innovators, let alone giving them space to experiment with unproven ideas, is out of the question. However, just like the railroads in Levitt's example, the hands-off approach of banks to innovation allows new entrants to develop new markets. This might have come with few risks when technology was a natural boundary to entry in the financial sector. But today, cheap and ubiquitous computing power allows anyone with a good idea and modest seed capital to rival banking services.

Even though several banks and other multinational companies fund FinTech accelerator programs, such as the *FinTech Innovation Lab* in New York, London, and Hong Kong,[8] they are largely on the sidelines when it comes to disruptive innovation. By their own account, in their programs, they "give early and growth-stage companies a platform to develop, trial and prove their ideas alongside the world's leading banks in a 12-week mentorship program."[9] There are several issues with this approach to innovation: some products that underperform today, relative to customer expectations in mainstream markets, will become those that dominate markets tomorrow. By "tomorrow" we mean five to ten years, not twelve weeks. At the same time, the business model of banks allows no margin for error. Disruptive innovation requires launching into untested, unproven markets where little confirmation exists. Any entrepreneur will cringe when a mentor asks him to develop, trial and prove an innovation in twelve weeks, and such a program will only attract those entrepreneurs that have already been in the market for a while. As a result, FinTech innovation labs will vet sustaining innovation, pass on the disruptive ideas, and not even attract those entrepreneurs with the biggest potential in the first place. The notion that disruptive innovation happens "alongside the world's leading banks" also raises eyebrows. As we will discover later in this chapter, innovation happens best in a secluded pocket, far away from the bureaucracy of a big company.

It makes sense for banks to keep their eye on the ball for another reason: small niches at the onset can grow into respectable markets and threats over time. Christensen describes the humble beginnings of minimills—small-scale steel mills that use scrap metal as raw material—that only produced low quality rebar in the beginning, a business the large steel manufacturers were more than happy to get out of. Regardless, the minimills invested their profits in new processes for angle iron, then structural steel, and eventually high-quality sheet metal, which in the end disrupted the entire steel industry.[10]

Christensen himself couldn't have picked a better example than FinTech as an exemplar for the Innovator's Dilemma. Most FinTech startups are unprofitable or barely profitable for a long time, which includes many of the large online lenders. It is rarely those startups that large multinationals agree with that will make waves in the long term. The world's leading banks and financial firms have no use for disruptive innovation because their existing customers and shareholders have no interest in it. As a result, by definition, the innovation they are promoting is at best the incremental improvement of their existing operations. To align themselves more closely with disruptive innovators, banks must incorporate fresh approaches to new business development. Discovery-driven planning is one of them.

4.1.2 The need for discovery-driven planning

Discovery-driven planning is a tool that acknowledges the difference between planning for a new venture and planning for a more conventional line of business. Conventional planning (or platform-based planning) requires that managers extrapolate future results from well-understood past experience. One expects predictions to be accurate because they spring from solid knowledge about the past rather than from wild assumptions about the future. In conventional planning, a project's deviation from a plan is a bad thing. Conversely, in discovery-driven planning, we know little and assume much. Instead of treating assumptions as facts, they serve as best-guess estimates that we frequently test and question. This systematically converts assumptions into knowledge while a venture unfolds. When new data emerge, they become part of the evolving plan, which helps managers discover the potential of the venture piece by piece as it develops. This approach needs different disciplines to those used in conventional planning, but they can be just as precise as established practices.[11]

Discovery-driven planning is the *modus operandi* of every startup. Several FinTech companies have modified their course over time. The robo-advisor Wealthfront, for example, started out as KaChing in 2008, which allowed users to replicate the trades of successful amateur investors.[12] It then pivoted to provide professional account management in 2010 and now boasts over $1 billion assets under management.[13] Discovery-driven planning only works in small companies with a relatively flat hierarchy and a quick product and release cycle. This kind of thinking is squarely at odds with the current practices of established banks and credit institutions. However, in order to play the FinTech game successfully, banks need to learn how to use discovery-driven planning.

4.2 WILL BANKS NOTICE THE NEXT FINTECH BREAKTHROUGH?

It is possible but unlikely that a bank or another market leader in the established financial system will produce the next FinTech breakthrough. At this point, most banks look at FinTech startups as a cheap R&D lab from which they can mix and match services that might be useful to them to increase margins. This is the major reason they sponsor FinTech innovation labs around the globe in the first place. But by now we know that there are two different categories of FinTech services out there: those that emerge with *sustaining innovation* that makes the existing operations of the established financial sector easier. Examples are Big Data analytics that make sense of financial patterns or customer behavior, or other tools that banks already use in one form or another. The second category has to do with *disruptive innovation*—things banks have not thought of, but that are potentially extremely useful to their customers. Banks are good at spotting sustaining innovation. They are already highly technical operations, with a long history of working with technology providers to streamline and improve their operations. Where exactly this innovation is coming from—a garage in Silicon Valley or the shiny office of a consulting firm in the City of London—matters less and less to banks. When they can get hold of solutions that help them do their work more efficiently, they are likely to acquire them. FinTech companies offering sustaining innovation can therefore expect that banks will have an interest in integrating their services. We might see a large number of acquisitions of such FinTech startups in the near future.

Things are different for disruptive financial technology startups. Integrating a disruptive startup into the fabric of an established bank is much more complex, as it inherently cannibalizes a bank's existing profit centers. Marketplace lending has the potential to be a disruptive innovation. A new approach to lending in the trillion-dollar credit market might make a big dent in how the financial sector works. Regardless, banks have little interest in changing their business model when offering credit, at least for the time being. On top of that, most banks doubt that marketplace lending will be serious competition for their loan business, and some of them believe that the disruptive innovation in the sector already happened years ago when the concept of peer-to-peer lending was first announced in 2005. The ticket size of individual loans currently tops out at $35,000. This might be fine for consumer loans, but the much larger and more interesting markets for real estate credit and corporate lending require a different scale. Marketplace lending will have to grow out of its marginal appeal to be a real game changer in the established financial sector. Until that happens, it is very likely that banks will dismiss it as either immature or not interesting enough to be a serious competitor.

When looking at the business models and strategies of banks and established credit institutions today, it is clear that they have little leeway to support innovation from within. They all portray themselves as innovators, but simply projecting something does not make it so. As a result, disruptive financial innovation breakthroughs will take place at the fringes of the established system, without the incumbents noticing. Success rarely relies on getting it right at the first try. Instead, it hinges on continuing experimentation until the approaches that work emerge. Only a lucky few companies start off with a strategy that ultimately leads to success. There are other reasons banks will probably fail to notice those FinTech innovations with the biggest potential in the long term, as the next paragraphs will examine.

4.2.1 Incentive misalignment between the short term and the long term

Imagine your job is to spot and carry out the innovations that improve the operations of a big bank. What projects are you most likely going to support? If you take a long-term perspective, you would support new products and processes that will be key to a bank's success in five to ten years in the future. However, the results of those efforts will only become evident many years later, after they have swallowed millions of dollars in trial and error. When they have finally proven their worth, you might have already moved to another division or another bank and whoever is at the helm at that time will claim credit for the innovation you stuck your neck out for. Even if you are still around to harvest the fruits of your labor in five to ten years, if you lose money nine years out of ten—even one year out of ten—you will have a hard time staying the course. Instead, if you focus on delivering results that are visible and measurable within six to twelve months—even with an inferior approach—you know that those assessing the innovation program will reward you. This is just how incentives in business work. You see each project as a stepping stone. With something to show for your good ideas and efforts, you hope to get a shot at an even bigger and better assignment the next time around.

An incentive system that rewards decision makers for short-term thinking often undermines the company's success in the long term. Investor Frank Rotman points out that big corporations have "long organizational memories" when it comes to failures. Failures are often pinned on executives for a long time, which makes matters even worse. If an executive can build a track record of success, he may be able to afford taking more risks and try something that may fail once in a while. In essence, the formula for career progression is to fail on smaller projects and succeed on the bigger ones. These bigger projects are those for which your boss is holding his boss responsible.[14]

It is important to reiterate that we have no intention of lambasting the financial sector, or banks in particular. Misaligned incentives and resource allocation are by no means reserved for banks. Governments, for example, are unable to change their social security and other entitlement programs, even though most of these programs are on the brink of bankruptcy. Why is that so? Politicians stand for re-election every few years. It is their conviction that it is in the best interest of the country to re-elect them, so they focus on delivering short-term results that stick in the minds of the electorate until the next vote. How entitlement programs could improve is widely known. Yet, so many people rely on these programs that a radical change would be highly unpopular. Anyone who cuts benefits for voters can be sure to lose the next election.

Introducing change is never an easy game to win. Yet someone has to assume responsibility for taking risks and making unpopular decisions when it comes to fostering innovation that will prevail in the long term. Unfortunately, the people willing to do so have a difficult time standing up for what they believe in, or they opt out of the corporate career path entirely and start their own thing. The loss for corporations is immeasurable.

4.2.2 Forcing banks to collaborate with online lenders

When change refuses to grow organically from within companies, it is of course possible to legislate it from the outside. In the summer of 2014, the UK's Chancellor of the Exchequer, George Osborne, revealed new rules under the Small Business, Enterprise and Employment Bill, that force banks that reject loan applications from SMEs to refer them to online lending platforms.[15] Concurrently, bank Santander and the lending platform Funding Circle announced the first partnership between a UK bank and a peer-to-peer lending platform.[16] In return for customers' referrals from Santander to the online lender, Funding Circle promotes the bank's current account and cash management service. In a similar move, the Royal Bank of Scotland (RBS) signaled plans to enter the peer-to-peer lending market in a tie-up with a third party operator.[17]

Is this good news or bad news for the future of the hybrid financial sector? A little bit of both. Despite the new rules for online referrals and cooperation, banks bring in products from the outside into their business units instead of growing new ideas from within. They are distributing products that established online lenders have produced, still without investing in their own core competencies. Forced collaboration may be a start, to show that it is indeed possible to break down conventional barriers in the financial sector. Nevertheless, it still fails to address the underlying problems that prevent innovation from emerging from within the sector where it could make a difference for banking customers in the long run.

4.2.3 Innovating in-house vs. buying innovation

Authors CK Prahalad and Gary Hamel provide a useful framework to address innovation and competency of corporations. Even though their theory is close to 25 years old, it is still an excellent approach to see the advantages for companies to grow innovation in-house instead

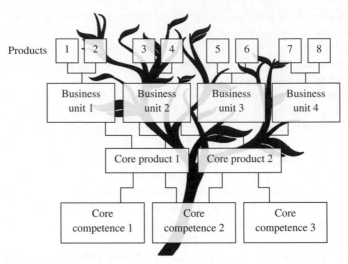

FIGURE 4.2   The corporation as a tree
Adapted from: Prahalad and Hamel

of purchasing it in the market. This is by no means the case with banks only. It applies to most large companies operating in mature markets. Prahalad and Hamel liken a company to a tree with several core competencies as its roots. These competencies are the "roots of competitiveness," that will eventually decide if a company will end up a market leader or a follower. Out of these core competencies, core products emerge as the tree trunk. Business units spring from core products as branches that finally produce products, the leaves and fruits of the tree. These leaves and fruits are the parts of the business that customers will interact with. Just as roots need time to grow, corporations build core competencies through a continued process of improvement and enhancement that may take a decade or longer. Companies that have neglected investment in building their core competencies will find it difficult to enter an emerging market. As a result, they might serve as a distribution channel for the products of other companies.[18] Figure 4.2 shows the structure of the corporation as a tree.[19]

The battle for leadership in a business sector takes place on the planes of core competence, core product, and products. An established corporation may win a battle on one plane but lose on another. With large investments, a company might be able to beat competitors to blue skies technologies, but it may still lose the race to build leadership with core competence. The only guarantee for a company to outpace its rivals in new business development is developing strong core competencies. This bottom-up strategy for innovation makes for a more resilient company than one that buys technology leadership piecemeal.[20]

4.3   WHY DO BANKS HAVE DIFFICULTY IN INNOVATING?

Several reasons exist why established companies may lose the battle for leadership in newly emerging markets. Among them are underinvestment in core competencies, imprisoned resources, bounded innovation, the tension between performers and producers, and the mismatch between current core competencies of banks with customer needs.[21]

4.3.1   Underinvestment in core competencies

In an organization like a bank, which consists of multiple strategic business units (SBUs), no single unit may be able to justify the investment required to build leadership in some new core competence. The managers of these SBUs will underinvest because none of them feels responsible for establishing a viable position in core products beyond the established strategy.[22] This is currently the situation, as none of the established online lending platforms or other financial innovation startups have emerged from the existing financial sector. Perhaps banks are overconfident—that they possess the underlying core competencies to address the financial needs of their customers—that they neglect product innovation. They also have the backup of governments and central banks who will bail them out when things go south. Believing they can always buy innovation when they need it, banks underinvest in the competencies that allow them to compete in the future. Instead of recognizing the need for long-term investment in new competencies, many banks focus only on that part of the FinTech sector with the most obvious payoffs. They try to cherry-pick the winners in the race for leadership in financial technology innovation, without learning how innovation works from the ground up. In a sense, this behavior has a tradition at banks: they have long relied on third parties to supply them with software solutions and other services. However, never before have suppliers been able to compete directly with banks. Today, they could decide to offer a service on their own directly to the market, which may net them billions of dollars in profit. None of the current trends in technology and innovation bode well for the banks when it comes to their market position in financial services in five to ten years from now. But even if they started innovating from within, they will still have to overcome other hurdles, such as their imprisoned resources.

4.3.2   Imprisoned resources

As SBUs evolve, they develop unique competencies. Typically, managers often see those people in an organization as the sole property of the business unit in which they earned their keep. Managers of other SBUs might want to "borrow" talented people from time to time to address challenges they are facing. However, SBU managers are often unwilling to lend their competence carriers, and they may actually hide talent to prevent the pursuit of new opportunities outside a particular SBU. We can compare this to residents of an underdeveloped country hiding most of their cash under their mattresses. The benefits of competencies, like the benefits of cash on hand, depend on the velocity of their circulation as well as on the size of the stock a company holds. When competencies become imprisoned, the people who carry these competencies never get assigned to the most exciting opportunities, and their skills begin to atrophy.[23] In the past, this may have had few consequences for banks. Employees could either play ball or look for another job. Luckily, today, anybody with competencies in financial technology innovation will have no problem finding plenty of venture capital to launch their own startup. If talented individuals feel they will be better off on their own, their loyalty to an employer becomes fragile. Several ex-bankers have already founded FinTech startups on their own. We expect this trend to continue.

4.3.3   Bounded innovation

If companies lack core competencies to compete, their individual SBUs will only recognize and pursue the low hanging fruit—those innovation opportunities that are close at hand. In the case of banks and financial technology innovation, this mainly covers marginal product-line extensions and automation. New disruptive technology will almost certainly stay under the radar of banks for this reason. Hybrid opportunities will emerge only when companies and their managers remove their blinkers.[24]

4.3.4 Performers vs. producers

Because people have better opportunities today to start their own ventures, imprisoned resources have become mobile across companies. In recent years, employees have begun to expect their employers to be aligned with them, not the other way around. This has spawned a new entrepreneurial class of innovators who have little interest in even pitching their ideas to large corporations. However, what might it have been like if companies had provided an environment that inspired innovators to develop their ideas in-house? What if the world's self-made billionaires had carried out their innovations at large corporations that hired them early in their careers? When examining these questions, we may want to distinguish between the mindset of performers and producers.[25] Performers possess skills in one key area but often fail to see the combinations that are necessary to convert an idea into a profitable business. Producers, on the other hand, see the potential for a new idea in the market, and they can execute on this idea to help it reach the greatest market potential. Creating breakthrough innovation and value for companies needs both skill sets in combination: the ability to follow through on processes and details to make the business work, and the vision to unite divergent ideas and resources into a blockbuster concept. However, performers lead today's great companies, and they primarily hire and reward other performers. This cultivates a performer-centric culture that pushes out those people with the greatest ability to create long-lasting value. Attracting producers into companies requires changes to the way organizations think and operate. Without a mind shift, companies will fail to attract—let alone identify—those people with the talent to ensure its competitiveness in the digital future.[26]

4.3.5 Divergence between core competencies of banks with customer needs

Just as "managers rise to the level of their incompetence," an organization's capabilities define its disabilities in another context.[27] Their systems, processes, and values ensure the continuation along an agreed upon trajectory. By definition, these capabilities shut everything down that diverts an organization from its projected path. Among the current core capabilities of banks are the following:

- Guarantee of their liabilities from central banks (via license)
- Capability in money management
- Capability in risk management
- Physical presence with branches
- Networks of ATMs
- Established proprietary channels of debit and credit card payments
- Experience in rolling out financial products and underwriting loans
- Strong legal departments

At the same time, trends in consumer behavior demand more than the capabilities in the list above. Customers are always on, hyper-connected to a variety of social networking sources, adopting new technology and services rapidly, and demanding mobile communication without onerous requirements to "know your customer," or KYC in short. Their demands look something like this:

- 24/7 availability for personal questions with rapid response beyond 9–5 business hours
- Well-developed digital channels that are accessible for two-way communication, not just one-way push advertising
- Low cost and transparency in financial services
- Easy to understand and transparent information about loans and products
- Ease of application for loans and products with rapid decision and availability of funds
- Painless and inexpensive ways to pay and receive funds

When banks deny loans to customers and businesses, borrowers are just clicks away from new solutions provided by online lenders, online payment providers, and mobile-first banks. As we learned when we looked at the social factors that enabled FinTech, customers have little patience for the onerous requirements of banks to comply with regulation, and fail to see why they should pick up the slack for past mistakes in the banking world that have resulted in a barrage of new regulation. Structural factors, such as increased regulatory requirements for banks, have made excursions into the murky waters of untested, unproven technology taboo. Yet this is exactly what disruptive technology demands: abandoning the safeguards and plunging head-on into a new adventure. It is already obvious that this is hardly what banks can and want to do. They need sure-fire wins, and they need them quickly. In light of the strong headwinds that banks face, what can they do to stay relevant in the financial sector in the future? They will have to develop core competences that allow them to innovate themselves. However, innovative capabilities are hardly an add-on. The wider ecosystem must shed beliefs that hinder innovation to give a company a realistic chance to keep and improve its market share.

4.4 DEVELOPING CORE COMPETENCE IN FINANCIAL TECHNOLOGY INNOVATION

To develop core competencies that allow banks to play in the emerging FinTech space, banks should do some fundamental soul searching. Corporations should ask themselves the following three questions to stay competitive:

- How long could we preserve our competitiveness in this business if we did not control this particular core competence?
- How central is this core competence to perceived customer benefits?
- What future opportunities will we miss if we lost this particular competence?

Without answering these questions and pointing out the obvious, banks are in desperate need to bolster their competencies in financial technology innovation. In the medium and long term, this will be the only way for them to establish leadership in newly emerging areas such as online lending. Staying on the sidelines and watching the sector emerge is dangerous, as new entrants amass experience and know-how in this sector that will further increase the knowledge gap to the incumbents. To stay in the race, banks should integrate innovation skills into their operations as soon as possible. This may mandate a rethink of their established practices, but it will be instrumental in the future. Unless they do this, they may suffer the fate of film manufacturers, who went under when digital cameras took over; or the music industry, which has ceded a large market share to new online vendors. In hindsight, it is always clear what companies that went from market leader to bankruptcy should have done to avoid their fate. Most likely, banks look at the existing examples of industries that technology disrupted, believing their situation will be different. Why is this so? Because it is easy to fall into the trap of marginal thinking.

4.4.1   The trap of marginal thinking

When a company has the option of making an investment in new technology or innovation, it will assess the innovation from the viewpoint of its existing business model. Based on the results of its number crunching, it will often decide against the investment if the marginal revenue is not worth the marginal cost of the investment. This is what author Clayton Christensen calls the "trap of marginal thinking."[29]

Companies can see the immediate costs of making an investment, but they struggle to understand the costs of not investing. When they deem the profit from a new product as insignificant while they still have an existing product with acceptable returns, they are blind to the future and the possibility of somebody disrupting the market under their nose. Assuming that the revenues from their legacy products keep rolling in forever, the consequences of the decision to wait are far from obvious. Companies remain on the sidelines and watch their competitors struggle with perfecting new innovative products. However, eventually, those companies that remained on the sidelines will have to pay a price, and that price can be very high. It may cost them not only the marginal cost of catching up, but the loss of an existing business line that the new innovation has disrupted. Henry Ford summed this up nicely: "If you need a machine and don't buy it, then you will ultimately find that you have paid for it and don't have it."

Throughout history, large incumbents have lost their shirts against new entrants. Just look at the battle between the video rental companies Blockbuster and Netflix. At its peak in 2004, Blockbuster had up to 60,000 employees and more than 9,000 stores. When it looked into the business model of a small startup called Netflix that pioneered DVD rentals by mail, Blockbuster management decided not to bother. Netflix profit margins were below those of Blockbuster and engaging in rentals by mail would only cannibalize their profitable stores. They concluded that Netflix's business model was not financially viable in the long term, and that they served a niche market. Was their assessment correct? By 2011, Netflix had almost 24 million customers. Blockbuster had declared bankruptcy the year before.[30]

Could this happen to banks? Author Brett King points out most banks linger in silo thinking, legacy organization structure, and traditional business models that frustrate change. Their use of digital communication as a one-way marketing channel, where customers are routinely told not to respond to emails they receive from banks, are hardly in sync with the demands of today's hyperconnected customer.[31] The attitude of marginal thinking shows itself in the statement of a senior U.S. banker at Barclays, who stated that "A widget company makes widgets, and a bank makes loans. If banks could make money on it, you bet you'd see more lending to small firms."[32]

4.4.2   The way forward

We realize it is easy to point out faults without offering encouragement for the initiatives that banks undertake. It is true that banks have come a long way in recent years, and that their digital and online operations have improved remarkably. The existing infrastructure becomes more and more efficient and automated, which will eventually lead to less interaction between the majority of customers and banking staff, with subsequently fewer branches. As we have examined in this chapter, sustaining innovation is what banks are masters of. However, disruption of the financial sector will happen sooner or later—it is only a question of time. There is no reason for banks to suffer the fate of other industries, which underwent massive reshuffling because of digital disruption. If they keep an open mind and build their digital strategy with innovation—not technology adaptation—at the core, they have a good chance of surviving the storm, even coming out on top.

4.5 CONCLUDING REMARKS

This chapter examines why FinTech emerged outside of banks. Part of the problem is that misunderstandings about innovation—such as the technology mudslide hypothesis—stop banks from being innovators themselves. Unfortunately, competing forces further diminish the ability of banks to invent and deliver products and services their customers want. In the end, they need to develop the core competencies to innovate, or they risk becoming another item in the list of industries that have failed to see the writing on the wall.

This chapter concludes the first part of this book in which we have examined the history and status quo of FinTech and its position in the wider financial sector. In Part Three we will offer more insights into the effective strategies for FinTech entrepreneurs and banks to compete in the hybrid financial world. Before we venture into strategy, we first change sides over to established financial institutions in Part Two. There, we examine how banks "do" credit, and how they assess the risk and profitability of loans. Then we will investigate difficulties and strategies on the road to the future of credit in Chapter 14, Digital Dilemmas, and Chapter 15, Digital Strategy.

NOTES

1. Kar, Ian (2014), "Here's How the Security Behind Apple Pay Will Really Work" (Bank Innovation, 12 September 2014), http://bankinnovation.net/2014/09/heres-how-the-security-behind-apple-pay-will-really-work/, date accessed 21 March 2015.
2. Gokey, Malarie (2015) "Apple Pay Takes Over 700,000 Locations, Many Coke Machines, and Works with Apple Watch" (Digital Trends, 9 March 2015), http://www.digitaltrends.com/mobile/apple-pay-partners-news/, data accessed 20 March 2015.
3. Isaac, Mike (2014) Dozens More Companies Sign Up for Apple Pay (Bits Blog of the *New York Times*, 16 December 2014), http://bits.blogs.nytimes.com/2014/12/16/dozens-more-companies-sign-up-for-apple-pay/?_r=0, date accessed 20 March 2015.
4. Christensen, Clayton (1997) *The Innovator's Dilemma* (Boston: Harvard Business Review Press).
5. Carroll, Lewis (1871, 2004) *Through the Looking-Glass and What Alice Found There* (New York: Barnes and Noble Classics).
6. Christensen, Clayton (1997) *The Innovator's Dilemma* (Boston: Harvard Business Review Press).
7. Levitt, Theodore (1960) "Marketing Myopia," *Harvard Business Review* 2004 Jul–Aug; 82 (7–8):138–49, https://hbr.org/2004/07/marketing-myopia, date accessed 17 July 2015.
8. Fintech Innovation Lab (2015a), home page, www.fintechinnovationlab.com/, date accessed 20 March 2015.

9. Fintech Innovation Lab (2015a), home page, www.fintechinnovationlab.com/, date accessed 20 March 2015.

10. Christensen, Clayton (1997) *The Innovator's Dilemma* (Boston: Harvard Business Review Press).

11. McGrath, Rita; MacMillan, Ian (1995) "Discovery-Driven Planning" (*Harvard Business Review*, July 1995), https://hbr.org/1995/07/discovery-driven-planning/ar/1.

12. McCracken, Harry (2009a) "KaChing: A Better Alternative to Mutual Funds?" http://www.technologizer.com/2009/10/19/kaching-a-better-alternative-to-mutual-funds, date accessed 14 November 2014.

13. Wealthfront (2014a) home page, https://www.wealthfront.com/one-billion, date accessed 14 November 2014.

14. Rotman, Frank (2015) "The Hourglass Effect: A Decade of Displacement," 13 April 2015, http://qedinvestors.com/frank-rotman-releases-the-hourglass-effect-a-decade-of-displacement/, date accessed 14 April 2015.

15. Fleming, Sam (2014) "George Osborne to reveal shake-up of SME loans" (*Financial Times*, 5 August 2014), http://www.ft.com/intl/cms/s/0/14a1ec8c-1cc4-11e4-88c3-00144feabdc0.html.

16. Funding Circle (2014a) "Funding Circle & Santander announce partnership to support thousands of UK businesses" (18 June 2014), https://www.fundingcircle.com/blog/2014/06/funding-circle-santander-announce-partnership-support-thousands-uk-businesses/.

17. Dunkley, Emma (2014) "Royal Bank of Scotland to enter P2P lending market" (*Financial Times*, 19 October 2014), http://www.ft.com/intl/cms/s/0/660447b0-5625-11e4-93b3-00144feab7de.html.

18. Prahalad, C K; Hamel, Gary, "The Core Competence of the Corporation" (*Harvard Business Review* May–June 1990).

19. Ibid.

20. Ibid.

21. Ibid.

22. Ibid.

23. Ibid.

24. Ibid.

25. Sviokla, John and Cohen, Mitch (2014) *The Self-Made Billionaire Effect: How Extreme Producers Create Massive Value* (New York: Penguin).

26. Ibid.

27. Peter, Laurence; Hull, Raymond (1969) *The Peter Principle: Why Things Always Go Wrong* (New York: William Morrow and Company).

28. Prahalad, C K; Hamel, Gary; "The Core Competence of the Corporation" (*Harvard Business Review* May–June 1990).

29. Christensen, Clayton; Allworth, James; Dillon, Karen (2012) *How Will You Measure Your Life?* (New York: Harper Business).

30. Ibid.

31. King, Brett (2013) *Bank 3.0: Why Banking is No Longer Somewhere You Go, But Something You Do* (Hoboken: Wiley).

32. Gordon Mills, Karen and McCarthy, Brayden (2014) "The State of Small Business Lending: Credit Access during the Recovery and How Technology May Change the Game" (Harvard Business School Working Paper, 22 July 2014), http://www.hbs.edu/faculty/Publication%20Files/15-004_09b1bf8b-eb2a-4e63-9c4e-0374f770856f.pdf.

Two

The Status Quo of Analytics in the Financial Industry— The Perspective of Banks

The second part of this book is about the way that banks assess loan portfolios. We will explain the different moving parts of credit analytics and will relate them to marketplace lending whenever possible. Before we delve into analytics, let's first revisit the journey banking has taken in recent decades and how this has shaped the way they conduct their business.

Banks play critical roles in societies. Among them is organizing the system of payments, giving credit to businesses in the economy, and safeguarding the funds of depositors. The banking system also allocates capital from those with a surplus of funds (depositors) to those with a deficit (borrowers). It does so by transforming small amounts of liquid deposits into large loans that are relatively illiquid. In a nutshell, by matching deposits and loans, banks provide liquidity to the economy. Intermediation traditionally takes place on the balance sheet of banks, but banks also engage in off-balance sheet operations, for example, offering loan commitments, letters of credit, and guarantees for customers' future investments. Banks further create and trade derivative contracts that allow counterparties to rein in their risks. If they carry out intermediation between creditors and borrowers efficiently, this benefits both individuals and the entire economy. Without readily available credit, economies would be by a magnitude smaller than they are today.

This relatively simple concept of banking has undergone a massive transformation in recent years. The largest banks in many countries have merged into financial service conglomerates that offer various products, including additional functions such as retail banking, asset management, brokerage, insurance, investment banking, and wealth management. Developments on the product side have occurred in parallel with the emergence of new funding sources. Driven by securitization, mostly of residential mortgages, banks have thrown off the shackles of their deposit base for lending. They have bundled assets on their balance sheets and sold them into the market to finance expansion. Off-balance sheet vehicles, such as Structured

Investment Vehicles (SIVs), allow banks to collateralize assets funded by short-term paper, which generates trading profits and enables them to raise capital to plug funding gaps.[1]

P2.1   BANKING IS INNOVATION

Banking is in flux, and financial innovation—heavy use of technology—has been widespread in the financial sector for decades. The image of banks that the popular media portrays, as lumbering stalwarts who turn a blind eye on innovation, is therefore largely inaccurate. Financial institutions have traditionally been at the forefront of technology, and new technology and innovation are playing a huge part in established banks. There have been many innovations both in the front office and in the back office of banks. By their nature, front office innovations, such as ATMs, credit cards, debit cards, and online banking, are most visible for customers. The first self-service ATM with commercial success was launched by Barclays Bank in the late 1960s. Since then, ATMs have revolutionized the banking habits of retail customers. They simplified the distribution of cash for customer withdrawals since their mass launch in the US in the 1970s and most of the rest of the world in the 1980s. After more than 40 years of operations, ATMs dispense about 75 percent of all cash in the UK to consumers. Cash machines have become an integral part of consumers' interaction with money.[2]

Next to those visible changes in banking, innovations in the back office of financial institutions are equally important. They sustain and enhance the operations of banks. For example, advances in computing technology, networking, and database technology allowed the accurate calculation of liquidity and intraday liquidity with near real-time transaction processing systems. Making use of powerful processors and algorithms has made the calculation of exposure and risk and other sophisticated analytics possible. Stress testing and scenario analysis are other innovations in the back office. Adapting technology early and aggressively has given rise to new kinds of financial contracts that include many moving parts. Finally, back office financial innovation is at the heart of the worldwide trading of contracts, which have massively increased the market for financial instruments. Most of these breakthroughs take place behind the scenes, and many people rarely see the back office of a bank. Nevertheless, the back office and its functions are actually the core of modern banking, at the forefront of innovation.

P2.2   BANKING GOES MOBILE

The fact that shaping the banking habits of customers has been expensive in the past has raised the barrier to adaptation of new technology by small players. In the U.S., it still costs banks about $1,700 per month to run one ATM on someone else's property and slightly less if the ATM is located at the bank's own branch. These high costs are a reason established banks have begun to scale back on their ATM and branch networks.[3] Computing power, networking, data storage, and software programming also come with hefty price tags that have made entry into financial services relatively unattractive for startups. In the last decade, however, barriers to enter the financial sector as a service provider have come down significantly. Ubiquitous smartphones give their owners secure access to sophisticated computing technology at a low cost, which has given people around the globe access to their finances on the go. A generational shift has further leveled the playing field, where the demands of emerging consumers have slowly displaced established banking habits. A study by Visa on the financial habits of millennials in Asia finds that 80 percent of those aged between 18 and 28 believe that they will soon be able to do all their shopping and bill payments online. Additionally, 73 percent believe this will be possible with a mobile phone, whilst 99 percent of millennials in Korea shop online. They use a mix of cards and cash for their financial transactions, presenting an opportunity for financial institutions to introduce more people to the convenience of using electronic payments. However, the cashless society is still a stretch: only half of the payments by millennials that they make on a monthly basis are done in cash.[4] Yet a future where electronic payments will displace physical currency is beginning to take form. Once customers have embraced using personal devices for payments and banking on a large scale, the last mile of established banks in their access to customers will have disappeared. Today's FinTech startups challenge mainly the banks' front office, which is experiencing slow attrition with fewer branches and ATMs.

P2.3 BANKS ARE FAR FROM DEAD

With the surge in peer-to-peer lending and the massive funding rounds by FinTech startups hogging the limelight in the media, it is easy to label the forays of startups into the financial sector the swan song of established bank lending. However, regardless of customers' new view of banking and attitudes towards money, the formal financial sector and traditional lending is a success, contributing close to 8 percent to the GDP of the United States in 2012.[5] To dismiss the knowledge of banks in designing new financial services in FinTech startups would be a foolish move. Despite criticism of established financial institutions, banks have established best practices in lending and operations that have worked well for many decades. Unless FinTech entrepreneurs understand how formal bank lending works, they will hardly be able to meaningfully innovate the credit sector. In fact, some online lenders are already on the path to making the same mistakes as the banks did in the run-up to the financial crisis of 2007/8: several platforms are selling their sub-prime loan portfolios in bulk to banks and hedge funds who securitize them for big insurers and asset managers.[6] Financial technology innovation should follow a better paradigm than "same, but different." Instead, it should help evolve the financial sector toward better ease of doing business, more inclusivity, and more stability. To achieve this, entrepreneurs with an interest in online lending get a head start if they stand on the shoulders of giants instead of trying to reinvent the wheel.

P2.4 HOW TO READ THIS PART OF THE BOOK

This part of the book explains the underlying logic of credit analytics in the back office of banks. Among other themes, we will discuss how financial contracts work, which risks play important roles, and how banks have been managing them successfully. To do this, we will use descriptive examples and financial mathematics to give both a qualitative and a quantitative perspective. But before we get started, a note of caution: banking and financial mathematics can be highly complex, much more so than a casual observer from the outside of the financial sector would expect. In some cases, this may alienate those readers without a background in finance or economics. However, we feel it is important to outline the moving parts and the mechanics of bank lending in detail. This will equip readers and aspiring and established entrepreneurs in the P2P lending space with a solid understanding of the viewpoint that a bank would take when building and analyzing a loan portfolio. In the third part of the book, we will then fuse the findings of Part One with those of Part Two to arrive at recommendations to pick the best of both worlds in a Hybrid Financial Sector.

Whenever possible, this part of the book starts each segment with relatively simple introductions, examples, and diagrams that give an outline of the subjects discussed in the chapter. As the chapters progress, we will then delve deeper into the mechanics of financial contracts, analysis of all financial risk factors, which will be important when quantitatively analyzing the financial events of debits and credits and applying the analytics into liquidity, value, income and risk. Those who simply wish to get an overview of the mechanics of bank lending may skip ahead when the details become overwhelming. Those who have a solid background in finance may find the introductions and examples overly simplistic. Feel free to skip past the introductions into the more financially analytical part of the chapters. Of course, entrepreneurs in the FinTech space can operate without getting a PhD in financial maths, but they should at least understand the process, the instruments, and analytics native to bank lending.

P2.5   WHAT WE DISCUSS IN THIS PART

The following list briefly describes the individual topics of this part and explains why they apply to banking, but may also be—or become—relevant for P2P lending in the future.

Chapter 5 (Financial Contracts) introduces the different types of financial contracts, the central element that defines the DNA of financial analysis. It provides a detailed description of all contract elements that we need to consider in mapping and analyzing financial contract events. It first focuses on the usability and challenges of time and its evolution, on both actual and simulated dimensions, which play a vital role during the lifetime of financial contracts. It then describes the mechanism of the contracts by identifying and describing all combinations of possible pattern events, executed in parallel within fixed or variable time cycles, constructing all financial events.

Chapter 6 (Market) covers the first input element of financial analysis defined as *markets*. Market risk factors, such as interest rates, are the input information linked to many rules defined in the financial contract. The chapter explains the reasoning of risk-neutrality, reflecting the arbitrage, risk, free assumption in valuing and pricing financial instruments. It describes the usability of yield curves and forward rates and prices aligned with risk-neutral expectations. It then moves to economic scenarios based on real world probabilities, by applying what-if, historical and stochastic scenarios. It then explains how spreads, such as credit and liquidity spreads, apply in extending the rates beyond market risk-free and thus discount the cash flows based on the real-worlds risk probabilities. Finally, it highlights the market risk elements in P2P finance.

Chapter 7 (Counterparties) refers to the *counterparty,* which is the second element of financial analysis. It describes the different possible roles which counterparties could play in financial contractual agreement. We then highlight the usability of the information referring to counterparty-descriptive characteristics. Moreover, the chapter identifies the distinction and usability of the two-credit status, default and non-default. It also describes the approximation of default probability based on credit spreads and expected recoveries. It also explains the usability for extending the default probabilities by applying credit ratings through different time horizons. It then discusses the differences of real world and risk-neutral default probabilities where the latter is the basis for applying credit spreads. It finally focuses on analyzing the links of counterparties via markets by considering the allocation of the obligors to their own specific risks and to specific or several markets, or by allocating several obligors to a single or several correlated markets.

Chapter 8 (Behaviour) is about *behaviour*, the third input element of financial analysis. It therefore explains the identification and modelling of *withdraws, prepayments, remaining principal* and *sales*, all fallen to market driven types of behavior. It then goes on to identify the defaults and downgrading probabilities as well as their migrations through time, driven by behavior characteristics. It also explains the behavior of using credit facilities, lines, and the extent of them for avoiding default. It finally explains the elements of identifying the expected behavior of recoveries.

Chapter 9 (Credit Exposure) covers the topic of *financial credit exposure*. The chapter goes through the identification and measurements of gross and net exposures, their distribution and evolution through time driven by the evolution of market conditions, counterparty credit status, market and credit behavior, valuation principles, and strategies and types of contracts. It then explains how credit losses are estimated under both default and non-default statuses. We finally explain how counterparties are linked via their credit exposures.

Chapter 10 (Credit Enhancements) refers to *credit enhancements* and explains their different types and structures. It thus provides an extended description of asset-based credit enhancements including financial and physical collaterals, intangible assets and close-out netting agreements. It then describes the counterparty-based credit enhancements, including guarantees and credit derivatives. The chapter also outlines the cases of allocating collaterals and guarantees to credit exposures as well as the challenges for valuing and adjusting asset-based credit enhancements. It then extends to the additional special elements considered in credit enhancements including the cases of double default, wrong way risk, maturity mismatch, payment times, and the dependencies of contracts and counterparties via credit enhancements. We finally discuss and propose approaches for employing alternative types of credit enhancements in P2P lending, such as by using real estate titles, phone contracts, loyalty points, and other stores of value, as well as life insurance and guarantor systems.

Chapter 11 (Systemic and Concentration Risks) covers the topic of *systemic and concentration risks*. The first part is about the identification and measurement of systemic risk, which depends on both credit exposure and counterparty analysis. The chapter explains in detail the development of chain reactions after both default and credit downgrading events. It then defines the results of systemic risk in regards to expected losses. The second part refers to concentration risk based on credit exposure and counterparty analysis. It shows how a single event, or a group of similar events, could result in large losses.

Chapter 12 (Liquidity, Value, Income, Risk & New Production) refers to *liquidity, value, income, and risk* as the main analysis output elements, and it also covers the topic of *new production*. The chapter starts with the topic of liquidity and describes its role in the performance of financial contracts. It then analyzes the time factor in liquidity and covers in detail the two important parts of liquidity analysis named market and funding liquidity risks. Moreover, the chapter describes the different methods for measuring and reporting liquidity and its risks resulted by considering the integration of market, credit and behavior risk factors, as well as by combining market and funding liquidity analysis. The chapter continues by covering the topic of value and income elements. It explains the main principles for estimating value and income, their projection to profit and loss analysis and the role of valuation principles. We then explain how to measure the risks on value and income based on deterministic, dynamic, and integrated stress testing, as well as a stochastic process. Furthermore, the chapter defines the measurement of economic capital based on risk measurements, their allocation and how its combination with financial performance is the basis of risk adjustment. It finally provides some key points in applying risk management. We also describe the main elements considered on the design of new production of new or reconstructed financial portfolios, including the considerations of time, dynamics of future markets, counterparties and behavior, definition of strategies of going concern and/or rolling over, targeted volumes, type of new contracts and counterparties and analyzing the output financial elements. Finally, the chapter covers the topic of treasury and funds transfer pricing, and it explains the role of the treasury in financial institutions as well as why and how employing funds transfer pricing. We then discuss the possible role of the treasury in online lending.

NOTES

1. Berger, Allen; Molyneux, Philip and Wilson, John (2010) "Banking, an Overview" in *The Oxford Handbook of Banking* (Oxford: Oxford University Press).
2. King, Brett (2010) *Bank 2.0* (Singapore: Marshall Cavendish International).
3. Son, Hugh and Tracer, Zachary (2012) "BofA Yanks Most Teller Machines From Malls, Gas Stations," Bloomberg News, 23 July 2012, http://www.businessweek.com/news/2012-07-23/bofa-yanks-9-percent-of-teller-machines-from-malls-gas-stations.
4. Visa (2012) "Connecting with the Millennials - A Visa Study," http://www.visa-asia.com/ap/sea/mediacenter/pressrelease/includes/uploads/Visa_Gen_Y_Report_2012_LR.pdf.
5. U.S. Department of Commerce, "The Financial Services Industry in the United States" (2014a), http://selectusa.commerce.gov/industry-snapshots/financial-services-industry-united-states
6. Devasabai, Kris (2014) "Hedge funds, securitisation and leverage change P2P game," Risk.net 12 October 2014, www.risk.net/risk-magazine/feature/2372612/hedge-funds-securitisation-and-leverage-change-p2p-game.

CHAPTER 5

Financial Contracts

T his chapter will describe the elements that banks need to consider in mapping and analyzing financial contracts. Markets, counterparties and behavior are the main input elements of all financial contracts, discussed extensively in Chapters 6, 7, 8. Time is a fundamental factor, which plays a central role during the lifetime of the financial contracts. There are two important parallel dimensions of time; these are the actual and simulated ones. However, the treatment of time contains some great challenges including its scale and the length of iterations set by day count conventions. Linking the above elements to the mechanism of the contracts, expressed as contractual rules and translated into mathematical functions, different patterns are defined with the most major ones referring to principal, interest, credit enhancements, and behavior. Here we describe the evolutions of such patterns driven by the contractual rule parameters and executed at fixed or variable time cycles.

5.1 CONTRACT ELEMENTS

The counterparties that enter into a bilateral or multilateral financial deal are in essence defining a contractual legal agreement with an underlying set of rules. Such rules describe the terms and conditions for exchanging cash flows during the lifetime of the contract. For example, a borrower and a lender who enter into a loan have to agree on several deal points: the amount of principal, the reference market interest that will be considered for the interest payments, the times for paying the principal and interest, and any possible options where the lender would prepay to the borrower and thus may terminate the contract. Financial contract agreements may contain many and more complicated rules. Based on these rules we can derive the financial events of the contract. In other words, we may identify what is likely to happen during the lifetime and in some cases after the maturity date of the financial contract.

In fact, the contractual rules are referring to characteristics of time, markets, and counterparties, and in some cases to certain behavior. These are the input elements to financial contracts that are related to the rules in a legal agreement of the financial contracts. Technically, the mapping of such rules, on a contractual level, is done by using attributes. Examples of such attributes are the amount of principal capital, the set dates of interest payments, the market reference, the counterparty ID, and many more.

The main characteristics of the counterparty are the ones referring to the credit quality, e.g., default probabilities and credit ratings; and of the markets are the yields and spread curves, prices, and rates as well as the applied accounting and discounting rules. These are the credit and market financial risk factors which are somehow correlating and interacting with each other as well as affecting the behavior analysis element.

Before—and even during—the lifetime of a financial contract, all counterparties involved in the deal are expected to fulfill their contractual obligations. The degree of accuracy of this assumption is associated with counterparty credit quality. Evaluating counterparties is an ongoing process. This is usually done by determining their ratings, default probabilities and credit spreads and monitoring them closely for changes.

In some cases, counterparties agree to have certain rights for making and employing their own decisions during the lifetime of the contract. Such decisions may influence the expected exchange of cash flows. For instance, a lender may have a right to prepay part of the principal amount at any time. However, the contract usually defines a fee the borrower has to pay in the event of prepayment.

Thus, think of a simple case when constructing a simple loan, the contract must be linked to an agreed predefined market interest rate in which the cash flows will be exchanged. The contract also belongs to the lender and borrower counterparties who agreed on assumptions for market conditions that will be considered to calculate the future interest payments. The lender also assumes that the borrower will pay back the principal and interest as agreed. However, we can expect there will be a difference between the assumed and actual market conditions and counterparty credit status. Therefore the contract is directly exposed to market volatilities and counterparties.

Market conditions, counterparties and behavior drive the financial events in a contract. Technically, what happens is that attributes are "decoded" as parameters in mathematical functions following algorithms for generating the events during the lifetime of the contract. These are including all expected cash flows such as payments referring to principal, interest, premiums, dividends, expected recoveries, etc. considering all contract rules at different points in time or through the cycle iterations. It is important to note that in most cases they are correlated and therefore influence each other's performance. For example, an increase in the market interest rate could influence the counterparty to prepay, partially or fully, the outstanding principal. If interest rates move against the counterparty's favor, this could prompt a borrower to default in his interest and principal payment obligations.

Figure 5.1, illustrates the main elements referring to financial contracts. In Chapters 6, 7 and 8, we will discuss the main input financial elements named "Markets," "Counterparty," and "Behavior". In the following paragraphs, however, we will go through the element of time and the patterns of financial events created by the contract mechanisms. As we will also see, financial events are the basis in liquidity, value and income analysis.

5.2   TIME IN FINANCIAL CONTRACTS

In financial analysis, time plays a central role. This means that time exists as a background dimension within the entire financial system. However, there are two parallel time dimensions in financial analysis: one is about the exact times set in contractual agreement; it also defines the historical actual financial event and the present point in time (PIT) where the future starts. The other dimension is the simulated and reported time. It refers to times, usually expressed as intervals, where we are considering the calculation and reporting of the financial events. Any calculation process of financial events follows this time dimension. Moreover, the estimation

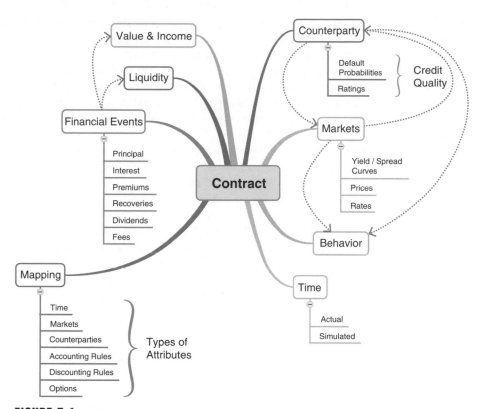

FIGURE 5.1 Main elements referring to financial contracts

of markets' evolution also considers such time dimensions. Dealing with the time dimension, we must also set the time where the analysis should start. This is for setting the point at which the pseudo-current (present) time analysis is defined and where the past and future periods are considered during the calculation process.

The rules defined are the agreement among counterparties that determines the *what, how* and *when* of a financial contract. In other words, what has to be done during the lifetime of the financial contract, how will it be done, and when? The *when* relates to two kinds of timing events. It is indicating a particular *point in time (PIT)* or *through the cycle (TTC)* iterations. This distinction informs the pattern of financial events in a contract.

In financial contracts, rules define the exact times at which actions are expected to be taken. PIT events indicate exact points in time that are non-recurring. Think for instance about the exact points when a contract starts and ends. TTC iterations represent the time cycles that are recurring, for example, when interest or principal payments will change hands between a borrower and a lender. However, some timing events are less clearly defined. When a contract includes options that the counterparties can exercise at their convenience, timing assumptions are less accurate. An option of prepayment, for example, may be exercised according to a strategy or rational behavior that takes into account the future. In this case, we use a model that takes into account these time imprecise assumptions.

The scale of the time can differ between minutes, hours, days, and years. The first two are only considered in intraday actions, such as trading activities, whereas the last two come into play in most short and longer term analysis. Using a time grid finer than daily can make most analytics almost impossible to use because, most likely, it increases the complexity of systems to a high degree.[1] For this reason, time attributes defined in a contract are set on a daily grid or higher, e.g., week, month, quarter, etc. Moreover, in most market conditions, counterparty and behavior characteristics consider time on a daily or higher scale. The time buckets (defined usually as Time Bucket System TBS) used in financial analysis and the corresponding reports are set on single or combination of time intervals as Day(s), Week(s), Month(s), Quarter(s), Half-Year(s), and Year(s).

Even a daily grid can still make analytics overcomplicated. A gap analysis based only on daily buckets will demand expensive computation and will result in overly detailed reports. A contract with a duration of 10 years has almost 3,600 intervals when applying daily buckets, which will result in an amount of data that is impractical to work with. However, in the simulation process, daily intervals may have an important use. Financial analysts want to look at simulation results on a daily interval grid. To control liquidity, it is common to have daily intervals of about 30 days. On the other hand, the more detailed the simulation, the more expensive it becomes. Computation time is proportional to the number of simulated buckets. Monthly buckets often suffice for most simulation. Long-term simulations might be done with even longer time intervals and lower precision. Keep in mind that accuracy and cost are a tradeoff. The longer the time interval, the less accurate is the forecast of market conditions, counterparty and behavior characteristics.

But that is still not the entire story. When calendars define natural time in terms of days, weeks, months, and years, there are some special issues that have to be considered. Days have certain time intervals for trading, weeks may have five or six business days, months have between 28 and 31 days[2] and years may be common or leap. All this becomes an issue when we are constructing algorithms that need to be accurate over several years or even decades. In many cases, the duration of each month is simplified to be considered as 30 days, i.e., January and February are both treated the same. Such a pseudo-regular calendar introduces errors in the analysis that are invisible on a monthly basis. Thus, for instance, daily basis in the analysis raises issues in calculating correctly the accrual on the 31st day of January. In addition, leap years introduce additional complexity when interest is accrued over years. Thus, financial analysts use different day count conventions such as A/A, A/365, 30/360 ISDA, 30E/360, 30/365, etc. Based on these conventions, interest accrues over time, and it can be determined more accurately. Moreover, exact quantification of time intervals is important in the discounting process.

Figure 5.2 illustrates the main elements of time discussed above.

5.3 CONTRACT MECHANISMS PRODUCING FINANCIAL EVENTS

Financial contracts range from maturity loans to indices and some derivatives. In light of what we have just learned about constructing financial deals, it is easy to imagine that an unlimited number of possible contracts exist. In fact, if you ask even people in the financial sector about their estimate of the number of different financial contracts in existence, they will often answer something along the lines "hundreds," or "thousands." Surprisingly enough, there are only three dozen types of financial contract that are able to map more than 98% of today's financial instruments. A well known financial contract is the annuity, used in many

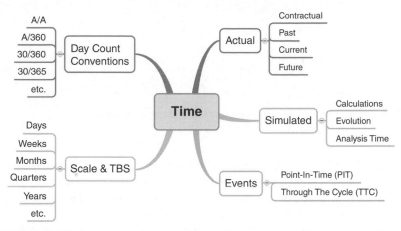

FIGURE 5.2 Main elements referring to time

loans in banking and P2P financial portfolios, principal at maturity (used in bonds), stocks, commodities, credit lines, etc. combination of them defining the derivative contracts. The mapping of such contracts is based on the elements discussed in Part Two of this book, and is illustrated in Figure 5.1. The reader can find a detailed description of the main contract types in other publications such as the textbook *Unified Financial Analysis*,[3] also under the *Algorithmic Contract Types Unified Standards* project.[4]

All contracts follow several fundamental patterns based on the contract rules and algorithmic mechanism, all combining to generate the financial events. In other words, we are describing financial contracts mathematically by using functions considering fixed or variable:

- Rule parameters, such as on payment and interest amounts, option of withdrawal of capital, etc.,
- Points in time (PITs) and through-the-cycle (TTC) iterations, applied for instance on re-pricing, times of payments, etc.

Thus, we can from now on identify and analyze the events based on the combination of the above factors. Note that patterns are in most cases interacting with, and interdepending on, each other; for instance, interest payments are based on principal amount and time of re-pricing. Table 5.1 illustrates the different combinations considered in the construction of the patterns for the financial events.

TABLE 5.1 Contractual rules and parameters applied within fixed and variable times

		Time			
		Fixed		Variable	
		PIT	TTC	PIT	TTC
Rule parameters	**Fixed**	Type I	Type II	Type III	Type IV
	Variable	Type V	Type VI	Type VII	Type VIII

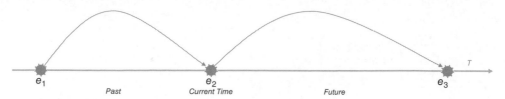

FIGURE 5.3   Past, current and future events according to time analysis

Types I and II define the events that are driven by rules with certain fixed parameters at times. Examples of such events are the defined (fixed) amount in principal payment of capital investment at the (fixed) PIT of value date (Type I), fixed interest rates and fixed principals (increase or decrease) paid TTC at fixed intervals (Type II).

A combination of fixed parameters arising through variable times fall into Types III and IV of event generation. Typical cases of such events are the predetermined fixed rates used in case of prepayment at any future PIT (Type III); another case could be a fixed interest rate applied through the cycles of payments that may be shifted to earlier or later time points (Type IV).

Cases where events result in variable parameters' of rules applied at fixed times fall into Types V and VI. Variable interest rates and payments at maturity date PIT or at fixed TTC iterations are typical examples of these types.

The most complex combinations are the ones where both rules and times that generate the events are variable (defined in Type VII and VIII). The degree of prepayment amount or use of a facility at any future PIT, based on a counterparty's decision, is a characteristic case of Type VII. Type VIII can be the case where variable interest rates and principal amounts (for instance, in an annuity contract) define the increase in payments and/or the maturity date, which may affect the corresponding increase and decrease in the cycle of payments.

In addition, we should identify whether the performances of the financial events are actual, expected, or unexpected. The first type, *actual*, is derived from the past historical events up to the current time, e.g., e_1 and e_2 shown in Figure 5.3. The *expected* and *unexpected* are referring to future events, e.g., e_3 shown in Figure 5.3, and are estimated based on predefined contractual rules as well as the expected or unexpected market conditions, counterparty status and their corresponding behaviors respectively. The performances of actual, expected and unexpected events are the result of strategies applied from the past to future times. Annex A, available on the website, lists the different types of time elements, cash flow and re-setting financial events.

We will now categorize and describe, in the following paragraphs, the most important types of patterns and their evolution through time, including the ones referring to principal, interest, behavior, credit enhancements, used to map financial contracts in any kind of lending situation, i.e., in banks or P2P lendings.

5.3.1   Principal patterns

The rules for defining the events of principal cash flow patterns, denoted as CF_{pp}, illustrate the evolution of the principal payments during and beyond the lifetime of a financial contract. The amount of principal cash outflows and inflows may be fixed or variable and may rise at fixed predetermined or variable points in time or through-the-cycle iterations. Based on Table 5.1

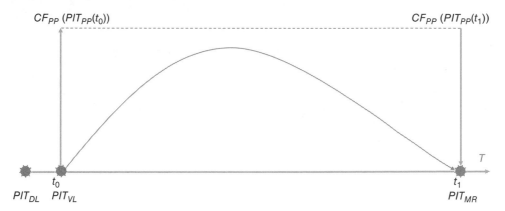

FIGURE 5.4 Cash flow pattern where the cash out-flow $CF_{PP}(PIT_{VT})$ is expected to be returned as cash in-flow $CF_{PP}(PIT_{MR})$

we can define the different types by combining the quantity of principal amount within the corresponding PIT and TTC intervals.

5.3.1.1 Type I & II: Patterns of fixed principal amounts arising at fixed PIT and within fixed TTC iterations
The pattern of fixed principal amounts appearing at fixed PIT and/or within fixed TTC iterations is driven by a deterministic set of contractual rules. Thus, the agreed exchange of the principal capital investment and the principal return defines such patterns. For instance, as illustrated in Figure 5.4, the cash outflow $CF_{pp}(PIT_{pp}(t_0))$ agreed upon at deal time (PIT_{DL}) and provided by the lender at a predefined value time PIT_{VL}; moreover, the principal capital, defined as cash in-flow $CF_{pp}(PIT_{pp}(t_1))$, is expected to be returned from the borrower at the maturity point in time PIT_{MR}. The exchange of the fixed cash "in" and "out" is expected within a predefined time cycle.

Within fixed cycle(s) there are expected cash flow patterns divided into a set of predefined fixed amounts according to the cycle iterations. Thus, principal payment cash flows paid at predefined TTC pattern are the step-ups fixed amounts for increasing the capital investment $CF_{PP(INC)}$, provided by the lender as shown in Figure 5.5, and the fixed step-down amounts, illustrated in Figure 5.6, for decreasing the return notional amount of the loan[5] $CF_{PP(DEC)}$, expected from the borrower.

5.3.1.2 Type III & IV: Patterns of fixed principal cash-flows paid within variable PIT and TTC iterations
These types of combinations are unlikely to appear under expected market conditions, counterparty characteristics and behavioral assumptions linked to contractually agreed terms. This is because the change in time dimensions, i.e., PIT and TTC, is very much linked and thus affects the principal payments and vice versa. However, under some unexpected "stress" conditions, a PIT, such as maturity time, may be shifted[6] to an earlier or later point. However, as the duration of the contract changes, the expected amount of principal cash flows may stay the same. On the other hand, the maturity time and cycles of decreasing the principal, i.e., paying back from the borrower to the lender, will change accordingly. Figure 5.7 and Figure 5.8 illustrate the examples of time variation where the expected principal payments are applied.

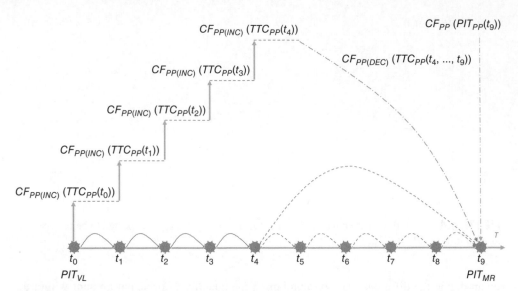

FIGURE 5.5 Expected cash flows of predefined fixed step-up principal amounts of capital investments, paid from predefined TTC time iterations divided by t_0 to t_4. The principal cash flow(s) from t_5 to maturity time t_9 could be based on a single amount, i.e., at t_9 the $CF_{PP}(PIT_{PP}(t_9))$, or on multiple divided amounts within TTC time iteration, i.e., $CF_{PP(DEC)}(TTC_{PP}(t_5, \ldots, t_9))$ as illustrated in Figure 5.6

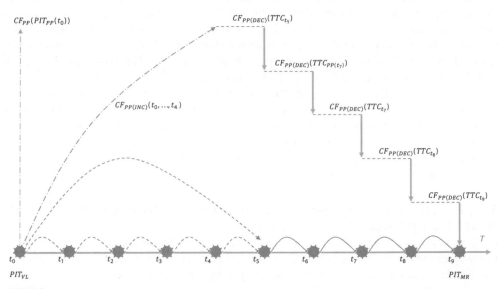

FIGURE 5.6 Expected cash flows of predefined fixed step-down principal return amounts, paid within predefined TTC time iteration, i.e., from t_5 to maturity time at t_9. The principal cash flows from t_0 to t_4 could be based on a single amount, i.e., at t_0 the $CF_{PP}(PIT_{PP}(t_0))$, or on multiple divided amounts within TTC time iteration, i.e., $CF_{PP(INC)}(TTC_{PP}(t_0, \ldots, t_4))$ as illustrated in Figure 5.5

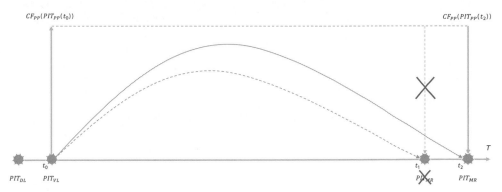

FIGURE 5.7 Cash flow pattern where the original maturity time PIT_{MR} is shifted and thus the cash in-flow $CF_{PP}(PIT_{PP})(t_2)$ is expected in a different time than originally agreed

5.3.1.3 Type V & VI: Patterns of variable principal amounts at fixed TTC and PIT

There are some contracts where the principal amount may vary at set TTC or particular PIT. A typical case of variable principal amounts within fixed TTC iterations is the annuity loan, where the sum of interest and principle are equal until the maturity; in such contracts, the principal increase and the interest deteriorates through time. Moreover, the cash flow evolution of credit line patterns, also called facilities, fall into this category; in this case any credit amount, up to the line, could be used until a predefined PIT, e.g., 45 days. As illustrated in Figure 5.9 there are different cash flow patterns reflecting the lending of a principal amount within a cycle of time $\{t_0, t_1\}$; thus, at PIT, t_1 the principal amount provided from the lender to the borrower may vary accordingly.

There are instances where the amount of principal cash flows may change during the TTC iterations. A typical case of such a principal pattern is when a counterparty executes the contractually agreed upon option of pre-paying part of the remaining principal at some time before the maturity time. Thus, as illustrated in Figure 5.10, a prepayment event at t_6 results in a reduction of the payment amount, set at t_5.

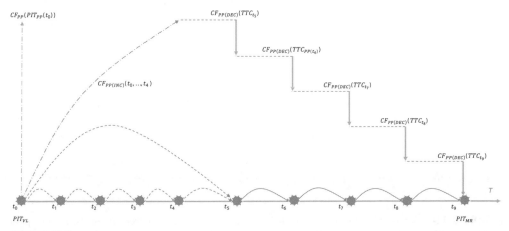

FIGURE 5.8 Step-down principal cash flows patterns of return amounts paid within modified TTC time iteration as maturity time is being extended (original pattern is as shown in Figure 5.6)

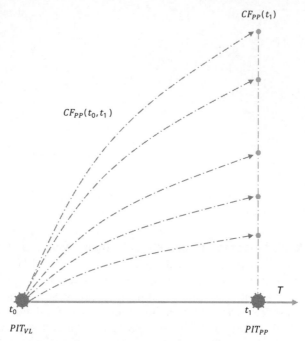

FIGURE 5.9 Cash flow patterns representing the options of a borrower to lend principal capital, within a cycle of time $\{t_0, t_1\}$. At any particular PIT t_1 when the borrower is using the credit facility, the principal amount may vary

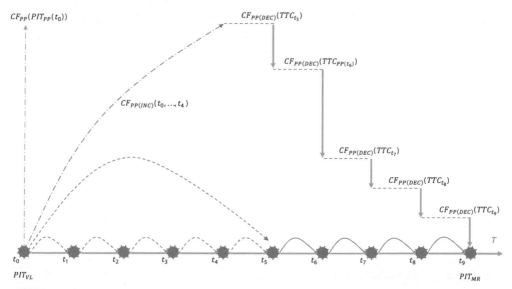

FIGURE 5.10 Variability of step-down principal return amounts due to prepayment event at t_6, paid within predefined TTC time iteration, i.e., from t_5 to maturity time at t_9.

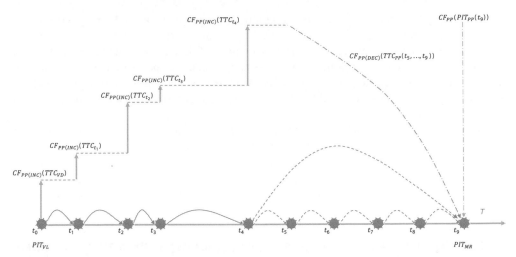

FIGURE 5.11 Cash flows of remaining principal amounts at step-up pattern driven by the credit needs within variable TTC time iterations from t_0 to t_4.

5.3.1.4 Type VII & VIII: Patterns of variable principal amounts at variable TTC and PIT
This case is the one with the higher degree of flexibility (variability) in regards to the patterns of principal cash flows and PITs / TTC iterations. A typical pattern falling to these types is the cash flows of remaining principal amounts at step-ups driven by the credit requests within variable TTC time iterations; see for instance the example of such patterns of cash flow evolution from t_0 to t_4 as illustrated in Figure 5.11. This is very much applied in the loans where a defined principal capital has been agreed, however different amounts distributed through variable cycles are drawn according to the borrower's credit needs, e.g., based on project evolution which is financed by the principal capital.

5.3.2 Interest patterns

In financial contracts representing a loan, the lender is expecting to earn an interest income, while the borrower sees interest as the price of getting credit. The two views are complementary and both parties should be able to understand and feel comfortable with the interest they have to receive or pay. Otherwise a loss or default may occur.

In terms of interest, it is important to understand the calculation parameters and the role of time in the payment process. Interest rates $R(t)$, notional or principal amount of the loan, valuation rules, as well as time are the main ingredients that are combined to calculate interest.

The interest rate can be fixed and thus independent of future market conditions. It can also be set as variable which implies that the actual or assumed changes in market conditions will be considered where the corresponding rates will be reset at predefined time intervals, for example, quarterly. The patterns of the notional or principal amount, discussed earlier, are combined with interest rates to calculate the interest payments; for instance, by simply multiplying the interest rates with the notional or principal amount. A more complicated approach could be employed by applying interest capitalization. In this case, instead of being paid out, interest is capitalized and added to the outstanding principal.

Based on the definitions made in the contractual agreement the interest payments are expected at predefined points in time, e.g., at value or maturity date, or through the cycle time intervals, e.g., monthly, quarterly, etc. The measurement of time *between* financial events, e.g., the time (t_i, t_{i+1}) between two principal or interest payments, is a challenging issue in financial analysis. As discussed earlier, the duration of each month is an unequal pseudo-regular calendar based on day conventions such as A/A, A/365, 30/360, etc., used in the calculation of interest accruals over time.

The interest payments falling at particular PITs or TTC iterations during the lifetime of a non-defaulted financial contract define the pattern of interest cash flow events, denoted as CF_{PP}. Interest payments can be fixed amounts. However, they normally vary TTC due to changes in principal and/or market evolution of interest rates. Interest payments are rather set at fixed PIT and TTC iterations; thus based on Table 5.1, we may expect the Type I, II, V and VI as discussed here.

5.3.2.1 Type I & II: Patterns of fixed interest occurring at fixed PIT and/or within fixed TTC iterations
This is the case where fixed interest rates are applied whereas the principal amount is not changed until the maturity, as seen in Figure 5.12. Fixed interest TTC iterations could appear in fixed-rate bonds where the principal is paid at the maturity PIT. A zero coupon bond also has one fixed interest at maturity PIT.

5.3.2.2 Type V & VI: Patterns of variable interest occurring at fixed PIT and/or within fixed TTC iterations
Most interest payments are variable due to contract agreements referring to the type of interest rates, i.e., variable, and/or the evolution of the principal amount. In the former case, interest payments are fully dependent on the changes of rates within the future time terms. For instance, the interest cash flows of variable-rate bonds, paid TTC

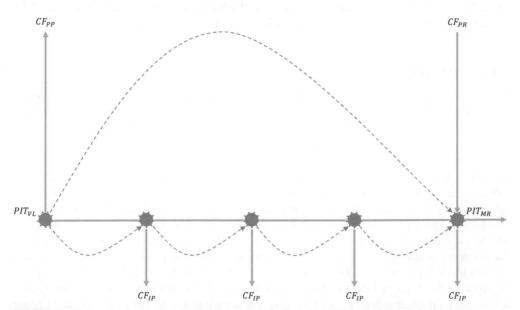

FIGURE 5.12   Equal Interest payments driven by fixed interest rates and steady principal amount

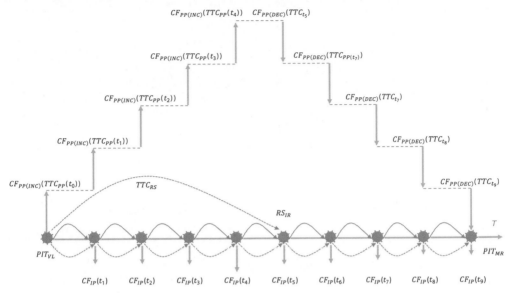

FIGURE 5.13 Cash flows of variable interest payments due to variable principles and interest rates

iterations, are expected not to be the same. In the latter case the future principal payments can be estimated or pre-defined, e.g., on annuity contracts or on loans with step-ups or step-downs as discussed earlier and illustrated in Figure 5.13. The example shown in this figure considers also the rate reset event TTC_{RS} at t_5. However, despite the type of interest rate, i.e., fixed or variable, applied in such contracts the interest payments are expected to be unequal within TTC iterations, due to principal changes.

5.3.3 Accrual interest patterns

There is a practical caveat in regards to interest that should be pointed out and carefully considered in interest calculations: the calculation of accrued interest payments that fall between the agreed time intervals. The borrower owes accrued to the lender, but has not paid them yet. The accrual over the interval beginning at t_b and ending at t_B is given by Equation 5.1.

$$AI(t_b, t_B) = \int_{t_b}^{t_B} R(t)P(t)dt \tag{5.1}$$

In practice, however, the principal and nominal interest rate change in a discreet rather than in a continuous manner and thus, Equation 5.1 can be simplified as shown in Equation 5.2 and Figure 5.14, where the accrual interest within the time intervals (t_i, t_{i+1}) is defined as follows:

$$AI(t_i, t_{i+1}) = R(t_i)P(t_i)\Delta(t_i, t_{i+1}) \tag{5.2}$$

where the interest rate $R(t)$ and principal $P(t)$ are constant in each segment.

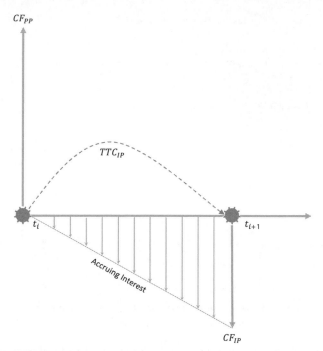

FIGURE 5.14   Accrual interest pattern

Note also that some important features are relevant to the correct calculation of accrual amounts. These are the *capitalization* of the interest, as mentioned above, the *compounding method* where implicit capitalization is assumed between successive interest payments and the *upfront payment* where interest is paid at the beginning of the accrual period instead of at its end.

5.3.4   Credit enhancements patterns

The cash flow events appearing after a credit event, i.e., counterparty default or downgrading, are results of the asset and/or counterparty based credit enhancements that we discuss in Chapter 10 (Credit Enhancements).

Particularly, for the assets based credit enhancements, the cash flow is a result of their liquidation.[7] Thus, their value at the time of exercising them is the amount of cash flow used to cover the counterparty credit losses. As such assets are driven by market conditions, but also by the underlying counterparty credit status,[8] their value may fluctuate over time and cannot be estimated precisely. Moreover, the exact time of such cash flows varies but is expected to occur shortly after the credit event assuming that the asset(s) are still liquid.

In the example shown in Figure 5.15, at t_2 a default will cancel all future expected principal and interest cash flows. However, at some time after the default, e.g., $t_{CE(1)}$ and/or $t_{CE(2)}$, new cash flow(s) are expected from the credit enhancement(s). Both the amount and the time are estimated but under stressed conditions this could be rather imprecise.

When counterparty-based credit enhancements are used, the cash flows are expected from the guarantors or protection sellers after the counterparty credit risk event. The amount of

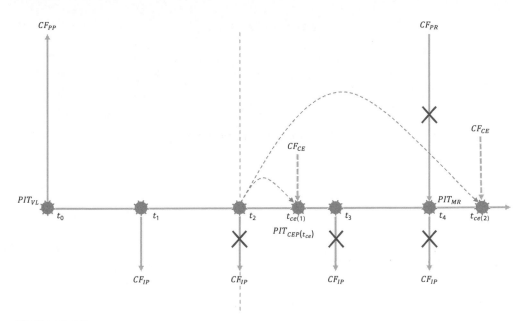

FIGURE 5.15   Cash flow of asset-based credit enhancements

the cash flows is expected to be equal to the value defined in the contractual agreements, i.e., guarantees or credit derivatives. The latter generates additional cash flow events referring to premiums paid to the protection seller until the maturity of the contract or until the time of the credit event. The time of the cash flows is normally defined in the contractual agreement[9] but is expected usually later than the ones from the asset-based credit enhancements.

5.3.5   Behavior patterns

As already discussed, financial contracts contain a set of predefined rules used to estimate the financial events under given counterparty and market conditions. However, there are some rules which are driven by the behavior of the counterparty; for instance the counterparty may have an option to prepay a loan, withdrawing cash from a current account, drawdown the remaining principal amount of a loan or from a facility to fulfil possible liquidity needs.

In addition there is some unwritten behavior that must also be considered; counterparties may decide to cancel the financial contract, i.e., default, recover part of the outstanding credit exposure, or may also try to avoid default by using other loans. Such behavioral characteristics are discussed in Chapter 8 (Behavior Risk).

Behavior introduces to the analysis some unclear rules and unexpected events. Note, however, that financial analysis depends entirely on clear rules that are expected to be followed among the counterparties and creates the expected pattern of financial events. Practitioners therefore are mapping the behavior patterns by using replicating portfolios. Replication mimics the behavior of the counterparty by using well defined principal and interest patterns similar to the ones discussed in the above paragraphs. Such a technique is widely accepted and creates the basis for all types of financial analysis.

As we discuss in Chapter 8 (Behavior Risk), the main parameters considered in mapping the behavior are the *amount* and *time*. Note that it makes no sense to map the behavior at a

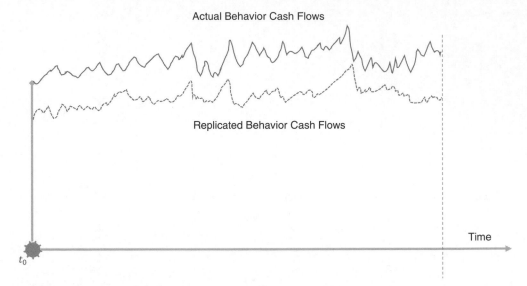

FIGURE 5.16   Example of actual and replicated behavior cash flows

single contract level; it is rather more practical to apply it at portfolio level as counterparties do behave in a similar manner. In replication portfolios, we are using financial contracts that take the role of shadow contracts and therefore substitute these two parameters. Take, for instance, the case of prepayment behavior where counterparties expected, statistically observed, to prepay an amount within a certain time horizon. A principal at maturity or annuity contract could mimic these expected cash flows.

Of course, different institutions may employ several replication portfolios to map the different behaviors of their customers and relative financial contracts. However, a perfect replication portfolio of mapping the behavior is very hard to construct (see an example in Figure 5.16). A good approach is to monitor the existing and mimic behaviors and adjust them later according to the current and future market and credit risk expectations. Under crisis and stress conditions the parameters of the replication portfolio should also be stressed accordingly. A well-defined replication portfolio should be able to align its stress parameters with the behavior stress factors.

5.3.6   Other patterns

In addition to the above, other patterns may also rise and be considered in the events' evolution of financial contracts, such as fees paid from obligors against prepayments, service fees, premiums that are agreed to be paid from protection buyers to protection sellers, dividends from stock and equities. These can be expected or unexpected financial events appearing at fixed or variable times, i.e., fall into one of the combinations defined in Table 5.1.

5.3.7   Example of financial events

Let us now describe a simple example illustrating financial events as shown in Figure 5.17. Let us assume a loan where at t_0 of value date, indicated as PIT_{VL}, a principal amount cash-flow

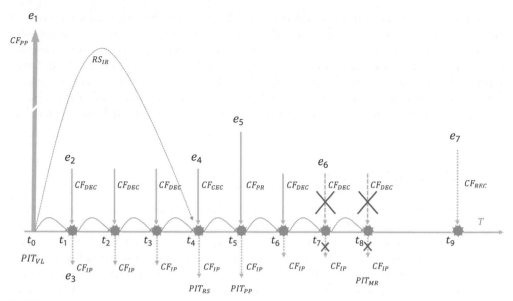

FIGURE 5.17 Example of financial events evolution

CF_{PP} event, denoted as e_1, is provided from the borrower to lender. At t_1 to t_8, the agreed principal payments CF_{DEC} and estimated interest payments CF_{IP}, paid from the lender to borrower, are the cash flow events denoted as e_2 and e_3 respectively; these events are expected to occur until the maturity date (PIT_{MR}) at t_8. Moreover, the interest rate is reset RS_{IR} at PIT_{RS} of t_4 and the loan is re-priced, e.g., based on the agreed corresponding referenced market conditions; such an event, denoted as e_4, will result in a revaluation of the future interest payment cash-flows. At PIT_{PP} of t_5 however, the lender decided to prepay part of the principal providing the corresponding cash flow CF_{PR}. Such a prepayment event e_5 may also affect the volume of the cash-flows for the future interest CF_{IP} and returns of principal payments. At t_7 an unexpected default, denoted as e_6, occurred; this implies that all future expected interest and principal cash flows, i.e., at t_7 and t_8, will be canceled out. However, at t_9 a future event e_7 may occur representing a cash flow due to expected recoveries CF_{REC} and/or possible credit enhancements, e.g., collaterals, that may be exercised after the default event.

The degree of the number and type of financial events that will be generated in financial contracts depends on the richness and complexity of the rules defined in financial contracts and is linked to:

- The type and number of market conditions, e.g., fixed or variable market expectations
- The counterparties, e.g., degree of credit ratings
- The behavior of the markets and counterparties, e.g., exercising the right to prepay

As we will see in Chapter 12, based on the financial events, the liquidity value, and income will be derived. Finally, the difference between the expected and unexpected performance of the input elements will influence the risk measurements in the output elements, such as funding and market liquidity risks, sensitivities, value and income at risk, together with the corresponding losses.

It is also important to understand that the cash flows of all contract types are received not only from the expected and unexpected future payments, e.g., principal, interest, etc., but also by the expected behavior, e.g., to get payments from recoveries and guarantors, as well as from the trading activities applied to financial collaterals. Still, we need to consider the different expectations in changes of market prices. Whether the contract holder is receiving these cash flows at the agreed time or unexpected future cycles or points in time, is fully dependent on market conditions, counterparties and corresponding behaviors to which the financial contract is linked.

5.4 CONCLUDING REMARKS

This chapter describes financial contracts as agreements regarding exchanges of cash flows that follow certain patterns. These patterns depend on market conditions, counterparty characteristics and behavioral assumptions; they may also depend on each other's performance. Writing these patterns, taking into consideration the above mentioned dependencies, using understandable and writable algorithms, and implemented by employing computer power, we are able to model nearly everything in financial deals and calculate the possible financial events.

The main types of pattern events refer to the results of principal and interest payments, use of credit enhancements, and behavior cash flows. As we have seen, their values and time can be from fixed to variable. The amount and types of financial events during the lifetime of a financial contract could reach a high degree. A transparent and easy analysis of the events is based on mapping and analyzing them based on their types and their interactions.

NOTES

1. The usage of the existing complex and dynamic transaction systems of intraday deals, executed within the time window of 10 am to 3 pm, may include some degree of speculation due to the fact that accruals can be earned during these five hours.
2. The months July and August were renamed for Julius Caesar and Augustus Caesar in ancient Rome. In honor of these great Caesars, both months were set to last 31 days. But, at the time, each month was only 30 days long, so days were taken from the last month of the year which was February at that time.
3. Brammertz, Willi; Akkizidis, Ioannis; Breymann, Wolfgang; Entin, Rami; and Rustmann, Marco *Unified Financial Analysis, The missing links of finance* (Wiley 2009).
4. See more information under the following link www.projectactus.org.
5. Principal amortization.
6. After renegotiation between the counterparties the contract is restructured in regards to maturity. This may happen for instance when avoiding a default event due to the incapability of the obligor (i.e., borrower) to pay back the principle at the predefined PIT or TTC in the original contract.
7. Assuming that the asset is tradable and is liquidated for covering credit losses; also there are no legal implications for passing the asset to the lender.
8. Credit rating and spreads.
9. Assuming that guarantors or protection sellers will not default in fulfilling their obligations.

CHAPTER 6

Markets

Banks differentiate between risk and uncertainty. *Risk* is—by definition—the possibility that something may happen away from the expected. If we foresee this possibility, we can then include the associated risk factors in the analysis, and thus the rate of return will be at "risk-free." On the other hand, *uncertainty* describes risks that are unforeseen. Managing uncertain risks is very difficult, and quantifying precisely their contribution to return is nearly impossible. Banks therefore embrace risk, but shun uncertainty. This is important to remember when we discuss markets.

Financial contracts directly link to market conditions described by certain factors. In financial analysis and risk management, we use several risk factors that are linked to markets. Such factors are interest rates and spreads, exchange rates, stocks, indices and commodity market prices. *Micro* and *macroeconomic parameters* influence these market risk factors directly and indirectly. For instance, interest rates take into account inflation, unemployment rates, and many more as risk parameters.

Analysts use only these sparse risk factors to achieve holistic and mutual usability and consistency in their analysis among different markets in a practical manner. Following this approach, the models they use for pricing interest rates should have the same underlying parameters and commonly accepted models, such as LIBOR. This results in consistency and transparency and gains acceptance from both markets and regulators. Moreover, the data that underlie these risk factors are commonly shared within the markets. Nowadays, past and current market prices of commodities, stocks, FX and interest rates from the entire global markets are easily accessible. Actual data represents the real-world view; however, future positions must be forecasted.

The forecast of the market risk factors at future times must be based on reliable and consistent market models. For this, we need arbitrage-free models that take into account the risk for profit taken beyond the risk-free return on capital. As we will see, yield curves and forward rate models play the role of arbitrage-free from current to future time models. As we will discuss in this chapter, using arbitrage-free reduces the complexity in applying financial analysis; it also aligns with the expected behavior of investors, which is to avoid risk whenever possible.

Being risk-averse implies that people try to reduce risk or choose an option with the minimum of uncertainty possible. In fact, investors are reluctant to accept a deal with an uncertain payoff. They will always prefer a deal with more certain, but possibly lower expected payoff. Consider the following example: somebody offers you the option between accepting

FIGURE 6.1   Main market analysis elements

$50 or flipping a coin where *heads* will give $100 and *tails* nothing at all. Which option would you choose? Most people will choose the sure bet of $50 and a minority will prefer to gamble with the unknown payoff. But based on the risk-neutral probability (heads and tails are equally likely with a probability of 0.5 each), both options have exactly the same payoff ($0.5 \times 100 + 0.5 \times 0 = 50$). Still, most people will be tempted to take no risks. Even if you offer $49 or less in cash, where a rational person should choose the option that is worth more, people will prefer the non-risky return instead of flipping the coin.

On the other hand, if the deal offered a choice between $1 and 49 cents, most people will prefer to flip the coin. This explains why people tend to be risk takers when the expected loss is low. This is exactly the perception lenders have with marketplace lending. Even though P2P loans come with a high risk of default, investors feel they are relatively safe. Most marketplace lending platforms advise investors to diversify across at least 100 loans. Nevertheless, the underlying assets by themselves still have the same risk as before.

Before we continue, let's briefly go back to our coin flipping game. Even though people are courageous when the stakes are low—as in gambling for $1 or getting 49 cents for sure—most of us get cold feet when the choice is between $1 million and $499,000 in cash. A high expected loss tips our animal spirits towards risk-averse decisions. This explains why most people choose to park their hard-earned capital in a low-yielding savings account at the bank. Despite minuscule interest rates, at least the payoff is certain, they reason. Most savers forget that savings accounts slowly diminish their savings because the interest rates are lower than inflation rates. In recent times, interest rates have even turned negative.

To sum it up, only a few investors are risk seekers who prefer to put their money into stocks that may have high expected returns, but also high risk and thus a chance of losing all of the capital or part of it. Uncertainty is the main element when quantifying risk.

Figure 6.1 illustrates the main topics discussed in this chapter.

6.1   REAL-WORLD AND RISK-NEUTRAL EXPECTATIONS OF MARKETS

The expectations for the future evolution of market risk factors are a fundamental concept in financial market analysis. All values and expected liquidity build on the expected future performance of the underlying market risk factors. Quantitatively speaking, the expectations that drive our decisions are naturally based on economic and risk-neutral probabilities. The former is based on our observed or simulated frequency of many possible different outcomes; the latter considers the risk taken in possible future outcomes.

The view of the real-world expectations of economic probability is looking at the future by taking into account the past and/or by deterministically or stochastically defining future scenarios to figure out the possible future outcomes of value and liquidity. In fact, real-world expectations are considering real-world probabilities, which can be determined through empirical studies. We can model them with economic scenario generator models, for example. Naturally, such models include future uncertainties of the market risk factors within the time evolution. These risk factors adjust their values according to market conditions.

Deterministic economic scenarios should be based ideally on nonbiased and more or less realistic assumptions that consider quantitative variables such as money supply, unemployment rate but also qualitative idiosyncratic factors of market behavior. Stochastic economic scenarios are mathematically driven and simulate the evolution and uncertainties of market risk factors.

Risk-neutral probabilities assume the absence of arbitrage. Based on the risk-neutral pricing approach, we can price an asset based on its expected payoff. With this, we can calculate the correct net present value (NPV) by discounting it with the risk-free interest rate. In the risk-neutral world, the present value V of a cash flow occurring at a future date t is given by the relatively straightforward formula (6.1)

$$V = \frac{1}{1 + r(t)} E(CF(t)) \tag{6.1}$$

where
   $r(t)$ is the compounded risk-free interest rate,
   E is the risk-neutral expectation with respect to the risk-neutral probabilities, and
   CF is the expected cash flow.

In risk-neutral valuations, the economic expectations of asset returns, or the probabilities of realistic economic scenarios, are irrelevant. Only the risk-neutral probabilities matter.

In summary, we can arrive at a valuation by using the following expectations:

- Risk-neutral expectations for cash flows and risk-free rates for discounting
- Real-world expectations for cash flows and risk-adjusted interest rates for discounting.

Risk-neutral valuation is mostly used by the analysts who are confident about the elegance of strictly mathematical approaches in an arbitrage-free "ideal little happy world." Practically speaking, it is easier not to bother with the probabilities and real-world expectations and uncertainties. In normal and liquid markets, this works quite well. However, the ugly truth is that markets can be illiquid. Uncertainties may occur in the future, even in markets that were stable throughout history. For this reason, real-world expectations and risk adjustments will always drive future expected cash flows and values.

6.2 ECONOMIC SCENARIOS BASED ON REAL-WORLD PROBABILITIES

A sensible estimation of the value, income and liquidity analysis must be based on economic scenarios which are based on real-world probabilities. Such scenarios may be less structured mathematically and thus cannot be defined in the same precise terms as those used to formulate arbitrage-free models. However, when it comes to the evolution of market risk factors in the future, they may be less biased—or they may at least attempt to be.

Even though there is no common agreement among economists about forecasting techniques to define economic scenarios, there are, technically speaking, three distinct methods for constructing economic scenarios:

- **What-if scenarios**. These are deterministically based scenarios where an analyst has the freedom to define the future evolution of market risk factors, e.g., a scenario of 1.5% of parallel shift of the yield curve over a one-year horizon can be defined. In practice, analysts may apply scenarios where the prices of risk factors remain constant throughout the simulation horizon. They may use a forward scenario in which all future spot prices are derived by forwarding the currently observed market prices. These scenarios make it possible to compare value and income effects over time.
- **Historical model scenarios**. These are based on statistical models which are based on historical data observations. Past stress periods can be a good benchmark for defining such scenarios. Of course, history does not necessarily repeat itself, and then not at the same frequency and magnitude.
- **Stochastic scenarios**. These are stochastically driven scenarios based on some economic research of the considered risk factors and algorithmic random scenario generators, e.g., Monte Carlo techniques. The number of generated scenarios is rather large. We consider such forecasted scenarios unbiased, but also difficult to examine at an individual level.

The definition and generation of economic scenarios requires considerable analysis of economic expectations, observations, as well as algorithmic approaches.

6.3   THE RISK-NEUTRAL EXPECTATIONS

Based on risk-neutral expectations, one can price using discount rates and applying high analytical approaches which result in well-defined, expected payoffs. Yield curves and forward rates and prices are the fundamental elements applied in the space of risk-neutral expectations.

6.3.1   Yield curves

A yield curve is a discount rate curve, with each point on the curve representing the discount average rates of discounting, starting from today and travelling along the points on the time axis. Because it is an average-rate curve, it tends to be smooth, even using linear or spline interpolations.

Yield curves may have different curve slopes and directions based on the expected market conditions, and they come in four basic shapes as illustrated in Figure 6.2:

- **Normal**: where the curve slopes gently upwards, usually at relatively short term
- **Upwards (rising or positive) sloping**: where the yield is historically a low level but the long rates are significantly greater than the short rates
- **Downwards (inverted or negative) sloping**: where the yield is historically a high level but the long rates are significantly lower than the short rates

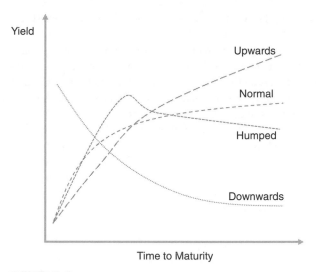

FIGURE 6.2 Example of basic shapes of yield curves

■ **Humped**: where yield curves are rising upwards, reaching the peak point at medium term, and then sloping downwards

Investors should act in line with their expectations. For instance, in the case of expecting a rise of short-term interest rates, they should only buy short-term loans and at maturity roll over the investment. It is safe to say that roughly 80–90 percent of yield curves have positive slopes.

Intuitively, we can say that short-term maturity investments are less risky than those with a longer maturity. The risk occurs because of the uncertainty of both future interest rates and the probability of the borrower not to fulfil the payment obligations. For example, lenders who invest capital for a three-year term will demand a higher interest rate and credit spread than if they had to lend it for a three-month term. Lenders tend to lend over a short term, but borrowers like to borrow over a long term.

In peer-to-peer lending, lenders and borrowers have much less flexibility. Most loan terms are medium, e.g., 36 to 60 months, with fixed interest rates. These loans are still relatively shorter-term compared to a 30-year mortgage. Regardless, if a lender invests in an illiquid product with a duration of five years and ends up being stuck in this investment in times of adverse market conditions, the illiquidity of these assets can become a problem.

6.3.2 Forward rates and prices

Forward rates[1] can be defined as the way the market feels about the movements of interest rates in the future. They do this by extrapolating from the risk-free theoretical spot rates which cannot actually be observed directly from the market. A forward rate curve is a curve of normal short-term rates as seen at different points in time in the future. For example, it is possible to calculate the one-year forward rate one year from now. Thus, to compute a bond's value using forward rates, you must first calculate this rate. After you have calculated this value, you just plug it into the formula for the prices of a bond where the interest rate or yield would be inserted.

Forward rates are calculated from current market rates following mathematical principles to establish what the market believes based on the arbitrage-free rates for dealing today, or at analysis date, at rates that are effective at some point in the future. The absence of arbitrage is one of the most important axioms in mathematical finance. It helps us to work out the price of simple contracts such as retail loans and deposits to derivative instruments. Let's consider a simple interest rate model where the yield quoted today for a one-year zero-coupon bond is 3% and the corresponding two-year rate r_2 is 5%. A loan starting a year from today and maturing in two years t_2 can be replicated by borrowing money for two years and investing the proceeds in a one-year bond. The forward rate r_{t_1,t_2} that applies to this forward loan is derived by the no-arbitrage condition that this loan should have the same value as the portfolio of the two zero-coupon bonds shown in 6.2:

$$(1 + r_1)^{d_1} \cdot (1 + r_{t_1,t_2})^{(d_2-d_1)} = (1 + r_2)^{d_2} \tag{6.2}$$

Where:

r_{t_1,t_2} is the forward rate between term t_1 and term t_2,

d_1 is the time length between time 0 and term t_1 (in years), i.e., in our example 1 year,

d_2 is the time length between time 0 and term t_2 (in years), i.e., in our example 2 years,

r_1 is the zero-coupon yield for the time period $(0, t_1)$, i.e., in our example a period of 1 year and a rate of 3%, and

r_2 is the zero-coupon yield for the time period $(0, t_2)$, i.e., in our example a period of 2 years and a rate of 3%.

Based on the above equation the forward rate per annum is $r_{t_1,t_2} = 0.07\%$. Any quoted forward rate that is higher than the above rate will allow an investor to lock-in a riskless profit, i.e., borrowing money for two years, investing the proceeds in a one-year bond and entering into a future deal to lock-in the higher one-year forward rate.

The absence of arbitrage is based on the market mechanism of adjusting supply and demand. However, it can occur locally and for short periods of time. As soon as arbitrage opportunities exceed a certain threshold, risk seekers find arbitrage opportunities. The threshold is determined by the costs of arbitrage, which means that in practice, only highly organized investors for whom these costs are minimal can profit from arbitrage opportunities. Such opportunities still exist in well-developed liquid markets.

Finally, forward rates are driven by market expectations and cannot fully predict future rates. The forward rate calculated in the above example of 0.07% may differ from the expected economic forecast for the one-year. In fact, if you compare the actual rates within a term structure of let's say three months with the forward rate curve for the same term structure, the rates will certainly not differ much.

If we interpret the forward rates as the economically expected future spot rate, interest rates should be rising most of the time. Yet, this is not necessarily true; the observed rates typically revert to a medium and longer-term mean. Arbitrage-free models of interest rate dynamics are well structured and mathematically well defined; however they are unable to economically forecast the interest rates, at least not in the medium and long term. We need to understand the expectations and related assumptions for building economic market models as realistically as possible.

The modelling and estimation of forward prices and forward exchange rates are relatively simple and rather straightforward. Knowing that spot prices are observed we can say that at the time t the forward price of a stock $F_S(t_0, t)$ with current price $S(t_0)$ is given by 6.3:

$$F_S(t_0, t) = S(t_0)e^{r(t_0,t)(t-t_0)} \qquad (6.3)$$

In regards to the forward exchange rates,[2] we need to consider the interest rate term structure of both domestic and foreign currencies that need to be exchanged. Thus, based on the current Foreign Exchange rate $FX(t_0)$ and the difference of the domestic and foreign spot interest rates $\Delta r(t_0, t)$ with term t, the equation for estimating the t-forward exchange rate is given by 6.4:

$$F_{FX}(t_0, t) = FX(t_0)e^{\Delta r(t_0,t)(t-t_0)} \qquad (6.4)$$

In the above equation 6.4 the forward premium equals the difference between domestic and foreign interest rates which is based on the assumption of interest rate parity under arbitrage-free conditions.

The reason we even bring up commodities in this context is that they may be collateral in a loan contract and the market may wish to price them. The estimation of the commodities' forward prices has some additional complexity due to the fact that we should also consider their storage[3] cost as well as the incapability for making available for consuming or producing within a short time; the latter issue makes the short selling very difficult which almost vanishes arbitrage opportunities. Thus, similarly to 6.3, at time t the forward price of a commodity $F_C(t_0, t)$ with current price $C(t_0)$ is given by 6.5:

$$F_C(t_0, t) = C(t_0)e^{(r(t_0,t)+c+cy)(t-t_0)} \qquad (6.5)$$

Note that in the exponential factor of the above arbitrage-free pricing formula of commodity forward prices 6.5 the additional term c represents the storage cost whereas the term cy, named convenience yield, represents the adjustment to the cost of carry, a physical commodity, which for instance is keeping a production process active. The convenience yield also ensures the equality in the commodity forward price function.

Even though practitioners use forward rates and prices, we should remember that they cannot predict future spot prices or future spot exchange rates. This is due to the fact that forward rates or prices are not economic forecasted rates. Instead, they are based on arbitrage-free conditions that lead to biased forecasting. The economic dynamics that influence the future interest rates or prices play no role in determining the forward price and rates. In fact future interest rates or prices are not only dependent on the market (investors) expectations of the future returns but also on the volatility and unexpected performance of this return, i.e., on the riskiness and future uncertainties. Considering real-world expectations allows a more realistic analysis of future investment performance.

6.4 BEYOND MARKET RISK-FREE RATES

Both approaches of risk-free rates and risk-neutral probabilities are used to analyze financial contracts. They work well in spot and forward markets. However, market arbitrage free models and risk neutrality do not consider other types of risks such as counterparty credit and liquidity risks that impact the value and liquidity of the contracts and investment portfolios. Markets fail to consider such factors at the contract level. For this reason, they introduce the concept of spreads. In theory, we may imagine spreads as the links between market, credit, liquidity and other risk-free rates, for which risk neutrality cannot be assumed only with market arbitrage free models. In other words, spread encodes the specific credit, liquidity and possibly other risks of the individual contract.

There are some important characteristics of spreads defined by the markets that we should highlight:

- Spread curves have the same properties as yield curves, i.e., containing terms and rates; spreads, however, display additional dynamics and may change independently of market risk-free rates. Therefore, they are independent risk factors and have to be modelled as such. Modelling spreads risk factors with the same properties as yield curves also allows the same risk analysis techniques to be applied as are available for yield curves, e.g., risk, sensitivity and stress scenario techniques.
- They are applied as an add-on on discounting risk-free rates impacting the value, income and liquidity.
- They normally refer to whole classes of contracts such as loans.
- They rarely move as much as risk-free rates; having said that however, spreads can be moved violently under uncertain and turbulent conditions.
- They can be represented as coupon or zero rates and it is possible to derive forward spreads in similar ways as in forward rates.
- Spreads are changing over time. However, under normal conditions, spreads are expected to move less than market risk-free rates.

Spreads aim to include credit, liquidity and possibly other types of risks linked to financial contracts. Therefore, spreads s are additive to the market risk-free rates $r(\tau)$ to finally determine the rate R used for pricing or discounting process, e.g., LIBOR plus s, as illustrated in 6.6:

$$R = r(\tau) + \sum_{i \geq 0} s \qquad (6.6)$$

where the index i indicates the add-on spreads, including credit discount, liquidity and other types of spreads.

6.4.1   Credit discount spreads based on risk-neutral default probabilities

Credit discount spread applied as an add-on factor above market risk-free is the indicator of the risk premium demanded by the investor, e.g., lender, against expected losses resulting from the credit event of the obligor, e.g., the borrower. Credit risk-free spreads are estimated from the losses considering the risk-neutral default probabilities discussed in Chapter 7. Moreover, as illustrated in Figure 6.3, credit spreads are associated with the counterparty credit ratings, which are a reflection of the risk-neutral default probabilities and the resulting expected credit losses within a time horizon. Used as discount factor such spreads directly influence the value and liquidity of the financial contracts.

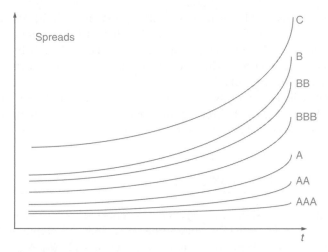

FIGURE 6.3 Example of spread evolution related to credit ratings

As explained in Chapter 9, the calculation of both gross and net credit exposures, and their evolution through time, will give good estimations of credit losses used in defining the premium through credit discount spread. Therefore, such spreads should consider current and/or expected[4] net exposure at the time of the revaluation process; we should avoid linking directly the spreads with credit enhancements, but rather with net exposures. Recoveries, which are driven by behavior characteristics, should also be avoided in defining discounting credit spreads unless they are very well measured.

The evolution of discounting credit spreads can be approached in a similar way as in market forward rates deriving the forward spreads.[5] Finally, using the analysis of the real-world probabilities, where spreads are stochastically changed or deterministically stressed, discounting credit spreads can be adjusted. The approaches of Credit Value (valuation) Adjustments[6] fall into this category.

6.4.2 Liquidity spreads

The failure to receive the expected contractual cash flows, i.e., the rise of funding liquidity risk, as well as the unfavorable trading of liquid assets due to market liquidity risk leads to unexpected losses as explained in Chapter 12. Even though liquidity risk is a result of market, counterparty/credit and behavior risks, practitioners[7] employ liquidity spreads in discounting process for evaluating financial instruments.

Thus, assets that are expected to be illiquid, i.e., not saleable or buyable, at a favorable price due to stress conditions will have high liquidity spread and vice versa. A similar concept could also be applied to the probability of continuation of the expected cash flows and capability of applying roll-over process.

Thus, the liquidity spread determines a premium[8] that counterparties need to pay, against market and/or funding liquidity risk. Such spreads can basically be applied to most investment, trading, hedging, credit enhancements, financial contracts/investments, e.g., loans/bonds, stocks, index futures, securities, options, credit derivatives, etc.

The liquidity spreads could somehow consider all financial risk factors and their integration; moreover, in many cases such spreads include future strategies and operational issues. They are adjusted by the real-world market expectations and default probabilities of the underlying market and credit risk factors. They are also driven by the market dynamics and thus are expected, over time, to be very volatile.

Additional spreads, on top of the ones mentioned above, could refer to profit and cost coverage, e.g., salaries, taxes, but also premiums paid for hedging or mitigating unexpected losses due to both financial and operational risks.

6.5   DISCOUNTING CASH FLOWS

As we mentioned earlier, risk-neutral expectations reflected by yield curves and discount spreads are used as factors in the discounting process. Then we are employing real-world expectation to readjust the risk-free discounting rates and spread. *Risk-free* is mainly applied on *static analysis* whereas *real world* is driven by *dynamic simulations* which are not always easy to obtain.

Based on the discounting factors we are defining[9] the discounted cash flows and the present value of future cash flows. In this process we are considering the time value of money as well as the risk or uncertainty of future cash flows within the investment time horizon.

Interest rate cash flows are the most important attribute in loans. Based on time value of money an investor is making at time t_0 an investment of $CF(t_0)$ and is expecting (or demanding) a higher return when the investment matures at time t as defined in 6.7. In fact interest rate $r(t_0, t)$ can be seen as the price the borrower has to pay to the investor for using the capital during the credit period. Moreover, by discounting the investment cash flow using the appropriate interest rate, the present value PV of the investments at t_0 that pays a cash flow $CF(t)$ at a future time t is obtained by using 6.8.

$$CF(t) = (1 + r(t_0, t)^{t-t_0} CF(t_0)) \qquad (6.7)$$

$$PV = \frac{CF(t)}{1 + r(t_0, T)^{t-t_0}} \qquad (6.8)$$

The main driver of the interest rates is the time horizon or, in other words, the term of the investment which is expressed by the yield curves.[10] There are many models proposed by the financial industry to construct yield curves. However, as they are also driven by the markets they are inherently following some assumptions—such as that they are following positive growth which only under uncertain conditions could turn to negative sign. The expected upward slope of yield curves implies a bias which is the case when arbitrage-free models are applied.

The term structure of risk-free interest rates, which excludes credit, liquidity and any other types of risks, makes the analysis rather easy and convenient. Thus, the single risk-free interest term structure is useful for estimating the interest cash flows and the value of the instrument. Moreover, deterministic shocks and stochastic evolution of risk-free risk factors can be applied in an easy and "clean" concept. In fact, a deterministic stress on a single term structure gives the ability to observe the effect across all financial contracts denominated in the same risk-free factor.

6.6 CONSIDERING MARKET ELEMENTS IN P2P FINANCE

You may have wondered why we treat markets and how banks use them in lending in a relatively detailed way. Establishing a baseline for discussion of P2P loans is important, otherwise we keep comparing apples with oranges. Let's now overlay what we discussed about markets in this chapter with the characteristics of P2P loans. When we look at them through the lens of established credit markets and the way banks lend, loans originated from marketplace lending platforms have a number of strange characteristics and oddities, some of which are red flags or stand in stark contrast with how the market actually works. For example:

- Loans are relatively risky, so lenders seem to be risk takers. This goes against what we discussed earlier in this chapter, where we implied that most people wish to avoid risk. A reason for taking risks could be the small exposure of individual loans, often as small as $25, as advocated by LendingClub.[11]
- P2P loans have a fixed rate, and they never re-price. This implies that the market never changes, which is incorrect, of course. Fixed rates only work precisely with short-term loans, for example, loans that last only one day and that roll over continuously under new terms. This makes sense in markets that are very liquid or where there exists a lot of trust between borrowers and lenders, none of which applies to the market for P2P loans. Fixed rates are profitable when they are much higher than actual rates. Nevertheless, in volatile markets they may result in great losses.
- Fixed loans also make sense in frozen markets where rates have nowhere to go. But because markets are not effectively frozen, applying real-world economic scenarios to P2P loan portfolios makes sense.
- The maturities of P2P loans are short to medium term. For this reason, there exists market risk because of potential high market volatility.
- High spreads between lending and borrowing rates imply high credit losses and a low credit rating for most counterparties.
- It is unclear how platform operators estimate the value of contracts. It is also unclear how they apply discounting. They consider risk-free yield curves and credit spreads; thus they should be available together with the applied valuation and accounting rules.

What does this mean, and what should we conclude from this list? If a loan portfolio at a bank had the characteristics that we just identified for P2P loans, a bank would advocate the following recommendations to deal with the portfolio:

- Apply analytics to estimate all returns, i.e., profits, fully understand all risks and calculate resulting losses of the loan book and achieve transparency about market risk.
- When looking at the entire portfolio of an individual or bank, short-term loans should be used for liquidity only, but not to generate long-term investment returns. Return projections should therefore not center on short-term loans, and they should only make up a small portion of the entire portfolio.
- Manage market risks by hedging fixed interest rates with interest rate swaps.

Because analytics are still a long way from providing the entire picture of the risk and return potential of P2P loan portfolios, this seems to be an ideal starting point to improve the

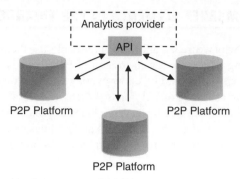

FIGURE 6.4   Analytics provider with API

sector. Only when retail and professional investors can compare potential investments across different platforms, both in the FinTech space and in traditional credit finance, will they be making informed decisions with their money. At the moment, each platform provides its own analytics, some better than others, but all of them a far cry from how banks and professional investors analyze their loan portfolios. A reason for this may be the lack of knowledge within marketplace lending platforms on how to do this, or the high cost involved in programming and deploying analytics. Analytics talent still resides in banks and professional financial services providers that cater to them. A full suite of industrial strength is costly to purchase and maintain, even for large banks. Unified analytics that P2P platforms could subscribe to would be an excellent opportunity to make marketplace lending more transparent. Such a system does not exist yet, perhaps because the current market leaders in the analytics space lack interest in the relatively small P2P lending space, or because platforms themselves fail to see the need. We imagine a system similar to how banks already use services of third parties. They normally provide an Application Programming Interface (API) through which clients can pipe in their data and then offer the output that they can display on their website. Figure 6.4 outlines how this works, and how different platforms could have comparable data.

6.7 CONCLUDING REMARKS

There are two main views in looking at and analyzing markets where both have unique and important roles. The first point of view is based on the risk neutral concept serving the need of applying arbitrage risk-free in the discounting process and pricing financial instruments. Thus, terms and rates of yield curves and the estimation of their future performance, e.g., by using forward rates, are trying to include the expected losses that may arise due to market risks. However, the future performances of markets may be slightly different or even far from the initial expectations and the ideal risk-free assumptions may turn to reduce the value, provide negative income and experience liquidity distress, all resulting in unexpected losses. This is the main reason why practitioners are taking a second view point by considering the real-world probabilities. Based on such probabilities market risk factors may change to a certain degree. These changes can be based on historical observation or by defining deterministic or stochastic scenarios. The former scenarios are mainly based on what-if future paths, and the latter on algorithmic evolution of a great number of possible paths. The results of these economic

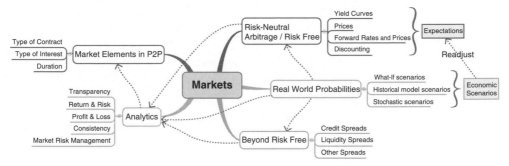

FIGURE 6.5 Detailed elements considered in financial analysis of markets

scenarios are used to readjust the initial arbitrage free assumptions. Thus, beyond the risk-free expectations additional spreads should also be applied, i.e., to include the counterparty, credit, liquidity and other types of risks, as well the consideration of earning profit, i.e., via profit spreads. Such analytics is aimed to increase the profitability and reduce the financial risks in order to provide transparent and consistent analytics in financial systems. It can also be the main toll used in designing the strategies for defining the types, interest and durations of contracts constructing the P2P credit portfolios. Figure 6.5 illustrates the elements and their relation considered in financial analysis of markets.

NOTES

1. Also known as implied forward rates.
2. The FX rates are applicable to deals that refer to different markets.
3. Commodities are physical assets that need to be stored and preserved.
4. Depending on the applied valuation rule.
5. A way to determine forward credit spread is by considering a risk-free benchmark security and spot prices for the risky security; then the forward yield can be derived from the forward price of these securities. Moreover, the difference of forward yields on a risk-free and a risky security is considered. The forward credit spread is estimated by employing the yields of the forward date and the yield to maturity. See *An Introduction to Credit Derivatives*, by Moorad Choudhry (Elsevier, 2004); and *Credit Derivatives Pricing Models* by Philipp J. Schiinbucher (Wiley, 2003).
6. Gregory, Jon (2012) *Counterparty Credit Risk and Credit Value Adjustment: A Continuing Challenge for Global Financial Markets* (New Jersey: John Wiley & Sons).
7. Liquidity spread is usually assigned and defined by the treasury.
8. E.g., based on the funds transfer pricing (FTP) system the liquidity premium is defined as the cost of carrying liquidity cushion averaged over total assets of the bank; see BIS occasional paper No 10 on "Liquidity transfer pricing: a guide to better practice" (http://www.bis.org/fsi/fsipapers10.pdf).
9. An extensive literature is available in regards to detailed explanation on how such cash flows are estimated; a good theoretical as well as practical description can be found in the book *Unified Financial Analysis, The Missing Links of Finance* (Wiley, 2009).
10. Also known as interest rate term structure.
11. Lending Club (2015a) "What is the minimum investment amount to open an account?", http://kb.lendingclub.com/investor/articles/Investor/What-is-the-minimum-investment-amount-to-open-an-account/?l=en_US&fs=RelatedArticle, date accessed 23 July 2015.

CHAPTER 7

Counterparties

A financial contract is a pattern of promises between the counterparties. Indeed, the great majority of financial contracts link to counterparties. The roles of the counterparties are different and well defined in each contract. In a loan, for example, the lender agrees to provide principal capital at the current time to a borrower in exchange for the principal and interest cash flows at future times; in a guarantee contract, however, the guarantor agrees to fulfill the obligations of an obligor, e.g., the lender, in case the obligor defaults; in a credit derivative, the counterparty who plays the role of protection seller agrees to cover any losses arising from another counterparty default or downgrade credit event.

Counterparties have their own qualitative and quantitative descriptive characteristics where some of them can be unique but others are fairly standard. For instance, counterparties have a unique name, could belong and operate in a certain industry, have a defined income, profit, and expenses. We must consider their descriptive characteristics because they can be very useful in identifying their expected credit behavior and correlation among counterparties. Promises given by counterparties are not always kept. Thus, there exists counterparty credit risk and this should be identified, measured and considered in both value and liquidity analysis. The main counterparty risk factors are the default probability, the credit ratings, the probability of the ratings to change, and the credit spreads. Counterparties influence each other. Moreover, the current and future market conditions also influence counterparties. Therefore, counterparty and credit analysis is integrated with market risk factors. Figure 7.1 illustrates all the main elements considered in counterparty analysis that this chapter will focus on, namely the types and roles of counterparties, their descriptive characteristics, default probability, credit ratings, credit spreads, and links and correlations among the different counterparties.

7.1 TYPES AND ROLES OF COUNTERPARTIES

Depending on the role that counterparties are playing in the credit system, they can have different functions: they can play the part of *borrowers, lenders* and *guarantors*. In some instances, *guarantors* play the role of *protection sellers*. Counterparties can play several or all roles at the same time.

Lenders are the counterparties that provide capital and thus they are aiming for a return of profit on their investment. In the case of loan contract (or portfolio of loans), lenders are expecting contingent cash flows resulting in the predefined rules and algorithmic mechanics

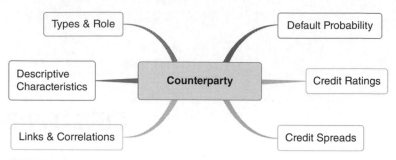

FIGURE 7.1   Main counterparty risk elements

of the individual contracts. In fact, these cash flows are expected payments from the lender, which split to the following categories:

- Principal cash flows, denoted as CF_{Prl}, whose sum equals the capital investment
- Interest income, denoted as CF_{Int}, which is driven by the market conditions, as well as credit and profit spreads

Moreover, the lenders may sell the loan deposits to receive liquidity and income.

Borrowers, also called obligors, receive capital, loan, for a predefined duration in exchange for interest and sometimes fees. These counterparties have an obligation to return the capital, as principal cash flows denoted above, based on predefined terms set in the contract rules.

Although financial contracts are legal agreements, there is always a probability that borrowers will default on fulfilling the agreed obligations. If they default, credit losses ensue. Therefore, financial contracts can be enhanced with additional rules defining the possible actions to cover such losses from other counterparties. As we will discuss in Chapter 10, in regards to counterparties, these enhancements are referring to *guarantors* and *protection sellers* in guarantees and credit derivatives instruments.

Banks play multiple roles as counterparties. When they act as lenders, they are very strong counterparties compared with P2P systems, mostly in terms of understanding and managing risk, maximizing performance, in size of assets, absorbing losses, and legal rights against the borrowers. On the other hand, banks are also acting as borrowers. They are more trustworthy counterparties compared to P2P systems because they have a good reputation, legal departments, and they provide collaterals including deposit guarantee from central banks. Finally, banks may act as guarantors/protection sellers. Compared to P2P systems they are more trusted, have a better knowhow and reputation in derivative markets.

In marketplace lending, the same counterparties exist as in bank lending. However, their roles are slightly different: lenders and borrowers interact directly with each other, where the platform abdicates risk management and guarantees to the lenders themselves. Borrowers and lenders still interact with the platform after it has underwritten a loan, but more in an administrative capacity. For example, when lenders decide to fund a loan, they do so via an account set up by the platform. In the event of delinquency, lenders will also depend on the platform to collect any outstanding payments and remind the borrower of his legal obligation to repay. The main difference lies in the part of guarantors. In marketplace lending, they are largely absent. Unless a platform has organized a third party to step in and take over administration of outstanding loans, nobody guarantees for the deposits of lenders in case of a collapse of the platform. Deposit insurance from central banks only comes with a banking license. At the same time, most lenders have no way of insuring their deposits with credit default swaps (CDS) because they do not exist yet for online loans. However, when larger borrowers, such as credit hedge funds securitize their loans, they may enhance them with a guarantee.

7.2 DESCRIPTIVE CHARACTERISTICS

There are characteristics that quantitatively and qualitatively describe the profile of the counterparty. Think of this as metadata, which helps in understanding counterparties, irrespective of their contracts. Such a profile can be used to identify the capability as well as willingness of the counterparties to fulfill the promises of cash flow exchange. Descriptive characteristics may be used in credit scoring analysis for identifying the probability of the counterparty to default or change the credit risk profile defined as credit rating. Moreover, the counterparty profile used in identifying the possible correlations among them, lead to system and concentration risk.

There are some typical characteristics used in counterparty description such as, for individuals: age, place of leaving, income, gender, job, educational background, or even religion. For business entities, e.g., SME, corporate, they are profit, sales, expenses, industry, sector of business, region of operations, and others. A sample of counterparty descriptive characteristic is shown in Table 7.1.

Descriptive characteristics may also be used to reflect possible financial behavior and credit needs. For instance, a young person with a good educational background has most likely the need for medium to long-term loans as well as credit lines (credit cards), whereas an SME will require credit facilities and short to medium-term loans.

The most useful characteristics in counterparty systemic, concentration and correlation analysis are the ones referring to the business sector in which a counterparty operates—for instance, the industry, region and country. Note also that some of the descriptive characteristics change over time. This is a great challenge because such information needs to be retrieved and updated on a frequent basis which is not always feasible. Thus, practitioners are trying to focus on those characteristics with a high likelihood of being fixed and most available.

TABLE 7.1 Sample of counterparty descriptive characteristic

Descriptive Characteristic	Type of Information	Variable
Region	Qualitative	No
Sector	Qualitative, e.g., IT	No
Industry	Quantitative e.g., Index	Yes
Performance	Quantitative e.g., income, sales, P&L, expenses	Yes
Age	Quantitative	Yes
Income	Quantitative e.g., salary	Yes
Profession	Quantitative, e.g., self employed	Yes

TABLE 7.2 Sample of characteristics of counterparties used in marketplace lending

Descriptive Characteristic	Type of Information	Variable
Region	The city, state, and zip code provided by the borrower in the loan application.	No
Assets & direct/ indirect income/expenses	The home ownership status provided by the borrower during registration. The values are RENT, OWN, MORTGAGE, OTHER.	Yes
Performance	Employment length in years. Possible values are between 0 and 10, where 0 means less than one year and 10 means ten or more years.	Yes
Income	The annual income provided by the borrower during registration.	Yes
Profession	The job title supplied by the borrower when applying for the loan.	Yes

Source: Lending Club

In marketplace lending, the descriptive characteristics are similar as illustrated in Table 7.2.

Online lending platforms may collect more data. These characteristics are quite similar to the ones that banks use. However, the credit scoring algorithm of platforms may be markedly different. They often take into account alternative data such as payment history on bills, and so-called fringe alternative data, such as posts on social networks, friends, and others. Platforms often consider more data than banks when scoring their borrowers. They may be more precise because counterparties know each other in real life as well. They may also be more transparent and easier to maintain and update as they work within a bilateral scale.

7.3 DEFAULT PROBABILITY

All counterparties have a probability of default (PD), even though it might be very low. Defining this probability is a complex exercise as there is a need for combining quantitative and qualitative information, historical data and future assumptions of the market risk factors. Thus, a spectrum of quantitative measurements comes into play, such as the current financial status versus the distribution of credit exposure, the correlation with other counterparties and market risk factors and, in case of default, the future value of the collaterals. On the other hand, based on a spectrum of qualitative criteria, assessments and hypothetical assumptions we are trying to identify the willingness (expected decisions) of the counterparty to comply with the agreed credit obligations and, in default cases, the expected behavior for recovering some of the credit losses. Moreover, statistical analysis of the past credit behavior, e.g., past payment delays, and future market conditions, e.g., high interest rates, applied to variable loans may also be used to define the default probabilities.

Default probability is the fundamental counterparty risk factor, which indicates the likelihood for the counterparty to default. Despite the existence of such probabilities, as long as there are no default events the contractual events, such as the expected cash flows, still occur as expected. Obviously the survival is complementary to default probability.

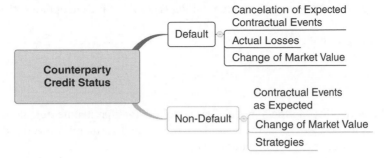

FIGURE 7.2 Impacts of default and non-default statuses

Regardless, default probabilities impact the market value of the financial contract through ratings and discounting credit spreads; it also drives the funding contingent strategies of the credit portfolio, explained in Chapter 12. Of course a default event immediately turns the status of counterparty to "default" which results in the cancelation of the expected financial events and actual credit losses, as explained in Chapters 5 and 9, whereas it impacts directly the value of the contract and portfolio that it belongs to. Figure 7.2 illustrates the impacts of default and non-default statuses.

There are two types of models applied to identify and estimate default and survival probabilities named structural and intensity (also called reduced form) models.

7.3.1 Structural models

Structural models[1] estimate the likelihood of default by considering the economic funda-mentals of a counterparty, e.g., company's debt and equity ratio. The value, V, of a firm at future time, t, is uncertain, due to many external and internal factors (economic risk, busi-ness risk, foreign exchange risk, industry risk, etc.). Structural models therefore are based on measurable endogenous and exogenous parameters, which impact the counterparty's value and inherently impact the financial capability to repay the debt. Thus, such models are mainly applied in corporate/company types of counterparty.

Following Merton's model, a firm's value V_t assumes the returns on its assets distributed normally and their behavior can be described with Brownian motion formulation:

$$dV_t = \mu V_t dt + \sigma_A V_t dW_t \tag{7.1}$$

with $V(0) = V_0$, W is a Brownian motion (random value taken from standardized normal distribution), σ_A is a constant assets volatility and μ a constant drift.

Consequently, the firm's assets value, assumed to obey a lognormal diffusion process with a constant volatility, is given by

$$V_t = V_0 e^{\left(\left(r - \frac{1}{2}\sigma_A^2\right)t + \sigma_A \sqrt{t}W\right)} \tag{7.2}$$

The debt value at $t < T$ with debt maturity, T, a debt face value L, and a possible company default at T is,

$$D_t = P(t,T)L - Put(t,T;V_t,L)$$

where $P(t, T) L$ is the discounted face value and $Put \left(t, T; V_t, L\right)$ is a put option with underlying V and strike L

The default probability is

$$PD = P(V_t \le D) \tag{7.3}$$

Note, however, that Merton's model does not allow for a premature default, in the sense that the default may only occur at the maturity of the claim. In principle however, default may occur at any time before or on the maturity date T.

Employing KMV Model, a default even is likely to appear when the firm's asset values reach a certain level defined as threshold, which could before the maturity date T. This threshold for defaulting is set as "Default Point" which is roughly approximated by the sum of all the Short Term Debt (STD) and half of the Long Term Debt (LTD).

$$DPT = STD + 0.5\,LTD \tag{7.4}$$

Then, an index called Distance to Default (DD) defines the distance between the expected assets value of the firm within an analysis horizon, and the default point, normalized by standard deviation of the future asset returns.

$$DD = \frac{E(A_t) - DPT}{\sigma} \tag{7.5}$$

Such distance to default can be calculated as absolute or relative value. The former is the sum of initial distance and the growth of that distance within the period T:

$$DD' = \ln\left(\frac{A_0}{DPT}\right) + \left(\mu_A - \frac{1}{2}\sigma_A^2\right) T \tag{7.6}$$

with μ_A drift rate, defining the expected rate of return of the firm's asset and σ_A the volatility of the underlying asset.

An extended approach to Merton's model, assuming that default actually can happen before the maturity date, is proposed by Black and Cox. In this model a time dependent safety barrier, $H(t)$, is introduced. Thus, the default either occurs when the value of firm's assets hits a lower threshold or at maturity date T. However, if the value starts away from the default barrier then the degree of survival probabilities tends, very quickly, to be equal to one. Another challenge is to specify the lower threshold appropriately. Thus, there are extensions of the Black and Cox Model where Barrier change may also be randomly employed.[2,3]

In the Hull and White structural model the default probabilities are consistent with those implied by bond prices and CDS spreads and where the joint probability of default across a large number of counterparties can be sampled from a multivariate normal distribution.

In such approach the Hazard Function is defined by credit indices (quality) and can be assumed to be driven by standard Brownian Motion. Moreover, given that default has not occurred by time t, the interpretation of the hazard rate represents the conditional probability of the occurrence of default in a small time interval $[t, t+dt]$.

7.3.2 Intensity models

In the intensity (also called reduced form) based credit risk models the risk of default event probability arrives exogenously. By employing an intensity model we attempt to model the pattern with which defaults arrive, rather than explain them endogenously. In such models, the implied default probability over a (small) time interval is modelled as proportional to the length of the time interval. The frequency of the events arriving in the time interval $[t, t + \Delta t)$ is described by a number called the intensity, denoted as $\lambda(t)$.

The risk of default event is modelled via a counting process $N(t)$:

$$N(t) = \sum_{s=0}^{t} \Delta N(s) \tag{7.7}$$

where

$$\Delta N(s) = N(t + \Delta t) - N(t) \begin{cases} 1 \; if \; event \; arrives \; in \; [t, t + \Delta \tau] \\ 0 \; if \; no \; event \; arrives \; in \; [t, t + \Delta \tau] \end{cases}$$

The counting increases incrementally and the time of default is the time τ of the first jump of N:

$$\tau = \inf \{ t \varepsilon^{\mathbb{R}} + | N(t) > 0 \} \tag{7.8}$$

Based on the Poisson process the probability that N jumps in the next small time interval $[t, t + \Delta t]$ is proportional to Δt. In other words, using the Poisson process, the local probability of a jump over a small time step is approximately proportional to the length of this time interval.

$$\mathbf{P}[N(t + \Delta t) - N(t) = 1] = \lambda \Delta t \tag{7.9}$$

The probability of no jump in $[t, t + \Delta t]$ is:

$$\mathbf{P}[N(t + \Delta t) - N(t) = 0] = 1 - \lambda \Delta t \tag{7.10}$$

Then we can subdivide the time intervals into n number of possible jumps having, therefore, subintervals of a length $\Delta t = (T - t)/n$. As the jump events across disjointed time intervals are independent, the probability of survival (no default) over the period $[t, T]$ is:

$$\mathbf{P}[N(t + \Delta t) - N(t) = 0] = \mathbf{P}[N(T) = N(t)] = (1 - \lambda \Delta t)^n \rightarrow e^{-\lambda(T-t)} \tag{7.11}$$

Thus, the probability of n default jumps occurring in $[t, T]$ is:

$$\mathbf{P}[N(T) - N(t) = n] \rightarrow \frac{1}{n!} \lambda^n (T - t)^n e^{-\lambda(T-t)} \tag{7.12}$$

The intensity λ is the hazard rate which is driving the default probability.

The first jump of the Poisson process, however, is a rather rare event. In order to achieve a more realistic model the default intensity and therefore hazard rate must be changed more dynamically through the time. The inhomogeneous Poisson process therefore has been introduced where the density of the time of the first jump, given that no jump has occurred until t is:

$$\lambda(s)e^{-\int_t^T \lambda(s)ds} \tag{7.13}$$

the corresponding hazard rates of default (assuming $\tau > t$ and $T > t$):

$$H(t, T, T + \Delta t) = \frac{1}{\Delta t}\left(e^{\int_t^T \lambda(s)ds} - 1\right), \tag{7.14}$$

$$h(t, T) = \lambda(T)$$

In the above paragraphs we highlight the main advantages and elements of most commonly used *intensity* and *structural* models. A more detailed description of these models can be found in Annex B, which is available on the website. In marketplace lending where the information referring to endogenous parameters of the counterparties is limited we propose that intensity rather structural models are more appropriate to be applied in defining default probabilities.

Default probabilities drive their usage in risk management and pricing of the credit portfolio. This means that, similar to the market expectation, a clear distinction between the risk-neutral and real-world default probabilities should be made.

7.3.3 Real-world and risk-neutral default probabilities

In Chapter 6 we discussed the real-world and risk-neutral expectations in regards to markets. Similarly, we now consider real-world and risk-neutral default probabilities. Both views and corresponding analysis serve different and complementary purposes.

As in the analysis of real-world market expectations, real-world default probabilities can be determined through empirical studies, historical observations and assumptions for defining scenario generator models of future credit events. Such real-world future default probabilities are very much applicable in risk management analysis. Indeed, real-world default probabilities are quantitatively assessing and measuring the probability of the counterparty to default, based on certain quantitative scenarios, and their impact on the outcomes of value and liquidity. In other words, it is defining the sensitivity of value, income and liquidity against the default credit events.

We have already discussed risk-neutral probabilities where we assume the absence of arbitrage; thus, unlike in the real world, the risk-neutral default probabilities are the basis of pricing approaches similar to the concept followed in market arbitrage-free models. Nevertheless, why are real default probabilities not part of such approaches? The answer lies in the expected behavior of investors who tend to avoid any possible losses. Let's imagine, for example, an investment where the expected outcomes are $100 with probability 99% and $0 with "default" probability of 1%. Investors with non-rational behavior would enter into such a deal, with a price of $99,[4] as the expected return has much higher probability than the one with entire loss. However, rational investors, who are by nature risk averse, are reluctant to accept a deal with a possible zero or negative payoff. Nonetheless, investors would take the deal with a reduced payoff but zero risk, let's say a $2 premium which will be used as compensation to risk of total loss. In fact, this default risk premium is used against the losses that result from the default probability of 1% in our example. Nevertheless, the $2 cannot cover the total loss of the defaulted investment. Such premiums make more sense when used against the expected losses of many investments placed at portfolio level.[5] As these premiums are driven by the arbitrage free discounting credit spreads they are reflecting the market price of credit spreads and used for discounting the value of the risk averse investments.

After all, investments are adjusting the instruments that are not risk-free by including in the discounting risk-free factors, e.g., interest rate r the real-world default probabilities, i.e., expressed as credit spreads s that reflect the additional risk and resulting losses. The additive spreads will obviously impact directly on the expected cash flows and value[6] of the financial contracts.

7.4 CREDIT RATINGS

Counterparties have at certain points in time (PIT) a specific default probability. Credit rating is a credit risk factor that reflects the counterparty default probability within single or multiple time horizons. Ratings are usually defined based on scoring systems, which use different sources of information to identify the credit profile of the counterparty, e.g., the counterparty descriptive characteristics, statistical observed data of past behavior, etc.

Driven by default probabilities, credit ratings indicate the probabilities of the counterparties to honor contractual obligations under different market conditions at given time horizons. These default/non-default probabilities vary within different time horizons. Normally, such probabilities increase exponentially when the borrower has a low rating, and exposes the lender to counterparty risks for a longer time. However, it may also depend on the type of financial contract; for instance, in a loan that pays back the principal at frequent time intervals, the default probability decreases with the duration of the contract and converges to zero toward the maturity date.

The evolution of default probability for multiple time horizons is aligned to the counterparty credit rating. An example that illustrates the discrete changes of default probabilities, for two credit ratings, within ten time horizons is shown in Figure 7.3. Moreover, the default

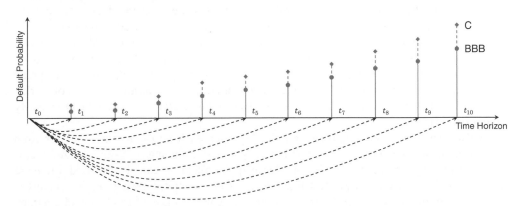

FIGURE 7.3 Degrees of default probabilities for two credit ratings BBB (•) and C (♦) within ten time horizons

probability of each obligor can be conveniently determined by its credit rating at corresponding time horizons.

Credit ratings of counterparties have some probability of changing, i.e., downgrade or upgrade, within a time horizon. Such probabilities are defined on a matrix called migration or transition matrix discussed in Chapter 8. The definition of such matrices can be a rather complex process based on statistical observation, economic assumptions, market conditions, idiosyncratic characteristics of the counterparties, etc.

The link between the counterparty ratings is based on their sensitivities to certain market risk factors, as well as the correlations among them using common and correlated sector analysis. This will be covered later in the section discussing the link of counterparties via markets. Finally, credit ratings in the view the risk-neutral default probabilities are associated with the counterparty credit spreads used in the valuation of the investments that contain the credit portfolio.

7.5   CREDIT SPREADS BASED ON REAL-WORLD PROBABILITIES

The premiums, mentioned earlier, against the risk-neutral default probabilities and resulting expected credit losses, are defined by using arbitrage free credit spreads. These credit spreads are applied as discounting factors as explained in Chapter 6. However, unexpected credit losses are defined based on real-world expectations of the default probabilities and credit ratings within a certain time horizon. Thus, both default probabilities and credit ratings driving credit spreads are risk factors which are applicable in risk management analysis. In such analysis credit spreads are stressed to a certain degree. In fact, we need to consider both spreads and ratings and observe their historic performance and/or applying scenarios based on what-if or a stochastic process analysis.[7]

The stress of credit spreads is linked to the stressed counterparties' ratings. It has been observed, however, that during credit crises, credit markets increase (adjusted) credit spreads even before the ratings have changed. Moreover, when sharp downgrading is applied, markets may tend to influence credit spreads more. Thus, any association of credit spreads with the credit ratings should be well defined and tuned within the credit spread modelling process. Of course, the adjustments of credit real-world probabilities will change the degree of expected credit losses and thus will impact the adjustments of discounting risk-free credit spreads.

As we will explain in the next paragraphs, credit spreads are also dependent on market uncertainties. This implies that the identification of credit spread fluctuation is based on future market volatilities and correlations. A good methodology for identifying credit spread fluctuations is to use the historical volatilities and/or simulating stochastic scenarios of market risk factors linked to counterparties' ratings. Analysis of fluctuations is also applied to identify the haircut on credit spreads.

Volatilities and stress conditions can also be observed from the markets such as from the premiums of single-name CDSs, bond prices and traded spreads of swaps. In addition, if no observations can be made, proxies or other mapping methods can also be used; these are defined based on some descriptive characteristics of the counterparty, e.g., region, industry, but also based on the counterparty credit rating and seniority class of the financial contract. Notably, under stress conditions markets tend to adjust spreads in a more dynamic manner than the actual real-world default probabilities and credit ratings.

Concentration and system risks also play a significant role in credit spread analysis. In fact, it is important to identify any systemic consequence to the market when a major concentrated counterparty defaults. This is also discussed in Chapter 11 (Systemic and Concentration Risks).

Finally, news and rumors in the market related to the counterparty or the sector(s) may also be considered and may impact the size of credit spreads. Such qualitative elements are very difficult to model and evaluate. Speculation is mainly based on qualitative, soft-risk parameters that influence the spreads. Deterministic stress on credit spreads may be applied to reflect such cases.

In marketplace lending, most of the interest rate that borrowers pay consists of credit spreads containing profit and counterparty risk. This makes the analysis rather complicated with low transparency because the individual spreads are all lumped together.

7.6 LINK OF COUNTERPARTIES VIA MARKETS

As already mentioned, counterparties are linked to markets. This is important to remember because, in this case, counterparties are not only exposed directly to each other, but they are also exposed to markets. The main markets that financial institutions consider for such analysis are the *currencies* and the *region(s)* where the counterparty is trading; moreover, to the stock, indices and commodities referring to counterparty's business *sector*.

Obligors can be linked to each other via the underlying "systematic" market risk factors that they are exposed to, i.e., market index of the sector that they belong to. Thus, the correlation and volatility of the risk factors define the corresponding correlation and volatility of the regions and sectors and consequently of the linkages among obligors.

The set of k markets at time t and the associated risk factors must be defined. For example, a market could refer to a sector, e.g. tourism, which is associated with corresponding *sector stock indices*. As obligors are allocated (linked) to markets, a risk allocation weight θ_{ik} of each obligor to the sector(s) must be defined.

There are two types of risk allocation weights:

1. The weight θ_{ik} is linked to single or several markets so that:

$$\sum_{k=1}^{N} \theta_{ik} \leq 1 \tag{7.15}$$

   where i is the number of obligor and $k = 1, \ldots, N$ is the number of systematic markets (factors), e.g., sectors, and
   θ_{ik} is the relative proportion of the obligor i in the market k.
2. The weight θ_{is} refers to the obligor's own specific idiosyncratic risk, so that:

$$\theta_{is} = 1 - \sum_{k=1}^{N} \theta_{ik} \leq 1 \tag{7.16}$$

   θ_{is} is the obligor's independent risk factor which is independent from other market exposures.

Given the different possibilities for allocating the obligors to different market risk factors, one has to define their structure and weights. The assumption in such analysis is that markets have an *influence on the performance of the participating obligors*. This also drives the *correlation*[8] of defaults between the obligors.

Markets that are linked to obligors can also be correlated. A general equation for defining such a correlation λ weight is:

$$\sum_{j=1}^{M} \lambda_{kj} \leq 1 \tag{7.17}$$

where: M is the number of market risk factors that are linked to the obligors, and λ_{kj} is the degree of weights where the sectors k and j are correlated.

The systematic markets (factors) can also be assumed independent (based on the applied model). Note that a model employing correlated factors, e.g., indexes of the same sector and geographic factors, interest rates, etc., could be transformed into one that is using independent factors; this can be done simply by linear transformation.

The performance of the markets can also be volatile. Such volatility σ_k can be defined via the volatility of the underlying market risk factors $\sigma_k = \sigma_{RF(k)}$.

Based on market volatility the correlation volatility between the obligors and the allocated markets σ_θ can also be considered and defined; a simple approach is by considering the standard deviation of obligors, i weights θ_{ik} to market volatility of σ_k, i.e.,

$$\sigma_\theta = \sum_{i=1}^{N} \theta_{ik} \sigma_k \tag{7.18}$$

The evolution of the markets will also impact the correlation between the obligors (linked to these markets).

At given counterparty the default or creditworthiness index is defined in 7.19.

$$Y_i = w_{is} \epsilon_{is} + \sum_{i=1}^{N} w_{ik} \epsilon_{ik} \tag{7.19}$$

where the weights w_{is} and w_{ik} refer to sensitivities of idiosyncratic and systematic factors respectively, given by:

$$w_{is} = \sqrt{1 - \left(1 - \theta_{is}\right)^2} \tag{7.20}$$

$$w_{ik} = \frac{\left(1 - \theta_{is}\right) \theta_{ik} \sigma_k}{\hat{\sigma}_i} \tag{7.21}$$

And where:

$$\hat{\sigma}_i = \sqrt{\sum_{k,j} \lambda_{kj} \theta_{ik} \theta_{ij} \sigma_i \sigma_j} \tag{7.22}$$

At time t_{q+1} the counterparty i has default probability $PD_{i,t_{q+1}}$ and expected rating state $R_{i,t_{q+1}}$ and defaults or change in its ratings, e.g., downgrades, if $Y_i \leq \Phi^{-1}(PD_{i,t_{q+1}})$ and $Y_i \leq \Phi^{-1}(R_{i,t_{q+1}})$ where: Φ is the cumulative normal distribution function and Φ^{-1} is the inverse. Thus, the default indicator of counterparty i is given by 7.23

$$DI_i = \begin{cases} Default \ if \ Y_i \leq \Phi^{-1}\left(PD_{i,t_{q+1}}\right) \\ Non\text{-}default \ otherwise \end{cases} \tag{7.23}$$

the rating change indicator of counterparty i is given by 7.24

$$DI_i = \begin{cases} Downgrade \ if \ Y_i \leq \Phi^{-1}\left(R_{i,t_{q+1}}\right) \\ upgrade \ if \ Y_i \geq \Phi^{-1}\left(R_{i,t_{q+1}}\right) \\ unchanged \ otherwise \end{cases} \tag{7.24}$$

In the following paragraphs, we examine how we can allocate obligors to markets. This helps financial institutions to identify the correlation among counterparties.

Marketplace lending may also have as high a degree of complexity as the banking credit portfolios, in regards to counterparty links and correlations. For this reason, investors in peer-to-peer loans may underestimate the risk of loans, because this risk is uncertain and difficult to quantify. When we think about applying the analytics that banks use for their loans to marketplace loans, we will need to think along the same lines for counterparty exposure in marketplace lending to specific markets. The practice of marketplace lending platforms to reduce all risk management to the scoring of borrowers, and the advice for lenders to diversify, is hardly doing justice to the complexity of the asset class.

7.6.1　Allocating obligor to its own specific risk

We may link obligors—or borrowers—to their own specific risk factors, such as to their own business. Thus, it is assumed that the fortunes of an obligor are affected by its own idiosyncratic factors specific to the obligor's characteristics, which are responsible for the possibility of the obligor's default rate. Although such a case is rather rare, it can exist for some counterparties; a typical example is Apple Inc. which has rather strong idiosyncratic specific risk characteristics that gives it a very low credit spread compared with other corporations in the IT sector. Even when other IT stocks perform badly, Apple has in the past outperformed. It seems to exist in its own universe with its own rules, which is to say that it has a high idiosyncratic sensitivity and a low sector sensitivity.

Such a model requires a market risk factor, i.e., spread, to identify the obligor's "idiosyncratic" i specific risk with a degree of weight θ_{i0}. Since such factor is driving the specific risk for a given obligor it affects that obligor only. Figure 7.4 shows such a model.

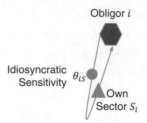

FIGURE 7.4   Allocating an obligor to own specific sector

7.6.2   Allocating obligor to specific market

In such cases, the obligor i is allocated not only to its own specific risk but also to specific market sectors, and the underlying market risk factors. The degree of weights θ_{ik} defines the sensitivity of the obligor to the market. Thus, the underlying factors of both its own specific sector and market k are responsible for the uncertainty of the obligor's default rate. Such allocation provides diversification benefit of obligors whose fortunes are affected by independent systematic factors.

Most counterparties fall into such allocations. For instance, most individuals and corporations belong to a specific region and corresponding currency. Figure 7.5 illustrates this case.

7.6.3   Apportioning obligors across several markets

In such cases, the obligor i is allocated to certain degree to several markets k with a degree of weights θ_{ik}. Thus, it is assumed that on top of the factors referring to its own specific risk, a number of underlying market risk factors also affect an obligor. These factors can also be responsible for the obligor's default rate.

Markets may also be correlated to each other with a degree of certain weight λ_{kj}. High degree of λ_{kj} implies that the obligor has lower degree of allocation into the correlated markets. In many cases counterparties could be linked, e.g., operate, to more than one correlated regions/currencies, or/a sector, e.g., tourism and aviation sectors. Figure 7.6 depicts this sort of correlated relationships.

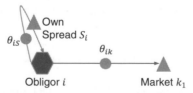

FIGURE 7.5   Allocating obligors to one or several sectors

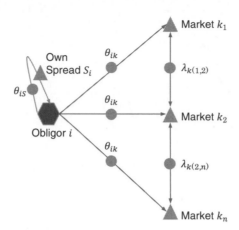

FIGURE 7.6   Allocating an obligor to several sectors

7.6.4   Allocating several obligors to a single market

This is the case where several obligors $i = \{1, 2, ..n\}$ are allocated to a single market k with a degree of weights θ_{ik}; thus, it is assumed that a single systematic factor affects the individual default rate of each obligor. In this case, a sector can be thought of as a collection of obligors having the common factor of being influenced by the same single systematic factor. A typical example is the fact that many obligors belong to the same region/currency or the same business sector.

Such allocations capture all of the concentration risk within the portfolio and exclude the diversification benefit of the fortunes of individual obligors being subject to a number of independent systematic risk factors. It also generates a prudent estimate of extreme losses. Figure 7.7 shows these types of cases.

7.6.5   Allocating obligors to several correlated markets

When obligors are allocated to several markets the possible correlation between the markets must be considered. Thus, as illustrated in Figure 7.8, a degree of weights between the market correlations should also be defined. In fact such a correlation is defined by considering the correlation of the market's underlying (market) risk factors. Thus, the correlation of obligors' default probabilities is identified by considering a) the degree of weights θ_{ik} where obligor i is allocated to one of several sectors k and b) the degree of weights $\lambda_{(a,b)k}$ where the sectors a and b are correlated.

This type of allocation is the most challenging as both degrees of weights θ_{ik} and $\lambda_{(a,b)k}$ need to be considered.

The above allocations' analyses are the basis for identifying the correlations among counterparties who are linked to specific and/or correlated markets. They are also significant in systemic and concentration risk analysis discussed in Chapter 11. In addition, they are applied in stochastic credit risk measurements, i.e., Credit VaR approaches. Concentration and systemic risks are big unresolved issues in marketplace lending where many borrowers and lenders connect to each other directly. It is very difficult to keep an eye on such risks when it is

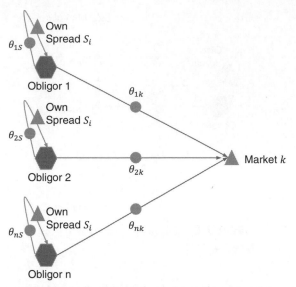

FIGURE 7.7   Allocating all obligors to a common single sector

unclear how individual counterparties are directly and/or indirectly linked to each other. At the same time, because the loan market in marketplace lending is nascent, it might be possible to collect enough information about individual exposures directly from platforms to understand concentration risk better. More research in this area is still necessary.

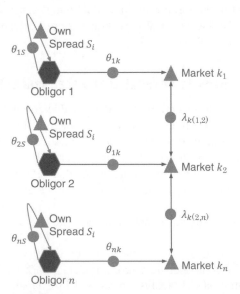

FIGURE 7.8   Allocating obligors to several markets that are correlated to a degree of weights λ

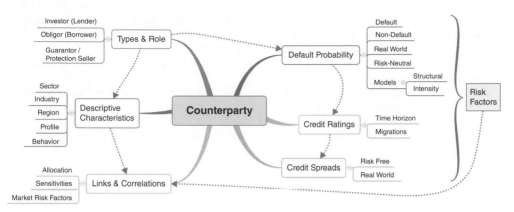

FIGURE 7.9 Main detailed elements considered in counterparty risk analysis

7.7 CONCLUDING REMARKS

In the credit markets, all types of contracts with very few exceptions (e.g., commodities), are directly linked to counterparties. As discussed in this chapter, there are three main types of counterparties, the investor (lender), obligor (borrower) and the guarantor or protection seller. The degree of credit quality of the guarantor must always be at a higher level than the obligor; this is not the case however for protection sellers who play the role of insurers against credit events by receiving premiums. Counterparties are characterized by a number of descriptive characteristics; most of them are used to identify the expected behavior characteristics whereas a few of them play a key role in concentration and systemic risk analysis. All counterparties have a certain probability to default at a future point in time. Structural and intensity models can be applied to identify and estimate default probabilities. Such probabilities have to be viewed in regard to risk-neutrality for pricing the credit portfolio; moreover they should also be viewed in regard to the real-world probabilities for applying stress conditions and readjust the risk-free assumptions. Default probabilities are reflected by credit ratings. Under stress conditions counterparties have certain probabilities to downgrade. Such probabilities are mapped with migration (transition) matrixes. Ratings also reflect the credit spreads. Such spreads can be used for discounting purposes, as discussed in Chapter 6 or stress testing considering the real-world probabilistic scenarios. Thus, at any time the expected impact in value, liquidity and resulting losses due to counterparty risk must be estimated. Finally, counterparties can be correlated. One of the most usable methods to identify the link between the counterparties is by their allocation and sensitivity to common or correlated market risk factors. This brings the analytics into a level of market and credit risk integration. To see how all the topics of this chapter interrelate with each other, Figure 7.9 includes in detail the main elements considered in counterparty analysis discussed above.

NOTES

1. Also known as asset value models.
2. H. Leland. Corporate debt value, bond covenants, and optimal capital structure. Journal of Finance, 49:1213–1252, 1994.

3. H. Leland and K. Toft. Optimal capital structure, endogenous bankruptcy, and the term structure of credit spreads. *Journal of Finance*, 51:987–1019, 1996.
4. The price based on such probabilities is $99\% \times \$100 + 1\% \times \$0 = \$99$.
5. The assumption behind the portfolio of investments is that within a time horizon the overall default probability and expected losses are very low.
6. Typical value adjustments at portfolio or accounting levels are the Credit and Debt Value Adjustment methodologies denoted as CVA and DVA.
7. Applying Credit VaR Approach.
8. The identification of both Obligors' and Sectors' correlation plays key roles in different types of analysis, e.g., Concentration and Systemic Risks.

CHAPTER 8

Behavior Risk

As already discussed, financial contracts contain rules used to sufficiently extract the financial events given the actual and assumed market and counterparty conditions. There are some contractual rules, however, which may give an additional degree of freedom, and which may change the expected financial events. Think for instance of a loan where a borrower has the option to prepay the loan at any time before the maturity. Moreover, a counterparty could always decide to terminate the contract and/or default. In this case the expected cash flows will change according to the time and amount of prepayment or default; additionally, other cash flows will rise, e.g., possible fees, recoveries, etc. All these are financial events, which are driven by the behavior analysis element.

Behavior is a very special type of risk as it reflects the decisions made by the counterparties. Such decisions are mainly driven by idiosyncratic as well as external factors such as market conditions. In the above mentioned example a counterparty could decide to prepay or default due to unfavorable market conditions, e.g., a loan of high fixed interest rates at the times where the market interest rate is very low. Behavior also refers to strategies, e.g., getting liquidity from selling the financial contracts/instruments. Nevertheless, decisions do not always make economic sense; counterparties may exercise their options by following other people or due to some "rational" behavior which sometimes is against their own interest.[1]

As already mentioned, behavior risk is one of the main input analysis elements, and thus impacts the value, income and expected liquidity of the financial contracts. In behavior risk analysis we are mainly considering the counterparty idiosyncratic characteristics but also the market-related risk factors. However, it is impossible or impractical to identify those characteristics and factors at individual counterparty and contract levels. On the other hand, counterparties with similar descriptive characteristics tend, in many instances, to behave in a similar manner for certain contract types and market conditions. Therefore, it is more than reasonable to apply our behavior assumptions at aggregated level.

Statistics could provide a good overview of past behaviors and could assist in approximating future assumptions. Thus, historic statistical information plays an important role in behavior risk analysis. Empirical research shows that, under normal conditions, counterparties behave in stable and predictable ways, whereas under stress conditions their behavior can become unexpected, and follow certain uncharted paths. When a critical mass of counterparties collectively follows an unexpected behavior, this can introduce great uncertainties into the financial system. Thus, deterministic and/or stochastic scenarios should be made and applied, to identify and measure the behavior risk. Even though there is no universal function to form

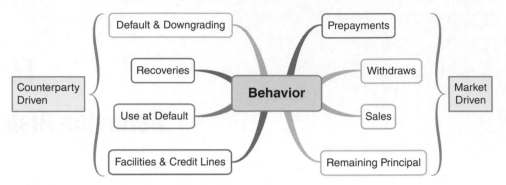

FIGURE 8.1   Classifying the main behavior analysis elements based on market and counterparty credit risk

the behavior element their effect on the cash flows must be clearly calculated. The default and prepayment behavior events, for instance, change future cash flows.

The number of behavior risk elements is not fixed; however we classify them as behavior driven by market risk and counterparty credit risk factors as illustrated in Figure 8.1. In banking financial instruments, typical market risk driven behavior elements are the prepayments of the loans, withdrawals of current and saving accounts, and the use/drawings of principal amount in loan contracts such as the ones used in a project development. Behavior of counterparty credit risks are the use of credit lines/facilities, the decision to default, reflected by the change of default probability, the expected recovery after the default event, and the use of credit lines to avoid the default event. Prepayment, default and downgrading, use at default and recoveries are behavior elements that should also be considered in the instruments provided in marketplace lending.

The pattern of the behavior is discussed in Chapter 5 (5.3.5 Behavior patterns).

8.1   PREPAYMENTS

Prepayment is an option of the obligor counterparty to prepay the remaining principal, partially or fully, before the contractual maturity date. In terms of liquidity, such behavior will cancel out all expected cash flows just after the prepayment option is exercised. Both exposure and value of the contract will be changed accordingly. To model prepayment, historical data and assumptions can give a good approximation of such behaviors. For instance, as illustrated in Figure 8.2 under stress conditions, counterparties are expected to change the prepayment, e.g., if interest rates deteriorate, counterparties tend to prepay more, and earlier than expected, of the fixed rated contracts and replace them with variable ones and vice versa.

The parameters considered in such behaviors are the PITs of prepayment date, the prepayment speed as a percentage that is paid back at each prepayment PIT, the payback value as the decrease in the outstanding notional amount, the valuation rule applied to remaining principal after the prepayment, the fees that may be paid and the payback rule.

Marketplace lending platforms have to communicate to lenders that borrowers might prepay their loans. In fact, prepayment comes with few repercussions for borrowers on most marketplace lending platforms. For example, when a prepayment option is exercised but no

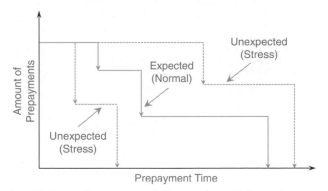

FIGURE 8.2   Pattern that illustrates the prepayment under statistically normal and stress financial risk conditions

charges, such as fees and penalties, are applied. The loser in this equation is the lender who will miss out on the promised interest and will have to look for alternative sources of fixed income. When loans at similar interest rates are abundant, this hardly matters. Lenders can simply select new loans and invest the capital they received prematurely from borrowers in these other loans. However, this may not be the case for an institutional investor with a large portfolio of marketplace loans who has carefully predicted and timed the liquidity in his exposure. When borrowers prepay, these liquidity predictions cease to be valid. Depending on the size of the portfolio, it might also be more complex to find new investments for a large amount of capital. This can be a headache when interest rates have significantly declined in the meantime. In any event, prepaid loans are something that lenders wish to discourage. This is why they should at least consider that borrowers may prepay, and they should adjust their investment strategy accordingly.

8.2 DRAW-DOWNS/REMAINING PRINCIPAL/FACILITIES AND CREDIT LINES

This behavior is the case of options where the borrower draws down the agreed remaining principal of loan gradually in accordance with liquidity needs. An example of draw-downs would be a loan applied to the construction industry, where the sum of the total pay-outs is agreed but not the exact payment dates. In most instances, the borrower will repay the principal plus the interest after the completion of the project and up to the maturity date.

Under normal conditions, credit institutions estimate the payouts based on project plans and statistical observations (see Figure 8.3). Interest payments are not always defined in advance, and thus the expected pattern of "cash ins" depends on future market conditions. Obviously, the value and the evolution of the credit exposure depend on the counterparty's behavior.

Under stress conditions such behavior may not be as expected, e.g., construction projects may slow down or even be postponed and thus the expected draw-downs may be delayed as illustrated in Figure 8.3. In such stress conditions, the credit exposure may be considered as a credit default.[2]

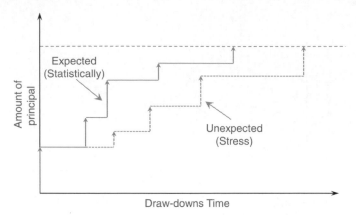

FIGURE 8.3   Pattern that illustrate the prepayment under statistically normal and stress financial risk conditions

Facilities have similar structure but they are rather short-term credits used mainly to fulfil the current liquidity needs whereas their credit lines define the restrictions and terms[3] of the corresponding draw-downs. The drawn part, as illustrated in Figure 8.4, is considered as an additional exposure that could be used by the borrower. The undrawn part is not considered as part of the current exposure but is the maximum future exposure indicating future expected credit loss. The pattern of the facilities/credit lines behavior is the same as of draw-downs except that the principal may or may not be exercised. Under normal conditions, facilities serve the liquidity needs whereas when the counterparty is under stress they can be used to avoid default events leading to the risk of *use at default*, discussed in the following paragraphs.

The important parameters of such behaviors are the draw-down dates, i.e., PIT time when draw-down happens, the draw-down amount, the maximal draw-down (in case of facility) and the interest rate adjustments.

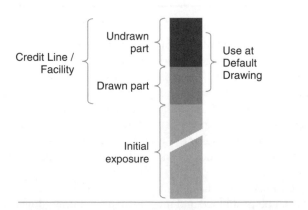

FIGURE 8.4   Facility exposure and the use at default drawing

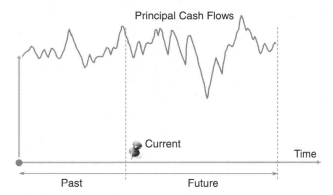

FIGURE 8.5 Example of pattern of past to future cash "ins" and "outs" of principal deposits and withdrawing at unidentified maturity saving account

8.3 WITHDRAWALS

In current and saving accounts which are typically non-maturity contracts, counterparties have the option to credit their own accounts at any time and they have the option of withdrawing the entire balance of their current and savings accounts at short notice or with no prior notice at all.[4] Thus, the expectations in regards to cash "in" and "out" flows cannot be exactly defined. Therefore, the evolution of the credit exposure can follow a random behavior as shown in Figure 8.5. However, under normal risk conditions, the behavior pattern of "cash in" and "cash out" is as expected and can be well modelled based on statistical analysis and mapped by using replicated portfolios as discussed in Chapter 5. On the other hand, scenarios should describe the unexpected behaviors resulting from stress conditions. Counterparties, for example, tend to withdraw more money under market stress while at the same time reducing the amount of their savings.

8.4 SELLING

Banks often sell assets to raise capital. Technically speaking, the behavior of sales is similar to the mechanism as in prepayment pattern. Thus, selling assets is a behavior that is driven by:

- Policies/strategies of the institution for managing their portfolios and accounts and profit planning.
- Market conditions, i.e., when mark-to-market valuation methods are applied.
- Requests for funding liquidity demands under normal as well as stress conditions.[5]

As mentioned earlier, under stress financial risk conditions, normally liquid products may become illiquid, which makes selling them more difficult.

The main parameters of modelling the sales behavior, in addition to those considered in prepayment are the difference between the book value and the current market value, the target income and sale amount.

Why is this important for marketplace lending? The option for lenders to sell their loans already exists on some platforms. Nevertheless, we are still a long way from secondary market liquidity of marketplace lending loans. Even though retail investors may still only dream about easily swapping the notes in their portfolios, institutional investors might already sell their loans to each other via intermediaries. This has no impact on the risk in the financial system in general, as investors simply swap exposure from one owner to another. The borrowers will not even know or care who lends capital to them, so counterparty risk and credit risk remain unchanged. When many peers share the exposure to loans, some defaults in the system may result in small individual losses. However, if one party concentrated their exposure to many loans in its portfolio, it may become unduly exposed to credit risk. This may be the case by holding many loans or by offering protection against their default.

In case of borrowers defaulting 'en masse', the investor may find himself unable to meet his own obligations to other exposures. This is especially problematic when excessive leverage is part of the equation. Examples in history abound. For instance, excessive leverage brought down American International Group (A.I.G.), the world's largest insurer. Even though the company did not own subprime loans, its London subsidiary A.I.G. Financial Products had amassed a portfolio of credit default swaps of roughly $500 billion from which it generated about $250 million in annual income in insurance premiums. Because this subsidiary was not an insurance company, it flew under the radar of state insurance regulators. When subprime loans defaulted in the financial crisis of 2007/8, its trading partners required additional collateral, which led to a liquidity crisis that essentially bankrupted A.I.G. The U.S. Federal Reserve Bank had to prevent the company's collapse, enabling it to post additional collateral to its CDS trading partners, and eventually ended up bailing out the insurer for $85 billion.[6] We are still some way off such large exposure or concentration in marketplace lending. However, if the sector continues to grow and reaches the predicted exposure of $1 trillion in peer-to-peer loans,[7] we will need to take the selling of assets into account to have the full picture of the sector.

8.5   DEFAULT AND DOWNGRADING

Counterparties may decide to default or may be under distress which implies an increase of probability to be unable to fulfil the contractual obligations. The latter results in a downgrading or, in other words, the change of credit quality into default over time. We classify default as a behavior element as it can be driven by the counterparty decision not to fulfil the agreed obligations. Moreover, it is mainly the idiosyncratic characteristics of the counterparty, e.g., decisions and plans of business strategies, operations, financial performance, etc., that indicate the credit rating.

As we discussed in Chapter 7, the default probability changes over time, which in fact impacts the credit rating. In the rating system, the changes in credit rating are mapped by employing transition[8] matrixes. As illustrated in Table 8.1, within a certain time horizon, a credit rating has a high probability of staying steady whereas there are some probabilities of migration to a higher or lower rating. For instance, in the example in Table 8.1, within a time horizon of one year, the BBB rating has 89.26% probability not to change, 4.83% to upgrade one notch, 4.44% to downgrade one notch, 0.12% to default and so on. The typical horizon of credit migration matrixes is one year. Of course the highest probability is for the rating not to change, which is the case under normal market and credit conditions. However, when such

TABLE 8.1 Example of a Transition Matrix where ratings may change from AAA to D (Default)

Rating	Probability of rating migration							
	AAA	AA	A	BBB	BB	B	CCC	Default
AAA	93.66	5.83	0.4	0.08	0.03	0	0	0
AA	0.06	91.8	5.8	1.3	0.9	0.14	0	0
A	0.06	2.27	91.86	5.09	0.29	0.26	0.1	0.07
BBB	0.03	0.25	4.83	89.26	4.44	0.81	0.26	0.12
BB	0.02	0.09	0.44	6.67	83.31	7.47	1.5	0.5
B	0	0.1	0.33	0.46	5.77	84.19	3.85	5.3
CCC	0	0	0.16	0.34	2.2	8.4	73.9	15

conditions are under stress, counterparties are likely to change their ratings. We can say that transition (migration) matrices describe the current and future behavior default probability of the counterparty.

As in all behavior elements, their main parameters are the time and degree of rating transition. Under stress conditions the real-world probabilities must be considered. This means that both parameters will be under stress, e.g., the probability of downgrading will increase or may become a reality. This will also be reflected in the corresponding default probability and credit losses. Let's remember that marketplace lending platforms refrain from changing the ratings of borrowers while loans are still current. Rating transition therefore currently has little merit for marketplace loans, but it may become relevant in the future.

The process and effort to identify such matrixes can be significantly high. Additionally, the complexity increases as they need to be updated, especially when market conditions are changing and/or new types of counterparties are linked to the contracts of credit portfolios. Even though there are many challenges in identifying transition rating matrixes, they play a key role in mapping the counterparty status over time. As such matrixes include the change of credit ratings, they also define the changes of the corresponding spreads and thus impact the pricing and valuation adjustment of credit portfolios. Finally, they are used in identifying the rating correlation among counterparties.

8.6   USE AT DEFAULT

Used at default is a special behavior case in the use of credit lines. Use at default means using credit facilities to avoid default. This is not a standard term, but it is an important consideration as it is related to credit exposure and usage of liquidity markets. Naturally, the use of facilities increase implies that there is available liquidity; it also means that credit exposure is increased. In lending liquid markets, borrowers under counterparty stress may use them as a resource of facility provider, for raising additional capital to avoid a default referring to their own existing credit exposure. In marketplace lending this could be the case.

It is very difficult to identify and avoid this behavior risk as a liquidity provider, i.e., lender. Liquidity providers may redefine the level of credit lines, but this can send the wrong signal to the markets. As already mentioned, this facility may or may not be used as it really depends on the counterparty's liquidity needs. When such needs are related to financial credit distress of the counterparty it may indicate an increase of default probability and expected credit loss. In the above mentioned case an obligor is using the facility as a last resort to avoid default of another loan. Although the default may not occur, the exposure of the facility is increased together with the overall expected loss of the exposures belonging to this counterparty.

The use of facilities to avoid default is difficult to measure and identify. It could be part of the drawing and potential undrawn exposure of the facility. As shown in Figure 8.4 there are two parts of the facility that are considered: the drawn and undrawn—the former defines the actual and the latter the future potential exposures. Both can be part of the corresponding actual and potential exposures referring to *use at default* case. A normal practice to identify such exposures is to have some statistical models of monitoring the use of facilities during the normal financial periods; any changes in the amount and time of exercising the facility option could indicate the *use at default* behavior risk. Institutions and liquid lending market places are trying to minimize the losses due to such behavior risk by readjusting the lines of the facilities. On the other hand, adjusting the limits of the facilities can increase the distress of the counterparties and default probability.

Does use at default matter in marketplace lending? A large share of borrowers use proceeds to refinance loans (58 percent) or consolidate credit card debt (28 percent).[9] However, to call this use of funds "use at default" may be a little harsh. Replacing a high-interest loan with a marketplace loan with a fixed lower rate may just be sensible and might have little to do with being at the end of one's rope. Regardless, it is important to know that loans have the potential to serve the purpose of default avoidance. In this case, we need to be aware that their exposure rises rapidly.

8.7 RECOVERIES

Having credit enhancements attached to the credit exposures investors can precisely estimate the net exposure, and thus losses, after the default event. Indeed, credit exposure is not always fully covered by the credit enhancements. Thus, additional recoveries[10] may be used for the remaining exposure and corresponding losses.

The degree of the expected recovery, after the credit enhancements, is mainly dependent on the seniority of the exposure. Thus, senior debts are paid out first and have a higher probability and amount of payment whereas subordinate and junior debts have rather lower probability (see Figure 8.6). The recovery rates are mainly defined by applying statistical analysis but also some qualitative assumption and mapped as a *recovery rate* pattern. Institutions define the *recovery rates* for mapping both the amount and the time in which the corresponding recovery cash-flows are expected. The recovery pattern describes how this amount is to be regained over time.

There are several parameters that need to be considered in recovery behavior analysis including the seniority class, the net and gross exposures, the expected amount of recovery, and the expected recovery pattern.

Portfolio loans constructed in marketplace lending are uncollateralized; thus interest income and recoveries may be the only sources of covering the credit losses. Defaulted borrowers may decide to recover part of the outstanding obligation for avoiding further down-grading and loss of reputation. Nevertheless, recoveries in marketplace lending are a rare occurrence, for example,[11] when a loan no longer has a reasonable expectation of further payments, it earns "charged off" status. The platform may sell such loans to a third party, and if the third party recovers the outstanding capital fully or partially, investors receive a pro rata

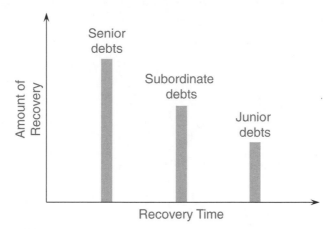

FIGURE 8.6 Expected recovery rates for senior, subordinate and junior debts

share of the sales proceeds or recovered capital. One marketplace lending platform admits that recoveries on previously charged-off loans are infrequent.[12]

8.8 CONCLUDING REMARKS

Behavior is one of the most important elements linked to most financial instruments. As it contains idiosyncratic characteristics, it brings challenges to map it with precise mathematical modelling.

Prepaying a loan may be a useful option for the obligor—in other words, cancelling an unfavorable loan to renew it with better conditions. On the flipside, it may reduce significantly the investor's income. In the models followed by marketplace lending, where no fees apply in case of prepayment, it is expected that any change of market conditions may encourage the obligors (borrowers) to prepay and indirectly roll over their loan with better rates. As we discussed in this chapter, the level, dates and speed of prepayments are modelled based mainly on historical observations. Any fees are estimated based on the remaining principal and duration of the loan. Finally, the valuation rule plays a significant role for estimating the prepayment amount.

The option of remaining principal draw-downs and the structure of facilities/credit lines contracts fall into the same category of behavior modeling. Note, however, that the former is mainly market and the latter counterparty driven. The level and the sequence of drawing the remaining principal and/or facilities are mainly following the counterparty liquidity needs. Thus, under liquid markets such types of behavior may have a low degree of risk; however under liquidity stress it may result in significant losses. Although credit finance provided via marketplace lending does not offer such options and types of contracts, the obligors joining credit deals may use them to pay the outstanding facilities and credit lines, e.g., credit cards.

For the behavior of withdraws, replicated portfolios are mainly used where they can be rather accurate under canonical expected conditions. At stress conditions, however, such behavior can damage[13] the credit financial system. To avoid such events institutions are setting certain limits. Note that such behavior does not exist in the marketplace lending model.

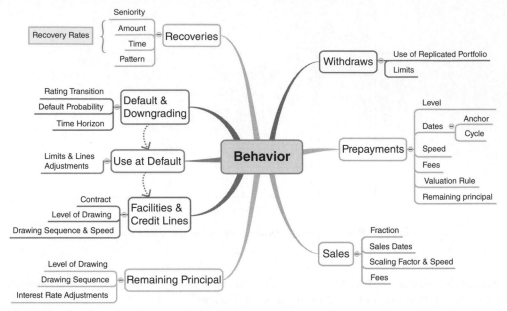

FIGURE 8.7   Elements of behavior analysis

Default and downgrading can significantly impact the value, income and expected cash flows of the credit portfolio. In the marketplace lending credit portfolios loans are uncollateralized with, in most cases, fixed and rather high interest rates, including market and credit spreads. Thus, borrowers may choose to default in case that future market conditions make the rules of the existing contractual loan agreement unfavorable. Furthermore, under stress conditions, counterparties at default may downgrade at significant degree and increase the credit speed. On the other hand, under liquid markets, counterparties may use facilities to avoid the default credit event. Primary marketplace lending is nowadays rather liquid, antithetically to banking lending market. Therefore, one can assume that some borrowers may use marketplace lending for avoiding default, indicating the use at default behavior risk.

As mentioned above, recoveries are the last resource for covering credit losses. Although in banking portfolios the rate of recoveries is rather well defined, linked to seniority class of the exposures, in the P2P model it is rather unknown whether recoveries can be expected, and to what degree.

Finally, the option of selling credit portfolios, fully or partially, can be useful in regards to funding and market liquidity as well as applying strategies for restructuring the existing portfolios. At the time of this writing, secondary market liquidity in P2P loans is still several years off.

Figure 8.7 summarizes all the main elements of financial behavior analysis.

NOTES

1. Due to lack of knowledge, laziness, negative feelings, or other reasons.
2. In the case of a delayed project there are, on the one hand, fewer requests for cash (expected draw-downs), but on the other hand this may be an indication that the project will not be completed. In

banking financial analysis, the latter case is considered as an indicator of credit default and thus the potential credit losses from the counterparty's inability to pay back the drawing up today will affect future liquidity.

3. I.e., committed and uncommitted, until further notice.
4. In most cases regarding saving accounts, however, credit institutions define some rules in regard to cash outs, i.e., notice and limits in withdrawals.
5. Liquidity funding management under stress financial conditions is defined in the contingency funding plans.
6. Morgenson, Gretchen (2008) "Behind Insurer's Crisis, Blind Eye to a Web of Risk," *New York Times* 27 September 2008, http://www.nytimes.com/2008/09/28/business/28melt.html?_r=0 &pagewanted=all, date accessed 21 April 2015.
7. Moldow, James (2014) "A Trillion Dollar market, by the People, for the People", https://foundationcapital.com/assets/whitepapers/TDMFinTech_whitepaper.pdf, date accessed 21 April 2015.
8. Also called migration matrix.
9. Bradley, Anthony (2014) "Debt Crowdfunding Holds Much Promise," Gartner Research, http://blogs.gartner.com/anthony_bradley/2014/10/22/debt-crowdfunding-holds-much-promise/, date accessed 25 May 2015.
10. Some practitioners are expressing recoveries as gross or net, i.e., gross recoveries include the effect of credit enhancements whereas the net recoveries are after credit enhancements. The natural way to define recoveries should be by using net recoveries as the credit enhancements are well defined whereas the expected recovery is driven by the counterparty behavior.
11. Based on Lending Club defaulting rules.
12. Lending Club (2015a) "What happens when a loan is 'charged-off'?" http://kb.lendingclub .com/investor/articles/Investor/What-happens-when-a-loan-is-charged-off, date accessed 25 May 2015.
13. In financial crises started in 2007, few credit institutions defaulted due to behavior of high degree and speed of withdraws exercised by the depositors of current and saving accounts.

CHAPTER 9

Credit Exposures

Investors, e.g., lenders, are exposed to the obligors, e.g., borrowers. Any default of the obligor from fulfilling the agreed obligations will result in losses, in most times, to all parties involved in the agreement. In a loan, for example both the lender and the guarantor are exposed to the borrower. Any credit event on default or downgrading of the borrower will result in economic losses to both lender and guarantor as well as loss in the obligor's solvency.

Credit exposure is a fundamental measurement in credit risk analysis. There are different types of credit exposures that an investor, e.g., credit institutions, or a lender in a market place lending system, must identify, measure and report. As illustrated in Figure 9.1, the gross exposure at a current or future point in time is separated into the net amount of credit exposure and the amount covered by credit enhancements. The former (also called exposure at default) contains the expected recoveries whereas the latter is expected to have fluctuations since it is market driven. Recoveries together with credit enhancements define the gross recovery of the exposure. When it substitutes the gross exposure, the loss given default is defined.

In this chapter, we will discuss the main types of credit exposures, with particular emphasis on the ones that are considered in the analysis of loan portfolios. Such exposures are mainly used to estimate the expected credit losses.

9.1 GROSS EXPOSURE

A single gross credit exposure $GE(t)$ at Point in Time (PIT) t is the maximum amount that the institution may lose in the event of the counterparty's default or downgrading, named counterparty risk. The former type of event, default, is considered when the exposure is held to maturity, whereas both events are considered when the exposures are traded at any time up to the maturity date.

The amount of gross credit exposure is measured simply by the *value* of all assets outstanding against the counterparty status linked to this exposure. The value therefore plays an important role in exposure calculations. Thus, the valuation rule(s) and the discount factors, e.g., risk-free rates, yields and spreads, must be well defined. At the time when the contract starts, the net present value may be used to measure the exposure, whereas at default or downgrading time mark-to-market valuation may be sufficient.

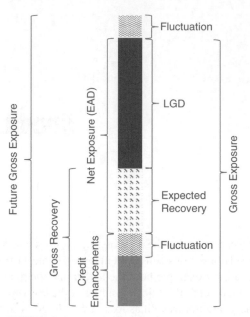

FIGURE 9.1   Defining credit exposures

9.2 NET EXPOSURE

In the gross credit exposure, we assume that neither credit enhancements (CE) nor recoveries are applied against the above mentioned events; in other words, it is an uncollateralized exposure. However, the riskiness of gross exposure against default or downgrading events can be covered by employing *credit enhancements*, which make up the collateralized net exposure. Thus, quantifying the amount of credit enhancements attached to gross exposure at any PIT t is essential. The general equation for estimating the current net exposure at time t of a default event, also called exposure at default (*EAD*), is defined[1] in 9.1

$$E_{net}(t) = E_{gross}(t) - CE(t) \qquad (9.1)$$

As discussed in Chapter 10 there are market and counterparty driven credit enhancements that may be applied at possible future time of credit event, i.e., default or downgrading. There are rules that must be applied when credit enhancements are employed, to mention a few: the guarantors must have higher credit quality rating than the obligor; also the financial collaterals may fluctuate based on market conditions and thus haircut analysis is applied; moreover, wrong way risk must be measured. Finally, a possible maturity mismatch,[2] between the exposure and the credit enhancements must also be considered. Any change of the value and employment process of credit enhancements will have an impact in net exposure and thus must be clearly identified, measured and monitored.

9.3 EVOLUTION OF THE GROSS AND NET EXPOSURES

Credit exposure can be estimated based on the current market, counterparty credit and behavior conditions. The value of credit exposures, over time, is not static, either at single contract or at credit portfolios levels. In fact, the future credit exposure is a time-sensitive measure. Thus, an important consideration for managing credit portfolios is modelling and estimating the evolution of credit exposure over time.

Different analysis elements drive the evolution of credit exposure, for instance:

- Evolution of market conditions.
- Counterparty credit status.
- Behavior.
- Type of contract.
- Valuation principles.
- Strategies.

The evolution of *market conditions* will impact the value of the contract at future, default, or trading time; for instance the present value of a variable loan is driven by the future interest rates. Moreover, market conditions will impact the value of market based credit enhancements, e.g., stocks, commodities, etc. and thus will modify the future net exposure accordingly. The expected potential exposure at future time *t* can be estimated based on its sensitivities to underlying risk factors. A general function for defining such sensitivity is shown in 9.2. The evolution of these factors should be derived using what-if or Monte Carlo simulation techniques, which are based on real-world expectations as discussed in Chapter 6.

$$E_{potential} = E_t \left(1 + \rho \frac{\partial VE}{\partial RF} \sigma_{RF} \right) \tag{9.2}$$

where
VE is the value of the exposure,
RF is the underlying risk factor,
σ_{RF} is the volatility of the risk factor within a time horizon, and
ρ is defining the confidence interval.

The *counterparty credit status* has some probability of change at future time(s). A counterparty downgrading will change the value of the traded exposure as well as any counterparty based credit enhancement; for instance, in the case of the guarantor having a lower credit rating than the obligor, the particular credit enhancement will entirely lose its applicability impacting directly the net exposure. The sensitivity of the potential future exposures, in absolute terms, to counterparty credit risk factors, e.g., PD is given by the equation 9.3.

$$E_{potential} = E \left(1 + \frac{\partial VE}{\partial PD} \right) \tag{9.3}$$

The *behavior of the obligor* may change the exposure in financial contracts when for instance options can be exercised, e.g., prepayments, use of credit lines/facilities (see Chapter 8) etc., as well as recoveries may be expected after the default event. A prepayment at future PIT will change the remaining exposure; moreover, the use of facilities based on liquidity needs will also impact the credit exposure. Note that when such usage is exercised to avoid a default event, it will dramatically increase the overall exposure and credit losses. In the defaulted contracts, the actual recovery will drive the net exposure and credit losses.

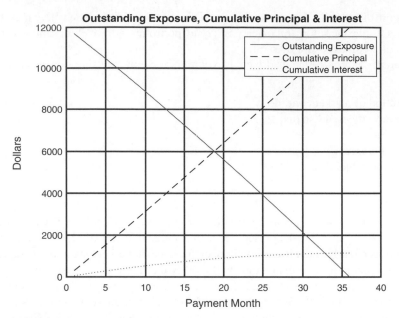

FIGURE 9.2   Evolution of credit exposures concerning principal and interest payments in annuity contract

Depending on the *valuation principles* applied to exposures and credit enhancements the future exposure may change. Thus, by applying mark-to-market, fair value, amortized cost, historic/write-off at the end, etc. will obviously result in different values of the exposure.

The *type of contract* which sets the evolution of principal plays an important role in exposure evolution. Consider, for instance, a loan contract, e.g., used in a project, where the principal will be provided according to the project schedule. The exposure could follow the corresponding project cash flow patterns and be mapped as discussed in Chapter 5 and illustrated in Figures 9.2 and 9.3, i.e., it increases till the completion of the project and reduces by paying back the principal until the maturity.

In the annuity type the interest and principal payments are reduced and increased correspondingly during the lifetime of the contract. As illustrated in Figure 9.2 the exposure and expected losses are reduced accordingly.

The exposure of a credit portfolio is very much driven by the *strategies* applied during the rollover process. In a portfolio, some contracts mature, some others default or downgrade. Portfolio managers decide about their reinvestment or replacement, i.e., new types of contracts, defining therefore the evolution of the portfolio. The absence of old contracts and the appearance of the new ones will therefore impact the credit exposure of the portfolio overall.

Finally, credit exposures can be changed according to strategies for the limits used to minimize the expected credit losses.

Based on the above, both gross and net credit exposures may change through time, e.g., from t_0 to t_n, as illustrated in Figure 9.3. Imagine the case of a variable interest loan used for a construction project. The nominal value of the loan is agreed between the lender and the borrower. The principal, however, will be provided at future times based on the project needs, e.g., at each project phase capital is needed and thus the exposure rises accordingly.

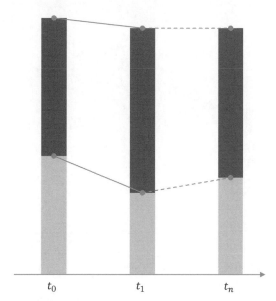

FIGURE 9.3   Evolution of credit exposures

In other words, the behavior (project need) is driving the evolution of the gross exposure. After the completion of the project the borrower pays back the principal capital, plus the interests, reducing the outstanding credit exposure. The borrower may also decide to prepay a percentage of the outstanding principal amount. The value of the contract also changes according to market conditions. Moreover, the physical collateral in this exposure is the actual building. The value of this collateral is driven by the phase of the project as well as the market conditions defining the corresponding market price. Any changes in the value of the collateral will modify the net credit exposure.

9.4   EXPOSURE DISTRIBUTION

The evolution of the credit exposure through time is not static as it is very much driven on analysis elements as mentioned above. However, there is no certain known path for such exposure evolution. In fact it depends on the future performance of the underlying parameters of these elements. For instance the performance of the market and counterparty credit risk factors will impact both gross and net future credit exposures.

A good way to identify the different possible paths of the credit exposure is to define a number of scenarios referring to the risk factors. Such scenarios are usually simulated, resulting in a distribution of the possible exposures at future time t as illustrated in Figure 9.4. Based on such distribution the Expected Exposure (EE) is estimated based on the mean (average) of the distribution of exposures at any particular future dates, defined by the simulation time intervals.

Typically, the expected exposure value is to consider many future dates up until the longest maturity date of the underlying instruments. Thus, a calculation of an expected exposure requires thousands of paths by simulating many future scenarios of risk factors for the given

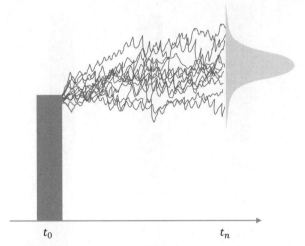

FIGURE 9.4   Evolution of credit exposures based on several scenarios

contract or portfolio. Once a sufficient set of scenarios has been simulated, the contract or portfolio can be priced on a series of future dates for each scenario. The result will be a matrix, or "cube," of contract values. The prices are converted to exposures after taking into account credit enhancements, e.g., collateral agreements as well as netting agreements where the values of several contracts may offset each other, lowering their total exposure.

The expected exposure is one of the main parameters in the calculation of the value adjustments of the credit portfolio as well as in the estimation of the expected credit losses, discussed in the next paragraphs.

There are more types of exposures that can be estimated based on the expected exposures, e.g., peak exposure PE, effective exposure EE, expected positive exposure (EPE), effective EPE, etc., which serve different purposes for measuring credit exposures. For instance, PE is a high quantile within the expected exposure distribution based on a certain confidence level, e.g., 99% at any particular future date which clearly is used in risk measurement.

9.5   CREDIT LOSSES

Credit exposure indicates, with a certain probability, the credit losses. The measurement of exposures and credit losses plays a key role in the pricing of the contract, that is, it defines the cost of a loan. Quantifying credit losses helps in the decision-making—for instance, defining and monitoring the type of contract that should be promoted and rolled over, as well as the kind of counterparty linked to this contract, the limits for type and amount of borrower lending, etc. Moreover, some of the elements in credit and liquidity risk management and monitoring are based on the credit losses, e.g., credit losses impact directly the expected cash flows.

We calculate expected credit loss based on two different assumptions: *non-default events* and *default events*. The former is based on the future expected exposures and default probabilities through the time intervals whereas the latter defines the actual estimated losses considering the expected collaterals and recoveries after the time of default event.

In the case of a non-default event, the consideration of time is defined up to T (i.e. maturity), or up to a given horizon date. The general formula of expected credit loss (ECL) for non-defaulted exposures is given by 9.4:

$$ECL = -\sum_i P_i \cdot PD_i \cdot EE_i \tag{9.4}$$

where

- The sum covers all time iterations.
- P_i is the discount factor from the current (analysis) date through the time interval (bucket) i to maturity / given horizon date. This factor includes the market risk free as well as any other discount spreads.
- PD_i is the probability of default, as discussed in Chapter 7, at the beginning[3] of each time interval (bucket) i.
- EE_i is the expected credit net exposure of the contract(s), based on the exposure distribution at future times, as discussed above, at the beginning of each time interval (bucket) i.

In the case of default the expected credit loss is given by 9.5:

$$ECL = GE - CE - REC \tag{9.5}$$

where

- GE is the gross exposure, discussed earlier, at analysis date (with past due amount),
- *CE* is the credit enhancements as discussed in Chapter 10 (Credit Enhancements), and
- *REC* is the recovery amount as discussed in Chapter 8 (Behavior Risk).

The above equation 9.5 is also defined as the Loss Given Default and expressed as $LGD = E_{net} - REC$

As we have already seen in the estimation of credit losses there are several elements that need to be considered. Thus, ratings and default probability define both obligor's and guarantor's credit status. These together with the expected recovery will indicate the loss probability and severity. Moreover, all market risk factors, including credit speeds, and their correlations/volatilities need to be considered when asset-based credit enhancements are applied. Finally, as already mentioned, the value concepts will impact both current and future credit exposures and corresponding expected losses.

9.6 LINK OF COUNTERPARTIES VIA CREDIT EXPOSURES

As illustrated in Figure 9.5, the lender and borrower are linked throughout an exposure of a certain value, e.g., loan, where they agree on exchanging cash flows. Moreover, a guarantor and/or protection seller is linked to the investor by covering any potential losses of the outstanding credit exposures; they are also linked to the obligor in that their protection is against counterparty risk. Therefore, the credit exposures impact directly and/or indirectly the

FIGURE 9.5   Evolution of credit exposures based on several scenarios

linkage and correlation among counterparties. We can say that a credit event in an exposure may impact several counterparties. The link we describe here is slightly different from the correlation via market sectors discussed previously in Chapter 7. Sector correlation describes a link by association to a group or locale, whereas the link via credit exposure has to do with co-dependency related to contractual cash flows exchanges and/or exposure value changes. We call the latter *wrong-way risk,* where the exposure increases when the credit quality of the counterparty declines. The International Swaps and Derivatives Association (ISDA) defines wrong-way risk as the risk that occurs when exposure to a counterparty adversely correlates with the credit quality of that same counterparty. Wrong-way risk, often called wrong-way exposure,[4] is discussed in Chapter 10.

As we will discuss in Chapter 11, minimizing concentration and systemic risk in regards to the exposures implies a significant reduction of the expected credit losses in case that single or minimum number of credit events may rise. Notably, the identification of the links and correlations among counterparties based on the concentration and systemic exposure analysis can be the basis of analyzing the interdependency of P2P counterparties.

9.7   CONCLUDING REMARKS

The identification and measurement of credit exposures plays a key role in financial analysis of credit portfolios. Uncollateralized instruments imply a high degree of exposures, i.e., in most cases equal to the gross amount. However, most contracts are collateralized and/or have good expectation of recovering rates. This reduces the net exposures which indicate the losses when risk events may rise during the lifetime of financial contracts. A great challenge in the exposure analysis is its evolution at future times. The main analysis elements considered in such evolution are the future market conditions, counterparty credit status, expected behaviour, type of contracts, valuation principles and future strategies of re-constructing the credit port-folio. Based on different paths of real world probabilities, a distribution of future exposures can be simulated. This is the basis for measuring additional types of exposures used mainly in risk and profitability management. Both market and counterparty risks result in credit losses. The estimation of the expected losses is defined by considering the credit exposures and the actual or potential status of credit events. Finally, credit exposures can be the basis of identi-fying the links among counterparties used in systemic and concentration risk, as discussed in Chapter 11.

NOTES

1. Some practitioners may also consider the expected recovery, discussed in Chapter 8 (Behavior Risk) in the estimation of net exposure that may result in further reduction. Such an approach however is mixing the well measured CE with unknown assumed expected behavior of recovery that is almost impossible to measure with high confidence of precision.
2. This appears when the duration of credit enhancements is shorter than the duration of the contract's life time.
3. Could be also another point with the time intervals.
4. ISDA (2001), "Letter to Mr Gresser, 7 September 2001," http://www.isda.org/c_and_a/pdf/ RGresserLetter-Sept701.pdf, date accessed 25 May 2015.

CHAPTER 10

Credit Enhancements

As we mentioned in Chapter 9, the status of a borrower and his contract is either "default" or "non-default." The latter includes three possible cases that relate to the credit rating of the counterparty. It may remain steady, or it can either upgrade or downgrade. Whenever a lender transacts with a borrower, the risk of default exists. Changing the loan status to "default" or "downgrade" will most definitely cause credit losses. To compensate for this risk and any potential losses, we apply a spread over the risk-free rate in addition to credit enhancements.

If a contract defaults, the contractual expected cash flows cancel out, and the value of the defaulted contract inevitably changes. However, credit enhancements as well as some expected recoveries generate new cash flows. Both credit enhancements and recoveries have the purpose of covering credit losses in full or in part. For instance, let's assume the case of a loan as illustrated in Figure 10.1 where the expected principal $CF_{PP}(t)$ and interest $CF_{IP}(t)$ cash flows cancel out after a default occurred at t_5. Despite the default we expect new cash flows at a time t in the future because the credit enhancements $CF_{CE}(t)$ and recoveries $CF_{RC}(t)$ start to be expected. We discussed recoveries in Chapter 8.

A non-default status indicates that no changes in expected cash flows will result from counterparty risks. However, an upgrade of the credit status of the counterparty will have a positive impact on the value of the contracts. On the other hand, a counterparty downgrade implies possible cancelation of the expected cash flows and credit losses, i.e., due to a higher default probability. In addition, it will negatively impact the value of the contracts. Any liquidation of such contracts will result in reduced expected trading cash flows. We could also expect a negative effect in the premiums of credit derivatives applied against a change in counterparty status.

In this chapter, we will go through the different types of credit enhancements named *asset based* and *counterparty based*. We examine what they are exactly and how they work going through the mechanics of credit enhancements. We will discuss why and how to allocate collateral and guarantees to different credit exposures, why asset-based credit enhancements could fluctuate, and how to measure such volatiles and what is the impact on credit exposures. We investigate the role of netting agreements and the challenges of employing credit derivatives. Then, we will explore some of the specific issues rising from the usage of credit enhancements including double default, specific and general wrong way risk, and maturity mismatch. Finally, we will propose some extending approaches for using credit enhancements in P2P lending models.

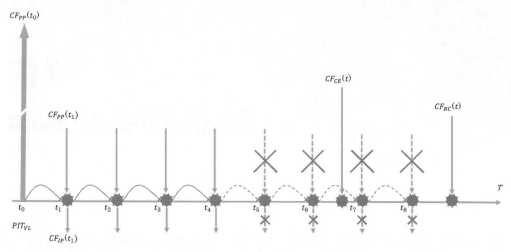

FIGURE 10.1   Cash flow cancellation and appearance after a default event

10.1   WHAT ARE CREDIT ENHANCEMENTS? TYPES AND STRUCTURE

Credit enhancements are financial contracts between counterparties with the goal of securitizing the credit exposure by mitigating the counterparty credit risk, e.g., default or downgrading. As illustrated in Figure 10.2, there are two main types of credit enhancements: *asset-based* credit enhancements and *counterparty-based* credit enhancements. The former concerns itself with financial/intangible and physical collateral and the assets linked to close out netting agreements. The latter are the contractual agreements between guarantors and protection sellers referring to guarantees and derivative instruments.

10.2   ASSET-BASED CREDIT ENHANCEMENTS

Physical, financial and intangible collateral are assets that reduce the net exposure of a contract and shield against credit losses. These assets legally belong to the borrowers, yet lenders have

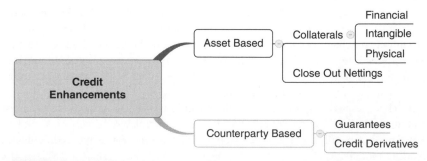

FIGURE 10.2   Main types of credit enhancements

the legal rights to liquidate them in case of a default event to cover credit losses. Whenever one can sell collaterals and readily turn them into cash, we speak of asset-based collaterals.

Physical collateral is one kind of asset-based credit enhancement. It describes tangible assets such as real estate and physical commodity goods, such as precious metals, oil, natural gas, etc. In a mortgage loan, typical physical collateral is the house that the borrower purchases with the loan. If he/she defaults, the house undergoes liquidation. It will go on sale to raise proceeds to reduce outstanding credit losses. Note that the market largely determines the value of physical collateral. Thus, in terms of price/value analysis, it is common to link them with price indexes. For instance, for mortgage collateral the House Price Index (HPI) is used to monitor the prices and their possible evolution over time. Note that we rarely link physical collateral to counterparties, so there is no direct counterparty credit risk.

Another kind of asset-based credit enhancement is *financial collateral* such as stocks, or bond contracts, that are available for liquidation in case of default. Both market and counterparty credit risk factors impact the value of such assets. For instance, credit spreads play an important part in the valuation of bonds, which are used as collaterals.

Intangible assets used as collateral can be intellectual properties, patents, copyrights, trademarks, trade secrets, and others. The value of such assets is hard to estimate accurately, especially after the event of default. For instance, the value of the trademark is expected to decline dramatically when a corporate defaults; however, the value of patents may hardly decrease at all. These collaterals are usually exercised as one of the last resources for covering credit losses.

Close-out netting is applied when a borrower has a number of predefined assets and agrees to make them available in case of default. Close out netting consist of two components: *close out*, which is the right to terminate the transaction with the defaulted counterparty and any contractual payments; and *netting*, which defines the right to offset amounts due at termination of individual contracts to determine a net balance (positive/negative values). In other words, the borrower may force these assets into liquidation to cover credit losses. For this agreement to be valid, it is obvious that the availability of the assets must be well set and defined.

Note that any change of rating (e.g., downgrading, default/credit spreads of the assets, considered in the close out process), will impact their values and thus must be counted in the net balance process.

10.2.1 Allocating collateral to credit exposures

Collaterals agreements can either be attached to specific exposures or to counterparties, such as the borrower. In the former case, they are only covering the credit losses of the particular exposures, whereas in the latter they are covering all possible exposures of the counterparty.

The structure of the applicability and use of collateral may have different degrees of complexity, depending on the types and number of collaterals attached to credit exposures. For instance, there are cases where a credit exposure is shared among counterparties, and a single exposure is attached to more than one collateral directly or indirectly. Let us think about the case illustrated in Figure 10.3, where a house mortgage contract M is shared, defined as M_1 and M_2, among counterparty CP_A and CP_B respectively; in such a loan the house is used as the physical collateral. Moreover, CP_B has two other contract loans L_1 and L_2; the former loan is collateralized by using a bond B_1, which has been issued by the CP_C. Finally, all the loans belonging to counterparty CP_B are also collateralized by the asset of bond B_2, which has been issued by the CP_D. Both house and bond B_1 will be used against losses that may occur

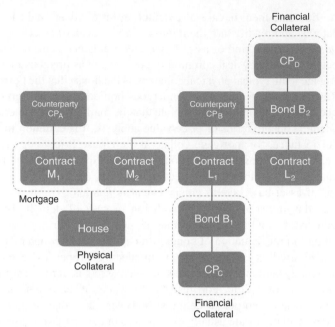

FIGURE 10.3 Example of applying collaterals to credit exposures

in the particular exposures that they are linked to; however, bond B_2 will be used to cover the credit losses initiated from any credit exposure of CP_B. The sequence of collateral usage may not be straightforward; the collateral management process usually defines it.

10.2.2 Valuing and adjusting asset-based credit enhancements

Depositors are eligible to liquidate asset-based credit enhancements that refer to borrower's credit exposures. During this liquidation process, the valuation rule plays a critical role. There are several approaches to valuation, such as nominal and fair value, mark-to-market, net present value, and more. Mark-to-market and net present value (NPV) are the most common when it comes to the liquidation of credit enhancements after the credit default event. The choice of several interpretations to value by applying different valuation rules is critical for estimating the net exposures and the marketability at the time of liquidation. For instance, using mark-to-market valuation for a mortgage loan, we need to approximate the price of a house at future possible time of default.

The value of asset-based credit enhancements can also fluctuate through time due to volatile market conditions. Prices of stocks, commodities, and real estate will hardly remain static and will always change in the future. A common way to adjust such volatilities is by applying haircuts. Typically, the approaches for estimating haircuts are based on statistical analysis, i.e., observing the market volatilities of such products, deterministic scenarios based on certain assumptions, and/or VaR models, e.g., historical, parametric, stochastic Monte Carlo, etc. Haircuts of credit enhancements are helpful in identifying their volatility and adjusting the net credit exposures; such value adjustment will also define the expected credit losses.

10.3 COUNTERPARTY-BASED CREDIT ENHANCEMENTS

There are contractual agreements where counterparties agree to cover credit losses. Such agreements defined as guarantees and credit derivatives are the counterparty-based credit enhancements. In a guarantee contract, a counterparty will continue to fulfill the agreed obligations in case the obligor, e.g., borrower, defaults. The counterparty protection seller in credit derivatives agrees to protect the protection buyer against credit risk events.

10.3.1 Guarantees

A guarantee is a counterparty-based credit enhancement where a counterparty agrees to cover the credit losses of a lender, partially or fully, in case the borrower defaults on fulfilling the agreed obligations. Therefore, in the case of a default, a guarantee effectively shifts the credit exposure from the borrower to the guarantor.

In fact, a guarantee is a legal promise to the lender, defined in a new financial contract. The new legal "promise" implies that there is an additional degree of trust between the borrower and the guarantor. This explains why, during the lifetime of the credit exposure, guarantors must always have higher credit rating than the borrower. Therefore, the credit rating of an additional counterparty must be monitored which introduces additional effort and cost when guarantees are used.

The actual value of the guarantee is defined by considering the valuation roles applied in the financial contract that the guarantor agrees to cover. Usually, the values of the exposures and of a guarantee contract are defined with nominal values (NVs).

Loans provided to corporate clients often use a parent or sister company or a related bigger corporate company as guarantors. The reason is that these companies have a higher credit rating, i.e., credit trust. In this case, the hierarchies and group structures of the counterparties can be very useful. The hierarchical levels define the role of the counterparties and the degree of dependency, e.g., who owns whom and how much. This could also be helpful in terms of collateralization. When considering, for example, that a parent company may guarantee all its legal subsidiaries, the collateralization process—the defining order and amount of credit exposure—plays a key role in loss coverage. Counterparty and guarantee dependencies using hierarchies can also be used in the identification of specific wrong way risk, as explained in the following paragraphs.

10.3.2 Allocating guarantees to credit exposures

As with collaterals, guarantees can involve a single or several counterparties or contract-specific exposures. When guarantors agree only to a single exposure, they promise to cover the corresponding potential losses; on the other hand, multiple coverage of credit exposure applies only if the guarantees attached to more than one exposure and/or to the counterparty have multiple exposures.

The degree of complexity for structuring the coverage of credit losses, based on guarantors, depends on the allocation of guaranteed contracts across the different exposures. Consider

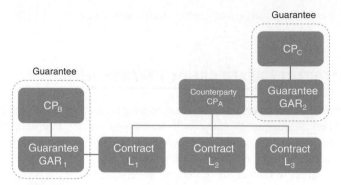

FIGURE 10.4   Example of applying guarantees to credit exposures

Figure 10.4, for instance, where a guarantee GAR_1 is allocated to (i.e., covers) a single exposure L_1, whilst a guarantee GAR_2 is attached to a counterparty CP_A and thus allocated to all related credit exposures, i.e., L_1, L_2, and L_3.

10.3.3 Credit derivatives

Credit derivatives are securitization products similar to guarantee contracts with the purpose of protecting investors against credit risk. At the same time, they are more flexible than guarantees. There are several types of derivative contract agreements such as credit default swaps (CDS), total return swaps (TRS), CDS on asset-backed securities, credit spread option, collateralized debt obligation (CDO), CDS index products, and many more. The thing they have in common is that at least one of the underlying variables refers to credit risk event. A more detailed explanation of the structure of derivatives is beyond the scope of this book. What follows simply highlights some of the important characteristics of derivatives that we will revisit later when we discuss marketplace lending.

There are three main counterparties involved in credit derivatives: the *obligor* (also called borrower) who is linked to the underlying credit exposure; the *protection buyer* (e.g., the lender), who is exposed to the associated credit risk; and the *protection seller* who provides insurance protection against a credit event and receives a premium. The protection seller guarantees the credit exposure against credit events and covers credit losses that occur, as specified in the derivative agreement. Figure 10.5 illustrates the main elements and simple structure of credit derivatives.

In a sense, the protection seller is acting as a guarantor, agreeing to insurance against a predefined credit event. However, it is sometimes unknown whether such an insurer will be able to fulfill the agreed insurance obligations. On the other hand, protection sellers may have an unclear understanding of the credit exposure and the credit status of the obligors linked to underlying credit exposures. A typical instrument that has fallen into this issue is the collateralized debt obligation (CDO) square financial products, which had rather high degrees of fuzziness in regards to the underlying exposures and credit quality of the protected counterparties.

Credit derivatives may have rules that are more flexible in regards to the counterparty credit events' definitions including, for instance, the credit event of default or downgrading

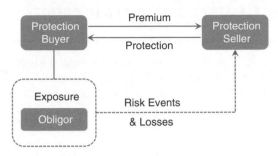

FIGURE 10.5 Simple diagram illustrating the main elements and structure of credit derivatives

of the counterparty rating status. Thus, it is very important that in credit derivatives contracts there is a precise definition of the credit risk events as well as a way to determine[1] when these occur.

Unlike the other types of credit enhancements, where cash flows appear only in a credit event occurrence (i.e., default), in credit derivatives a steady cash flow of the premium, paid to the protection seller, must be considered and counted as an expense. Moreover, credit events, including defaults, upgrades and downgrades, also cause changes in the market pricing which result in downstream gains or losses in a mark-to-market[2] accounting regime.

As mentioned above, there are several credit derivatives in the market. The type(s) of the underlying instruments, the status of the counterparties and the definition of the credit events may increase the complexity in regard to the analysis. Financial institutions are always inventing and structuring new credit derivatives for insuring their credit portfolios and mitigating financial risks. We all know by now how investment banks use this reasoning when packaging subprime loans, turning them into AAA-rated investments. We may witness history repeating itself, right in front of our eyes, with structured portfolios of loans issued from the marketplace lending environment.

10.3.4 Lack of credit enhancements in marketplace lending exposures

The world of marketplace lending is devoid of credit enhancements, such as collateral, that may shield investors against counterparty risk and credit losses. Marketplace lenders have stripped away those processes that make bank lending tedious and hard to comply with. Currently, marketplace lending platforms have very nimble operations and are hardly in a position to assess and accept collateral for their loans. For this reason, loans originated on marketplace lending platforms are entirely uncollateralized. When lenders diversify across several loans[3] the lack of collateral may not result in large losses in a loan portfolio. At the same time, if marketplace lenders wish to play in the big league with banks, they need to graduate into the realm of real estate credit. This will require a rethink of their business model and practices. When they have to assess collateral, this will most definitely result in larger overheads, and regulatory requirements for compliance. At this point, marketplace lenders become more like banks. It is uncertain how their loan origination will change when they make the jump.

10.4 ADDITIONAL ELEMENTS CONSIDERED IN CREDIT ENHANCEMENTS

In the identification and analysis of credit enhancements, credit institutions must also consider the possibility of double default—of both obligor and guarantor—the specific and general wrong way risks which can be also be linked with double default, the maturity mismatch between the exposure and the collaterals, as well as the dependencies of contracts and counterparties via credit enhancements.

10.4.1 Double default

A double default occurs when both the obligor (lender) and the guarantor default at the same time. Even though a guarantor promised to cover losses in case of a default, he may find himself/herself without the necessary capital to fulfill this obligation in times of need. When large parts of the market are under stress, the risk of double default is at its highest. A few additional considerations with double default are important.

Credit enhancements are directly or indirectly linked to counterparties. Guarantors on guarantee agreements and protection sellers in credit derivatives are counterparties who agree to cover losses stemming from counterparty credit risk. Most financial collaterals, except commodities, are also linked to counterparties; which implies that any downgrading will affect the value of the bond.

With the help of credit enhancements, banks migrate the risk, directly or indirectly, from the obligor to a third counterparty. In the case of counterparty-based credit enhancements, direct mitigation of the counterparty risk is applied. Thus, institutions treat the credit exposure as if it were an exposure from the guarantor rather than from the original creditor. Depending on the type of credit enhancement, we should consider the following cases:

1. Obligor (borrower) defaults or downgrades; guarantor or protection seller is capable of recovering the agreed amount of the corresponding losses.
2. Guarantor downgrades (at a lower degree of credit rating than the obligor), or defaults; obligor is still fulfilling the agreed obligations; as there is no credit event, no loss needs to be recovered. As the guarantee contract is invalid, the net exposure is estimated by excluding the collateralized amount agreed by the downgraded or defaulted guarantor or protection seller.
3. Double default: both the obligor and the guarantor or protection seller default. The credit exposure that the guarantor agreed to cover is now an additional, to net exposure, actual credit loss.

In the analysis of double default, we should make two different assumptions about correlations between the parties:

1. The two parties, obligor and guarantor or protection seller, are independent of each other; thus, the likelihood of double default is expected to be rather low. Statistically, the joint default probability is defined as $PD_{double\ default} = PD_{obligor} \cdot PD_{guarantor}$.
2. There is correlation between the two parties. That is, the same or correlated risk factors influence them at the time of default of the obligor. This case falls into general wrong way risk, which we will discuss later.

We can also apply the above combinations and analysis in a similar way with asset-based credit enhancements, for example:

1. Only the obligor (borrower) defaults but not the asset-based credit enhancements, therefore the asset recovers the credit losses.
2. Only the counterparty linked to the asset defaults, but not the obligor. Net exposure does not consider the defaulted asset.
3. Double default, this is both the obligor and the asset defaulting at the same time. The remaining net exposure, excluding the defaulted asset, will be the actual loss.

The assumption that the underlying risk factors linked to the obligor and asset-based credit enhancements are independent can be risky. Indeed, under general wrong way risk, a strong dependency exists. Moreover, when financial collateral belongs to the obligor, additional expected losses are indicated. This gives rise to additional types of risks named specific and general wrong way risk as discussed in the following section.

10.4.2 Wrong way risk

Another special type of risk is so-called wrong way risk. This risk has to do with identifying and measuring the *unfavorable dependency* between the counterparties' default probability with the current and future credit exposures. This dependency can be direct, which we describe as specific wrong way risk. When the dependency is indirect, we speak of general wrong way risk. In both kinds of wrong way risk there is a direct and indirect link correspondingly between the obligor (e.g., borrower), with the collateral attached to the credit exposure.

Let us imagine a case where a corporate borrows an amount A and uses, as financial collateral, its own stocks or other assets that have a value C. The resulting net exposure, estimated as $N = A - C$, is under specific wrong way risk. This is because if the corporate downgrades or defaults the value of the applied collateral will be changed, i.e., reduced, and adjusted accordingly to $C_{adjusted}$. In fact, the net exposure changes to $N = A - C_{adjusted}$ due to the obligor's change of credit status.

The size of credit exposure under specific wrong way risk is often not fully transparent; indeed, there could be cases[4] with an additional degree of complexity to the one mentioned in the above example. Normally, practitioners and regulators[5] focus on exposures where there is a legal connection between the obligor and the counterparty linked to the underlying credit enhancement(s). There are examples where collateral does not directly belong to the obligor but to a third party that has a legal connection with the obligor (for instance, a parent company).

The identification of general wrong way risk is usually more complex than the specific one. Such risk usually arises when the counterparty credit status of the obligor is dependent on the market conditions referenced to credit enhancements applied to the credit exposure. A typical case in this category is the use of collateral stocks or indexes belonging to the same sector as the obligor; assuming that the obligor has no strong idiosyncratic sensitivity, we expect that both obligor credit status and such collateral value will deteriorate synchronously. Another instance would be when an obligor, such as a financial institution, is using governmental bonds. In practice, there is an alliance between the downgrading of the governmental bonds and financial institutions belonging to the same country/region. In fact, there are several financial instruments[6] affected by general wrong way risk.

We can therefore say that general wrong way risk indicates the unfavorable dependencies between the counterparty's credit quality, i.e., rating, with general market risk factors. Such factors could be the region, industry, sector, and other categories that are germane to the descriptive characteristics of the counterparty. Moreover, the idiosyncratic strength of the counterparty and the degree of sensitivities against the market risk factors, discussed in Chapter 7, are essential parameters used in the identification of general wrong way risk.

10.4.3   Maturity mismatch and payment times

The duration where the credit enhancements are valid plays an important role in exposure and credit loss analysis. Imagine a case where a financial collateral, such as a bond, matures in six months covering an exposure that matures in one year. This means that for the first six months in the calculation of the net exposure, we can consider this collateral but not for the last six months. Thus, the maturity mismatch between an exposure and recognized credit enhancements must be well identified and considered.

How should one deal with maturity mismatch? One way is to try to quantify the mismatch in advance and monitor it closely for each particular exposure. However, this is complex and tedious. For this reason, institutions may apply adjustment factors[7] at the portfolio level for approximating the maturity mismatch.

Another important variable to consider is time: the point-in-time where the credit enhancement will recover the credit losses. Thus, for the financial assets the degree of market liquidity, discussed in Chapter 12 (Liquidity, Value, Income, Risk and New Production), plays a key role; that is, liquid assets can be liquidated almost after the default event whereas illiquid assets introduce time delays. The payments from the guaranties have further uncertainties in regards to time; legal issues and administrating processes may also cause unexpected delays.

10.4.4   Contracts and counterparties dependencies via credit enhancements

As we have seen, different types of credit enhancements are attached to a single or several counterparties and/or to specific contract exposure(s). This means that due to credit enhancements there may be dependencies between different contracts and counterparties. Technically speaking, such dependencies are usually mapped by grouping them using multidimensional matrixes.[8] Thus, as can be seen in Figure 10.6, if counterparty CP_B ensures the exposure for contract L_1 of counterparty CP_A through a guarantee GAR_1 and L_1 is also covered by a financial collateral bond B_1, which belongs to CP_C, then CP_B, GAR_1, contract L_1, bond B_1 and CP_C belong to the same group. Groups are useful to measure and report the counterparty and contract dependencies.

10.5   EXTENDING CREDIT ENHANCEMENTS IN MARKETPLACE LENDING

Just as in the established credit sector, credit enhancements in marketplace lending take two principal forms: securitization via simple to advanced credit derivatives, and use of collaterals. Securitizing credit portfolios originating from marketplace lending platforms have some additional challenges. We know that many counterparties who are applying for credit

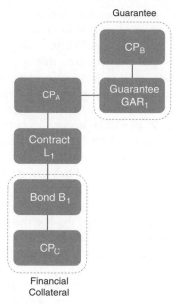

FIGURE 10.6 Example of applying multiple credit enhancements in a credit exposure

using marketplace lending systems may be those with limited or no other access to credit from established financial institutions. This implies that the expected default rate is higher. In addition, as marketplace lending is most attractive when markets are volatile, some additional market and behavior risks will have an additional impact on counterparty risk.

The above gives rise to products for securitizing bundles of loans provided by marketplace lending; e.g. against counterparty defaults and credit losses, which can then be sliced into "tranches" and sold to the market. By securitizing their portfolios, marketplace lenders can allow creditors access to funding for loans at lower rates. Banks, including Citigroup, Capital One, Bank of Montreal, Barclays and Deutsche Bank, are exploring how to finance or securitize such loans into large bundles that can then be sold to big investors.[9] Even though the loan volumes that marketplace lending platforms originate are still small, they nonetheless feed into the relatively unregulated and opaque shadow banking sector. There is a fear that credit institutions outside of the formal financial sector may end up repeating the mistakes that helped fuel the subprime mortgage crisis.

On the other hand, financial collateral and other types of guaranties have not been used so far. In other words, credit exposures are fully *un*collateralized. This means that lenders are exposed to the full amount of the principal provided to borrowers, which equates to expected credit losses. This also implies a higher default probability, especially under stress conditions, as the willingness and priority for fulfilling the agreed-upon obligations is expected to be less than in instances where collateral is in place. In simple terms, when obligors post a valuable asset as collateral, they make a strong effort to keep the promise, even in times of stress. In any event, guarantors prefer not to have to cover credit losses and are therefore enforcing obligors to fulfil their obligations. For this reason, when valuable collateral is in the mix, borrowers have skin in the game and loans perform better across the board.

Alternative ways to attach credit enhancements in marketplace lending credit exposures could be also applied. Let's look at some of them in more detail in the following paragraphs. Before we do this, let's agree on the fact that virtually anything could in theory serve as collateral for a loan as long as both parties agree that it is valuable. For collateral to be valuable—which is a prerequisite for it to serve effectively as a credit enhancement—the borrower needs to have an attachment to the asset he pledges as a security for a loan. Of course, the most obvious choice here is real estate. Borrowers will be in real pain when the bank forecloses on their house, so they will in most instances go the extra mile to avoid repossession. Another prerequisite for collateral is a recognized and indisputable value. If an asset has no value whatsoever, it will yield no additional cash flows when it should compensate for cash flows that a default has cancelled out. When the value is in the eye of the beholder, similar issues arise. For example, someone may see enormous value in his collection of vinyl records, but objectively assessing and transferring this value to a new owner will be a challenge. A situation may exist where both the lender and the borrower agree to accept collateral that is hard to value and enter into a contract. For the sake of argument, we will only focus on situations where the value of collateral is relatively straightforward. Whenever there is an official record, such as in a real estate registry, or a contract that outlines fees and services, collateral will be easier to value. Also important is that existing analytics apply to new kinds of collateral. With the examples we discuss here, this would be possible. We should classify collateral into asset-based and counterparty-based, and then feed them into the same analytics that already exist with more conventional kinds of collateral.

With this in mind, let's think about other situations where potential collateral has both characteristics—attachment and value. Examples we will discuss here are real estate, phone contracts, membership points, life insurance, and personal guarantors.

10.5.1   Real estate titles

Just as in established mortgage finance, real estate is a powerful asset-based credit enhancement that can provide security for lenders against default. We won't go into the mechanics of this here, also because real estate is already widely accepted as credit enhancement in deals. Still, for marketplace lenders to accept real estate as collateral, they will have to change their business model significantly. At this point, most platforms have purely digital processing of cash flows with a limited capacity for servicing physical collateral. Their structure for contracts is relatively simple and standardized. When real estate enters the picture, this has to change. Marketplace lenders have to add a physical component to their operations, where they have to manage recoveries more closely. Accepting real estate is therefore a low priority for most platforms, even for the big ones. Nevertheless, in small and closely regulated markets, accepting real estate comes with fewer obstacles. Their high valuations aside, the real estate markets in, for example, Hong Kong, Singapore, and Switzerland are closely regulated and relatively transparent. Marketplace lenders in these markets may have a better opportunity to accept real estate titles as physical collateral than those in fragmented and opaque markets.

10.5.2   Phone contracts as stores of value

Other situations where people have stores of value or commitments sitting in accounts unused are more common than we think. A mobile phone, for instance, may have a certain number of minutes of airtime or bandwidth available either in a long-term contract or in prepaid plan. These minutes can serve as collateral and asset-based credit enhancement for any loans a counterparty may take out. If this seems ridiculous, just think about it from a different angle: Apple lists the price of the iPhone 6 between $199 and $399 with a two-year contract at the time of this writing. The device is quite useless unless you connect it to a mobile network and data, and the cost of doing so is far less transparent. In the U.S., depending on the operator, two years of iPhone use costs between $470 and $1,120.[10] Any smart phone contract has therefore a potential value of up to $900. Imagine now that a phone company made loans from marketplace lending available to their subscribers. As a requirement for borrowers, it could demand they pre-pay their accounts partially, and it could take the device as physical collateral. The company could then relatively easily net the value of subscribers' contracts with their loans. If a borrower is late, the phone company simply forfeits the prepaid amount to the borrower and turns off the phone service. When a loan defaults, the company could repossess the phone. We can also imagine a situation where borrowers and lenders connect on a platform operated by a third party, independent from the phone company. For this to work, the phone company should recognize that subscribers may want to use their accounts as loan collateral, so it could offer a service to process collateral assignment and transfers of contracts to new owners.

Does this seem far-fetched to you? Perhaps in the developed world, but in emerging markets, there exists a vibrant market for pre-owned smart phones with stalls selling them at most shopping malls. Mobile payments made on cell phones and smart phones have already taken off. Large players like Apple and Google have entered the mobile payments market, but functional services have been in operation for many years already. For example, take M-Pesa, a mobile-phone based money transfer service launched by Vodafone in 2007 in Kenya and Tanzania. Now also available in Afghanistan, South Africa, India, and Eastern Europe, M-Pesa allows users with a national ID card to deposit, withdraw, and transfer money easily with a mobile device.[11] Mobile payments extend financial services to the so-called "unbanked," up to 50 per cent of the world's adult population.[12] These services could expand their offering from payment to lending and, because they have collateral built into their existing business model, may actually be ideal candidates to do so. Of course, it is a stretch to use $10 or even $100 in collateral for a loan that is many times that amount. But for small loans that cover single small expenses, it may suffice.

We realize that thinking of collateral in this way might be a bit of a stretch. Most people would hardly recognize a cell phone contract as collateral, and a $900 value seems paltry compared to the size of most loans. We won't even go into the headache and switching cost that is currently in place with most phone companies. However, to imagine new ways of extending credit, let's put these doubts aside for a minute and explore some ideas without pretending we have all the answers. Not all ideas will be brilliant, but at least they will form a basis for the discussion in the third part of this book where we will explore solutions for the hybrid financial sector. Of course, there needs to be an additional infrastructure in place for this new kind of collateral to serve as a feasible and credible credit enhancement. For example, phone companies need to have a process for "liquidating" contracts in case of a default. We will skip this discussion in this book. Regardless, we should recognize that the ancillary infrastructure also yields business opportunities in the hybrid financial sector. Just as mortgages need a servicer who deals with the physical property, new assets pledged as collateral will only work when the market has processes in place to liquidate or transfer them.

10.5.3 Loyalty points

Just as in the example with the phone contract, loyalty points could serve as some kind of asset-based credit enhancement. Most people collect membership points of some kind, be it airline miles, points from paying with a credit card, or loyalty points from a grocery chain. The evolution of such points is a simple form of analytics to see the performance of a counterparty. When someone has many points, we can get a picture of that person quite easily. Just imagine someone who has amassed 1 million air miles: you immediately have a picture of that person as a cool frequent flyer who zips in and out of airport lounges and flies at least business class, or first on upgrades. Naturally, this person must have a high-paying job, perhaps as an executive or successful entrepreneur. One glance at the point score triggers all these associations. This is much more efficient than reading between the lines of a person's salary history or job description. There already exist several marketplaces for loyalty points. Several companies specialize in loyalty commerce transactions with the goal of enhancing the monetization of loyalty currencies, including airlines and hotel chains.[13]

When a lender and a borrower connect through a marketplace lending platform, loyalty points could serve as collateral. They could easily transfer to the lender in case of delinquency or default. Of course, a borrower would have to find a lender to whom such collateral is valuable, but isn't this what marketplace lending is all about? When lenders and borrowers agree that a certain number of membership points fulfils the requirements for collateral in a default event, they have a deal. Again, servicing and facilitating the transfer of points is another story that still needs to be streamlined.

10.5.4 Life insurance

Most people have insurance of some kind, with life insurance policies being the most valuable. Life insurance already serves as collateral in credit agreements, and some businesses will accept life insurance as collateral. Processes to assign the policy to another party are already in place. A collateral assignment of a life insurance policy appoints a lender as the beneficiary of an insurance benefit. If the borrower fails to pay back a loan, the lender can cash in the life insurance policy and recover the outstanding loan balance. If a borrower passes away before repaying the loan in full, the lender receives the amount owed out of the death benefit. The remaining balance then goes to other listed beneficiaries. Such an arrangement effectively insures lenders against credit risk.

Lenders can accept any kind of life insurance policy for asset-based credit enhancement as long as the insurance company allows assignment of the policy. A permanent life insurance policy with a cash value is the most useful credit enhancement because it allows the lender access to cash immediately without having to wait for the policy to pay off. For this to work, the owner of the policy should have restricted access to the cash in the insurance policy to protect the collateral as long as the loan is current. As soon as the loan has been repaid, any restrictions or assignment to a third party are removed and the lender has no more claims on the insurance payouts. Not all insurance companies like to deal with collateral assignment and they are often slow to update changes of beneficiaries. Still, life insurance would be an ideal asset that should enhance the quality of loans significantly.

10.5.5 Guarantor systems

The ability and willingness to pay back a loan can drastically improve when a third party guarantees to step in to cover losses or exert pressure on delinquent borrowers. In small villages, for example, people lend to each other more efficiently than to strangers. When all people know each other well and do business with each other on a regular basis, a loan default will have repercussions that borrowers need to avoid at all costs to save their social standing in the community. Many societies use guarantor systems, most prominently the Japanese. When renting a flat in Japan, the leasee, the landlord, the real estate agent, and a personal guarantor are necessary to complete the contract. Without the personal guarantor in the deal, no transaction takes place. The leasee and the guarantor are jointly responsible for liabilities to the landlord that may arise. If a leasee fails to pay the rent, the landlord can legally seek payment for rent from the guarantor. This arrangement goes still farther: if the lease causes any trouble with neighbors, the guarantor steps in as an intermediator. Traditionally, family ties and other strong relationships served as guarantors. However, being on the hook for the behavior of a third party can quickly become a headache for a guarantor and, naturally, an industry has formed to turn this pain into profit. Guarantor services for rental contracts are available for a fee; typically one month of rent and an annual fee of 10,000 yen (about US$80 at the time of this writing).[14] It is easy to see how this arrangement could extend to providing personal guarantees for borrowers as well.

In corporate credit, guarantees are common. Typically, a related entity such as a parent company guarantees for loans of a subsidiary. When measuring net exposure, contracts with a guarantee become much stronger with very low default rates. The guarantor pushes a borrower to perform. In addition to asset-based and counterparty-based credit enhancement, guarantor systems use pressure on the counterparty to get them to comply with loan agreements.

Even though banks can use counterparty-based credit enhancements to shift the net exposure entirely to another party at no cost to them, guarantor systems come with a cost for borrowers. When formal ties or family ties exist, using guarantor systems may look like asking for a favor, but the economic cost can be significant. Unless a guarantor has an incentive to provide a guarantee, he will rarely shoulder the risk of having to step up to the plate when there is a default. A system that relies on guarantors to altruistically help their fellow community members will ultimately fail. Unless a deal fairly compensates all parties involved, the system will eventually unravel. When a third-party provides trust to a borrower, the system can become fuzzy very quickly. Guarantor systems therefore have more in common with insurance than actual trust. When insurance is not readily available, asset-based credit enhancements are therefore stronger than those relying on a counterparty.

10.6 CONCLUDING REMARKS

Everybody agrees that credit enhancements are a wonderful tool to mitigate risk and reduce net credit exposure. Let's summarize what they do and why they are important. In regard to analytics, the asset-based credit enhancements (i.e., financial collaterals and close out netting), are driven by both market and credit risk factors. This implies that market fluctuations and counterparty risk can directly influence the credit exposures and credit losses. On the other hand, counterparty analysis is applied to guarantors and credit derivatives. Even though credit enhancements have great impact in exposure analysis, some important issues must be attended to, including the probability of double default, the identification and measurement of specific and general wrong way risk, and the management of maturity mismatch and time of default event. Even though the great majority of credit portfolios issued by the credit institutions are attached to credit enhancements, in the marketplace lending model they are missing. Some alternative approaches for using financial collaterals and guarantor systems are proposed in this chapter.

After all, credit enhancements are vital when mitigating credit risk exposure, minimizing and absorbing the credit losses and aiming to keep the financial system and markets steady. Therefore, they consume a great part of management and financial analysis. Both credit financial institutions and regulators ensure that most of the credit exposures are linked, fully or partially, with credit enhancements. The construction, selection and management of all types of credit enhancements play an essential role in counterparty credit risk management.

NOTES

1. For instance the U.S. and European CDS Indices define credit events differently: for the U.S. indices, only bankruptcy and failure to pay trigger a default; restructuring is not deemed a credit event, even though most underlying single-name CDS contracts treat restructuring as a credit event; European indices trade with the same credit events as the underlying CDS contracts, including modified restructuring, bankruptcy, and failure to pay.
2. Book value accounting ignores these.
3. For instance, market leader Lending Club recommends they diversify across at least 100 contracts.
4. E.g., credit default swaps.
5. See BIS paper BCBS189 §101/58.
6. E.g., Interest Rate Contracts, cross-currency swap, FX Contracts, Commodity SWAP, etc.
7. Adjustment factors are also proposed by regulatory bodies.
8. Referred to also as "grapes."
9. Eaglewood Capital, a New York-based hedge fund manager, completed a $53 million securitization of Lending Club loans in October 2013 in a first-of-its-kind transaction. A large global reinsurance company bought all the senior tranches.
10. Bott, Ed (2014) "How much does an iPhone 6 really cost? (Hint: It's way more than $199)" (ZDNet, 18 September 2014), http://www.zdnet.com/article/how-much-does-an-iphone-6-really-cost-hint-its-way-more-than-199/.
11. M-Pesa (2014a) home page, https://www.mpesa.in, accessed 12 November 2014.
12. Demirguc-Kunt, Asli; Klapper, Leora (2012) "Measuring Financial Inclusion" (World Bank, Policy Research Working Paper 6025, April 2012), http://elibrary.worldbank.org/doi/pdf/10.1596/1813-9450-6025.
13. Points.com (2015a), website, https://www.points.com/.
14. University of Tokyo (2015a) Japanese Culture specific Guarantor System, http://dir.u-tokyo.ac.jp/en/topics/0804housing/1-06.html.

CHAPTER 11

Systemic and Concentration Risks

Systemic and concentration risks play a significant role in the stability of the financial system. We analyze these types of risk based on the direct and indirect interlinkages among counterparties and credit exposures. Systemic risk analysis can be a complex process. This is because a full analysis of the possible chain reactions among counterparties and exposures, after the default or downgrading credit event, is necessary. Concentration risk can cause high losses and may heavily affect the financial system within a short period. In this chapter, we discuss systemic and concentration risks that arise from credit exposure and counterparties.

As we will explain in this chapter, there are cases where contracts are linked directly or indirectly to several counterparties or other exposures; many counterparties or contracts can also be linked to a single exposure or counterparty. Such cases indicate systemic and/or concentration risk. Financial loans from marketplace lending are attached to many obligors; in other words, many counterparties are linked to a single exposure and underlying counterparty. At the same time, loans may have exposure to very similar counterparties who might act identically under stress. Yet it is unclear how exactly this may impact the financial system. Investors in marketplace loans should therefore think about potential exposure to counterparty risk and the mitigation of this risk.

11.1 CREDIT EXPOSURE SYSTEMIC RISK

Interlinkages and interdependencies of credit exposures can cause systemic risk. This can arise when a credit event of a single exposure or cluster[1] of exposures, causes cascading credit events that ripple through other exposures. Credit events are the default or downgrading of the underlying counterparties linked to the credit exposure. These are the obligor of the exposure and may also be the guarantor or protection seller covering part of the exposures via counterparty credit enhancements, as we explained in Chapter 10.

As we will discuss in Chapter 12 about the principles of the treasury model, banking institutions are acting as investors via their lending activities. Moreover, as we explained in Chapter 7 they are also obligors because they are borrowing capital via, for instance, inter-banking and retail markets. Finally, banks can take on a third role: they may also act as guarantors and protections sellers, for example, by offering derivative products.

Exposures may default or not, but change their value due to the obligor's credit distress, i.e., downgrading. In both cases, the defaulted or downgraded exposures may affect the value and counterparties of the credit enhancements that they are also attached to. In addition, both investors and obligors attached to these exposures suffer a sequence of losses. Finally, they may affect other exposures sharing the same counterparties or by using the defaulted or downgraded exposures as credit enhancements. The following two sections describe the main chain reactions after default and downgrading credit events.

11.1.1 Chain reactions after default credit event

A default credit event of the obligor's credit exposure may trigger the following sequence of defaults, downgrading and losses to other exposures and counterparties as is explained in more details in the following paragraphs.

1. The credit enhancements have to be exercised; thus, considering that there is no specific wrong way risk:[2]
   a. The asset based credit enhancements will be most likely under liquidation, at short term, covering the credit losses. Indeed, a liquidation of high volume of assets, e.g., stocks or bonds, especially under stress market conditions will influence negatively their market value. In other words, market liquidity risk may be the result, which will increase the actual net exposure and credit losses.

      When those types of assets are also used as collaterals to other exposures it will directly affect their exposure at default.

      Moreover, under stress market conditions, the loss of the assets' market value may influence the credit status of the underlying counterparties that they belong to. This may result in further systemic counterparty risk as the influenced counterparty will affect all other exposures that it is linked to.
   b. In the counterparty-based credit enhancements, the guarantor or protection seller will be asked to cover the credit losses. These losses may impact any other exposures that the guarantor or protection seller may be linked to. In other words, they may negatively influence their credit rating which can result in higher risk and expected credit losses.

      Overall, as illustrated in Figure 11.1, the systemic elements of credit enhancements are the counterparties, market liquidity and credit losses.
2. In the event of credit default, the investors (e.g., lenders) will have a credit loss equal to the loss given default as explained in Chapter 9. However, where the recovery is negligible or is not expected within a short term, the credit loss is equal to the net exposure, i.e., EAD defined in Chapter 9. Moreover, the defaulted exposure will result in funding liquidity risk, discussed in Chapter 12, due to the cancelation of the contractual expected cash flows.

   Banks are not only acting as investors but also as obligors to other exposures. Thus, the losses in value and liquidity of the defaulted contract that they are exposed to, may influence their capability to fulfil their future obligations, i.e., against the outstanding loans and/or derivative contracts that they are committed to. In such cases, banks have to use their own capital buffers[3] liquidating their own assets, which may affect their market value. Where such a buffer is not sufficient, the bank may default or get downgraded, which impacts systemically all of its outstanding exposures and credit enhancements which they are linked to. Such distress will also influence the continuity of the future

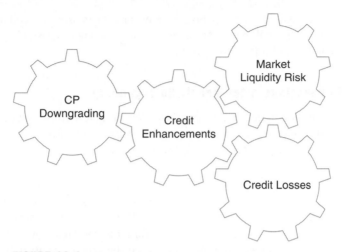

FIGURE 11.1 Credit enhancements are linked counterparties, market liquidity and credit losses

business and relative credit exposures. Most possibly however, financial institutions are getting bailouts, for avoiding default but not downgrading events, which turns to systemic risk and loss distribution within the markets,[4] i.e., exposing markets to the defaulted credit portfolios.

Figure 11.2 illustrates the systemic elements referring to investors.

3. The obligors (e.g., the borrower) of the defaulted exposure will increase the probability to default and thus the credit spreads of the other exposures that they are linked to. As a result, the value of these exposures will be reduced. Moreover, both changes in default probability and value of the exposure will further increase the expected credit loss.

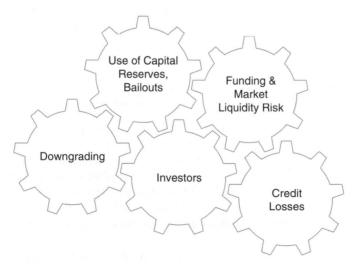

FIGURE 11.2 Systemic elements referring to investors

4. The defaulted exposures, such as bonds, may have been used as collaterals to other exposures. Thus, there will be direct impact on the linked net exposures, increasing their expected credit losses for the investor(s).

11.1.2   Chain reactions after credit downgrading

In the event of credit downgrading the probability for default and the corresponding credit spread of the credit exposure increases, whereas the actual value of the exposure is reduced. Thus, a chain of events may happen in the following ways:

1. Where such exposure, e.g., governmental or corporate bond, is used as asset-based credit enhancements the loss of value will directly impact the linked net exposures.
2. The expected credit losses, for the investors (e.g., lenders) of these downgraded exposures will be increased and therefore there is a need for more capital adequacy/buffer that may be used against these losses; this may introduce the employment of limits in further exposures and business development.

    In addition, if the investors are also obligors, such credit distress will possibly increase the default probability causing possible further impact to all credit exposures that are linked to.
3. The increase in default probabilities and spreads implies that the obligor is downgraded. Thus all other exposures linked to such an obligor will increase the probability of default, credit spreads and expected credit losses, and reduce the market value of these exposures.
4. Any counterparty based credit enhancements (e.g., credit derivatives) will be exercised against value change of the exposure due to the rise of credit spread (downgrading event). Thus, the protection sellers, who may also be playing the role of obligor, may go through financial distress.

The analysis of systemic risk, based on credit events, may be a complex exercise, as it involves most financial analysis elements, as illustrated in Figure 11.3. However, it is very important for managing efficiently the credit exposures and ensuring robustness of the entire financial system against financial risks.

11.2   COUNTERPARTY SYSTEMIC RISK

Counterparty systemic risk appears where a failure of an individual or a cluster[5] of counterparties impact a great majority of the other counterparties that are directly or indirectly linked. This implication can range from the downgrade of a credit rating to a credit default event, which can result in a collapse of the entire value of credit portfolios. As we have observed, during the crisis of 2007/8, the great majority of portfolios had significant losses which were due to downgrading rather than to default events. However, what should we consider in systemic risk portfolio value and liquidity analysis and where do market counterparty and behavior characteristics play a role?

In counterparty systemic risk analysis, the degree of *correlations* among counterparties in regards to their credit worthiness (expressed as credit ratings) should be identified. In

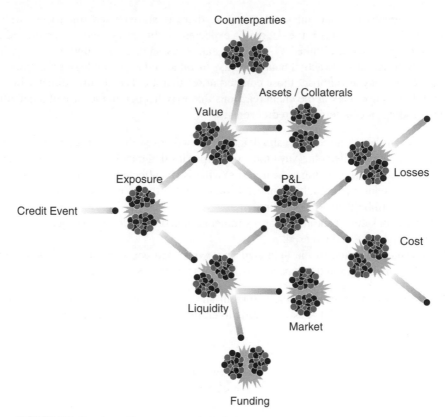

FIGURE 11.3 A credit event, e.g., default, in an exposure may cause a chain systemic risk reaction

such correlation analysis we need to identify whether and how an event of a counterparty's downgrades or defaults will influence the degree of other counterparties' *credit rating*. The most applicable way of performing such analysis is to consider the common and correlated market risk factors where counterparties are linked. This linkage is defined by analyzing the counterparties' *sensitivities* to these factors as discussed in Chapter 7. Typically, such factors are market indices, e.g., referring to the business sectors, currency, etc., to which the counterparty belongs. Thus, we should also consider the corresponding volatilities and correlations among these market risk factors. In addition, the *idiosyncratic* sensitivities, which indicate the level of the counterparty's strength to have the least sensitivity with the index factors, are also considered. Sensitivity profiles are behavior driven parameters and they are defined based on statistical observations together with expertise assumptions; thus, they are subject to change in the future.

Counterparties can be interlinked and interdependent of an event on a single counterparty or cluster of counterparties. This may systematically cause credit events on the other counterparties and exposures that they are linked to. As we already know in a loan contract, we typically need to consider three types of counterparties: the investor (the lender), the obligor (the borrower), and the guarantor or protection seller.

When counterparties default or downgrade, there is an expected impact on the value and size of the net exposures, the degree of expected credit losses, and the credit rating of the counterparties that are linked to it. For instance, as soon as a counterparty of a bond downgrades or defaults, the actual bond decrease in value and expected losses rise; moreover, the credit event may also impact those counterparties that are directly or indirectly linked to this bond. Let us now look at the chain reactions that may happen in the case of a default and the downgrading of counterparty credit events:

- Contracts linked to the counterparty default event will lose value whereas the expected cash flows will be cancelled out. Any other counterparties that may be linked to these contracts (via joint accounts or acting as guarantors) will also be affected. If such contracts are used as credit enhancement, such as financial collateral, to other exposures their corresponding net value will be changed accordingly.
- The net exposures of the financial instruments linked to the defaulted guarantor or protection seller will be increased.
- Counterparties linked to the defaulted or downgraded counterparty may increase their default probability and the expected losses of the contracts they are linked to.

As illustrated in Figure 11.4, the two main views of systemic risk for counterparties are based on identifying the linkages in regards to credit exposures and to other counterparties.

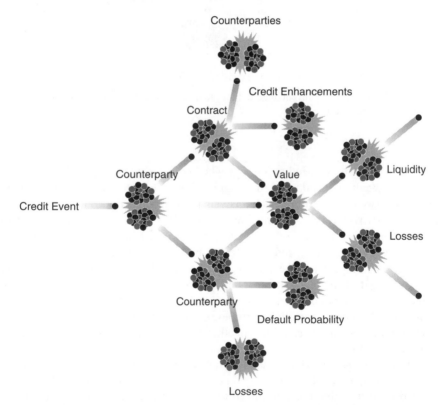

FIGURE 11.4   A credit event, e.g., default, in an exposure may cause a chain reaction of systemic risk

The former is based on exposure analysis of counterparties whereas the latter focuses on their allocation within the markets.

We can estimate the future correlation of the counterparties and corresponding systemic risk by simulating the evolution of the performance of assets and their sensitivity profiles. In such a process, one may simulate the market evolution in the future. We can do this with what-if market scenarios or by throwing the dice for the market conditions by applying Monte Carlo stochastic processes. Then, via the market correlations and sector sensitivities, one can determine the new ratings of the counterparties. A more advanced approach can be applied if, for the future time steps, one also throws the dice or deterministically changes the future ratings of a particular counterparty or a group of counterparties. In this dynamic analysis of the systemic risks, the new (future) counterparties and market conditions (sectors and indices) can also be considered.

11.3 SYSTEMIC RISK EXPOSURES AND LOSSES

The systemic risk losses are defined by analyzing the systemic interaction between the risk factors of particular market sectors, counterparty ratings as well as the sector and idiosyncratic behavior characteristics linked to financial contracts. The unexpected systemic events of the financial contracts, derived from the systemic risk, define the exposures to systemic losses expressed as losses in value, income and liquidity.

In marketplace lending, even though lenders bear all the risk of the loans they fund on lending platforms, the sector may create potential systemic exposures that might become significant. If the sector achieves a significant degree of market share—such as $1 trillion in originations by 2020[6]—then it could become systemic. The fact that returns are satisfactory with few losses under ideal conditions is no guarantee that this will continue under stress conditions. It is therefore sensible to look into exposures and their impact on the financial system beyond individual counterparties.

A high correlation among markets and high degrees of sector sensitivities of the counterparties indicate that the probability of increasing the amount of contacts that are under systemic risk is higher. Even a portfolio where the majority of the interconnected counterparties have low probability of downgrades or resulting default events, under stress conditions, systemic risk losses can be high. This is due to the fact that a small number of counterparties and markets could be vulnerable to stress conditions and thus could directly impact the correlated counterparties and markets that both impact the financial events of the linked financial contracts. Especially when securitizations of marketplace loans increase in size, some investors or funds may concentrate large exposure to the asset class. Because marketplace borrowers may act similarly under stress, such a concentrated exposure might become extremely volatile very quickly. Even a financial entity in the shadow banking sector can become systemic and may need capital injections if a rescue mission is necessary. For instance, the hedge fund Long-Term Capital Management (LTCM), after celebrating returns in the first three years, lost billions in just a few months following the 1997 Asian financial crisis and 1998 Russian financial crisis, and eventually required financial intervention by the U.S. Federal Reserve. Even though funds investing in marketplace loans are still nowhere near the size of LTCM at its peak, the danger for concentration by an unregulated entity exists.

The credit spreads together with the market curves are used to calculate the value and the expected cash flows, expressed as value and liquidity exposures of the financial instruments. In fact, these exposures can be distinguished as the ones where counterparties are holding and the ones that are exchanged. The former indicates the implications in losses of the portfolio value and liquidity in case the counterparty defaults or downgrades. The latter, that is not always available, indicates the degree of systemic exposure and interdependency between the counterparties. For instance, in a portfolio with governmental bonds, the information referring to both types of exposures is available.[7]

Future exposures can be defined based on stochastic process analysis or deterministic assumed market and credit risk factors. Any fluctuation of the exposures due to market volatilities is also considered to define the degree of haircut applied in future exposures. Haircuts can also be used to define the collaterals provided for absorbing future systemic losses. Future systemically correlated exposures are used to estimate the potential systemic losses.

Finally, it is important to bear in mind that the consideration of gross exposures could help to avoid the implications from general and/or specific wrong way risk discussed in Chapter 10.

11.4 CREDIT EXPOSURE CONCENTRATION RISK

In regards to the credit exposure or cluster of exposures belonging to a single portfolio, concentration risk indicates the concentrated interlinkages and interdependencies between the following two factors:

1. Particular exposure or cluster of credit exposures with several
   a. Assets or cluster[8] of assets
   b. Counterparties and/or cluster of them (Figure 11.5(a)).
      For instance, the former case could be when a number of assets (e.g., stocks) are used as collaterals to a single or to a portfolio of exposures; in case of a defaulted exposure such assets will be under immediate liquidation which may impact their value. The latter case could be when a number of counterparties are acting as guarantors or protection sellers to a particular exposure. A default event of such exposure will impact these counterparties.
2. Several credit exposures or clusters of them, linked to particular
   a. Asset or cluster of assets
   b. Counterparty and/or cluster of them (Figure 11.5(b)).
      For example, think of a case where several exposures are collateralized by a single asset or cluster of assets driven by a single market risk factor, e.g., gold commodity; this refers to the above first point. For the second point we could think of a case where many exposures may use a single guarantor/protection seller or cluster of guarantors belonging to the same sector. Finally, assume a more general case where exposures belong to a counterparty with the same or similar credit rating. This could be the case in marketplace lending, especially when ratings converge under stress.

In regards to credit risk analysis, we focus on the default and the non-default but down-grading events of the concentrated elements. In such credit events, the concentrated exposure

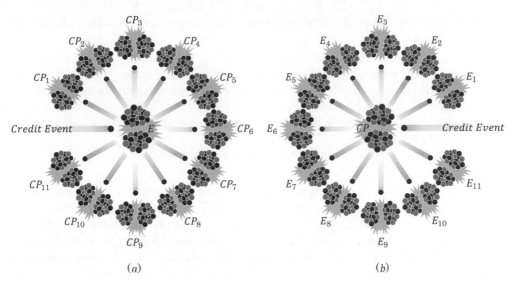

FIGURE 11.5 The impact of a credit event in (a) concentrated credit exposure E linked to n number of counterparties $\{CP_1, CP_2, \ldots CP_n\}$, (b) concentrated counterparty CP linked to n number of credit exposures $\{E_1, E_2, \ldots E_n\}$

will have a direct impact on the concentrated assets and/or counterparties that are directly linked to each other. Thus, all linked counterparties and assets will be impacted directly; for instance where they are used as credit enhancements, they will have to cover the losses of the credit event. A simple way to measure the concentrated risk in regard to credit exposures is by applying the formula[9] as defined in 11.1. H fluctuates between 0 and 1 indicating well diversified and highly concentrated exposures respectively.

$$H = \frac{\sum_i E_{net_i}^2}{(\sum_i E_{net_i})^2} \tag{11.1}$$

In a credit event applied to concentrated asset or counterparty there will be expected losses in the credit exposures that they are linked to. This may be due to a loss in value of the exposure.

The total losses in both cases can be significant and will depend mainly on the type of the event, value of the exposures, the number of the links and the possible systemic risk that may result.

11.5 COUNTERPARTY CONCENTRATION RISK

Counterparties may also be under concentration risk where a single event is expected to cause significant disturbance at the very same time to many counterparties of the financial system.

The analysis of concentration risk is based on the following concentrated interlinkages and interdependencies:

1. Counterparties are concentrated around a particular exposure or cluster of exposures
2. Credit exposures are concentrated around a particular counterparty and/or cluster[10] of counterparties
3. Counterparties are concentrated around a particular central counterparty and/or clusters of counterparties
4. Counterparties are concentrated around a particular market

In the previous paragraphs we have already discussed the first two. In the case of point 3, counterparties are linked to a central counterparty (single or cluster) in a sense that if the central counterparty defaults or downgrades it will immediately impact the interlinked counterparties (see Figure 11.6a). For instance, most banks have a strong correlation to governmental rating status; also several companies may act as suppliers to a big corporate. Where a government and/or a big corporate defaults it will directly impact the rating status of the correlated counterparties.

Finally, as illustrated in Figure 11.6b, counterparties may be exposed to a common market, e.g., business sector of telecoms. As discussed in Chapter 7 (7.6 Link of Counterparties via Markets) several counterparties can be allocated to a single market. Any event in the concentrated sector may cause an immediate impact in surrounding linked counterparties.

Counterparty concentration risk can be minimized by allocating the exposures of the counterparties that have different credit and descriptive characteristics and operate in uncorrelated markets.

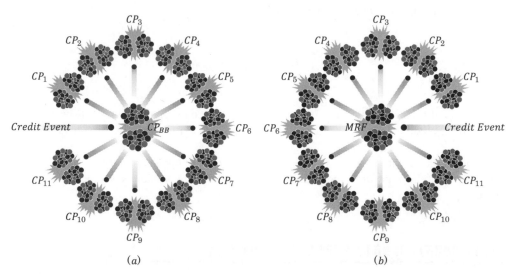

(a)   (b)

FIGURE 11.6   An event to a central counterparty (a) e.g. CP_{BB}, or (b) to a common market risk factor (MRF), may impact the interlinked surrounding n number of counterparties $\{CP_1, CP_2, \ldots CP_n\}$

11.6   SYSTEMIC RISK AND PORTFOLIO DIVERSIFICATION

The degree of systemic and concentration among the counterparties together with the corresponding degree of the corresponding credit exposures define portfolio diversification. Portfolios should be adjusted by considering both systemic and concentration risks. High systemic correlation and exposure or counterparty concentration indicates high risk losses and vice-versa. An optimal portfolio should be balanced based on the systemic and concentration parameters as indicated in this chapter. This is important for loans provided by marketplace lending platforms because they have a tendency to concentrate exposure narrowly. At the same time, they are seemingly allocated across many investors, which might lead regulators to underestimate exposure by one single counterparty. The potential for a large exposure by a single entity exists, especially in light of an uptrend in securitizations of marketplace loans. At the same time, analytics of the asset class in aggregate are lagging behind, which might mask these issues.

Both systemic and concentration risk analysis is based on integrated market, counterparty credit and behavior risk. A diversified portfolio can minimize these risks by applying a contract-based and integrated risk management approach.

11.7   CONCLUDING REMARKS

Systemic risk requires complex analysis. It can be seen from the view of identifying and analyzing the interlinkages and interdependencies of the credit exposures and counterparties where there is an expected chain reaction after default and downgrading credit events. Such events will affect the value of their exposure, which may influence other counterparties, other assets, collaterals and the P&L as well as both market and funding liquidity of the portfolio that it belongs to. Credit risk events to counterparties will have direct impact on the value and liquidity of the financial instruments that they are linked to. Moreover, they may affect other counterparties. As a chain reaction to other exposures and counterparties, systemic risk is expected to cause a significant degree of unexpected losses. Such losses must be well defined and measured quantitatively.

The interlinkages and interdependencies of specific instruments and/or counterparties with other financial instruments and counterparties may cause concentration risk. Indeed, in such a risk a credit event on an exposure and/or counterparty could immediately impact many other counterparties and/or exposures.

In the modelling of both concentration and systemic risks we need to integrate market, credit and behavior risk factors in a sense to understand, identify and measure their correlations and co-movements in both canonical (i.e., expected) and stress (i.e., unexpected) volatile conditions. Then we need to measure their impact in value, income and liquidity. Thus, financial analysis plays a key role in managing concentration and systemic risks.

The participants and credit exposures in marketplace lending may suffer from concentration and systemic risk. We need to understand what would happen to the entire system if certain groups of counterparties fail to fulfil their obligations, and how this would influence the credit quality of other correlated counterparties. What could happen if a contract with certain characteristics (e.g., linked to a number of obligors with a range of credit quality) partially defaulted? What might be the impact to the investors? In fact, in marketplace lending financial contracts, if a borrower defaults, the credit event impacts many lenders.

Indeed, there are many cases referring to systemic and concentration risk, depending on the structure of the contracts and credit portfolios. In this chapter, we have aimed to highlight the main combinations to be considered in building a framework for a complete model to identify and manage these types of risks.

NOTES

1. Clusters can be a group of exposures with a combination of similar characteristics, e.g., have the same contract type, belong to the same portfolio, have the same credit quality, influenced by the same market conditions, etc.
2. Explained in Chapter 10 (Credit Enhancements).
3. E.g., based on Basel regulation a capital adequacy against losses must be held by the financial credit institutions.
4. Via central banks, governments and thus tax payers.
5. Cluster is a group of counterparties that may share similar characteristics, e.g., are linked to the same sector, region, belong to the same credit quality/rating class, have similar descriptive characteristics, etc.
6. Moldow, Charles (2014) *A Trillion Dollar Market By the People, For the People: How Marketplace Lending Will Remake Banking As We Know It.*
7. See for instance the exchange of governmental depths among Euro-Zone countries.
8. Cluster indicates group of assets influenced by the same or similar risk factors, i.e., interest or FX rates, prices, etc.
9. It is based on the Herfindahl index.
10. A cluster of counterparties or assets implies a group of them that share similar characteristics, e.g., have the same credit quality, belong to the same (or correlated) sector, region, etc., influenced by same risk factors, etc.

CHAPTER 12

Liquidity, Value, Income, Risk and New Production

So far, we have been exploring the input financial analysis elements, which are the *market conditions*, *counterparty characteristics* and *behavioral assumptions*. In this part of the book, we will go through the output elements of financial analysis namely *liquidity*, *value*, *income* and their *risk measurements*.

As we discussed in Chapter 5, the centerpiece of the input–output elements is the financial contract. In this chapter, we will go through the financial analysis elements considered in both market and funding liquidity management, their risk measurement and management and the strategies applied to ensure sufficient liquidity. We will see how liquidity management and risk analysis are based on the full integration of all types of financial risk factors. In addition, we will discuss the role of credit enhancements in liquidity management and the different types of liquidity reports. Then we will analyze value and income, which are driven by the referenced risk factors and valuation principles. We will explore their roles in profit and loss analysis and how they affect the strategies of new production. In addition we will illustrate how to measure and manage value and income risks, and how they are used in the management of economic capital as well as their effects in liquidity risk. We will also see how we can adjust risks by using the risk and profitability measurements. We will then explore the applicability of integrated stress testing and stochastic process emphasizing the key points in applying risk management. Then we will discuss all the different elements that define new production including the parameters of strategies, e.g., going concern, portfolio structure, etc., setting of targeting future volumes and their allocations, as well as the types of new financial contracts and counterparties constructing future portfolios. We will then see that the new production must consider and manage liquidity, value, income and risk and future profits and losses by considering the time evolution and dynamics in markets and counterparty risk factors. We will finally explore the key roles of treasury and funds transfer pricing in managing the evolution of new productions, the profit and losses as well as the exposure to financial risks. Figure 12.1 illustrates all the main elements considered in the above mentioned financial analysis.

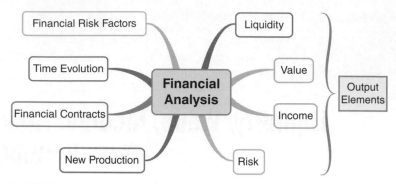

FIGURE 12.1   Main financial analysis elements in regards to liquidity, value, income, risk and new production

12.1   LIQUIDITY

In a sense, a financial contract is a vehicle that carries and shifts cash flows among counterparties. However, too much available liquidity may cause investors additional exposure to risks such as interest rate and price volatilities. Lack of liquidity implies frozen markets where investments cannot move further. The liquidity element is one of the most important analysis elements in finance. As long as cash is flowing as expected the market is performing at a stable status, any other case may cause high disturbances and great losses. When there is too much liquidity in the system, counterparties are in for a bumpy and volatile ride. Conversely, if liquidity freezes, counterparties are stuck without credit and need to wait until the ice thaws again.

As liquidity refers to the past-to-future cash flows, time is a fundamental element in such analysis. There are two main types of generating cash flows, the contractual and the ones resulting from trading activities. The former is leading to funding and the latter to market liquidity analysis whereas their combination provides a full picture of liquidity risk. Moreover, it is the basis of defining the strategies on liquidity management for all types of existing and future development of new financial instruments including credit enhancements. Finally, reporting liquidity provides a strong overview of the cash flow management and precise warnings regarding survivor probabilities to liquidity risk. Figure 12.2 illustrates the main elements of liquidity analysis discussed in this chapter.

FIGURE 12.2   Main elements of market and funding liquidity and their risk management

12.1.1   Financial contracts and liquidity

The basic financial instruments provided, or traded, by banks, are fixed income maturity and non-maturity instruments, stocks, commodities and typical credit risk contracts.[1] Basic instruments can be combined to create synthetic contracts such as swaps and forwards, futures, options, as well as credit risk derivatives, other structured securitization products, etc. The expected cash flows for market participants result from the contractual payments, such as interest, principal, etc., but also from any financial trading activities due, for instance, to sales activities of liquid assets, driven by market expectations. The former refers to funding and the latter to market liquidity. It is also important to remember that the main cash flows from credit enhancements and other derivatives are expected when they are exercised, i.e., for hedging and covering losses.

All expected cash flows depend on whether the counterparties are fulfilling their obligations and whether the market conditions and behavior risk factors are performing as expected. Thus, a default event will cancel out all expected cash flows whereas new cash flows will be generated due to credit enhancements and expected recoveries. The evolution of market conditions will affect the interest cash flows, and the values and prices of the financial instruments. At any time of trading, activities will generate immediate cash flows. Both market and counterparty driven behavior such as drawing, prepayments, recoveries, etc., will directly impact the expected liquidity.

The two main dimensions in liquidity analysis and reports are the time and the evolution of the business that will generate the cash flows. The main views of liquidity analysis are the funding and market liquidity. All are used to project the liquidity reports and identify whether the investment portfolios are producing the expected liquidity.

12.1.2   The time factor and types of analysis in liquidity

Inherently, the element of time is always considered in liquidity financial analysis, classified as *liquidity horizon* defining the time period when cash-flows returns will be considered, e.g., 90 days. As we will explain in the next paragraphs cash flows result from historical, static analysis and dynamic simulation.

In terms of liquidity, historical analysis is used to observe, from the view of a historic horizon, the actual cash flows generated up to the analysis (current) date; moreover, it is also important in *back testing* processes to examine how past market movements and counterparty status and behavior affected the liquidity of the actual cash flow events.

Static analysis examines the future expected cash flows based on the current and assumed performance of all financial risk factors linked to financial contracts, e.g., prices, discount factors, credit spreads, etc., at the current time of analysis. Current and assumed future conditions are considered to value the financial instruments and thus to identify their degree of liquidation in any possible trading activities.

Typically, the expected liquidity of the current investment portfolios and accounts are projected on so-called *static* views of:

- Current positions and the up-to-date expected assumptions of market and economic conditions;
- Current and expected credit status of the counterparty; and
- Expected behavior risk factors.

Dynamic simulation is applied to consider the future evolution of cash flows based on the corresponding evolution of market conditions, counterparty status, behavior assumptions and future business. This implies future changes in the performance of the contracts, investment, trading of the portfolios and accounts through time. This is very much applied in the process of restructuring and building new future portfolios. Indeed, by keeping only the existing financial portfolios the size of investment will roll down as financial contracts mature. In reality, as time passes, new business usually generates growth in portfolios and accounts, whereby the future changing in financial risk factors must be considered.

Financial institutions and investors are applying dynamic simulation for the "going-concern" view, based on new business analysis. In credit portfolios, new business means constructing new loans or rolling over the existing financial instruments. There is a strong link between new production and the projected market conditions, which enables forecasting of the performance of the future financial contracts. Thus, valuation, income and liquidity analysis should be based on the assumed future market and economic conditions and changes in credit spreads. The production of new business is defined by an institution's strategies, policies market/economic and credit risk conditions. This influences future portfolios and accounts and is usually a vital source of future cash flow to support cash out demands. Thus, it needs to be incorporated into the liquidity risk management framework.

12.1.3   Market and funding liquidity risks

Liquidity risk can be thought of in terms of changes in expected contractual cash flows from the existing and future contracts as well as in traded financial contracts. These two initiatives of unexpected cash flows are called funding and market liquidity risks.

Market liquidity risk is about the inability of the financial institution to trade (sell or buy) financial assets of the favorable price at a requested time. For instance, due to unexpected price movements, higher bid-offer spreads and market impacts from trading, the revenues from the sale of assets may be less than expected (or the cost to purchase assets may be greater). Note that market liquidity risk is itself associated with market, counterparty credit and behavior risk factors that may transfer a liquid asset to illiquid; moreover, trading costs tend to be greatest when such factors are most volatile.

In fact market liquidity is very much contingent on the:

- Performance of the financial risk factors
- Strategic trading decisions e.g., for selling and/or buying liquid assets

The expected losses of this type of risk are estimated by comparing the estimated value of the assets under stressed conditions to their value in tranquil conditions. We therefore simply revaluate, let's say, the fair price of financial instruments such as bond type, by discounting back the future cash flows taking into account economic scenarios based on real-world probabilities of market, credit and behavior stress risk conditions. Finally, note that asset-based credit enhancements that are exercised after default time can be heavily impacted by market liquidity risk.

Funding liquidity is about contractual obligations and management of contingent cash flows. Contractual cash flows are conditional on the pre-defined rules, options and algorithmic mechanics applied on the level of the individual financial contracts. Thus the expected cash flows,

- For the *loan contracts*, i.e., from the obligor, are split into the following categories:
  a. Principal payments defined at the contractual agreement (as illustrated in Chapter 5);
  b. Interest payments (as illustrated in Chapter 5) which are derived by the market and credit conditions
- For the *stock* and *indices* are due to expected dividends
- For the *derivative* contracts are predefined premium payments, provided from the protection buyer to protection seller; also, in case of credit event, are the recoveries of financial losses
- For the *options* have been agreed and may be exercised, e.g., prepayments, use of facilities, etc., cash flows may be generated.

Any unexpected changes of the above contractual cash flows—for instance, due to stressed market conditions, counterparty defaults, etc.—will result in unexpected cash flows incurring liquidity contingency issues and possible losses. This will possibly impact the value and thus market liquidity of the financial instruments.

Funding liquidity risk is about the inability of the counterparty to fulfil its contractual funding obligations under expected "normal" and unexpected "extreme" conditions. During normal financial risk conditions the demand for funding liquidity is usually steady. Under extreme conditions, however, some of the expected contractual cash flow: may be cancelled out (perhaps due to a default event), and/or resulted by exercising credit enhancements, or appear unexpectedly (for example, due to prepayments). Moreover, large market movements, for instance, may result in margin calls, changes in the degree of interest income, an increase of default probability, requests for additional collateral, etc. Naturally, there will be an impact on both liquidity and the value of such contracts. In such cases financial institutions may be forced to sell additional liquid assets. To make matters worse, in this type of scenario the (normally) liquid instruments lose their value and may become illiquid,[2] thus they are under market liquidity risk. That is, they cannot be traded quickly enough on the market, at a favorable price, to support liquidity demands or to prevent a loss. Finally, under funding distress the new expected business may shrink.

Practitioners may apply a specific spread against market and funding liquidity risks. They also need to readjust[3] their portfolios based on these types of risks.

In terms of analysis and measurement of liquidity risk, what-if scenarios may be applied for shifting the market conditions to a deterministic degree, whereas Monte Carlo methods may simulate stochastically the fluctuations of the markets, credit ratings, etc., to define the degree of resulting losses. Moreover, liquidity spreads may also be stressed. Thus, analysis due to unexpected conditions and resulting losses is the key element in both market and funding liquidity risk management. Finally, the behavior of sales, driven by idiosyncratic and strategic decisions, also plays a key role in market liquidity; for instance, structuring an inefficient credit portfolio or overselling particular assets may drop their value and turn them to an illiquid level.

In most analyses, funding and market liquidity are integrated due to their close connections. Market liquidity risk often leads to idiosyncratic funding liquidity risk and vice versa. In this context "idiosyncratic" refers to issues unique to the particular firm rather than market-wide liquidity issues. To map such integration, we need first to classify the analysis characteristics of both market and funding liquidity under normal and stress financial conditions and then analyze how and when they interact with each other as indicated in Table 12.1.

The first column/row of Table 12.1 refers to market and funding liquidity respectively; which, as discussed above, is driven by the impact of market and credit risks on value and

TABLE 12.1   Integration of Market and Funding Liquidity

		Funding Liquidity	
		Expected	**Unexpected**
Market Liquidity	**Expected Risk Factors**	Case 1	Case 2
	Stressed Risk Factors	Case 3	Case 4

expected cash flows under normal and stressed conditions. Both static analysis and dynamic simulations can be applied, driven by current and future expectations, producing corresponding cash flows for liquidity analysis. For analyzing stressed conditions, deterministic or stochastic shocks can be applied to risk factors, including changes in spreads, to projected measures of market and funding liquidity risks. The shocks may relate to market/economic conditions as well as counterparty idiosyncratic characteristics.

The cases of combining funding and market liquidity risks where liquidity obligations and idiosyncratic liquidity funding management are integrated with the market value of the liquid assets can be summarized as follows:

- **Case 1:** The parameters of market and funding liquidity are performing as expected. In this case, the exchange of cash flows resulting from the expected prices, discount factors, spreads, trading activities, credit losses, recoveries, etc. are as expected. Therefore, the liquidity funding process is supposed to be able to support the expected liquidity obligations.

  Under normal, expected conditions, this is the most common case that markets and institutions have to deal with.

- **Case 2:** Although the cash flows from the assets under market liquidity are as expected, the demand for liquidity outflows, from liabilities, is exceeding the expected degree and cannot be compensated for by the existing contractual inflows and liquidating process of liquid assets. In this case, the obligor is unable to fulfil the funding outflow liquidity obligations due to idiosyncratic inefficiency and/or distress.

  Investors and obligors usually fall into this category due to inefficient structure of portfolio management lacking efficient liquidity management and thus may not be able to survive under stress conditions without external[4] support.

- **Case 3:** Market conditions may be under stress and thus liquid assets become illiquid resulting in minor and unfavorable cash flows. On the other hand the contractual cash flows from the existing portfolios provide the expected funding liquidity. The funding inflow liquidity may or may not be capable of overcoming the resulting loss, due to trading activities under market liquidity, and thus will be unable to fulfil possible additional cash flow requests and funding outflow obligations.[5]

  Obligors facing such liquidity risk conditions may be able to survive during market liquidity turbulence due to their efficient portfolios and liquidity management as well as low idiosyncratic risk.

- **Case 4:** The worst case scenario in terms of liquidity risk rises is when both market and funding liquidity are under stress, e.g., financial assets become illiquid and there are unexpected or cancelled contractual cash flows.

Obligors falling into this category—typically during a financial crisis—have little chance of surviving without external support.

Both investors and obligors must identify any combination of the above cases of market and funding liquidity risks. Institutions have a full range of liquidity risk management strategies and policies where contingency plans are in place for dealing with the extreme cases and liquidity needs.

12.1.4 Measuring and reporting liquidity and risk

The most applicable ways to measure the liquidity status are by projecting both contractual and tradable cash flows and identifying how long the obligor can survive without external support. The cash flow projections are reported via marginal liquidity gap reports whereas the liquidity survival period is estimated and reported via cumulative liquidity gaps.

The marginal liquidity gap is about considering all contractual and tradable cash inflows and outflows, aggregating them at the points in time defined through the cycle iteration (e.g., daily, weekly, monthly, etc.) of a predefined time bucket system, and making them visible in a single report. Thus, as shown in Equation 12.1, at each point in time t_i the cash flows are aggregated within a time step s. Figure 12.3 illustrates a marginal liquidity gap report, where the single bars show the expected contractual net liquidity cash flows at a future time period.

$$ML(t_i) = \sum_i^s CFL(t_i) \tag{12.1}$$

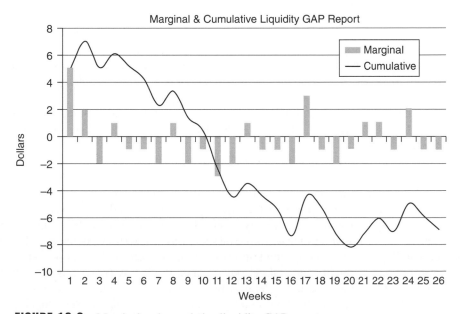

FIGURE 12.3 Marginal and cumulative liquidity GAP report

Cumulative liquidity gaps are based on marginal liquidity and are used to identify the time length of survivor period. Equation 12.2 shows the function for estimating such liquidity gap projection, where the cumulative liquidity CL at time t_k is defined by aggregating the marginal liquidity cash flows. Cumulative liquidity reports are more intuitive and are extensively used in liquidity analysis.

$$CL(t_k) = \sum_{i=1}^{k} ML(t_i) \tag{12.2}$$

The liquidity survival period $SP(t)$ within a liquidity horizon is defined as point at which the cumulative liquidity gap turns from a positive to a negative sign, i.e., the exact time when the cumulative liquidity will be equal to zero as illustrated in Figure 12.3.

Residual liquidity gap identifies the remaining cash flow position at a future point in time considering that no business will be renewed. The estimation of such a gap, as shown in Equation 12.3, is defined by considering the nominal value of the initial position at t_0 minus the cumulative gap.

$$RL(t_k) = NV(t_0) - CL(t_k) \tag{12.3}$$

Based on market liquidity analysis the assets can be evaluated, and kept as a buffer, in regards to the level of their liquidation; on the other hand funding liquidity is about contracts cash *in* and *out* flows. Institutions assess[6] their exposure to contingent liquidity events by calculating a liquidity coverage ratio. Such a ratio is equal to the stock of liquid assets,[7] driven by market liquidity risk, over the total net cash outflows,[8] and influenced by funding liquidity risk. Such a ratio must be over 100%. Equation 12.4 defines the general liquidity coverage ratio.

$$Liquidity\ Coverage\ Ratio = \frac{Liquid\ Assets}{Total\ Net\ Cash\ Outflows} \tag{12.4}$$

As already discussed, liquidity risk analysis is about integrating analysis of all financial risk factors which are not necessarily considered as risk-neutral but rather stressed into real-world probabilities. The key questions that we need to answer are the following:

- What are the cash *in* and *out* flows during the lifetime of the contracts and the portfolio?
- What is the maximum risk for losing liquidity survival period at a certain confidence level and liquidity horizon?
- How much are we exposed to contingent liquidity events?

When financial risk factors are deterministically defined and may be stressed, the resulting cumulative liquidity gap will illustrate the liquidity survival period. Moreover, where that risk factor or factors have been historically changed or will be changed based on different (stochastic) scenarios over time, then we have a distribution of the resulting cumulative liquidity gaps which will illustrate the corresponding distribution of liquidity survival periods. Based on the distribution of liquidity survival periods the liquidity at risk (LaR) can be estimated. Under stress conditions the expected cash flows may be cancelled out and replaced with others; moreover, under market and/or funding liquidity risk the expected liquidity contingency may be under risk.

12.2 VALUE AND INCOME

Value and the resulting income are two fundamental output elements that are considered in financial analysis. All financial risk factors together with valuation rules affect value and income, which are the main drivers of both market and funding liquidity, as discussed in the previous sessions. The results of income (positive or negative) are used as the basis in profit and loss analysis. Maximizing profit and optimizing risk are the main targets when defining the evolution in a new business production. Institutions employ both deterministic and stochastic approaches for measuring value and income at risk. The ratios of risk together with profit and loss measurements define the economic capital. Figure 12.4 illustrates all elements linked to value and income analysis.

12.2.1 Estimating value

Actual and expected cash flow events include and drive the value and income of the financial contracts. As we have already seen above, the main input analysis elements that impact these cash flows are the market, counterparty and behavior risk factors. In measuring value, moreover, the applied valuation method plays a key role. We can illustrate the above by defining the value of fixed income financial contracts using the following Equation 12.5.

$$V^m(t) = NV(t) + P/D_{NV}^m(t) \tag{12.5}$$

The indicator m defines the valuation method, $NV(t)$ is the nominal value at time t and P/D^m is a premium or discount function of NV based on valuation method m. The evolution of P/D is linked to the notional cash flows (which also determine the nominal value) and their degree is derived by the risk-free market conditions, e.g., discounting the outstanding principals by referring to interest rates and calculating the interest payments that will finally adjust the initial value of the contract. In a sense P/D corrects the NV over time. Thus, at future time t, in fixed-income contract, the P/D^m will derive the interest payments whereas

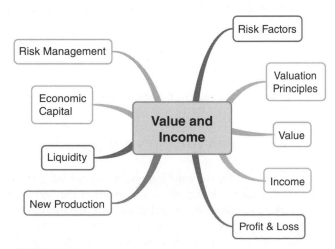

FIGURE 12.4   Main elements of value and income analysis

the nominal value $NV(t)$ is derived by the principal cash flows CF^P between t and maturity time as shown in Equation 12.6.

$$NV(t) = \sum_{t_i > t} CF^P(t_i) \tag{12.6}$$

Therefore, nominal value is the base of any valuation concept which is, however, independent from valuation method. As aforementioned, nominal value is equal to the sum of outstanding principal payments, this definition becomes necessary if premium/discount is involved; on the other hand, interest payment cash flows are not involved in such value estimation.

We should then conclude that to estimate value we first need to recognize the nominal cash flows and then understand the derivation of P/D^m_{NV} as a function of the valuation principle and expected risk conditions.

In fact, for fixed income instruments, all valuation principles take into consideration the initial value (i.e., at value date), and the final value (i.e., at maturity date of the contract); they also define the path taken between these values through the time of the contract.

For the stocks and commodities, where there are no principal cash flow payments, only the premium/discount factor P/D^m_{NV} defines the corrected "adjusted" value; thus, as defined in Equation 12.7 we can say that

$$V^m(t) = P/D^m_{NV}(t) \tag{12.7}$$

In regards to off-balance sheet transactions, the aggregation of the underlying principal payments is equal to zero as they are balanced within the asset and liability positions, or the underlying contest is a forward transaction where the initial principal payment is balanced by the subsequent payments.

12.2.2   Estimating income

Income is derived by the changes of the above value over time considering the evolution of the financial risk factors as well as the valuation principle. Equation 12.8 illustrates the basic function of income.

$$I^m(t) = \frac{\Delta V^m(t)}{dt} \tag{12.8}$$

As we consider time the discretization of the above function could be usefully defined as illustrated in Equation 12.9.

$$I^m(t_i, t_{i+1}) = \Delta NV(t_i, t_{i+1}) + P/D^m_{NV}(t_i, t_{i+1}) \tag{12.9}$$

Where $\Delta NV\left(t_i, t_{i+1}\right)$ defines the nominal income NI by considering the change of the value within time t_i and t_{i+1} and is independent of valuation methods; on the other hand $P/D^m_{NV}\left(t_i, t_{i+1}\right)$ is employed to estimate the actual income from premium or discount process by considering the evolution of risk-free market conditions and risk-neutral default probabilities. In many cases, such evolution is defined via a simulation[9] process. The view of this evolution is dependent on the chosen applied valuation method or principle. Again, as mentioned above, P/D_{NV}^m can be seen as the correction factor of the nominal income which depends on the valuation principle.

12.2.3 Profit and loss

Income is used to project the profit and loss analysis. Positive income indicates profit, whilst negative income indicates losses. Both positive and negative performance, together with the associated risk measurements, can be used to calculate the actual and expected returns as well as adjust the investment portfolio for resulting maximum profitability and minimum expected loss.

In profit and loss analysis all from existing past to simulated future value changes, positive and negative nominal income, the $\Delta P/D$ values, as well as expenses or cost cash flows are registered and reported. The projection of future profits and losses together with the risk measurements are also used in the decisions of rolling over and/or constructing new portfolios, as will be discussed later.

12.2.4 Valuation principles

There are two types of valuation principles based on a) market dependent methods and b) time dependent or accrual methods. The former implies that the time evolution of P/D_{NV}^m depends mainly on market prices whereas in the latter the time evolution of P/D_{NV}^m does not depend on actual market conditions. The main time dependent principles are the nominal/write-off at the beginning, historic/write-off at the end, linear to maturity/reprising and amortized cost. Market dependent principles are the mark-to-market fair or observed values, *lower of cost or market* reflects the "principle of prudence" interpreted in a very strict manner. A full description of these rules is beyond the scope of this book; however, the reader can refer to the textbook *Unified Financial Analysis*.[10]

12.2.5 Risk on value and income

The main element that defines the value and income is the P/D which is directly linked to the financial risk factors. Any contract that is sensitive to changes and/or fluctuations of these factors during its lifetime will directly impact the corresponding value and income. The risk analysis is about identifying, measuring and managing these sensitivities over time. Risk is more related to "shaking" the real world rather than the risk-neutral expectations of markets and default probabilities as well as stressing the economic scenarios based on real-world probabilities as discussed in Chapters 6 and 7.

Investors must be able to identify their strength as well as robustness against unexpected and extreme performance of the financial risk factors that their financial contracts are exposed to. They directly impact liquidity, value and income. Moreover there are many side effects, e.g. in the exposures to concentration and systemic risks. It is therefore very important that financial institutions are able to absorb any possible resulting losses due to unexpected real-world conditions but at the very same time are able to fulfil any other obligations against other counterparties that they may have. This will also imply that risk conditions will have the minimum impact on the entire market.

There are two important approaches[11] in risk analysis: a) deterministically stressing and b) stochastically fluctuating the financial risk factors.

12.2.6 Stress testing

Deterministic scenarios can be applied for stressing at certain level(s) financial risk factor(s), in an individual or integrated manner, to measure the resulting unexpected losses. For instance, let's say a shock on an interest rate may be increased, within a quarter time horizon, up to 200bp whereas under such stress market condition counterparty(ies) are expected to downgrade one to two notches.

The assumptions of stress scenarios can be defined by the investor, the financial institution itself or by regulators and central banks. These assumptions can be driven by *historical*, *current* and *future* expected stressed market conditions. Thus, *historic models* and *what-if scenarios* can be applied. Note, however, that history doesn't necessarily repeat itself and even if it does, not necessarily at the same cycles. Additionally, the current conditions do not remain steady whereas the future expectations may have several different paths. The problem becomes more complex as market risk factors usually interact with each other as well as with the other types of credit and behavioral risks. For instance, during a period of recession it is expected that interest rates will decline over time whereas some commodity prices may increase their values; moreover, due to market stress, borrowers may lose part of their strength to be able to fulfil the agreed credit obligations which indicates an increase of credit spreads.

The definition of a scenario is a process looking from the past to future and defining meaningful stress conditions in a consistent manner. As markets are not static, stress conditions should also be applied considering also the evolution of these factors overtime.

12.2.7 Designing dynamic and integrated stress testing

Business is not static and there are existing contracts that may rollover after they mature; on the other hand, new contracts structure the production of new accounts and portfolios through time. The strategies on the evolution of new production must consider stress scenarios.

As mentioned, financial risk factors interact with each other; such interactions must be considered in the design of stress testing scenarios. Strategies also play a key role in stress testing. Table 12.2 illustrates a matrix of four different combinations that can be used to define an integrated stress testing scenario where both market conditions and counterparty status are considered in assumed (expected) stress cases. These obviously will drive the financial events,

TABLE 12.2 Combination of Market Conditions, Credit/Counterparty Status, behavior characteristics and new production in the design of stress testing

		Credit/Counterparty Status	
		Assumed	**Stressed**
Market Conditions	**Assumed**	Expected Financial Events (Expected Behaviors & Remained Strategies)	Financial Events change due to Idiosyncratic Stress (Stressed Behaviors / Reviewing Strategies)
	Stressed	Financial Events change due to new Market Conditions (Unexpected Behaviors & Reviewing Strategies)	Unexpected Financial Events (Unexpected Behaviors & Change of Strategies)

the P&L as well as the behavior characteristics. Then, strategies and portfolios/accounts may be reviewed or restructured accordingly aligned with possible stress evolution of risk factors. So, there are four main combinations that we could employ:

- The market conditions performing as assumed whereas there are no changes in counterparty credit status. In such case financial events appear as expected. Strategies may remain unchanged.
- The market conditions are under stress whereas counterparty credit status is steady. Financial events are expected to change whereas strategies will be reviewed and possibly changed.
- Market conditions are stable but counterparty credit status is under stress. Financial events will be changed due to counterparty idiosyncratic stress. Strategies should be reviewed and renewed.
- Both market conditions and counterparties are under stress. Unexpected financial events will rise and strategies will be changed

12.2.8 Stochastic process

By using deterministic scenarios it is very difficult to cover all possible cases of real-world probabilities of the risk factors performances. Thus, stochastic process can also be applied to generate many different scenarios, which can be used to define a distribution of future values or prices of risk factors. As a result, the corresponding values of the portfolio contracts/instruments are obtained from such distributions which finally lead to the value distributions of the portfolio. This concept, defined as Value at Risk (VaR), has the scope to identify the notion of the maximum loss of a portfolio[12] for a certain confidence level and pre-specified holding period.

There are different *analytical* and *numerical* methods for estimating VaR including Delta-normal, Delta-gamma, Parametric, Monte Carlo, Historical, Benchmark, etc. For instance, employing the very popular Monte Carlo approach, scenarios are generated for all risk factors in a random fashion, based on a variance-covariance matrix and a dynamic capital market model.

A more advanced approach is the dynamic VaR which is constructed based on the main market risk factors, a set of scenarios and strategies as well as the valuation concepts. The main additional feature of the dynamic Monte Carlo approach is the full integration of the time dimension. In contrast to the conventional static VaR, which has proven to be a consistent and reliable framework to measure short-term market risk, i.e., normally up to three months, the dynamic VaR methodology provides an answer to the market risk measurement problem when the relevant time horizon is long, from one to two years. While the static VaR consists in "instantaneous price shocks" of the market condition applied to the current balance sheet, the dynamic Monte Carlo method generates many market scenarios over a certain time horizon and simulates the activity of the financial institution over each of these scenarios. The relative impact in the income simulation, considering future strategies of the business evolution, can be used to measure the dynamic Income (or Earnings) at risk (usually denoted as IaR or EaR).

There is intense research and development of VaR approaches and relative systems and models implemented by both academia and the financial industry. Although there has been criticism of the stochastic process, especially during the crisis times, we should recognize the advantage of such approaches for considering a spectrum of risks and identifying as well as measuring the degree of risk and resulting economic losses which lead to a definition of the corresponding economic capital.

12.2.9 Economic capital allocation and risk adjustments

Economic capital reflects the measurement of risks in terms of economic realities, i.e., scenarios, based on real-world probabilities, e.g., VaR calculation. Naturally, the measurement process involves converting a risk distribution to the amount of capital that is required to support the risk and absorb the resulting losses. The risk refers to both financial and operational instances. However, the former is more amenable than the latter. Economic capital provides a standardized unit measurement (i.e., a dollar of economic capital), and can become the basis for comparing and discussing opportunities and threats during the risk management process. As such, economic capital offers a language for pricing risk that is related directly to the principal concerns of strategies and profitability management.

The allocation of economic capital should be structured efficiently. Too little capital may not be able to absorb all losses; but setting aside a lot of capital, though safer, is costly. Thus, finding an optimal capital structure involves finding the right balance between the need for safety and the desire for maximizing return on capital. The idea is to assign capital charges to individual business and assigned portfolios based on their risk measurements. When risk-based capital allocation is used, the cost of managing (adjusting) the risks becomes a very important aspect. Such a method refers to the decision made on what type(s) of risk management should be applied, e.g., accepting, avoiding, hedging, transferring/mitigating. Risk is always linked to returns and available assets; therefore, a complete form of capital allocation should be driven according to the return on capital or assets and the ability of their risk adjustments. The general formula of risk adjustment is defined in the following Equation 12.10.

$$Risk\ adjustment = \frac{Return}{Economic\ capital\ at\ Risk} \tag{12.10}$$

Using risk-adjusted performance measurement (RAPM) models, the risks and returns are compared against capital investments. The commonly used RAPM models[13] are based on the return of capital (ROC) or return on assets (ROA). Risk-Adjusted Return on Capital (RAROC) is a model of RAPM, derived by the ROC function, which is mostly recognized by the financial industry. Equation 12.11 illustrates the RAROC function:

$$RAROC = \frac{Performance}{Risk} \tag{12.11}$$

where the term *performance*, in the numerator, includes revenues but excludes expenses and expected losses and the *risk* in the denominator refers to capital reserves excluding, however, the ones referring to expected losses. A high degree of RAROC implies, therefore, a degree of risk, e.g., VaR, in relation to economic profit and vice versa. Consequently, a high degree of RAROC implies low requirements on a percentage (%) for the economic capital and vice versa. Thus, the ratio between economic capital and RAROC can be used to define the capital allocation as defined in Equation 12.12.

$$Economic\ capital\ allocation\ (\%) = \frac{Economic\ capital}{RAROC} \tag{12.12}$$

We could conclude therefore that combining risk measurements and profitability provides powerful and efficient ways to allocate capital against risk and unexpected losses and thus ensuring the stability of the portfolio through time.

12.2.10   Some key points in applying risk management

Finally, we would like to highlight that in the process of identifying risks the following characteristics should be considered:

- *An efficient degree of complexity.* The selection of the approach and the identification and calculation of the risk measure should be simple but not simplistic. The degree of complexity for identifying, computing and reporting risk should be aligned with the complexity of the underlying risk factors and their integration.
- *Effectiveness, sensitivity and robustness.* A small degree shock in the risk parameters that have been considered should cause not minor but rather significant impact to value, input, liquidity and relative losses. Moreover, risk measures must not be overly sensitive to modest parameters.
- *Transparency.* All risk measurements should be available, explainable and understandable to the investors and the market participants.
- *Risk decomposition.* The risk measurements should be decomposed within the responsible portfolios and linked to relative units and business lines. This will make the risk management simple and more applicable. This will also help in distributing and diversifying the effects of the corresponding losses as well as allocating the economic capital.
- *Consistency.* The scenarios applied in risk factors must be consistent and provide coherent risk and profitability measurements, e.g., a stress of default probabilities should be aligned, and not in opposition, to stress credit spreads. Moreover, if for instance the impact to a portfolio A is less than in portfolio B then the latter is less risky than the former.
- *Intuitiveness.* After all, even considering many risk factors driven by deterministic or stochastic scenarios the risk measure and reports should be meaningfully aligned somehow to the intuitive notion of the underlying real-world factors and probabilities.
- *Optimization.* Risk management is about optimizing the portfolios to maximize profitability and minimize losses under economic scenarios based on real-world probabilities.
- *Cockpit.* Just as a pilot in a cockpit does, a risk manager should be able to understand the exposures to different risks, where all relevant risk measurements are considered to ensure that businesses are running safely and profitably as well as ensuring that the system is robust in turbulent times.
- *New production.* Risk management must always be linked to profitability analysis and strategies for restructuring the current, and planning the future, business. Thus, new production must always be linked to the evolution of parameters referring to risk and profitability.

12.3   NEW PRODUCTION

Businesses are going concerns, and investors need to plan the future of their new portfolios. New production is a forward looking process where time evolution is the underlying factor. Time drives the dynamics of market evolution, credit status of both existing and new counterparties. Thus, these dynamics are considered in estimating the future performances of financial risk factors (i.e., market, counterparty and behavior), and also the idiosyncratic characteristics of the investors. All future assumptions of the financial risk factors are considered in the strategic decisions on whether the performance of the portfolio structure will be based on run-off or rollover and going concern processes. Moreover, how the risk management will be applied is also taken into consideration. Based on the investors' strategies the following decisions have to be made:

a. The target volume/size of the investment performance with a certain time horizon
b. The type of business in regards to contract terms and conditions made among the counterparties, i.e., lender and borrower
c. The investment and re-investment process for structuring or restructuring the portfolios respectively based on the new business types and/or the targeted volume.

After all, at future times, the expected value, income and their risk measurements will result in the corresponding evolution of profit and losses to evaluate the worthiness of the new production.

We would like to list all the above elements that should be considered during the new production process:

- *Time.* The future time is set in regard to the horizon and time buckets/intervals where the evolution of financial risk factors, patterns of the financial contracts and financial events will be aligned.
- *Dynamics.* The expected evolution of market conditions and future credit status of the counterparties are the dynamics considered in planning the production of the future businesses. For instance, yield curves, prices, credit spreads, etc., to be started at future points in time should be defined. Furthermore, such evolution is expected to impact, directly or indirectly, both market and counterparty behaviors.
- *Risk Factors.* The risk of the above dynamics to move away from the initial expectations is part of the constant changes in financial risk factors. Moreover, some idiosyncratic characteristics, of the investor, may change through time.
- *Strategy.* The investor must decide whether only the existing contracts in the current portfolios will be considered at roll-down/run-off liquidation process or a roll-over process will be applied. Moreover, new contracts may enhance the future investments at going-concern view. As such, where a process is applied at portfolio (or account) level its structure must be also defined. Finally, the management of financial risks should consider the future evolution of risk factors, i.e., dynamic stochastic or deterministic.
- *Volume.* The target degree in the volume of the future business, for a certain time horizon, must be defined by the investors. Thus, based on their strategies three different options may be considered:
  - Reducing the volume by rolling-down/run-off of the existing business without reinvesting in the same or different types of business, i.e., financial contracts/portfolios. This may happen when investors would like to sunset the existing portfolios following the maturity steps, at future times, of the financial contracts.
  - Keeping the volume steady by rolling-over the existing (old) type of business after they mature, i.e., re-investing in the same types of financial contracts/portfolios. In this case, the investor is most probably happy with the returns and thus enhances the portfolio with

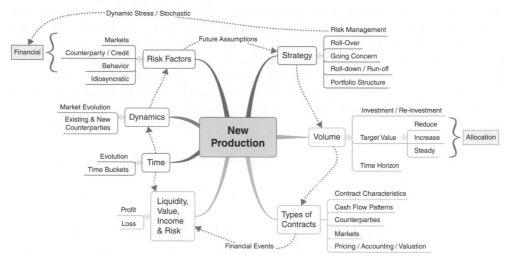

FIGURE 12.5   The elements and processes of a new production

the same types of financial contracts—assuming, however, that the market conditions and counterparties' credit status stay steady and/or the current portfolio has a favorable degree of robustness against risks.

- Increasing the volume by adding new contracts, discussed in the next point referring to types of contracts.

A combination of the above investments and re-investments defines the business allocation and portfolio structure of the new production.

- *Types of contracts.* Adding new contracts (type of business), investors must decide and define their characteristics, i.e., the terms and conditions that will define the pattern of cash-flow exchange, types of counterparties and possible options that could be exercised. Moreover, the markets linked to these contracts, pricing assumptions and the applied accounting/valuation rules.
- *Liquidity, value, income and risk.* Both current and existing financial contracts will result in liquidity, value, income and corresponding risk measurements leading to profit and loss analysis.

Figure 12.5 illustrates the above elements and process considered in a new production.

In marketplace lending the investment on a single capital, provided by the lender, is in fact sliced to a number of loans, constructing therefore a portfolio of loans linked to several borrowers. Having said that we can argue that the risk and portfolio management discussed in the above paragraphs can be naturally applied following the same guidelines.

12.4   TREASURY AND FUNDS TRANSFER PRICING (FTP)

So far in this chapter we have discussed value, liquidity, income, risk and the development of new businesses. The question now is who is coordinating them, managing the different types of financial risks and is responsible for the profit and loss of the institution? A key role in the financial institution is played by the treasury department. In a sense the treasury department is a *bank within a bank* or, in other words, *the heart of the bank* which pumps liquidity to different business entities managing the value and income, balancing the assets and liabilities and mitigating financial risks. Let us explore now the main principles of the treasury.

Just as a bank classifies deposits and loans differently in their balance sheet, from an accounting perspective, loans can be considered from the position of the lender and the borrower:

- For the lender the loan is an asset where an income is received from the expected interest payments or trading activities.
- For the borrower the loan is a liability that defines the obligation to pay interest expense.

In the banking system, liabilities represent the majority[14] of capital, which the institution borrows from the markets and thus an obligation of future expense is defined. On the other hand, in lending this capital back to the market it becomes an asset where income is expected to be generated. Based on this model, assets cannot exist without liabilities and, therefore, both sides of the balance sheet have to be considered at the same time.

Regarding its loan business, the bank must make sure that:

- It has access to capital markets to borrow funds to fulfil future expense obligations.
- It lends capital to trustworthy borrowers in the market who will fulfil the loan obligations until the maturity of the loan agreement.
- Assets and liabilities are balanced, over time, in a way that:
  - the value of the assets is higher than the liabilities,
  - the cash-inflows are higher than the cash-outflows, and
  - the expected income is higher than the expenses, which allows profitable operation.
- Any losses can be absorbed and thus the financial system is stable and robust despite any risky conditions.

Links between financial contracts placed in the liability and asset sides are obtained via the funds transfer pricing system. To see how such a system works, assume a bank has three profit centers and FTP framework as illustrated in Figure 12.6, which has the following functions:

1. The liability profit center which is responsible to get deposits from the market.
2. The asset profit center which provides loans to the market.
3. The treasury department which acts as a bank within a bank.

One of the main functions of the treasury department of a bank is to manage the bank's balance sheet and to ensure that all departments in the bank can access the capital they need for their daily activities. As mentioned above, the goal is to maximize margins, manage risk and provide the necessary liquidity of funds. The management of risk especially has a high priority. The treasury is also responsible for the securitization of assets to free up equity capital. It may also interact with regulators who set rules, e.g., regarding capital requirements and liquidity.

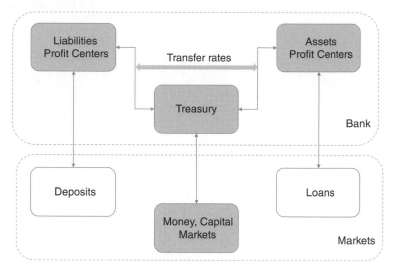

FIGURE 12.6   Profit centers and FTP framework

12.4.1   Funds transfer pricing (FTP) and transfer rates

The treasury buys the loans from the liability side, and it is connected to the outside world via the money and capital market. It finances the asset side with credit, where the different transfers of capital among profit centers have certain rates called *transfer rates*. Once transfer rates are determined, these rates should be used to split income; however they cannot impact, add or deduct, the total income.

A simple example, illustrated in Figure 12.7, shows how such transfer rates are set. Let's say at time t_0 the liability profit center borrows for one year a deposit at a rate of 1.5% whereas the asset profit center is lending a five-year loan at a rate of 5.8%. The treasury plays the role of the intermediator between the two profit centers: it buys the one-year liability with the risk-free rate of 2.2% and then finances the five-year loan for the current risk-free fixed market rate of 5%. In this example, the one year deposit bought by the treasury pays a margin of $2.2\% - 1.5\% = 0.7\%$ to the liability profit center. At the same time, the asset profit center for the five-year loan makes from the treasury a margin of $5\% - 5.8\% = 0.8\%$. The treasury receives a net margin of $2.2\% - 5.0\% = 2.8\%$.

You may wonder why the treasury should play such a role and receive this margin in the first place. In our example, for the next five years (i.e., from t_0 to t_5) the asset profit center receives from the loan the agreed rate of 5.8% whilst still passing 5% to the treasury, and thus is keeping the margin constant at 0.8% regardless of any possible changes in the market conditions. After one year however, at t_1 the deposit with rate of 1.5% matured. Assume now a situation where at t_2 the market is under stress and the new yield curve shifts to higher rates as illustrated in Figure 12.8. This means that the liability profit center will have to pay a higher rate of 3.6% to borrow the new loan deposits. Consequently, the treasury must also adapt to new market conditions by buying the new liability with the higher risk-free rate of 4%. Both liability and treasury margins will be adjusted accordingly resulting in lower margins of 0.4% and 1% respectively. Note that from the new yield curve it is expected that the rates increase dramatically in years three and four which implies that the treasury profit will become

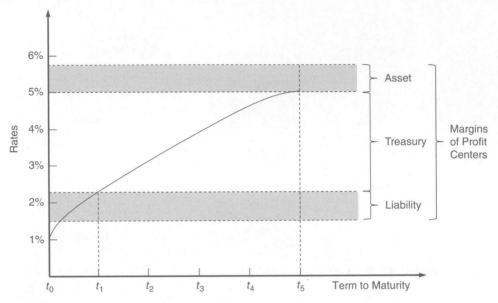

FIGURE 12.7 Margins of FTP centers

negligible or even negative, which indicates losses. The problem becomes even worse where the asset profit center is lending at t_2 a five-year loan at a rate of let's say 5%. This implies that the treasury will have to finance this loan with fixed market rate lower degree and thus shrink out the final margin.

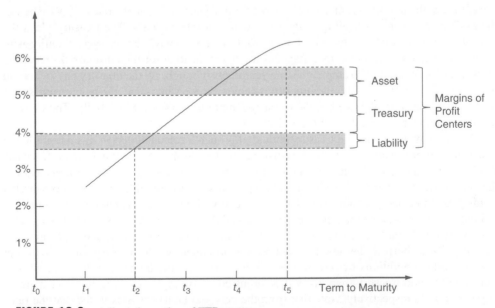

FIGURE 12.8 Adjusted margins of FTP centers

Another question is: what if, due to stress market conditions, accessing capital from the liability side has become difficult and thus the bank cannot provide liquidity to the asset side? Or what if there is an excess of cash from profit centers that the bank cannot lend to the market? In both cases, the treasury will buy or sell the missing capital required or excess liquidity by using its link to money and capital markets. Moreover, the treasury may trade liquid assets to access liquidity. In a nutshell, we can say that the treasury acts as a buffer between the asset and the liability profit centers of a bank, ensuring its profit margins stay intact.

Banks transfer their financial risks to the treasury. Therefore, beyond the role of splitting the profits, the treasury is responsible for managing liquidity, value, income and associated risk as well as absorbing, by hedging or mitigating the risks, any associated losses.[15] Therefore, on top of the transfer rate discussed above, transfer rates should include different types of margins:

- **Credit margin** which is considering the counterparty risk of the loan credit exposure.
- **Liquidity margin** used for the liquidity[16] that should be held against short-term liabilities.
- **Treasury margin** for the bank's treasury profit. [17]
- **Institution-specific margin** which refers to the institution's own credit rating that impacts the cost of funding.
- **Add-on margins** that may include additional profit margins, operational risks and cost, behavior risks, and cost referring to new strategies.[18]

Banks apply financial analysis to manage risk and optimize profitability. These margins balance asset and liabilities, which both incur risk.

12.4.2 Treasury in P2P finance

After all, financial institutions, with a support of treasury, try to ensure that the lender has positive interest income for the duration of the loan and the borrower enjoys fair market and spread rates. This happens by considering the evolution of future performance of risk factors as well as by considering and influencing the strategies applied in both asset and liability sides.

Does a marketplace lending platform also need a treasury? With the current business model, most likely not. Since they connect lenders and borrowers directly, marketplace lenders have no need to raise funds in the money market. Because the loans they originate never enter their balance sheet, all credit and market risks lie with the lender, so there is no financial risk to offload. The unique selling proposition (USP) of marketplace lending platforms lies in their streamlined operations that reduce operating costs, new rating algorithms to score borrowers and their performance, and in the ability to connect counterparties directly without using their own balance sheet. In this sense, they have a limited need for a specialist who can access credit markets rapidly to generate liquidity. However, what they do need is a way to assess the financial health of the system of which they are after all a part. If there were a financial crisis that led to defaults *en masse* on a particular marketplace lending platform, this could be catastrophic for the entire sector. The health of the capital markets will inevitably influence the performance of their loan book. Of course, lending platforms do monitor financial markets and certainly have a good overview of the macroeconomics going on around them and of the performance of their current loans. But how the actions that take place on their platforms and the loans that they originate influence the economy beyond the platform will be more complex to assess. Without models of the expected performance of their loans that assess marketplace loans in similar ways to the rest of the formal financial sector, including expected profit and loss for platforms, banks, and individual counterparties, platforms will only have half the picture. Even though their liquidity arises on the spot when a lender and a borrower connect, transparent and consistent analysis will give them a clearer picture of the risk of loans and of the expected market liquidity that borrowers and lenders cumulatively shape. Platforms need to operate with awareness of their impact on the markets so they can secure robust revenue streams for their lenders. This is where treasury services can fill in the information gap—namely between individual platforms and their impact on the financial sector on the margin.

12.5   CONCLUDING REMARKS

The source of liquidity risk is, in most cases, a combination of all financial risk factors and thus the risk management of liquidity demands integrated risk analysis. The evolution of cash *in* and *out* flows is monitored and estimated from past to future times respectively. Market liquidity analysis answers the question as to how liquid a financial instrument is; thus, it is very much linked to its pricing characteristics and trading activities. Funding liquidity refers to contingent contractual cash flows; for instance any risk event (e.g., default) will cancel the expected cash flows, and may initiate the ones from credit enhancements and recoveries. Liquidity managers must consider both types of liquidity analysis, assessing and driving the strategies for rolling over and/or defining the future businesses accordingly. The combination of funding and market liquidity is the basis of applying risk management based on real-world probabilities. Liquidity risk is a result of market, counterparty and behavior risk factors and thus, institutions acting as investors should apply the different types of risk analytics discussed in the previous chapters. Therefore, liquidity risk is measured based on deterministic or stochastic scenarios. Moreover, institutions also assess their strength against contingent liquidity events. Liquidity and its risks are viewed mainly by using ratios and gap reports of historical to future cash flows. Investors must pay great attention to identifying and managing both market and funding liquidity ensuring liquidity survivor under any stress conditions. They apply strategies to manage liquidity and to keep the business and credit enhancements always liquid. Figure 12.9 illustrates in detail the main elements considered in liquidity risk analysis.

In value and income analysis, the main parameters are the nominal value and the delta of values over time, whereas premium and discount are employed to adjust them. Moreover, valuation principles play a critical role in estimating values. Of course, all financial risk factors based on risk free assumptions affect value and expected income. Stressing deterministically and/or stochastically these factors, by employing risk management, will result in changes in value and corresponding possible negative income, i.e., losses. Income and losses reflect the profits and losses which, together with risk measurement, give an estimation of the economic capital. Based on dynamic simulation, income drives the profit and loss together with strategies for the evolution of new production. Finally, as mentioned, value plays a key role in managing both market and funding liquidity. The correct estimation of the value of an asset indicates the degree of the cash results from the liquidation process. Moreover, both value and income will indicate the expected contractual cash flows over time, which may be used in funding liquidity management. Figure 12.10 illustrates in detail the elements and their relations used in value and income analysis.

FIGURE 12.9 Main elements of market and funding liquidity and their risk management

As businesses evolve there should be a new production of credit portfolios. In such cases, institutions are simulating the dynamics in market and credit risk factors evolution. This means at future time intervals reevaluating both market conditions and credit quality of the existing as well as new counterparties; in addition considering their future behavior under normal and stress market conditions. The above means simulating the evolution of value and income as well as the possible losses. Based on these dynamics as well as the idiosyncratic characteristics of the investors they are defining the strategies for rolling down or rolling over under stress or going concern scenarios. The aim is maximizing profitability and minimizing losses whilst ensuring enough liquidity even under stress conditions. Such targets can be reached by investing, re-investing and allocating on the same or different types of financial instruments within a certain time horizon. In fact the characteristics of the new contract and counterparty must be defined and analyzed using their outcomes under assumed and uncertain conditions.

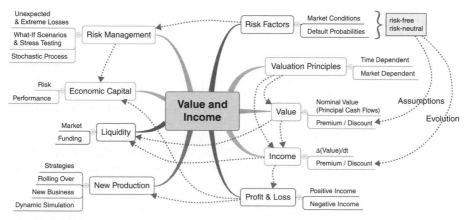

FIGURE 12.10 Main elements of value and income analysis

Because banks need access to capital markets, they need an experienced specialized center, i.e., treasury, to access these markets. On the other hand, the treasury can support and influence the management of assets and liabilities that would otherwise weigh down the balance sheet of the bank. The advantages of working with a treasury department are clear-cut for banks: they can increase their spread and increase returns for investors; the treasury identifies exposure to financial risks and manages these risks by absorbing or mitigating possible losses; the separation of risk and front-end operations can increase the stability and robustness of a bank. The treasury itself fulfils these functions by pragmatically applying analytics on liquidity, value, income, and risk measurements. It also measures and balances profit and risks for exposures to borrowing and lending.

Individual marketplace lenders will hardly need a treasury department, but several platforms together—or the entire sector, for that matter—could benefit from a centralized entity that would provide treasury-like services for all of them in an aggregated manner. The benefits of such a system are to ensure positive interest income for the lenders on one hand and fair market and spread rates for the borrowers on the other—under both canonical (expected), and stress (unexpected) market, liquidity and behavior risk conditions.

The aim of applying risk management is to increase profitability, ensuring at the same time robustness of the financial system against unexpected conditions. The applied methods should have a sufficient degree of complexity, whereas the risk scenarios should have effectiveness sensitive to risk factors. All models and approaches must have a high degree of transparency, available to the market. This will ensure consistency in the disclosure reports. Overall, counterparties involved in the financial deal should make decisions by having a good view and understanding of the existing status as well as any assumptions made for the future. The efficiency of such decisions is a result of an optimal combination of analytics and intuitiveness.

NOTES

1. Typical credit risk contracts are financial collaterals and guaranties.
2. Before the credit crunch in the financial crisis of 2007/8, financial securitization products were considered highly liquid due to their high quality of senior and mezzanine tranches; ironically, many of them became highly illiquid due to stress market and credit conditions.
3. See also the approaches on Funding and Liquidity Valuation Adjustment denoted as FVA and LVA.
4. Use other source of liquidity, typically for financial institutions via additional facilities or bailout from central banks.
5. Under market liquidity stress, the institutions may be forced to carry out trading activities (mainly sales) of their liquid assets with additional discounts; they may also request to access funding facilities and deposits with probably high cost.
6. See also BIS paper bcbs238 on Basel III: The Liquidity Coverage Ratio and liquidity risk monitoring tools.
7. Defined as high quality with certain degrees of liquidity.
8. Based on the regulation from the Bank of International Settlements (BIS), the total net cash outflows considered in the estimation of the Liquidity Coverage Ratio are the ones occurring over the next 30 calendar days.
9. Income analysis is also called income simulation.
10. *Unified Financial Analysis, The missing links of finance*, by Willi Brammertz, Ioannis Akkizidis, Wolfgang Breymann, Rami Entin, Marco Rustmann (Wiley 2009).

11. Sensitivity analysis can also be a cause for measuring the impact of risk factors' fluctuation to value; however, in this book we will be focusing on real-world probabilities based on stress testing and stochastic process analysis.

12. The size of the portfolio is not important for the VaR method; it can consist of only one contract or of all the contracts in the entire organization.

13. Commonly used ROC models are Risk-Adjusted Return on Capital (RAROC), Return on Risk-Adjusted Capital (RORAC); moreover, there are well known ROA models which are Return on Risk- Adjusted Assets (RORAA), Risk-Adjusted Return on Assets (RAROA).

14. The minority is received by the stake holders which defines the equity.

15. Of course, if the market had moved in the opposite direction the profit of the treasury would have increased.

16. Usually as cash or highly liquid assets.

17. Deal-making profit center.

18. New markets and contracts.

Three

Toward the Future of the Hybrid Financial Sector

If a boom-to-bust expansion of consumer credit defined the last era in retail banking, a push toward digital will be the overarching theme of the current one.[1] As we said in Part One of this book, the FinTech space is diverse and moving fast. The fact that marketplace lending platforms gain ground is just one of many attacks on established financial institutions taking place. In the face of imminent disruption, banks feel an urgent need to act. Some analysts give banks an ultimatum of three to five years to become digitally proficient or lose the battle for the digital banking customer.[2] Nevertheless, doomsayers of the established financial sector often miss an important point: many FinTech products and services rely heavily on existing infrastructure and services that are under the control of established financial institutions. For example, payment processors require users to link their accounts with their existing bank accounts or debit cards, and marketplace lending platforms need banks when funding and issuing loans. On top of that, established players in the financial sector are some of the best customers of marketplace lending platforms: banks and large hedge funds have bought and securitized portfolios of loans from several marketplace lending sites.[3] This stands in stark contrast to the vision of the nascent online lending industry doing away with banking as we know it.[4] In any case, the future of credit will hardly be an either/or proposition. Rather, it will be important for the established financial sector to incorporate new ideas from FinTech entrepreneurs, who in return should take advantage of the experience and know-how of banks when it comes to risk management and financial analytics of complex portfolios.

In Part Two of this book, we learned that banks have incorporated digital services in the front and back offices for decades. To say that banks need to become "more digital" therefore misses the point. Globally, several incumbent banks and financial institutions already embrace digital and upgrade their value chains aggressively. All banks offer online banking, and many of them use mobile technologies and are actively investing in FinTech innovation. Banks have realized that the habits of today's digital customer differ from those of the boomer generation or even the first generation that grew up with the internet, generation X. By no means are the banks asleep at the wheel, as some advocates of FinTech innovation want us to believe. At the same time—and we explored this in Part One of this book—banks are large bureaucracies that are hardly exemplars of rapid innovation and deployment of new technology. Even though they are hesitant to admit it, they are in general risk-averse and prefer to wait on the sidelines until their customers are sure to embrace a new technology. This is the weak point of established market leaders. Dominant players in an industry are in a poor position to judge which new technology will usher in a paradigm shift, and even well-managed companies fail to stay leaders in their industries when they confront changes in technology. Throughout history, the decisions that led to the demise of established companies were made when their leaders were widely regarded as the best in the world. They saw the markets through the lens of their past successes and existing customer base, not from a fresh perspective that allowed for trial and error over a long period of time.[5]

P3.1 DANGERS OF A BIG BANG APPROACH TO CATCH UP WITH TECHNOLOGY INNOVATION

The opportunity to disrupt finance and build a new financial sector is large, and much advice about how to tackle it has emerged. Most of it centers on encouraging banks to upgrade their digital strategy and align their business models more with those of IT companies to integrate FinTech startups into their existing value chains. However, innovation is a more complex beast. It is not only technical issues that play a large part in the financial system of the future, social and organizational challenges are also important drivers. Recommending that banks get on the bandwagon and transform themselves into tech companies misses the point. To applaud technology startups indiscriminately as the harbingers of the future, despite the fact that many of their services are unprofitable, lack transparency, and come with a host of privacy and security issues, bears an eerie resemblance to the irrational exuberance of the first dot.com boom around the millennium.

In the run up to the year 2000, several established multinationals with firm roots in the so-called *old economy* felt a pressing need to catch up quickly with promising technology startups. Authors Catherine Chu and Steve Smithson describe the case of a large American-owned multinational car manufacturer that aggressively drove e-business across the whole company in 1999 to avoid missing the boat on e-commerce.[6] The new CEO of the company believed in the need for a "technology and business revolution" that he spearheaded by recruiting senior staff aggressively from tech companies and forging partnerships with new tech companies. This hasty "big bang" approach to innovation cost the company dearly. The business culture of existing staff members clashed with the culture of the new hires. The absence of quick wins of the new strategy, despite the heavy use of outside consultants, undermined the credibility of the costly initiative. An e-business gap emerged between established and new divisions that was impossible to bridge. When the company posted a loss twice the size of its profits of the previous year in 2001, and the dot.com euphoria showed the first signs of weakness, the new CEO was fired. The company assumed a back-to-basics strategy—after writing off millions of dollars that it had sunk into the push toward digital.

Although technical barriers play a role in the implementation of new technology, organizational and social issues are more important. It is naive to assume that established market leaders in finance and banking will be able to turn their organizations upside down overnight just to catch up with new technology that is not even proven to yield sustainable advantages. Despite their good ideas, FinTech startups and entrepreneurs hardly have all the answers when it comes to a sustainable and robust financial system of the future.

P3.2 THE NEED TO COLLABORATE IN A HYBRID FINANCIAL SYSTEM

Instead of assuming that the end of the established banking sector is near and that newly emerging financial technology startups will rule the world next year, it may be better to analyze the challenge from a distance. In Part One, we explained the status quo of FinTech and their aspirations for the future. We also briefly touched upon the business models and operational processes of online lending platforms to help us understand the position of marketplace lending in the FinTech ecosystem. In Part Two, we examined in detail how banks operate when they underwrite loans, and laid out the framework for robust financial analytics. In this third part of the book, we will now combine the two viewpoints. Instead of comparing FinTech and established bank lending and declaring one or the other the winner, let's think of a way to merge the best of both worlds. When we acknowledge the strengths of both actors, we lay the foundation on which they can collaborate constructively. Both sides of the equation are already aligned, and banks and FinTech startups overlap in many ways. When they both integrate each other's expertise, they can strengthen their business models to align them with the demands of digital customers.

This part of the book begins with an analysis of the profitability and risk of a portfolio of marketplace loans. A stress test will serve as the basis to develop more robust analytics that should help professionals and investors in making better informed financial decisions about marketplace loans. We will then examine the digital dilemmas that banks and FinTech companies face, which leads us to several strategies to cope with the challenges. The emergence of a hybrid financial sector still has several hurdles to overcome, but if banks and FinTech companies manage to tackle them, we might end up with a financial system that is more transparent and more resilient. The final two chapters chart a path to the hybrid financial sector and introduce unified analytics as the starting point.

NOTES

1. Broeders, Henk and Khanna, Somesh (2015) *Strategic choices for banks in the digital age* (McKinsey and Company), http://www.mckinsey.com/insights/financial_services/Strategic_choices_for_banks_in_the_digital_age.
2. Ibid.
3. Jenkins, Patrick and Alloway, Tracy (2015) "Democratising Finance: Big banks eye marketplace lending push" (*Financial Times*, 28 January 2015), http://www.ft.com/cms/s/0/93837c4a-a6db-11e4-9c4d-00144feab7de.html.
4. Ibid.
5. Christensen, Clayton (1997) *The Innovator's Dilemma* (Harvard: Harvard Business School Press).
6. Chu, Catherine and Smithson, Steve (2007) "E-business and organizational change: a structurational approach" (*Information Systems Journal*, 10/2007), http://onlinelibrary.wiley.com/doi/10.1111/j.1365-2575.2007.00258.x/abstract.

CHAPTER 13

Profitability and Risk of Marketplace Loans

To understand marketplace lending better, we apply a banking risk-management approach to a portfolio of marketplace loans. In this chapter, we conduct a financial analysis and stress test of a publicly available loan portfolio of marketplace loans for the year 2014.[1] We also use the loan books for previous years to approximate default probabilities and prepayment characteristics of different rating classes. Some platforms publish their loan books, both in the U.S. and in the UK. Nevertheless, we felt that the loan book of Lending Club, the U.S. market leader, might be a good proxy for the sector in general. We could run this analysis, based on our models and systems, with any loan book that a marketplace lending platform might make available.

The model and the datasets we used in the analysis are available on the companion website for this book.

Disclaimer: Because Lending Club makes their loan books available online, we were able to conduct this analysis with real market data. We are grateful to Lending Club for sharing these data and applaud them for spearheading transparency and openness in the sector. Banks are nowhere near as open with their portfolios. If lenders are transparent about their loan books, this helps regulators and investors analyze exposure more effectively, which could be the first step towards a safer financial system.

The results of our analysis are simulated and are not describing gains and losses under real market conditions. It shall not serve as an endorsement for or against investing in marketplace loans. Even though we arrive at negative returns in our analysis when we apply stress conditions, this does not mean that investments in marketplace loans or Lending Club will incur a loss with certainty. The purpose of the analysis in this chapter is a what-if scenario analysis that might help us understand the asset class under different assumptions.

13.1 UNDERLYING ASSUMPTIONS OF THE ANALYSIS

Marketplace loans are, in effect, simple annuity contracts. We explained the structure of expected financial events of annuities in Chapter 5 (5.3 Contract Mechanisms Producing Financial Events) and their risk (market and credit defaults). These are the steps we applied in the model.

13.1.1 Getting the input data

We use the following information provided by Lending Club: counterparty id, principal amount, value date, duration of the contract, cycle of payments, interest rates, and counterparty ratings and sub-ratings.

13.1.2 Time

The analysis date is set on 1 January 2014. The Time Bucket System for the simulation intervals is defined as monthly to align with the actual contractual time intervals.

13.1.3 Risk factors

Based on the above data, we set the following model parameters for the market, counterparty and behavior risks:

- Market parameters are only referring to market interest and credit spread rates. They are used for discounting and they drive expected cash flows, value and income.
- All counterparties have a rating—A, B, C, D, E, F and G—from best to worst. Each rating class has five sub-ratings, such as A1 to A5, B1 to B5 and so forth.
- Ratings drive default probabilities, spreads and recovery rates.
- We consider two behavior characteristics: prepayments and recoveries in case of default.

13.1.4 Mapping the financial contract

We derive the amortization schedule of the payments by using a fixed rate annuity contract type for mapping the financial contract. The main attributes of such contract are:

- Value date (starting point of the contract)
- Principal amount (present value of the loan), set value date
- Annual interest rates
- Cycle of interest and principal payment derived by the number of payment periods and the total duration of the loan

13.1.5 Calculating contractual financial events

The computation engine provides all financial events including all expected cash flows, values and incomes at both points in time and through the cycle iterations.

13.1.6 Constructing portfolios

Based on the available provided data of the contractual deals, we randomly generate 1,000 portfolios containing 1,000 contracts each. For each contract of these portfolios, the model calculates all financial events.

13.1.7 Analysis outputs

We perform liquidity, value, exposure, profit and loss analysis at the contract and portfolio level under canonical conditions and two different stress scenarios—A and B—with different levels of stress. The model generates several types of report.

Figure 13.1 illustrates the layout of this model. It includes most of the considerations about profitability and analysis that we outlined in Part Two of this book.

In the following paragraphs, we describe the results of the model in more detail. Without intending to spoil the surprise, we conclude that returns are good when conditions stay as they are. As soon as defaults rise under modest stress, portfolio returns decrease to low single-digit returns over the holding period, or turn negative.

We are unsure if investors are in a position to perform analytics as described in Part Two of this book. Risk management (i.e., by performing stress testing) could help platforms offer advice to investors to optimize their portfolios.

Table 13.1 shows the results of the return distribution of three scenarios under canonical (ideal) conditions and the two different stress scenarios, both annualized and for the full duration of the holding period. Scenario A applies "mild stress," Scenario B applies "medium stress." This table shows the changes in portfolio performance under the different scenarios. We will explain the underlying assumptions of each scenario under the heading "Stress test scenarios."

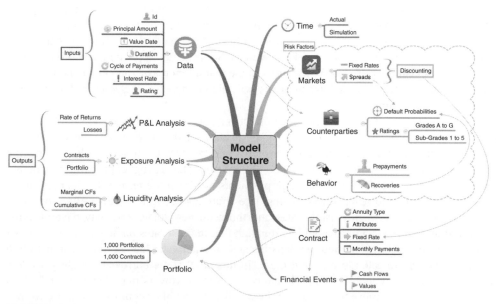

FIGURE 13.1 Layout of the model

TABLE 13.1   Summary statistics of the model portfolio under canonical conditions and stress conditions

	Mean		Standard Deviation		Median		Skewness		Kurtosis	
Scenario	Full Duration	Annual	Full Duration	Annual	Full Duration	Annual	Full Duration	Annual	Full Duration	Annual
Canonical	23.8979	6.6262	0.2068	0.0090	23.8962	6.6262	0.0898	0.0386	2.7082	2.9557
Scenario A	4.0136	1.4286	0.0378	0.0091	4.0129	1.4287	−0.0230	−0.0194	3.0609	2.9392
Scenario B	−14.7135	−4.0096	0.1002	0.0171	−14.7105	−4.0094	−0.0920	−0.1130	2.7321	2.8617

A more in-depth conclusion follows at the end of this chapter. Let's now go through the model parameters and analysis of this model step by step. Figure 13.1 shows the layout of the model.

13.2   RISK FACTORS

Several factors impact the performance of a portfolio of marketplace loans, namely market risk, credit and counterparty risk, and behavior. Below, we look at these variables and their drivers to understand how they might influence the performance of the loan portfolio.

13.2.1   Market risk

Interest rates of marketplace loans are fixed over the term of the loan, and counterparty ratings set the amount of the initial rate. However, these interest rates[2] include both market risk-free rates and discounting spreads, as we discussed in Chapter 6. Because market risk-free rates can be very low or negative in an interest-rate environment that follows a crisis, spreads may make up most of the interest income. As the rates are fixed,[3] contracts are not repricing over time. This implies that market volatilities will have no impact on the value and future cash flows. In a sense, fixed interest rates intrinsically neglect market volatilities, but they may increase counterparty and behavior risks as well as the strategies applied in new production or restructuring existing portfolios. When stress in the market increases, and the market becomes volatile, market interest rates for new loans will either increase or decrease, but they will hardly remain the same.

Higher interest rates have a negative effect on borrowers. Because they have to pay a higher rate on new loans, they come under stress as they see the alternative credit system, their lifeline for capital, at risk. New loans under these conditions are unattractive. Those borrowers who agree to new—and in effect, worse—conditions might have a higher probability of default because they will be shouldered with high payments for the entire term of the loan, normally three to five years. However, lower interest rates may also have a negative effect on loans. If a gap opens up between existing rates and those on new loans, this may have an effect on default and prepayment probabilities. Imagine that interest rates on new loans were lower than rates in the previous period, perhaps because marketplace lenders must compete with new entrants who threaten to undercut them. In this case, some borrowers might get a loan elsewhere and prepay their existing obligations. Other borrowers may decide to default on their existing loans because they perceive the conditions as unfair compared to those for new borrowers. Prepayments and defaults lead to a loss of interest income to lenders.

Marketplace lending platforms depend almost exclusively on their credit scoring algorithms for risk management. They consider a wider spectrum of data than credit scores alone, so they often get a better picture of potential borrower behavior. Because they offer fixed interest rates, marketplace loans may become a bad investment if the interest falls below the real market interest rate. Regardless, next to predicting borrower behavior, platforms take little account of expectations of how market conditions might change. The margin between the lender and borrower is steady, but accounting considerations, such as measuring fair value, are also absent.

Fixed rates may matter little when banks pay no interest at all. Lenders will be happy to get at least some interest and pay little attention to whether it is fixed or variable. However, when the market improves, or when inflation sets in, fixed rates are a bad deal for lenders. It remains to be seen how lenders will react to this feature of marketplace loans when they find themselves locked into deals that lose money in comparison to other investment options.

Of course, one could contend that fixed rates have worked fairly well in the bond market. Because marketplace loans are similar to a corporate bond market for private lending, they might as well use the same recipe and offer fixed rates. Bond markets offer zero coupon loans, or fixed loans, where the interest rate is often lower than inflation. The difference between the bond market and marketplace loans is that in the bond market, all counterparties are professional investors who do their homework regarding profitability and risk management. To expect the same from retail investors in marketplace loans is impossible. Even though some data and analytics are available on some of the larger marketplace lending platforms, investors will hardly have the capacity to program an advanced risk model which would allow them to price risk fully.

13.2.2 Counterparty credit risk

Default probabilities and credit ratings often have a strong connection with spreads and expected recoveries. As discussed above, the interest rate in marketplace loans consists of the market interest rate and a credit spread. We assume that the market risk-free rate is small,[4] whereas the counterparty credit spread defines the bulk of the rate in marketplace lending.[5]

We apply intensity models, discussed in Chapter 7, to estimate the conditional default probabilities[6] driven by frequency of the events arriving within time interval,

$$
PD_{con}(t) = 1 - \exp\left[-\underbrace{\frac{spread}{1 - recovery}}_{hazard\ rate} \cdot t\right]
\tag{13.1}
$$

where, the first part of the exponential function implies the *hazard rate* of default defined by discounting the credit spreads and recovery rates, whereas the second part, i.e., t, defines the future periods.

In Chapter 7 we looked at how conditional default probabilities[7] through time[8] can be estimated based on a *hazard rate* function. In this analysis, spreads are derived from the available interest rates. The recovery rate is defined as the expected interest income earned through the interest payment cycles. Any stress in credit rating will result in a shock in credit spreads, which impacts the default probabilities through the *hazard rate* function. This function assumes that default probabilities (PD) of counterparties can increase exponentially from year to year, based on spreads and recoveries. It may seem overly harsh, but the degree of risk is indeed changing exponentially under stress conditions; this explains why regulators[9] also require banks to assess their credit portfolios under such an assumption. In bank loans, counterparty spreads are relatively small because they mostly lend to high-quality borrowers. However, in marketplace lending, counterparty spreads are extremely high in comparison. A 5-year low rated loan contract with a PD of 20 percent in the first year could easily reach 100 percent probability of default in the final year if we apply the hazard rate function. In marketplace lending, applying a hazard rate therefore only makes sense for stress conditions, not expected market conditions.

13.2.3 Behavior

The only behavioral characteristics in our analysis are prepayment and the change of the probability of default discussed in Chapter 8. Both of these characteristics have underlying drivers. For instance, markets and idiosyncratic factors drive prepayments. Past observations indicate expected prepayment rates and times under normal and expected conditions. However, under stress conditions, prepayment rates may change in regards to the time intervals. Moreover, borrowers may use prepayments as a strategy for rolling over their loans for better conditions.

Market and idiosyncratic borrower characteristics drive changes in the probabilities of default. For lenders, probabilities of default indicate changes in the expected credit exposure and losses. Borrowers may decide to default if they recognize that their payment rates are higher than market rates and the contractual conditions have tilted against them. If the terms of an individual loan agreement diverge significantly from the terms that have become the new standard in a market, the willingness of borrowers to fulfill their obligations may deteriorate rapidly.

13.3 PORTFOLIO CONSTRUCTION

We have already learned that the type of contractual agreement is based on a fixed rated annuity type of financial instrument where the obligor pays out a stream of principal and interest payments where their sum is always equal through the payment time intervals. Therefore, the payments of interest (i.e., income) are decreasing, and payments of principal capital are increasing through time.

To construct a portfolio that contains loans with a certain target allocation, we first modeled a *direct* approach to portfolio construction, where an investor invests in a certain number of loans and funds them fully. We investigated a portfolio that allocates capital across the top-rated rating classes A to G according to the target allocation recommended by Lending Club. Table 13.2 shows this target allocation.[10]

To simulate the *direct* investment approach, we select loans from each loan grade from the entire population of loans. For example, to arrive at an allocation of 27 percent of A-rated loans, we randomly select 270 A-rated loans from the entire Lending Club loan book. To make sure that they contain each sub-rating, we split the selection evenly across sub-grades A1 to A5, which turns out to be 52 loans of each sub-grade for A-rated loans (270 divided by 5). Then we follow the same procedure for the remaining loan grades and selected 420 B-rated loans, 130 C-rated loans, 100 D-rated loans, 50 E-rated loans, 20 F-rated loans, and 10 G-rated

TABLE 13.2 Recommended target allocation across loan grades

Loan grade	Target allocation
A	27%
B	42%
C	13%
D	10%
E	5%
F	2%
G	1%

Data source: Lending Club, as of May 21, 2015

loans, again evenly distributed across sub-grades. We end up with a portfolio consisting of 1,000 loans spread across all sub-ratings.[11] This is a simplification to approximate the target allocation, which is somewhat imprecise because the nominal amounts of each loan vary in size. Still, it approximates the exposure of institutional investors to marketplace lending.

Conversely, private investors practice an *indirect* investment approach. They allocate capital across several loans in small tranches. For example, an investor may choose to allocate an amount of capital across different rating classes with a tranche of $25 per loan. To model the indirect approach, we need to make sure that lenders have equal exposure to each loan, so we multiply the expected profit or loss with a weighting factor that corresponds with equal exposure. To model the indirect approach, we sum the loans of each loan grade and calculate their share of the entire portfolio. Then we adjust this share to match the target allocation from Table 13.2. We now hold a portfolio with partial loans that models how a retail investor might invest in Lending Club.

For simplicity's sake, we assume that investors allocate their capital all at the same time and then hold the portfolio until the term of the last loan has completed. We understand that lenders will re-invest capital when it becomes available, but we have omitted this here to keep things tidy. Figure 13.2 shows the distribution of the capital investment for 1,000 sample portfolios in the indirect investment approach.

13.3.1 Portfolio exposure

Because marketplace loans are unsecured, the exposure of the portfolio is inherently collateralized, or recovered, by using the interest income. In this case, the net exposure is correlated to interest income and counterparty risk[12] that is when a counterparty defaults it will directly impact the degree of net exposure; in other words the portfolio is also exposed to specific wrong way risk. On the other hand, due to the fact that the market interest rates are fixed, market volatilities will not impact the net exposure.[13] As we already discussed, markets, i.e., interest rates, drive the net exposure and counterparty risk. Figure 13.3 shows the exposure of one sample portfolio that consists of 1000 randomly selected Lending Club loans across loan grades A1 to G5. Net credit exposure indicates the expected credit losses in the event of default. As can be observed from Figure 13.3 the greatest degrees of exposures appear in contracts 350 to 700 which are rated between B and C. Contracts with ratings B and C make up the lion's share of portfolios of marketplace loans. As a result, when borrowers with credit ratings B and C underperform, portfolio performance suffers disproportionately.

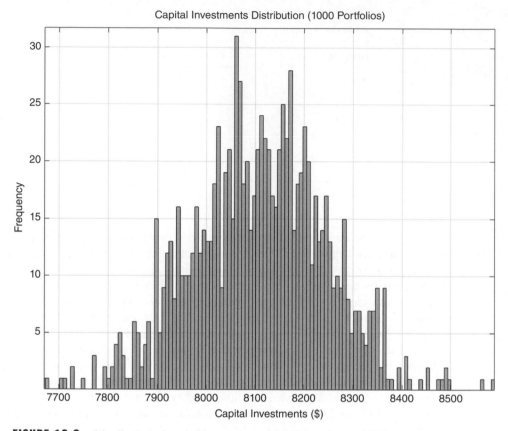

FIGURE 13.2   Distribution of capital investment, of 1,000 sample portfolios

13.4   MODELING PORTFOLIO PERFORMANCE

The performance of the constructed portfolio is measured based on income simulation and expected liquidity. These have to be evaluated under both canonical expected conditions and stress scenarios.

13.4.1   Income performance

To estimate the return on investment of the portfolios, we need to estimate the performance of the sample portfolios under canonical conditions. Such conditions imply that all borrowers fulfill the agreed obligations. In an ideal world, the default probability is zero because none of the obligors will default. They will execute all principal and interest cash flow events as agreed without late payments, and they will also refrain from early payments, so the prepayment rate equals zero.

The return performance is based on a simple typical return of investment estimation, i.e., the net profit over the initial investment. Thus, the distribution of contract returns of a single

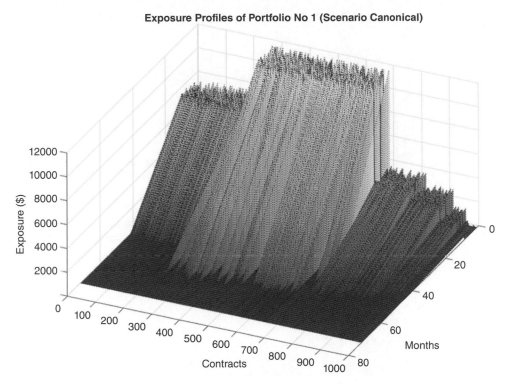

Exposure Profiles of Portfolio No 1 (Scenario Canonical)

FIGURE 13.3 Portfolio exposure for scenario under canonical expectations

sample portfolio is as illustrated in Figure 13.4. Figure 13.5 shows the distribution of the returns referring to 1,000 sample portfolios.

These returns look good. The median total return of our sample portfolios is 23.9 percent during the overall duration[14] of the contracts. The lower bound is 23.31 percent and the upper bound is 24.54 percent. The annual mean arithmetic return is 6.62 percent. Table 13.1 at the beginning of this chapter shows additional summary statistics of the different scenarios.

Let's remember that this is the return under canonical conditions, where the market and all borrowers behave in exemplary fashion and get an A+ for their behavior.

13.4.2 Liquidity performance

In regards to liquidity, every single contract results in expected principal and interest cash flow payments. As the portfolios in marketplace lending are not tradable, only funding liquidity is of interest in our analysis. In such analysis two types of liquidity reports are rather important: marginal and cumulative. Marginal liquidity focuses mainly on the view of *in* and *out* flows through time. Cumulative liquidity illustrates the evolution of the cash flows, where the investor can see the growth or deterioration of the expected cash *in* and *out* flows. Examples of these types of reports are illustrated in Figure 13.6 where marginal and cumulative liquidity GAP reports based on aggregated cash flows for portfolio number 1 under canonical conditions are shown; moreover, detailed evolution, of individual contracts of the portfolio, is illustrated in Figure 13.7.

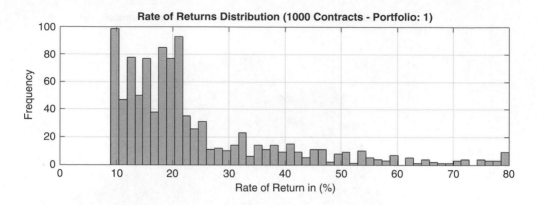

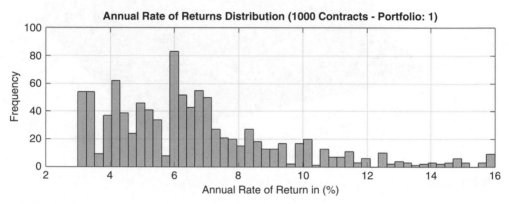

FIGURE 13.4   Rate of return distribution of a single sample portfolio during the entire duration of the investment

Moreover, Figure 13.8 illustrates the evolution of expected liquidity gaps of the entire distribution of 1,000 portfolios. When contracts mature, their cash flows become flat. Still, investors hold them until the last contract has matured.

Under normal conditions, we can say that "returns are quite good as long as the music plays." Let's now investigate this claim by stressing the portfolios.

13.4.3   Stress testing

Under stress, portfolios perform differently from what we expect under canonical conditions. To simulate this, we stress the *ratings, time of default, prepayments rate,* and the *point in time of the prepayments*. We define these parameters based on the scenarios.

We assume that higher rated borrowers default less often than lower rated counterparties. When they do, defaults are expected to happen late. At the same time, they prepay more often than lower rated counterparties. When they do, they do so early. The point in time where the default or prepayment occurs is defined as a percentage in regards to the duration of the contract; for instance an event (default or prepayment) at point in time 90 percent means that if a contract lasts 60 months, the default happens in month 54.

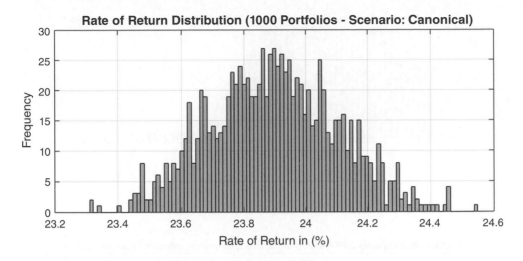

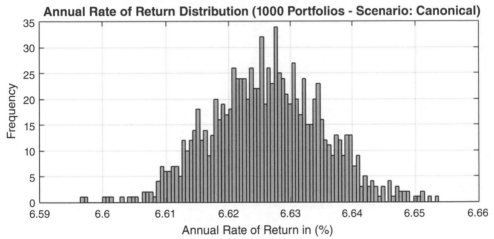

FIGURE 13.5   Distribution of the rate of returns under canonical conditions among all 1,000
sample portfolios

As aforementioned, and discussed in Chapter 7, we derive the default probabilities through
annual time iterations, by using the *hazard rate* function defined in Equation 13.1, which is
driven by the credit spread and recovery[15] rates. The market risk-free fixed rates are set to
1.5%; to capture any volatility of this rate we apply an add-on random factor that may increase
the above rate up to 2.5%. The remaining degree from the interest rate set in each contract
defines the credit spread.

Obviously, a borrower with a higher rating pays a lower interest than a borrower with a
lower rating, where the rating is the sum of market interest and the credit spread. Because
these are all unsecured—uncollateralized—loans, nothing can compensate lenders in case of
a default. We have therefore used the accumulated interest income that lenders receive as
de-facto collateral or recovery just after the default against which we compile losses that occur
in the event of a default. With this in mind, what is worse under these circumstances: defaults

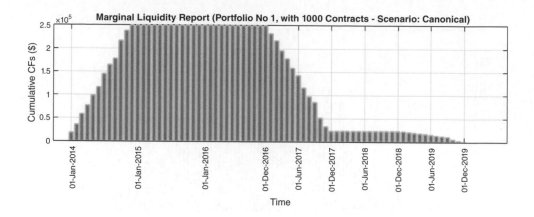

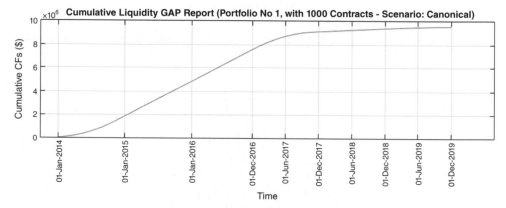

FIGURE 13.6   Marginal and cumulative liquidity GAP reports based on aggregated cash flows for portfolio No 1 resulted under canonical conditions

of higher rated borrowers or lower rated borrowers? Both result in losses, but because the higher rated borrowers pay much less interest than lower rated counterparties, their de-facto collateral is much smaller. When they default, they can wipe out the accumulated interest over the period, quickly racking up losses. Investing in only the higher grades is therefore a bad risk mitigation strategy because defaults eat up the lower interest almost immediately. As a side note, Table 13.3 shows the interest rates that lenders can expect from each loan grade.[16]

We used the default probability to estimate losses from cancelled interest and principal cash flows, after the point in time of default.

We stress the risk factor of credit spreads by applying deterministic shock that ranges based on the rating scale, i.e., from A1 to G5. Default rates for the two scenarios are described in the next paragraphs. Notably, the point in time of default plays a key role in the estimation of returns and losses.

Let's move on to prepayments. Market conditions affect both default and prepayments. The latter impact investors' interest income and the liquidity of the portfolio. Moreover, they impact the net exposure because we use interest income as collateral/recovery to cover losses. Prepayments therefore have an effect on the size of losses in case of defaults.

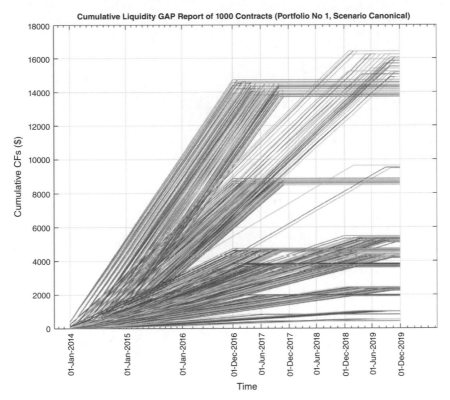

FIGURE 13.7 Cumulative liquidity GAP reports for each of the 1,000 contracts in portfolio number 1 under canonical conditions

13.4.4 Stress test scenarios

As we discussed in Chapter 6, the main market risk factors are currencies, asset prices, yield curve and market interest rates, and product interest rates. Marketplace loans only have indirect exposure to market conditions; these also drive the probability of default and prepayments. Roughly speaking, in marketplace lending, all possible scenarios impact the same two things, either positively or negatively: default probability and prepayments. Let's now look at three different scenarios, summarized in Table 13.4.

13.4.4.1 Baseline case: Canonical conditions in the ideal world This is the outcome we all would like to see with our investments where they perform as expected. We hardly need to describe this in more detail, as we have already looked at its results at the beginning of this chapter.

Scenario A: Shock in the economy If the economy in general is under pressure with interest rates at low or negative levels, credit from formal channels may remain inaccessible for most counterparties. The market has little faith in counterparties to improve their economic prospects in the future, which would allow them to meet their obligations as borrowers. Stress in the market implies liquidity problems and insecurity. All parties in the economy have a

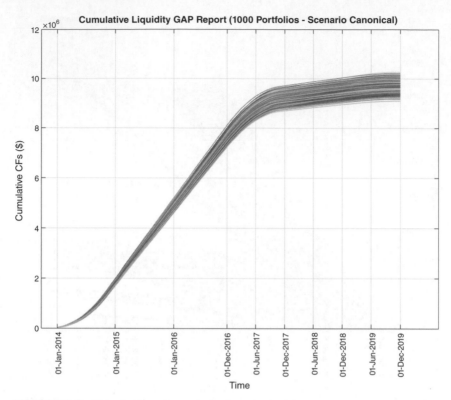

FIGURE 13.8   Distribution of cumulative liquidity GAP reports out of 1,000 portfolios

difficult time; some people may lose their jobs, and those who run a business will have to brace themselves for rough weather ahead. Borrowers of marketplace loans pay high fixed interest rates for a relatively long duration of three to six years. They may have signed up for a high rate loan because they were hoping for a market upswing. Being stuck with such a loan is especially severe for small businesses. They may have borrowed to improve their business prospects, but in an economic slump, customers fail to materialize. The longer that very low

TABLE 13.3   Interest rate and ARP Lending Club

Loan grade	Annual interest rate	Origination fee	36-Month APR	60-Month APR
A	5.32%–7.98%	1%–4%	5.99%–9.97%	7.02%–9.63%
B	8.18%–11.53%	4%–5%	10.98%–14.38%	10.38%–13.80%
C	12.29%–14.65%	5%	15.90%–18.31%	14.58%–16.99%
D	15.61%–17.86%	5%	19.29%–21.60%	17.98%–20.28%
E	18.25%–20.99%	5%	21.99%–24.80%	20.68%–23.49%
F	21.99%–25.78%	5%	25.82%–29.70%	24.51%–28.40%
G	26.77%–28.99%	5%	30.71%–32.99%	29.42%–31.70%

Data source: Lending Club, as of May 21, 2015

TABLE 13.4 Stress test scenarios and their simulation

	Canonical conditions	**Scenario A**	**Scenario B**
Description	Nothing changes	Shock in the economy, the whole market underperforms	Shock in the economy with extra stress on alternative borrowers
Assumptions	Prepayments → Defaults →	Prepayments ↗ Defaults ↑	Prepayments ↗ Defaults ↑
Simulation	No change of expected defaults and prepayments	Stress on counterparty spreads and prepayments	Stress on counterparty spreads and prepayments

interest rates persist—a sign that the economy is doing badly—the higher the likelihood of a behavior change in borrowers. We must assume that market conditions change eventually, that they will not stay the same. With this in mind, it becomes apparent that fixed interest rates are riskier than we expected. In the long run, nothing stays the same. When market conditions change, borrowers may choose to default because they simply lack the funds to pay back the loan. People have fewer options to make more money, and the default probability is increasing. On the flipside, few highly rated counterparties prepay their existing loans because they simply lack the funds to do so. We simulate this scenario by stressing the counterparty spreads across all grades and decreasing the frequency of prepayments marginally.

Scenario B: Shock in the economy with extra stress on alternative borrowers   When the economy tanks, it often affects all people in one form or another. This is roughly what Scenario A is all about. In Scenario B, we put added stress on borrowers relying on credit outside the formal financial system. Defaults in the sector may occur for several reasons. For example, platforms may have a hard time underwriting marketplace loans. Reasons for this may be that their cost of capital has gone up through time, or that regulation has stepped up the rules, which have made it more difficult to service middle to low-rated borrowers. If marketplace lending runs into liquidity problems at the same time that the economy is under shock, a vicious cycle begins: borrowers come under stress as they see that the alternative credit system, their lifeline for capital, is at risk. Shouldered with high fixed interest rate and a relatively long maturity, borrowers may default. As a result, their credit scores suffer and they become even less eligible for credit. As a group, marketplace borrowers might act similarly in economic turmoil. Lower-rated loans have a high default probability and credit spread, so their defaults in times of stress are less of a surprise. Conversely, when high-rated counterparties default—those that we assumed would be secure—it takes investors by surprise. How prepayments behave in this scenario is unclear. They may remain steady but most likely they will be reduced due to liquidity problems. A higher frequency of prepayments on the other hand may be the case if competitors decide to take advantage of the weakness of those platforms that are under the heaviest scrutiny by offering lower rates that allow borrowers to prepay; however they will rather look for the higher rated counterparties. Higher rated counterparties may therefore prepay to restructure their portfolios. Sources of stress for platforms are manifold. Another possible cause for distress for the sector might be that lenders lose the appetite to invest in their loans. We simulate this scenario with a higher rate of default and a high frequency of prepayments, expected from highly rated borrowers.

13.4.4.2 Simulating scenarios We simulate our scenarios by stressing three variables: the risk factor of the credit spreads, the times of default, and the probabilities of prepayment rates and the time of prepayment. The following paragraphs explain each variable.

Stressing risk factor of credit spreads Spreads have been shocked[17] based on the underlying counterparty rating in contracts. The default probabilities, starting with initial spreads linked to rating classes, are changing over time based on hazard rates. The new default rates range from 8% for rating A1 to 99% for rating G5. This actually defines the shocks of the ratings, which will immediately affect credit spreads. For instance, within the duration of the contracts, in Scenario A the spread for counterparties rate A1 may rise, but only 0.1%. However, in Scenario B, the spread for the lowest rated counterparties may rise by up to 99%.

Stressing times of default Default events occur at an expected point in time, depending on a contract's counterparty rating.[18] We expect contracts with high ratings to default later in the term, and contracts with low ratings earlier. In Scenario A, counterparties rated A1 default at or after 84% of the life of the contract, while contracts rated G5 default at or after 20% of their life. For instance, a contract maturing in 36 months with a default time of 84% is expected to default after 30.2 months. Figure 13.9 and Figure 13.10 illustrate the default rates and times applied to all 1,000 contracts in the analysis according to their sub-grades A1 to G5. To make the simulation more pragmatic, we increase the volatility of the rates and times by adding a small noise factor between zero and ten percent.

Default rates and times shown in Figure 13.9 were aligned with Scenario A where lower rated counterparties are expected to default. The first 690 contracts (rated A1 to B5) have defaulted with a rate from 6% to 36%. As expected, the PITs of such defaults appear late— from 72% to 84% of the duration of the contracts. The 310 remaining contracts default with a rate from 40% to 100% at the PITs from 36% to 71% of the life of the contracts. On the other hand, in Scenario B (Figure 13.10), the default rate increases for the contracts with median ratings B and C. The first 690 contracts with A1 to B5 ratings have a default rate of less than 48%, and these defaults occur late. The remaining contracts default from 49% to 100% at the PITs from 20% to 49% of the contracts' life.

Stressing probabilities of prepayment rates and the time of prepayment The top prepayment rate is 25.5% for Scenario A and 60% for Scenario B. The time of each prepayment is set as a percentage of the contract's duration. Figure 13.11 and Figure 13.12 show the amount and times of prepayments for each contract. In Scenario A, the PITs of prepayments range from medium to late—35% to 99% of the life of the contract. In Scenario B, prepayments are higher. The first 690 contracts, rated A1 to B5, will prepay 46% to 60% of their principal during the first third of their duration. The remaining contracts will be also prepay, but will prepay smaller amounts, and later in the life of the contract.

13.4.4.3 Outcomes Based on the above scenarios the system calculated all financial events for the 1,000 contracts of the 1,000 portfolios. As we mentioned earlier, the return performance is based on a simple typical return of investment estimation. The distributions of the returns for the 1,000 sample portfolios, based on Scenarios A and B, are illustrated in Figure 13.13 and Figure 13.14 respectively.

In Scenario A, the median total return of our sample portfolios is 4.02% during the overall duration of the contracts. The lower bound is 3.9% and the upper bound is 4.12%. The annual

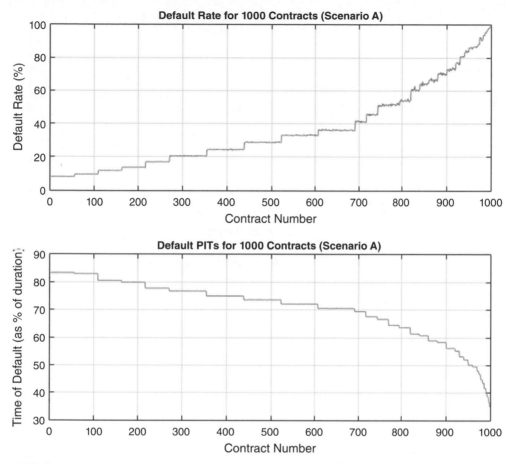

FIGURE 13.9 Default rate (in percentage) and the time of default as percentage of individual contracts' duration applied, for Scenario A, to each group, classified from A1 to G5 ratings, of the 1,000 contracts constructing the simulated portfolios

mean arithmetic return is 1.42%. Returns for Scenario A are still positive but rather close to what an investor could get from the established financial institutions which also provide 100% guarantee of returning the full amount of the capital.

In Scenario B, the median total return during the overall duration of the contracts, reaches a negative return on investment of −18.3%, with the lower and higher bounds estimated at −18.68% and −17.94% respectively. Moreover, the annual mean return is −5.1%. In this case, investors are suffering losses that the interest income cannot cover.

The distribution of cumulative liquidity GAP reports out of 1,000 portfolios for both *Scenario A* and *Scenario B* are illustrated in Figure 13.15 and Figure 13.16. As we can see, the cumulative cash flows have been reduced 24.8%.

From Figure 13.17 and Figure 13.18 we can observe that the evolution of the contracts' net exposures have increased over time. This is because due to stress scenarios the interest income, which is considered as the amount to collateralize the gross exposure, has decreased;

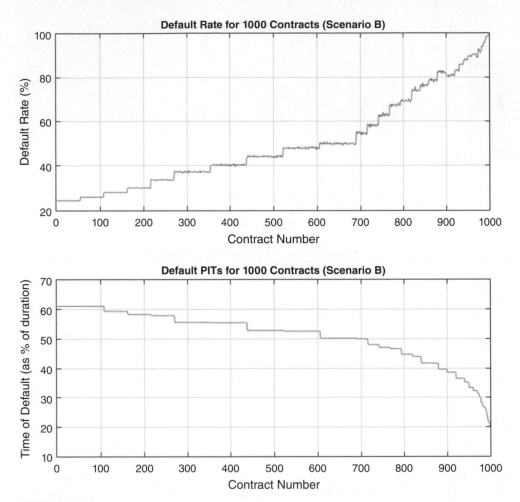

FIGURE 13.10   Default rate in percentage and the time of default as percentage of individual contracts' duration applied, for Scenario B, to each group, classified from A1 to G5 ratings, of the 1,000 contracts constructing the simulated portfolios

thus, the net exposure has been increased accordingly. Figure 13.19 illustrates the evolution of the portfolio exposures under the three scenarios (i.e., Canonical, A and B).

13.5   RISK MANAGEMENT

The idea of risk management is not to increase the premiums but rather to optimize portfolios and minimize the losses under stress conditions. As we saw, defaults of higher rated borrowers result in higher losses than those of lower rated borrowers. Risk mitigation only through diversification across loan grades can look different from what we might expect. Higher-paying, lower-rated contracts are essential to buffer investors against unexpected losses.

Ideally, a portfolio under stress would have no losses. Yet, in the real world, even the carefully constructed portfolios of large banks incur losses under unexpected circumstances.

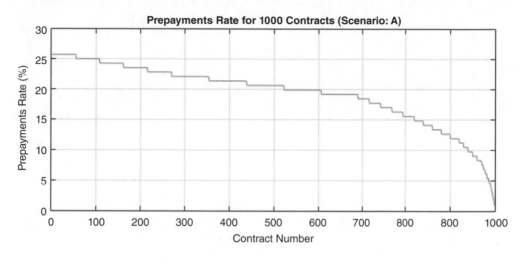

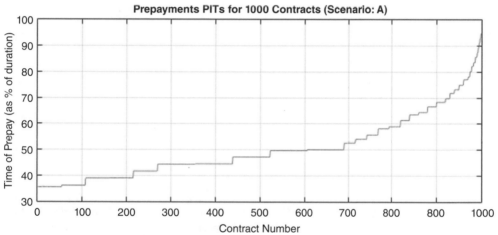

FIGURE 13.11 Prepayment rates as percentage of the remaining principal amount and prepayment point of times as percentage of individual contracts' duration, applied for Scenario A, to each group, classified from A1 to G5 ratings, of the 1,000 contracts constructing the simulated portfolios

We learned this painfully in the financial crisis of 2007/8. Banks thought they had perfectly mitigated all risk, but their assumptions turned out to be wrong. To use this as an excuse to forgo risk modeling of marketplace loan portfolios would be missing the point. Sure, banks used models and they still incurred losses in the end. However, they overestimated the value of the assets on their books, they overestimated the performance of high-rated assets under stress, and they underestimated the impact of market and counterparty risk on their portfolios. Their models were too optimistic in their expectations, which required the intervention of the central bank to bail out many banks. In a nutshell, banks used the wrong models and they used them in the wrong way. As the saying goes: "A fool with a tool is still a fool." Underestimating risk using advanced models and systems with poor parameters is unsustainable. We can learn from past mistakes to construct and understand better the risk models and take into account

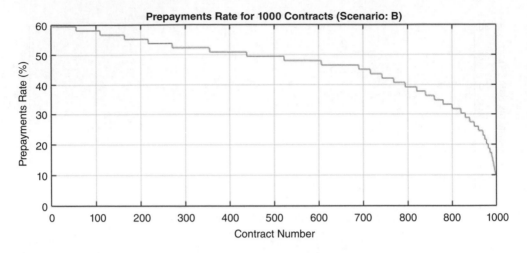

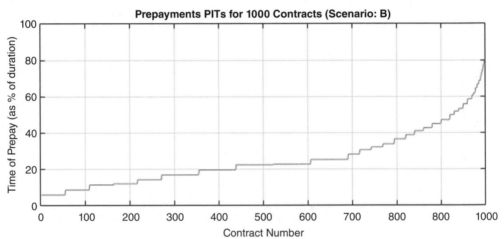

FIGURE 13.12   Prepayment rates as percentage of the remaining principal amount and prepayment point of times as percentage of individual contracts' duration, applied for Scenario B, to each group, classified from A1 to G5 ratings, of the 1,000 contracts constructing the simulated portfolios

more severe stress scenarios. The credit sector can only profit from this. This is true for the credit sector beyond marketplace lending, including the entire financial system.

When regulators look at credit exposure today, they mainly request use of determinist stress scenarios rather than relying on VaR models. Because the central bank and tax payers bear the losses of financial institutions in the end, regulators want to avoid unexpected losses. Regulators want to see portfolios with no losses, even in stormy markets.

It is true that it is not the lending platforms but the individual lenders who hold this exposure on their books. Nevertheless, if the asset class at large suffers, the originators should at least know the extent of the losses that the loans they sold to investors might incur.

As we pointed out in Chapter 11 about concentration risk and systemic exposure, regulators will want to understand the cumulative losses of the asset class to accurately model the impact they could potentially have on the economy at large. If regulators looked at the asset class

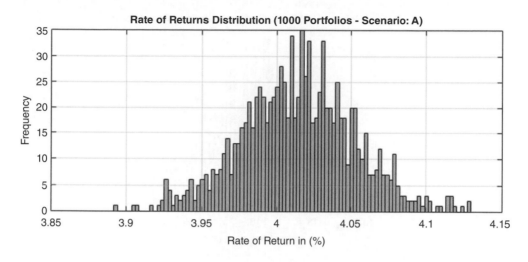

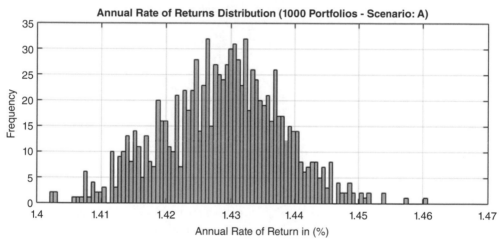

FIGURE 13.13 Distribution of the rate of returns under stress Scenario Λ: Stressing the spreads one notch

with the same microscope they apply to banks, they will want to know that risk-free rates and spreads can absorb expected losses. Regulators could also inquire into how lenders structure their current and future operations to survive in times of increased stress. Unless lenders have enough capital to remain liquid under stress conditions, they are vulnerable.

13.5.1 Operational risk

Even though it is not part of the analysis, marketplace platforms have operational risk. Platforms follow regulations for operational risk, which ensures they follow know-your-customer (KYC) procedures to verify the identity of borrowers and lenders. However, lenders cannot rely on deposit insurance for their loans. At the same time, the larger platforms have safeguards in place where an independent party takes over the servicing of the loans in case something

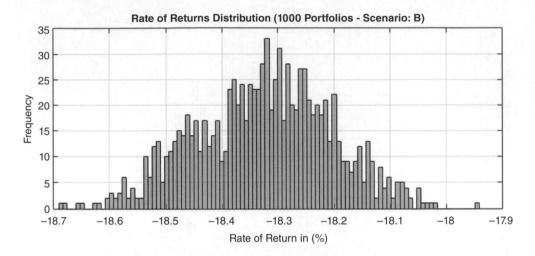

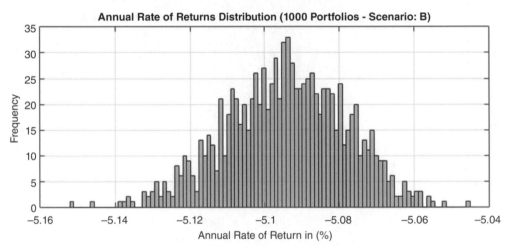

FIGURE 13.14   Distribution of the rate of returns under stress Scenario B

should happen to the platform. Regardless, in case of bankruptcy of a platform, lenders will have no recourse against the platform. Operational risk is less of an issue today because the larger platforms have proven their worth. Lending Club, for example, trades on the NYSE and is valued at roughly $8 billion. Such an operation will hardly disappear overnight. Bankruptcy is not around the corner for the well-established marketplace lenders, but a financial crisis could change that. Lenders should be aware that some operational risk persists. Operational risk can cause high losses with a low probability, which could impact the value of the whole portfolio.

13.5.2   Likely overestimation of borrower quality in marketplace lending

An analysis of the expected probability of default in Lending Club's loan book of 2007–2011 indicates that the credit scoring algorithm used by the platform slightly overestimates

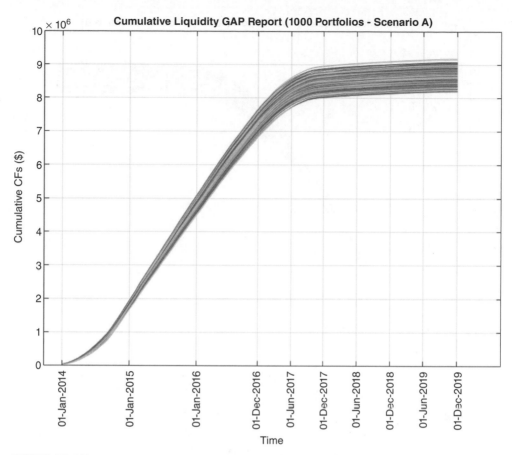

FIGURE 13.15   Distribution of cumulative liquidity GAP reports under Scenario A

borrowers of the lower loan grades. Compared to the number of loans issued, the platform incurred a disproportionate amount of losses in 2007–2011 from borrowers with medium grades, and[19] the probability of default is inconsistent with their grading system of borrowers. Perhaps this has to do with the fact that marketplace lenders never downgrade a borrower, even if his loan becomes delinquent. Figure 13.20 shows how the frequency of ratings diverges with the frequency of defaults.

In Part One of this book, we raised the question as to whether marketplace lending platforms serve as a storefront for subprime loans that hedge funds and banks are more than happy to take off their hands. Lenders like to point out that they mainly lend to borrowers with high credit scores. Regardless, almost 40 percent of all new loans for autos, credit cards and personal borrowing in the U.S. went to subprime customers during the first 11 months of 2014.[20] This is the highest level since 2007, when subprime loans represented 41 percent of consumer lending outside of home mortgages. Somebody must be underwriting these loans. For instance, online lending resource Biz2Credit underwrote roughly half of its loans to subprime borrowers in 2014.[21] Credit bureau Equifax defines subprime borrowers as those with a credit score below 640 on a scale that tops out at 850. Some marketplace lenders accept only borrowers with higher scores, others accept subprime borrowers.[22]

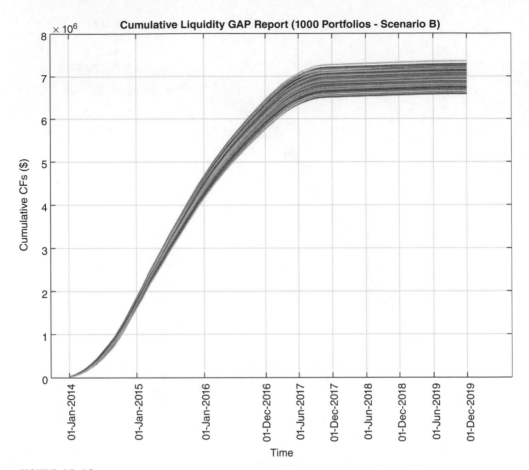

FIGURE 13.16 Distribution of cumulative liquidity GAP reports under Scenario B

Even though marketplace loans—like any other investment—come with certain investment risks, the comparison with subprime loans that stood at the center of the financial crisis 2007/8 is not entirely fair. The largest amount of credit that borrowers can get on a marketplace lending platform is $35,000 at the time of this writing. This is relatively modest compared to the average subprime loan in the run up to the financial crisis. It is also important to remember that marketplace loans only make up a tiny fraction of the credit markets.

Regardless, most marketplace borrowers use their loans to refinance their credit card balances at better rates. Marketplace lenders do check borrowers' credit scores and update their credit scoring algorithms often. Additionally, they use alternative data—such as consumers' monthly bill payments—and so-called fringe alternative data—posts and connections on social networks—to determine borrowers' credit worthiness. Even though the predictive value and fairness of fringe alternative data are up for debate, fringe alternative models attempt to fill in the gaps that freeze some consumers out of the credit markets, reaching even further than mainstream alternative models. These underwriting standards are a long way from what banks demand from their creditors, but they are a step up from those of the fly-by-night stall in the mall that sold subprime loans by the dozen.

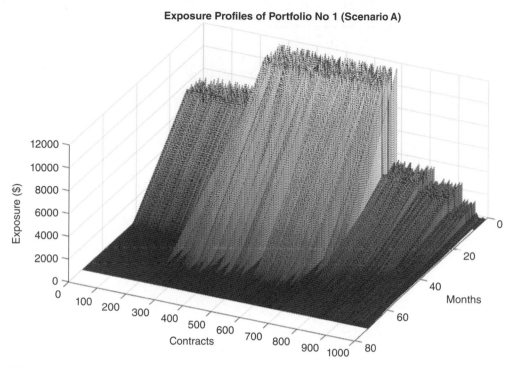

FIGURE 13.17   Portfolio exposure for Scenario A

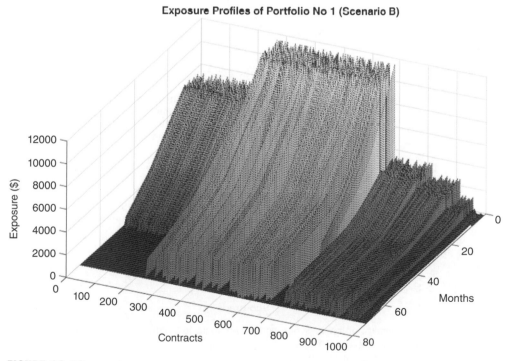

FIGURE 13.18   Portfolio exposure for Scenario B

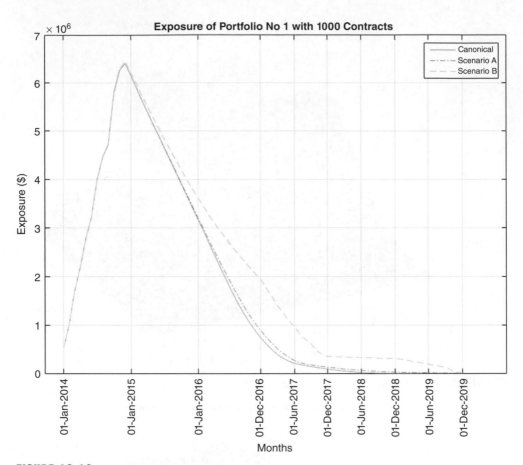

FIGURE 13.19   Evolution of the portfolio exposures under three scenarios: Canonical, A and B

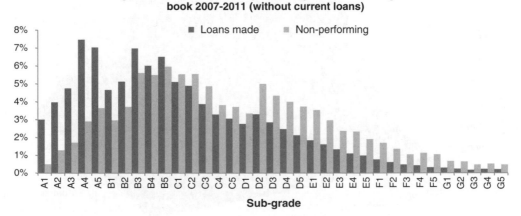

FIGURE 13.20   Percentage of loans vs. non-performing loans in Lending Club's loan book
2007–2011, excluding current loans
Data source: Lending Club, as of May 21, 2015

Regardless, the fact that marketplace loans are uncollateralized makes them risky, and predictions about the actions of borrowers under stress are difficult to make. Even the pioneers among the marketplace lenders have only lived through one recession so far. How the business model of marketplace lenders will fare in future financial crises is unknown. Borrowers may honor their loan agreements or they may default *en masse* with little consequence because their loans are uncollateralized. This would be a disaster for both individual lending platforms and the entire sector.

Every loan comes with investment risk. Even bank loans with the highest rating and high-quality collateral can default. Even though a certain degree of risk is necessary to have meaningful returns above the risk-free rate, banks avoid uncertainty at all costs. When they can assess risks beforehand, they can manage them. When the risks are unknown, they cannot. Marketplace lenders, on the other hand, do very little to remove the high uncertainty that exists in their loan books. Even though they like to point out that they lend to borrowers with high credit scores, they still originate a healthy number of loans with a subprime grade. Furthermore, some of the information that borrowers provide is not even verified. This adds unnecessary uncertainty into the equation. Sensible lenders will sooner or later ask marketplace lenders to improve the quality of borrowers to drive down counterparty risk and default risk. For a lender who has diversified his loan portfolio across hundreds of loans, individual defaults may not matter. Nevertheless, every default that could have been avoided by better screening borrowers is unnecessary.

13.5.3   A note on portfolio restructuring and optimization

There is a sweet spot in the number of loans in a portfolio of marketplace loans. Beyond a certain point, adding more contracts reverts performance to the mean which actually reduces the return. This is the case because large portfolios become concentrated as counterparties are acting in similar ways. The recommendation to diversify across 200 contracts with certain scales of ratings is too general; it may work under normal conditions, but if there is stress in the system, a portfolio that invested in fewer selected loans may actually outperform. Because interest rates are high, investors can make profits in good times when there are few defaults. Yet, the interest income will fail to cover losses when they occur under less than perfect conditions. If we had more information about borrowers, we could analyze the correlation between them. This would give a more comprehensive overview, and we could accurately model concentration and systemic risks. Platforms have this information, and they can easily investigate how and where credit exposure concentrates. Ideally, we would have this information from more than one platform, so we could stress the entire market of online loans in general.

The ability to restructure portfolios is the most straightforward solution to making marketplace loans more resilient in times of market stress. If platforms perform good analytics, they can allow different durations for contracts; by simulating the performance under different assumptions, they can play with the duration and the loan amount to optimize the performance of a loan. When the market is likely to come under stress, platforms should shorten the duration of loans and readjust their interest rate. Platforms should define the rules under which loans perform best. To leave this up to the investor fails to take into account that most retail investors have no means to accurately model and understand marketplace loans. Yet for platforms, additional analytics like the ones we outline in Part Two of this book are relatively straightforward to implement. Loan originators should make sure that contracts are profitable under various conditions that go beyond ideal circumstances.

13.5.4   A note on collateral and hedging exposure

When defaults occur that exceed what originators expect under normal conditions, loan portfolios are at a high risk of performing badly. In our analysis, we used interest income as collateral. However, marketplace loans could benefit from other forms of collateral as well. Especially when they lend to small businesses, several ways to collateralize exposure are possible. Some marketplace lenders already move into auto loans, others offer refinancing of student loans. It will only be a matter of time before marketplace lenders fund the first mortgage. Having collateral in the mix would drastically improve the performance of loan portfolios under stress.

For medium-term high fixed-interest uncollateralized contracts, the default probability will almost always be too high, even when the slightest sign of stress in the market appears. Under stress, lenders can either increase interest or hedge their exposure. It would be relatively straightforward to design a derivative to cover the losses for lenders in stress conditions, and this would make the most sense when we have achieved secondary market liquidity of marketplace loans. Originators could add the premium for this insurance to the interest rate that borrowers pay, or they could offer the insurance as a service to lenders for a fee. In any event, adding insurance should hardly increase interest too much, but it could potentially transform the asset class. Increasing the interest rate for loans is a fine balance: too high an interest rate will result in the same situation that bank lending imposed on marginal borrowers. However, if platforms do nothing and simply wait for the first crisis to occur, they risk tarnishing the sector before it can develop its full potential. If platforms do nothing and pursue a business-as-usual strategy, lenders will suffer losses under stress with certainty.

13.6   THE ROAD FORWARD

The marketplace lending model is interesting and profitable under expected market, counterparty and behavior conditions, but it is far from complete. Vital components are missing, such as the ability to compensate lenders for losses under stress. Banks could be part of the road forward in several ways. They could offer derivatives, they could be protection sellers by applying their own analytics to the asset class, or they could buy a part of the portfolios, for instance, highly rated loans that offer relatively modest interest. In terms of secondary market liquidity, banks could also play an important role in the evolution of the sector.

It is possible to complete the business model for marketplace lending. Analytics in this analysis, which are described in Part Two of this book, are straightforward, and banks have the in-house talent to perform and deploy them. Marketplace lending platforms should take advantage of this know-how: by tapping into the banks' pool of experience, they could become stronger in their analytics and could become intermediaries. This would change the positioning of marketplace lenders from the underdog to the next generation of credit institutions. Online originators have the potential to do what banks do, and more. Then—and only then—will they be competitors to established credit institutions. At the same time, the potential to make a bigger splash hinges on the collaboration of platforms and banking institutions. The maximal utility of the innovation in marketplace lending lies in its integration in the hybrid financial sector.

Analytics are the first low-hanging fruit for improving the operations of marketplace lending platforms massively. Platforms can certainly claim that providing analytics is the sole responsibility of investors, but if a crisis happens, platforms are the players in the game with most to lose. They would benefit from a unified analytics engine that works among all platforms. When this is in place, regulators will be able to plug in as well. This is an interesting opportunity for regulators to experiment with an innovative credit business model because the scale of marketplace lending is still relatively modest and platform businesses are new and their size manageable. This would not only reinvent credit, it would also reinvent regulation. Chapter 16 will focus on the hybrid financial sector in more detail.

13.7   CONCLUDING REMARKS

We identify the trend in portfolio performance by applying only three consistent scenarios scaled up from canonical to extreme conditions. We showed that, under canonical conditions, a diversified portfolio of marketplace loans, based on our sample portfolios, stands to earn roughly 23.9 percent over the term of the investment (60 months), or 6.63 percent per annum. However, under mild stress conditions, the total portfolio returns decline to roughly 4 percent or 1.43 percent per annum. Under stress, total returns turn negative to −14.71 percent or −4 percent per annum. This is by no means horrible, but it is also a far cry from the sure-fire value proposition that entices retail investors into marketplace lending. Notably, we performed more simulations using different portfolio sizes (e.g., from 100 to 2,000 contracts per portfolio). The results, however, under the same scenarios are very similar to the ones presented in this chapter. The reader is welcome to apply the analysis described in this chapter, considering the predefined or their own sample data and model parameters, by using the software accompanying this textbook.

Instead of median expected returns under ideal conditions, investors must be aware of the real possibility of their investments turning negative, with no way to cash out before the term of the illiquid investment has run its course. Holding on to an investment with a negative return over five years might do much damage to the public perception of the sector. Marketplace lending platforms should do everything they can to avoid lenders experiencing returns such as in Scenario A and Scenario B.

Nevertheless, platform operators argue that it is the responsibility of the lender to analyze the risk-and-return characteristics of loans on their platforms. They are only partially right. Platforms oversimplify the asset class by showing only the expected returns under fair weather conditions and omitting the potential losses that might occur under stress. It would be good practice to improve transparency in this regard. It should be in the interest of platforms to offer suggestions to lenders that help them avoid losses even in difficult markets. Platforms have no empirical experience of a full credit cycle, so they need to use models to simulate potential outcomes. We hope they run similar analyses like we have done in this chapter. Unless they do so, platforms risk saddling their investors with losses they didn't see coming. This may drastically decrease the appetite of the investing public in the asset class. Also, if the return of a loan book of a platform is negative, how exactly will marketplace lending platforms uphold their high valuations? Lending platforms should aim to offer their investors the ability to structure the best portfolios possible that will be profitable under various conditions.

Institutional investors and other professional investors that allocate capital to marketplace loans have access to sophisticated analytics of third parties that simulate scenarios like the ones we have investigated in this chapter. However, relying on institutional capital only can be a risky strategy for lending platforms. Because their funding sources closely correlate, platforms risk a freeze in funding liquidity under stress conditions. This could be the death knell for many players in the sector. With this in mind, what should platforms and investors do? They must identify the following key issues in their portfolios.

- What are the risks that portfolios are exposed to?
- Which are the contracts that are most sensitive to these risks?
- What is the impact of stress on performance and losses?

After clarifying these questions, platforms have the following options:

a. Restructure portfolios by employing contracts that are least sensitive to risk and providing best performance. Investors can do this over time by rolling over their portfolios or by selling the underperforming contracts and replacing them with new ones.

b. Collateralizing and/or mitigating risk exposures. The former needs additional effort of identification, measurement and monitoring, whereas the latter increases the cost of loans.

c. Do nothing and hope that investors' assumptions will come true and no additional uncertainty creeps up.

Most practitioners apply a combination of the above, and investors in marketplace lending should do the same. With the appropriate tools, platforms and their investors should be in a strong position to bolster portfolios against unnecessary volatility.

NOTES

1. Provided by Lending Club and referring to the year 2014, available on their website; Lending Club Statistics (2015a), Download Loan Data, https://www.lendingclub.com/info/download-data.action, date accessed April 20, 2015.
2. Based on Lending Club data, the interest rate varies from 6 percent to 26 percent, Lending Club Statistics (2015a), Download Loan Data, https://www.lendingclub.com/info/download-data.action, date accessed April 20, 2015.
3. Variable interest rates tend to adjust the contract's value and liquidity according to market conditions.
4. 1% to 3% for a duration of 30 to 70 months.
5. In our case study we interpolate the spreads based on interest rates defined in Lending Club Statistics (2015a), LoanStats3c.xlsx. In this case study they range from 1% to 35% for A1 to G5 ratings per annum
6. The approach of conditional default probabilities based on a hazard rate linked to credit spreads and recovery rates is also the basis of Basel III credit and counterparty risk and valuation adjustment of credit portfolios (see BIS paper bis.org/publ/bcbs189.pdf).
7. The approach of conditional default probabilities based on hazard rates linked to credit spreads and recovery rates is also the basis of Basel III credit and counterparty risk and valuation adjustment of credit portfolios (see BIS paper bis.org/publ/bcbs189.pdf).
8. Using normal annual time interval.
9. E.g., BIS in Basel III regulatory papers.
10. Lending Club (2015a), "Automated Investing Allocation Summary" under account, https://www .lendingclub.com/portfolio/primeReport.action, date accessed 21 May 2015.
11. A detailed illustration of all sub-rating distributions among 1000 contracts can be seen in the file "Loans.xlsx" in the software model accompanying this textbook.
12. This impact of counterparty credit status to credit exposer, named specific wrong way risk, is discussed in Chapter 11 (Credit Enhancements).

13. General wrong way risk occurs when market performance impacts negatively the exposure.
14. 30 to 60 months.
15. In this exercise we use the interest income as recovery.
16. Lending Club (2015a) "Rates and fees," https://www.lendingclub.com/public/borrower-rates-and-fees.action, date accessed 21 May 2015.
17. Detailed data referring to shock factors are provided in Annex B, available on the website, together with the model.
18. Detailed data referring to applied default PITs are provided in Annex B, available on the website, together with the model.
19. Lending Club (2015a) https://www.lendingclub.com/info/demand-and-credit-profile.action.
20. http://www.wsj.com/articles/lenders-step-up-financing-to-subprime-borrowers-1424296649.
21. http://www.biz2credit.com/research-reports/analysis-bank-failures-2009-2014-identifies-credit-desert.
22. Dugan, Ianthe Jeanne and Demos, Telis (2014) "New Lenders Spring Up to Cater to Subprime Sector," *Wall Street Journal*, 5 March 2014, http://www.wsj.com/articles/SB1000142405270230473 28045794216532069820 12, date accessed 18 July 2015.

CHAPTER 14

Digital Competencies and Digital Dilemmas

For hundreds of years, credit has been a bricks-and-mortar business. When people needed a loan, they would naturally go to a bank. The last few decades have challenged the traditional banking business model: new ways to lend and borrow capital with electronic distribution have developed rapidly, and they are here to stay. The two approaches to lending co-exist for certain types of loans, but banks still deal with the big-ticket items, such as mortgage loans. Giles Andrews, CEO of the first marketplace lending platform, ZOPA, points out that his company has no intention of replacing banks. Instead, it is focusing on doing a slice of banking more efficiently.[1] The requirement for a banking license prevents online lending platforms from offering credit cards and current accounts. Yet, in underwriting for small business loans and personal loans, marketplace lenders might gain significant market share.

The threat of disintermediation puts the established market leaders in the financial sector on the defensive. Most banks are firmly rooted in the 20th century. Even though they offer online banking and mobile banking, they will need to continually embrace electronic platforms and digital technology and upgrade their operations to meet the needs and demands of customers. Unfortunately, the debate about the future of finance is often one-sided. It often pits the crusty banks that have trouble catching up with innovation against the nimble FinTech startups that seem to have all the answers. This picture is inaccurate. Banks need to roll up their sleeves to help reinvent the financial system; but so do online lending platforms—to streamline their processes and analytics to make them more transparent and robust.

To usher in the next generation of lending, banks and online lending platforms need to become aware of the dilemmas they face. At the same time, most recommendations for the lending institution of the future assume that the model of branchless FinTech startups is the ideal model for banks to strive for. As we saw in Part Two of this book, marketplace lending platforms have a lot to learn from banks when it comes to risk and profitability management and analytics that make their loans comparable and transparent. When it comes to maturity and experience with credit cycles, they have nowhere near the expertise that banks have collected over many years in business, and that include plenty of stressful situations.

14.1   DIGITAL COMPETENCIES

Let us first focus on the ways banks could improve their operations to serve the digital customer better. Authors Henk Broeders and Somesh Kannah outline a framework consisting of four dimensions along which banks can create value with digital competencies.[2] These dimensions are:

- Connectivity
- Decision making
- Automation
- Digitization

Broeders and Kannah believe banks need to build stronger connections to their customers by using digital technologies in their operations. Opening new communication channels also improves the connectivity between their staff and their suppliers. By using Big Data and advanced analytics, banks may make better decisions, for instance in sales, product design, pricing, underwriting, and user experience for their customers. Paperless operations, automation and straight-through processing (STP) already help banks to streamline their workflows. But they can also automate recommendations to customers, such as information about new products or trading opportunities in their portfolios, which would reduce the overhead that banks need to spend on customer relations. The final goal is for banks to adopt a digitally centered business model in which digitization enables rapid innovation, automation, and communication. Does such a recommendation make sense? It does, but we believe it could still go farther.

It becomes clear when looking at the Broeders and Kannah framework that banks already are keenly aware of those areas in their operations that need innovation. Many financial institutions already invest heavily to acquire these competencies and move aggressively to adopt new technology. Several securities exchanges and major banking houses have already integrated STP, the prime example of automation and digitization.[3] Barclays launched its Pingit app for exchange marketplace payments by smartphone two years before most of the other banks even considered it.[4] However, exactly where banks should invest to make the leap into the 21st century is a difficult decision. The popularity of apps and their platforms can change within a few months, which can destroy years of development and investment in a specific infrastructure. It is less about ticking boxes to show that banks have fulfilled certain key performance indicators for their digital strategy, and more about creating long-lasting competitive advantage and value for customers.

14.1.1   Banks lag in some areas and lead in others: Analytics

At the same time, online lenders already use technology heavily to improve their operations along the four dimensions we have just discussed. In that regard, they should be the ideal examples of companies that banks should emulate. However, lending platforms have glaring deficits in other areas, such as analytics and risk management. It might seem simple, but analytics for marketplace lending are extremely complex, much more so than assessing the risk in the loan book of a bank. Marketplace lending has no central entity—it connects lenders

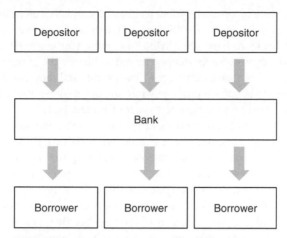

FIGURE 14.1   Financial system with banks as intermediators

and borrowers directly—so it is easy to argue that investors are solely responsible for the risk they take on. Still, even if each investor bears the risk of his own investments, the aggregate exposure to potentially risky assets weakens the stability of the financial system. If push comes to shove, we should have an idea what might happen with this exposure under stress conditions. Because many feedback loops exist between lenders and borrowers in marketplace lending, getting an idea of the risk that such lending imposes in the financial system is a complex exercise.

Compare Figure 14.1 and Figure 14.2: Figure 14.1 shows a simplification of how the formal financial sector works. With banks at the core of the interaction between depositors

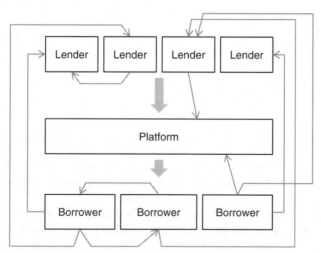

FIGURE 14.2   Complex system with marketplace platforms as intermediators

and borrowers, the system has relatively few feedback loops between individual parties in the economy. Sure, the financial crisis of 2007/8 was a harsh reminder that uncertainty still exists despite the claim of banks to have securitized risk and uncertainty. However, instead of an implosion in the crisis, central banks stepped in and stabilized the system by infusing capital in banks. Banks can also be borrowers in their own right, and they can lend the capital they borrow. However, this introduces nothing new into the discussion about linear systems versus complex systems, and therefore we have left it out of Figure 14.1.

Granted, banks are complex organisms in their own right, and so is the formal financial sector. Despite their complexity, both have succeeded in reducing uncertainty and shifted it towards risk that they can manage. By compartmentalizing the moving parts of a complex system into manageable and separate segments, banks have gotten a grip on uncertainty.

The picture is different when marketplace platforms facilitate credit between individual borrowers and lenders. In Figure 14.2, multiple interactions between individual parties in the economy exist. Even with a limited number of lenders, borrowers, and platforms, there will be countless permutations of possible linkages and feedback loops between agents. Of course, feedback can be positive or negative, where it either increases or decreases the actions of another party. Simply put, if individual borrowers default, they impose stress on individual lenders. If these lenders are also borrowers, perhaps even on other, seemingly unrelated platforms, the initial stress cascades from one actor to the next. Untangling the source of the stress can be extremely difficult, and it is unclear whose responsibility it is to mitigate stress and stabilize a complex system.

Compared to banks, platforms have not managed to reduce uncertainty. They may mitigate risk with diversification, but the uncertainty still remains in the system. Because of an almost unlimited number of feedback loops between the actors in marketplace lending, understanding the relationships of individual agents is difficult. More work is necessary to gain a clearer picture of the risk in complex financial systems.

We already know that platforms make the point that individual lenders are responsible for the risk they choose to take on. However, not even marketplace lending platforms themselves are modeling the complexity of the interactions they facilitate. They would have some of the necessary information to do so, but they often claim that their job in analytics only goes as far as rating borrowers. Risk management and risk analytics beyond counterparty risk are still entirely borne by lenders. At the same time, the only analytics available on platforms are limited. They mainly focus on expected rates of return, without taking into account expected nominal losses. Digging deeper and analyzing the loan books that some platforms make available—as we did by modeling potential losses in Chapter 13—adds a few more pieces to the analytics puzzle. Still, it hardly captures the overall picture of risk in the shadow banking sector.

Marketplace lending platforms recommend diversifying investments across many different loans. When investors do this, the risk in the underlying contracts still remains. What will happen if a crisis hits the economy and borrowers default *en masse*? In the absence of historical data, given the young age of the online lending sector, it is tricky to make a prediction of possible losses in a portfolio of marketplace loans under stress.

When it comes to financial regulation, marketplace lenders operate on a different playing field to the banks they are trying to disrupt. Most online lenders have a limited set of rules to comply with, and they are largely flying under the radar of regulators. It is unrealistic to assume they will be able to duck this oversight forever. The recommendations of Broeders and Kannah for banks to create value with digital competencies are a starting point. Stephen

Hawking pointed out that he thought the next century would be the century of complexity[5]—coping with it will be the next challenge that banks and online lenders face.

14.2 DIGITAL DILEMMAS

At the present, financial institutions and marketplace lenders should confront the dilemmas they can solve. Tackling complexity in the financial sector right out of the gate will be too ambitious a goal, and being aware of the challenge ahead might be enough for the time being. Digital dilemmas on the road forward face in both directions: they matter for the established banking sector, as well as the newly emerging FinTech companies. Both need to incorporate those parts of the business models of their competitors that are strongest and use them as the baseline for innovation.

Even though interactions between parties in the economy are also physical, we believe these dilemmas are mostly digital, and technology can solve them for the most part. Therefore, the first order of action for banks and FinTech companies boils down to formulating a digital strategy. We will first start with the questions surrounding digital strategy and the digital dilemmas for competitors in financial services.[6] Without answering them definitively, the dilemmas we focus on here are:

Dilemma 1: Disrupt or defend?

Dilemma 2: Cooperate or compete?

Dilemma 3: Diversify or concentrate?

Dilemma 4: Keep digital businesses separate or integrate them?

Dilemma 5: Buy or sell businesses in the portfolio?

In the rest of this chapter, we will visit each dilemma and examine how it relates to banks and to FinTech companies, in particular marketplace lenders. Figure 14.3 summarizes the digital dilemmas and their focus.

14.2.1 Dilemma 1: Disrupt or defend?

When the market leaders in offline retail commerce were afraid around the millennium of "getting Amazoned" by new online competitors, some retailers started a mad rush to leapfrog into the internet age. However, the line between a disruptive and a defensive strategy is

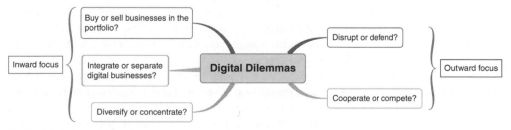

FIGURE 14.3   Digital dilemmas for competitors in financial services

seldom so clear. For established banks, adopting a disruptive strategy is easier said than done. Their internal processes are often at odds with taking risky bets on unproven technology. Regulations and high legacy overheads lock banks into a conservative stance, whereas tech startups with nimble teams have more freedom to experiment. Venture capital firms who back tech companies understand that their investment may be a total write off, so they encourage startups to swing for the fences. By ducking any form of red tape and taking wild bets with frequent experiments, the expected payoff is large. Regardless, new ventures cannot remain in the startup phase forever. Their business models will have to mature at some point, and they will have to comply with regulations and laws governing the sector in which they compete. "Disrupt or defend" is just a starting point to frame the discussion about strategy. Especially in a sector such as banking that is already highly technical and highly regulated, we need to consider several gray areas instead of choosing between black or white.

It makes sense for banks to defend their stance when they are under attack—at least for a while. They can invest in new technologies and digital channels and upgrade their traditional channels at the same time, such as by trying out new formats for their branches or using their ATMs to sell additional services. However, disruption of their existing business model may be a valid option for banks as well, especially for smaller banks without strong brand recognition. When they launch their own disruptive pilot projects, they may find that these projects are so successful that they cannibalize the traditional operations of the bank. At this point, a bank may choose to rebrand itself, wind down their traditional operations, and fully focus on its digital operations.

Marketplace lending platforms are by definition disruptive. Their digital dilemma therefore works in the other direction than that for banks: while banks may wish to operate more in the digital realm, marketplace lenders may feel the pressure to boost their physical presence. Most people believe that bank branches are a thing of the past, and they may well be—for established banks. In the same way that Apple stores have helped the brand improve its mass appeal, large online lenders may want to expand their physical footprint and position themselves more like banks with physical stores. These might not be branches in the traditional sense, but stores that resemble information booths, genius bars, or cafes. Some banks are already experimenting with new branch concepts that focus more on information, and less on transaction.[7] It is possible that online lenders will do the same. In this case, the digital dilemma for online lenders will be whether to make the leap from bits to bricks by investing in physical storefronts and sales staff.

14.2.2 Dilemma 2: Cooperate or compete?

In the UK, under the Small Business, Enterprise and Employment Bill, banks that reject loan applications from SMEs must refer them to online lending platforms.[8] Several banks have announced collaborations and partnerships with marketplace lending platforms, such as bank Santander and Royal Bank of Scotland (RBS).[9,10] Despite a law telling them to do so, it may be in the interest of banks to cooperate with marketplace lenders by their own volition. Online lending is not just subprime lending by default.

An example of this kind of cooperation might be funding for entrepreneurs. After entrepreneurs have become wealthy by graduating to successful business owners, most banks will happily welcome them as clients. Conversely, the situation for entrepreneurs without a track record is entirely different. To build the trust of business owners earlier, banks—and private banks in particular—may find it sensible to partner with an online platform that can secure funding for early stage companies from private individuals. As an advisor, the bank may simply provide support for both parties in deal making without lending capital itself. The bank provides a service to wealthy individuals who might wish to invest directly in promising startups, and it also gets on the good side of entrepreneurs, who might enlist it when their companies need later stage funding or when they go public. Such a partnership costs relatively little, and it may be a good investment in the long run for a bank. It would also help the market-place lender because the tie-up with a bank would lend immediate credibility to its services. Entrepreneurs would be happy, too: they would get into the pipeline for larger funding later down the road right at the beginning.

For the time being, banks often frame the discussion about FinTech in terms of a frag-mented marketplace, where FinTech companies occupy a niche in the sector, and the banks dominate the most lucrative parts. The argument that the provision of this or that service is "not what we do" is still the common answer we hear when we broach the subject with banks. The dilemma for banks is that they fail to see an advantage in cooperating with online lending platforms—or other FinTech startups, for that matter. Most banks prefer to keep FinTech companies at arm's length, unless the partnership results in immediate process optimization. However, banks will profit in the long term when they can begin to see themselves not only as buyers of FinTech startups, but also as providers of services and knowledge to them. Even though banks often have bigger guns than startups in marketplace lending and could fight them relatively easily, they may choose to cooperate. Running a seed accelerator for startups is hardly the core competency for most banks. If they outsource a seed program to a FinTech startup, banks can access new customers or offer new services to their existing client base.

Cooperate or compete is an important digital dilemma that banks face, not only in the digital space. Regardless, this dilemma is perhaps more important for FinTech companies. Even though many of them rely on services provided by banks somewhere in their value chain, most of them have little interest in integrating with banking operations. When they provide sustaining innovation, they might be more aligned with how banks think and operate, and the gap might not be as big. But for those disruptive FinTech entrepreneurs who offer financial services that banks have difficulty understanding, there exists a chasm between the two worlds.

A difference in corporate culture is just one issue: it is of course much cooler to work with a small creative team in a loft in the Mission District in San Francisco than having to succumb to dress code and adhering to business hours in the cavernous back office of a bank. For many entrepreneurs, more important than a big paycheck is launching their own company and making an impact. The feeling of being a maverick, a game changer, is something that only true entrepreneurship can provide, warts and all. Sure, it helps if there is a billion-dollar payoff at the end, but even without it, most entrepreneurs will not want to miss the experience. Banks have nothing to offer in this regard, and they seem terribly unattractive to entrepreneurial spirits. At the same time, if banks can provide ways for entrepreneurs to innovate in-house, entrepreneurs might see benefits from cooperations more readily. The services of a FinTech startup that partnered with a large bank would enjoy an immediate boost in credibility, and their reach might be much bigger if they can tap into the large customer base of an existing network. The infrastructure for cooperations between startups and banks is still missing, but if banks reached out to entrepreneurs more actively, both sides may benefit.

For marketplace lenders, the question of whether to cooperate or not extends to partners other than banks. When online lending comes of age, regulators will demand cooperation without an option to opt out. Even though there are several regulations in place for marketplace lenders, such as money laundering rules and regulations that prevent misselling to the public, the sector has still nowhere near the regulatory overhead that established credit institutions grapple with. Going up against regulators has proven a bad strategy for marketplace lenders. For instance, lending platform Prosper, the first of its kind in the United States, chose to challenge regulators in its early days.[11] Whether this is the reason it ceded its leadership position to Lending Club is up for debate. The fact is that Lending Club cooperated with regulators early on and plans to keep doing so. This seems to be a winning strategy that triumphs over confrontation, at least in marketplace lending.

14.2.3   Dilemma 3: Diversify or concentrate?

When a bank makes the decision to enter a new field, it faces the next dilemma: to diversify across several initiatives or concentrate resources on one venture. The decision to start a corporate venture is often stretching the comfort zone of a bank. Therefore, suggesting that a bank start several FinTech initiatives at the same time will require from the bank a lot of trust in the team leading these ventures. Diversification can reduce risk, but the payoff is that the bank will have fewer resources available per venture. Especially when they are moon-shot ideas that might take a long time to mature; the key to success is a long runway. To come up with a real game changer, a bank should allocate enough time, money, and human resources with strong leadership qualities to a project. For example, the Australian bank Westpac unveiled its mobile strategy in 2012 that included several small projects that it launched at the same time. When some of them took off, it integrated them in a digital platform and focused its investments.[12]

While diversification reduces the risk of a portfolio, some successful investors recommend putting all of one's eggs in one basket and watching that basket carefully. The same applies to digital strategy: venture capitalists seed multiple ventures and then double down on those with the most potential. Banks should follow the same model, funding several digital innovations at the same time. When some of them show promise, banks should focus more capital on the winners to scale their operations.

The first part of this decision—diversifying their digital initiatives—is already under way in some banks. They fund FinTech platforms and innovation labs and thereby keep their digital competitors close. However, seriously scaling up those ideas that bubble to the top still runs into problems, for several reasons. One of them is that new ideas often take years to develop their potential. To request proof-of-concept within a few months is unrealistic, yet it is how most FinTech accelerators and innovation labs function. Banks will need to take a much longer view on their technology initiatives to be able to spot the next disruptive trends. When they have supported a new idea over the longer term, they are in an excellent position to scale it up when it shows signs of success in the market. If they demand quick results and abandon those entrepreneurs that don't fit in the current paradigm, they will alienate the innovators with truly disruptive potential. These innovators are the ones that will unseat banks in the longer term, and they will remember it if banks have pulled the rug from underneath them.

Instead of diversifying, banks could also concentrate their efforts on just a few digital initiatives. However, it is unlikely that one digital idea is so strong that it warrants all the attention and resources of a bank. Diversifying digital strategy therefore often makes much sense. However, banks need to be aware that they can no longer remain passive investors in new ideas. They need to take an active part in implementing these ideas in the marketplace. For this to be successful, they need to build entrepreneurial competencies in leading digital projects on the ground. This competency is still sorely lacking at banks. Attracting the talent in the first place that allows banks to diversify across several digital initiatives is yet another challenge they face.

The question of diversification vs. concentration matters less to FinTech companies, at least in their current iteration. By definition, being relatively young companies, their focus is narrow, and they will lack the resources to diversify their efforts across several projects at the same time. However, they might want to consider several options within one overarching idea. For example, there are different ways to acquire new customers, some of which might include collaborations with established banks. FinTech companies should diversify not across projects, but across strategies for business models, marketing and business development. When they have grown past the startup stage and it is time to diversify their product offering, they may drive a similar strategy as banks that spin off products into new verticals instead of keeping them under the same umbrella. Nonetheless, once FinTech companies expand past their core competency, they risk giving up their advantage of being nimble and agile.

14.2.4   Dilemma 4: Keep digital businesses separate or integrate them?

One goal of banks in their digital strategy is to provide multiple channels of interaction to their customers. By integrating a digital operation that they have purchased or developed, banks can multiply their communication channels quickly. For example, Lloyds Banking Group integrated digital initiatives in its traditional business, but the rest of the group kept new technologies separate in a digital hub that improved the customer experience.[13] On the other hand, Banco Bilbao Vizcaya Argentaria (BBVA) decided against integrating into its existing operations the online bank Simple, which it had acquired. Instead, BBVA runs Simple as a test lab to better understand the behavior of digital banking customers.[14]

Some banks integrate their digital initiatives into their traditional business. This is often the best scenario for customers, as they have access to several services on one platform. Other banks completely separate their digital businesses from their established operations. They may launch them under different names or are simply standing on the sidelines as investors. Both approaches work. However, in the long run, the traditional banking model will inevitably pivot towards a more digital experience, so integration makes sense when technologies have proven to add value for the customers of banks.

The dilemma of separating digital initiatives from more traditional operations will require care, especially when the continuity of a well-established banking brand is at stake. When starting initiatives in marketplace lending, banks can run a platform as a separate entity, whilst providing the same backend services, analytics, and risk management that they already use for their other loan portfolios. This way, banks can optimize their learning about customer behavior in a new sector, enabling them to understand first-hand how marketplace lending might be useful in their other lending operations. At the same time, banks are in a strong position to provide a superior service over other platforms. They already have a multimillion-dollar infrastructure in place that could support marketplace lending operations. The dilemma of separation vs. integration need hardly be a tough one to solve; banks could integrate new digital services into their existing operations on a sliding scale.

14.2.5   Dilemma 5: Buy or sell businesses in the portfolio?

Different segments of the financial sector are undergoing a digital transformation at different times. When faced with the need to upgrade their operations with digital capabilities, some banks invest heavily in their own infrastructure or in the acquisition of potential attackers. Other banks decide to shed those business units most in need of revamping. For example, a bank with a traditional lending operation may decide to move forward aggressively by launching their own marketplace lending initiatives or by backing existing platforms in the market. Alternatively, a bank may choose to jettison its small business lending operation altogether and focus on other segments as their core business. Where banks want to compete comes down to their long-term strategy and vision. Not every bank can and should try to please all possible customers—only key customers that are most important in the long run. Focusing on one specific segment may be more successful than juggling too many balls at the same time.

14.3   CONCLUDING REMARKS

In this chapter we have discussed four digital competencies that banks need to learn to stay relevant in the credit sector of the future: connectivity, decision making, automation, and digitization. We have also introduced the digital dilemmas that come with those competencies, such as "disrupt or defend," "cooperate or compete," "diversify or concentrate," "separate or integrate digital businesses," and "buy or sell portfolio companies." Banks and FinTech companies need to understand the digital dilemmas they face. If they are clear about their options, they will be able to focus on formulating their digital strategy. Even though the five dilemmas here are by no means an exhaustive treatment of all the potential challenges that banks and marketplace lenders face, they are a useful starting point to raise awareness and frame the discussion. With this in mind, the dialogue on strengthening the financial sector will become more focused and actionable.

Nevertheless, more important than deliberating about dilemmas in the financial sector—digital and other—is taking first steps towards their resolution. This chapter highlights the dilemmas but stops short of prescribing how banks and marketplace lending platforms should resolve them. No one-size-fits-all approach exists to build the future of credit. Both bank lending and marketplace lending are dynamic sectors that are continually evolving. The challenge to integrate the two is large. Possible approaches to tackle this challenge with digital strategy is the subject of the next chapter.

NOTES

1. King, Brett (2014) *Breaking Banks: The Innovators, Rogues, and Strategists Rebooting Banking* (New York: Wiley).
2. Broeders, Henk and Khanna, Somesh (2015) "Strategic choices for banks in the digital age" (McKinsey and Company), http://www.mckinsey.com/insights/financial_services/Strategic_choices_for_banks_in_the_digital_age.
3. Croxford, Hugh; Abramson, Frank and Jalbonowski, Alex (2005) *The Art of Better Retail Banking* (Hoboken: Wiley).
4. Skinner, Chris (2014) *Digital Bank: Strategies to launch or become a digital bank* (Singapore: Marshall Cavendish Business).
5. Hawking, Stephen (2000) *San Jose Mercury News* (January 23, 2000).
6. Broeders, Henk and Khanna, Somesh (2015) "Strategic choices for banks in the digital age" (McKinsey and Company), http://www.mckinsey.com/insights/financial_services/Strategic_choices_for_banks_in_the_digital_age.
7. King, Brett (2013) *Bank 3.0* (New York: Wiley).

8. Fleming, Sam (2014) "George Osborne to reveal shake-up of SME loans" (*Financial Times*, 5 August 2014), http://www.ft.com/intl/cms/s/0/14a1ec8c-1cc4-11e4-88c3-00144feabdc0.html.

9. Funding Circle (2014a) "Funding Circle & Santander announce partnership to support thousands of UK businesses" (18 June 2014), https://www.fundingcircle.com/blog/2014/06/funding-circle-santander-announce-partnership-support-thousands-uk-businesses/.

10. Dunkley, Emma (2014) "Royal Bank of Scotland to enter MARKETPLACE lending market" (*Financial Times*, 19 October 2014), http://www.ft.com/intl/cms/s/0/660447b0-5625-11e4-93b3-00144feab7de.html.

11. The Economist (2015) "Shredding the Rules: A Striking Number of Innovative Companies Have Business Models That Flout the Law" (*The Economist*, 2 May 2015).

12. Broeders, Henk and Khanna, Somesh (2015) "Strategic choices for banks in the digital age" (McKinsey and Company), http://www.mckinsey.com/insights/financial_services/Strategic_choices_for_banks_in_the_digital_age.

13. Ibid.

14. Groenfeldt, Tom (2014) "BBVA Makes Banking Simple" (Forbes, 7 March 2014), http://www.forbes.com/sites/tomgroenfeldt/2014/03/07/bbva-compass-makes-banking-simple/.

CHAPTER 15

Digital Strategy

By now, we have an overview of the operations of marketplace lending platforms and we have examined the inner workings of bank lending. We have also looked into some of the advantages and disadvantages of each, and pondered the question as to what marketplace lenders and bankers can learn from each other. Facing their digital dilemmas, they will need to formulate a roadmap along which they could transform and improve their operations. At the same time, we realize that a discussion about digital strategy can fill entire volumes. Several authors have tackled the question as to how organizations can compete and excel in an increasingly digital marketplace, and they discuss some excellent approaches at length. This is by no means an exhaustive manual on developing or implementing digital strategy for lending institutions of the future—that book remains to be written. Nonetheless, this chapter highlights some important points to consider when formulating a strategy to operate a modern lending institution; no matter whether it is an established bank that wants to integrate digital business models or a FinTech company with the desire to grow past the confines of a startup. This chapter will introduce some approaches and models that banks and lending platforms can use to put their strategy into context.

15.1   WHO NEEDS DIGITAL STRATEGY?

In the last chapter we discussed some of the digital dilemmas that banks and marketplace lenders face. This should help us understand some bottlenecks and roadblocks on the way to the hybrid financial sector. Yet knowing about challenges on the road forward is just one part of the equation. We also need tools and strategies to solve those problems. Let's agree that marketplace lending has made a big splash in recent years and that the idea of connecting lenders directly with borrowers is here to stay. This is good news for entrepreneurs founding or operating marketplace lending platforms, but how can they improve the odds that they will reach escape velocity from the startup stage? How will they compete in the battle for larger market share with the incumbent financial institutions in the prime lending sector and mortgage finance? At the same time, those incumbent banks may be scratching their heads as well. They need to gain innovative capacities to stay relevant in the digital future, but where should they begin? It is uncertain if there is still ample time to come up with a strategy after waiting for a FinTech shakeout over the next few years, or if the last chance to catch up with the innovators has already passed. Examples abound of large multinationals disrupted by upstarts and in bankruptcy within a few short years. What can banks do to avert the same fate?

In any event, banks need to embrace digital technology in their interactions with customers. Simultaneously, to become more relevant to a larger pool of investors and borrowers, marketplace lending platforms will need to leave behind the stigma of subprime and move forward into the prime and mortgage finance sectors. Both players need to face their digital dilemmas and formulate a solid digital strategy. As always, no sure-fire recipe will guarantee success. The dominant players in the marketplace lending space might change a few times until the sector has matured to the point where it can challenge on credit on a larger scale. By integrating into their own operations some of the innovations related to marketplace lending, banks will also become more attractive for digital natives. Learning on both sides will make the credit sector safer and more attractive to lenders and borrowers.

At the heart of formulating strategy is the analysis of the lay of the land. Several frameworks for this exist. The next paragraphs will introduce some of them.

15.2 FRAMEWORKS TO ANALYZE THE IMPACT OF INNOVATION

To examine how innovation spreads in the market and how companies should react to innovation by competitors, we find the following three frameworks the most helpful: Rogers' concept of the *Diffusion of Innovations*, Gartner's *Hype Cycle*, and *Big Bang Disruption* put forward by Downes and Nunes. Let's briefly examine what each of these ideas is about and then explore their usefulness for marketplace lending and the hybrid financial sector. As a guide to these frameworks, Figure 15.1 outlines the different relevant aspects in analyzing innovations that are common to all these models. This includes the timing of market entry, types of customers, adoption rates, diffusion and market share, hype and disillusionment, the reactions of competitors, maturity and staying relevant.

15.2.1 The diffusion of innovations

In 1962, author Everett Rogers formulated the theory of the diffusion of innovations.[1] Figure 15.2 shows the well-known graph that most companies and entrepreneurs have adopted as tried and true.

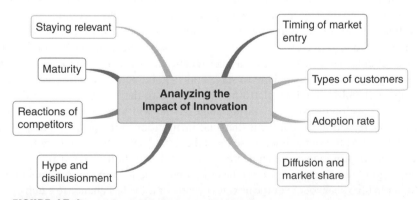

FIGURE 15.1 Analyzing the impact of innovation

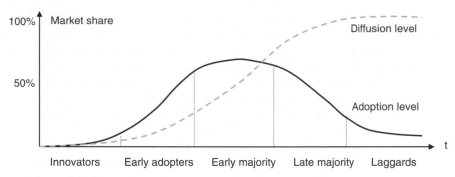

FIGURE 15.2 Diffusion of innovations curve
Adapted from: Rogers, Everett

According to the diffusion of innovations theory, companies that introduce new technology slowly build their market share over time. *Innovators* and *early adopters* are among their first customers who beta-test the unfinished technology and iron out its bugs and shortcomings. When the technology has spread wider, customers in the *early majority* embrace it, followed by the *late majority*. Finally, at the point where the technology is nearly ubiquitous, *laggards* jump on board as well. This approach gives companies some breathing room to roll out and improve new technology. When they see adoption picking up in the market, they know that they are on the path to greater market penetration and can scale operations accordingly. The theory is also useful when segmenting customers.

15.2.2 The hype cycle

Gartner's hype cycle, another well-known methodology, describes how technology matures in the market.[2] This concept is a staple in technology marketing. Despite several shortcomings, the model is relevant in the context of FinTech and marketplace lending as one way to forecast the adoption by the market, and eventually the market share of a technology. When venture capital is flowing into lending platforms at unprecedented rates, the sector might be in the run up to the peak of inflated expectations. Figure 15.3 shows the hype cycle.

The hype cycle starts with a *technology trigger*, a potential technology breakthrough that makes headlines in the market. At this stage, the product is often still buggy and unproven.

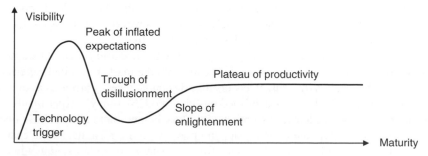

FIGURE 15.3 Hype cycle
Adapted from: Gartner

In the following *peak of inflated expectations*, early success stories mix with false alarms and accounts of fatal flaws in the new technology. When it fails to deliver, interest in the technology decreases, and it descends into the *trough of disillusionment*. Some early supporters fold their operations, others help improve the technology. If they succeed, useful applications of the new technology become more obvious on the *slope of enlightenment*, and ancillary products emerge. More and more investors fund pilot projects and, finally, when the technology reaches the *plateau of productivity*, the mainstream—the late majority and laggards—adopt it. At this point, the technology has established a level of visibility that remains fixed.

Even though they are well-known and make sense intellectually, the theories of the diffusion of innovation and the hype cycle have one flaw: they fail to take into account exponential growth. Some digital businesses take a while to take off, but once they have reached critical mass, a large number of customers switch to the new service without ever reverting back to the competition. The pace of gradual customer adoption and slow market penetration hardly accounts for impulse decisions. A good example is the emergence of social networks. One of the earlier social networks, Myspace, attracted 75.9 million monthly unique visitors in the United States at its peak in December 2008. NewsCorp had bought Myspace for $580 a few years earlier[3] but, in 2011, NewsCorp sold the social network again for $35 million. It had roughly 30 million monthly unique visitors then.[4] In a short period of time, Myspace had ceded most of the market share to Facebook, which currently boasts more than double the monthly users of Myspace at its peak and a valuation of over $200 billion.[5,6] The transition looks like it unfolded slowly, but when customers feel they better abandon a sinking ship in favor of the next trend, firms will rarely know what hit them until it is too late.

Another shortcoming is the notion of the plateau of productivity in the hype cycle. This phase is hardly a plateau but a slippery slope in the digital world. If market leaders rely on these frameworks to assess their prospects, they will be at a disadvantage when combatting aggressive new entrants.

15.2.3 Big Bang Disruption

Instead of the slow diffusion of innovation and the gradual slope of enlightenment, we need a better way to chart disruption. Frameworks that accurately describe gradual—non-exponential—adoption of technology have trouble describing innovations that follow the law of accelerating returns. For those innovations, we need a more complex framework: enter *Big Bang Disruption*.[7] The approach greatly speeds up Rogers' diffusion of innovations curve. When competitors disrupt a market with innovative technology, established companies may lack the time to leisurely tweak their business models. Before they know what happened, their market share has eroded and they find themselves without a working business model in a new reality. Figure 15.4 shows what Big Bang Disruption looks like.

A big bang that unseats incumbents seldom comes without warning signs. Disruptors, who often come from outside the sector, make their entry into the market as failed experiments in the first stage of the *singularity*. Market leaders may discount these occurrences as random, but they often foreshadow trouble for established business models. Today's experiments may not be scalable, but an unprecedented disruption could lurk behind them all. As those disruptive experiments unfold, entrepreneurs may happen upon a winning formula. In the ensuing *big bang*, customers across all market segments—from innovators to laggards—quickly embrace the technology and abandon legacy products. Incumbents struggle to stay relevant. In the *big*

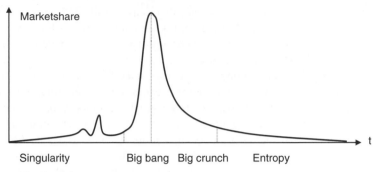

FIGURE 15.4 Big Bang Disruption
Adapted from: Downes and Nunes

crunch, incumbents rapidly crumble. At the same time, the disruptors mature themselves. Their innovation is no longer disruptive but incremental and sustaining. Finally, *entropy* sets in: the disrupted incumbents who are struggling to stay relevant in the new ecosystems may or may not find uses for their remaining assets and their intellectual property. The next disruption is already on the horizon, and those who unseated the incumbents now find themselves at risk of disruption themselves.

Each of the three frameworks to chart innovation has its shortcomings. However, when FinTech entrepreneurs and those responsible for digital strategy in banks analyze their options, all three theories come in handy to frame the discussion about the way forward. When we talk about marketplace lending and the future of finance, we might still be in the early stages. The market share of marketplace lending platforms is but a small drop in the ocean of the entire credit sector. However, startups in the lending sector have managed to generate significant interest from the media and investors, and innovators and early adopters are already flocking to the sector. In recent years, we have seen some singularities, such as high valuations of marketplace lending platforms in the public markets or announcements for high profile collaborations between startups and established banks. The longevity of marketplace lending is still up for debate, but banks have had more than one wake-up call to get busy with a digital strategy of their own.

15.3 SPOTTING SIGNS OF TROUBLE ON THE HORIZON

Since its beginnings in 2005, marketplace lending has emerged in niches, and this *modus operandi* is likely to continue. One or several new entrants will erode the market share of banks piece by piece, or they will slowly build up a new niche market entirely. However, the issue for banks is hardly individual lending platforms that service a few niches. More troubling is the fact that customers might be able to re-combine several FinTech services into their personal modular bank. Another issue is that niche lenders might slowly amass a war chest of cash and expertise that allows them to encroach farther and farther on the turf of established credit institutions. We discussed both scenarios in the first part of this book.

Looking for signs of disruption in the dynamic between marketplace lenders and banks misses the larger picture. It may be too easy to decide that FinTech startups are still too small to matter. It is also a simplification to pronounce that marketplace lending will turn the entire credit sector on its head. The larger implication for the banking sector loom on the horizon, and the biggest one of them has its origins directly in banks: banks have become unable to cultivate customer-centric innovation on their own.

From the perspective of entrepreneurs in marketplace lending, the premise for digital strategy is relatively straightforward: they are the new disruptors with nimble business operations who launch experiment after experiment until something sticks. Those lending platforms that have been around for a while may already have high valuations and high profile partnerships. At the same time, their market share of the overall lending market is still modest, and their products far simpler than what banks have on offer. To grow, they need to find ways to attract those lenders and borrowers who still transact with banks. They become a threat when they can fund loans for larger ticket items—such as real estate or credit lines for small and medium business operations—at the same or lower rates than established banks. However, to do this, the new competitors would have to play by the same rules as the banks they are trying to disrupt. They would have to come out of the shadows, comply with the same financial regulations as banks, and start requiring collateral for their loans. Additionally, marketplace lenders would have to offer the same kinds of liquidity for their investments as banks. They should also think beyond competing in a fragmented market. Most marketplace lending platforms claim they have no ambitions of replacing banks but only wish to service a slice of the market more efficiently. Nevertheless, when several marketplace lending platforms compete for the same niche, they will drive down margins with ever greater concentration of credit exposure.

If one thing is for certain, then it is that time is accelerating in the digital world, not slowing down, and the strategy of marketplace lenders should already concern itself with the way that they will operate on the declining end of their business cycle. How exactly lending platforms could evolve their business model will be the subject of Chapter 16 (The Hybrid Financial Sector). Banks have a little bit more to worry about in the short and medium term. For this reason, the rest of the chapter will examine how banks could formulate strategies to cope with disruptions in the credit sector.

Banks are still the undisputed market leaders in the credit sector, so they might dismiss the recent forays of marketplace lenders onto the scene. In the analysis in Chapter 13, we found that the marketplace lending model is promising but still incomplete for lack of analytics, among other issues. However, as we have seen in recent history, complacency is a poor strategy to deal with new entrants. When startups in the sector fetch multi-billion dollar valuations, something is afoot, and banks should brace themselves. At the same time the business cycle of lending institutions is already in the very late stages: their market share is almost 100 percent with even late adopters and laggards as their customers, their business models are at a plateau, and in some cases they even retrench. How banks can upgrade their business models towards one that incorporates FinTech innovations of recent years is unclear. So, how should they behave at this point?

In Part One of this book, we discussed the fact that the business structure of a bank is hardly compatible with that of a tech startup. The initiatives of banks to fund FinTech innovation and collaborate with startups are a promising beginning, but these moves will hardly transform banks into innovators themselves. At the end of the day, they will have to find sensible ways to foster a more entrepreneurial culture in their operations. This will be a longer-term process, which will require radical shifts in their business model.

15.4 HOW BANKS CAN OVERCOME THE INNOVATOR'S DILEMMA

In Chapter 4, we introduced the Innovator's Dilemma. We examined how new technologies can get the better of established companies and destroy their market share unless they focus on disruptive innovation themselves. We have already examined this in Part One where we learned that large multinationals are ill-suited to spearheading disruptive technology they might have invented themselves when they focus on their existing operations and markets. In this chapter, we focus on strategies for market leaders to overcome this dilemma. There are ways for market leaders to stay on the edge of innovation if they avoid certain pitfalls. Clayton Christensen explains how established companies can become innovators in potential new markets that don't even exist yet.[8] He puts forward four different strategies to achieve this: develop disruptive innovation in a separate company; plan to fail cheaply; let those in charge of innovation formulate their own rules and processes; and find new markets. The following paragraphs briefly describe each of them.

15.4.1 Develop disruptive innovation in a separate company

By definition, innovation always starts small. Sometimes, it needs several years to achieve even tiny market share. It is easy for managers of large companies and large divisions to drop projects without an immediate or foreseeable payoff. High-performing companies have excellent systems for weeding out those ideas that their customers have no use for. This is why most companies under-invest in disruptive technology and lower-margin opportunities.

Instead of developing them firmly in-house, projects related to disruptive innovation should be placed in small companies separate from the main company. Some companies and banks already do this, for example, by financing spin-off companies from universities or sponsoring innovation platforms. However, innovations still have to filter back into the larger company to gain velocity for positive impact on a larger scale.

Small teams and companies can get excited about modest opportunities and small wins, which is the only way disruptive innovation can flourish. In addition, only a satellite company can provide the framework for innovators that will help them perform at their peak. As long as entrepreneurs and innovators have to comply with corporate processes in a rigid structure, they will hardly find their stride. Banks should therefore create innovation labs separate from their main organizations that can fly under the radar of public scrutiny. Of course, this may be a political challenge. Especially in a field such as FinTech that garners much media coverage and has a fresh and innovative flavor, a bank's top management may wish to position themselves as those who bring a fresh wind into a crusty institution, but without taking imprudent risks. They might want to use high profile initiatives with quick results to bolster their public personas.

Obviously, this approach will defeat the purpose of working with innovators. Just as politicians before an election will steer clear of any issues that might end in failure, a bank's top management has little interest in taking risks with unproven innovations. As long as managers are at the helm of innovation initiatives, they will only invest in the sure bets with a certain payoff. We already know where this will lead: towards an innovation culture that focuses on rapid return maximization without concern about the longer term. Instead, FinTech innovation should be a low-profile affair with banks, but one they take seriously enough to buffer with ample funding and then leave in the hands of the innovators themselves. Such an approach has the potential to foster an innovation culture that eventually spawns new financial products, and looks beyond the immediate bottom line.

There is another argument for separating the regular operations of incumbents from the innovative business units. When big organizations are supposed to innovate, a division opens up between those forces in favor of the status quo and those who seek radical change. Author Salim Ismail notes that it is important for big companies to assign potential change agents to the edges of the organization and give them free reign to experiment with new business models that cater to digital customers.[9] Ismail calls information-enabled, rapidly scaling organizations *Exponential Organizations* (ExOs). Their growth potential is not linear, but explodes exponentially because their lean structures take advantage of technology with every step. Leaders in FinTech and marketplace lending are ExOs. To understand how banks could partner with them or replicate their business models, banks should leverage the strengths of their internal change makers.

In the best case, a cutting-edge ExO that emerges from the edges of a bank can serve as catalyst to transform the rest of the business, which might eventually create a new core business that replaces the legacy operation. Again, banks cannot expect that all their innovation programs will produce ExOs with bottom lines in the billions. Creating exponential growth may take a long time. It needs trial and error and the will to persevere even when moving ahead is counterintuitive and unpopular. This is only possible when innovation takes place outside of the limelight—on the periphery, in a structure that is separate from main operations.

15.4.2   Plan to fail cheaply

Successful disruptive innovators plan to fail early and inexpensively in the search for product-market fit for their technology. Their markets often emerge through an iterative process of trying, failing, learning, and trying again. The perception of failure always looks bad in the press, no matter how much positive spin a PR department might pile on it. Most managers prefer a definitive, long-term strategy that they can budget for and stick with. However, such a strategy stifles innovation before it begins. Successful innovation needs room to fail and fail again, until it no longer fails almost by coincidence. There is no need to point out that this idea, too, will be hard to swallow for most banks. They will gladly leave the failing to startup entrepreneurs, and will only work with successful FinTech companies.

We have already examined why banks should build innovative capabilities in-house when we discussed Prahalad and Hamel's classic model of the corporation as a tree in Chapter 4. In-house core competence is at the heart of being able to compete in the long term, and the ability to fail is an integral part of building competence.

15.4.3   Let those in charge of innovation formulate their own rules and processes

For innovation to thrive in larger organizations, innovators should have the opportunity to utilize the resources of the organization without leveraging its processes and values. Innovators should have the leeway to create their own rules that allow them to experiment with a disruptive technology. We have already discussed part of this approach, postulating that innovation should take place in a small satellite company that lives on the fringes of a larger corporation. A good example of this approach is Lockheed's *Skunk Works*, a program that successfully developed military aircraft in WWII. As a separate and secret unit, a small team of engineers with an anything-goes mentality was shielded from the bureaucracy of the main company. Because they were free to approach their challenges anyway they pleased, they managed to deliver a jet—from idea to finished product—in just 143 days.[10] Many companies have copied the *Skunk Works* model, and it would work well for banks also.

15.4.4 Find new markets

By now, we already know that new products in their early stages will rarely be compatible with the demands of existing customers of large multinationals. Large companies often adopt a strategy of waiting until new markets are "large enough to be interesting." This is understandable. Markets that don't exist are impossible to analyze, and large companies never launch into an unknown market. Demanding market data where none exists is hardly a successful strategy to foster disruptive ideas. Regardless, new and unknown markets are where disruptive opportunities lie. Successful innovators need to find or develop new markets that value the attributes of their disruptive product, rather than search for a technological breakthrough so that the disruptive product could compete as a sustaining technology in mainstream markets. New ideas developed in small companies are a better fit for small markets.

Innovation is more than knowing *what* to do. It also has to take into account *why* and the *how* we do something. Part of this is looking at the markets in which banks currently have little traction and interest. If they were already in these markets or scrambled to get a share of them, they would hardly be the markets that yield the largest gains in the future. Of course, in their main operations, banks must still pursue their home markets. These markets are the turf of banks, and they know them inside and out. However, finding new markets will be like entering a dark room without knowing where the light switch is. Market discovery—like planning to fail—will demand from banks that they overcome the stigma that has to do with doing what is less obvious when they focus on innovation.

15.5 FROM PRODUCER TO SUPPLIER AND MOVING TO A NEW SINGULARITY

Disruption on a large scale has not happened yet in the credit sector. But when it is on the horizon, banks should have at least some thoughts about how to cope with it. To overcome entropy and irrelevance, authors Larry Downes and Paul Nunes see two ways for those companies that have been disrupted by aggressive new entrants: making the switch from producer to supplier and moving to a new singularity.[11] As unspectacular as the first proposition may seem, companies in entropy can shut down their retail operations and transform into suppliers for innovators. In a sense, banks are already suppliers for marketplace lending platforms and other FinTech companies because most platforms depend heavily on banking relationships and financial networks. They use banks to hold the capital of lenders in savings accounts and to underwrite the loans.

The second approach, the move towards a new singularity, is also already afoot: several banks are reaching out to early stage FinTech entrepreneurs as collaborators. They fund FinTech hackathons and global FinTech innovation centers and lend their brand recognition to FinTech innovation labs. This is a smart strategy. Keeping their future competitors close when their technology takes off is often the main motivation. When new ventures seem promising, some banks acquire startups and incorporate them into their own operations or run them as test labs. They also invest directly in new startups together with other investors and venture capitalists. By sponsoring FinTech innovation labs, banks are on the inside track as far as innovation is concerned. However, there is still one issue: are banks simply keeping their thumb on new ideas by investing and buying them up or are they truly interested to incorporate innovations into their operations? We believe they would be well advised to do the latter. In that case, we must ask whether banks are capable of making the most of the innovations they acquire.

15.6　FROM CLOSED INNOVATION TO OPEN SERVICES INNOVATION

It has become clear in this chapter that banks may need to re-examine their definition of innovation. At the same time, FinTech startups may believe they know all about innovation, but they, too, need to keep an open mind and should look at all possible options to becoming excellent companies. A useful framework for this process is *Open Innovation*. It describes an approach for firms to advance their technologies by using external ideas, and internal and external paths to markets. Open business models transcend the narrow confines of existing structures and incorporate inputs, processes, and outputs from outside firms.[12] Open innovation gives companies a chance to transcend the "not invented here" syndrome and keep an open mind about those innovations that might help them become stronger. Some banks are moving from a closed innovation model to an open innovation model. They might have taken first steps towards profiting from emerging technology in the lending space, but this trend is still in the early stages. At the same time, most products in finance are commodities: capital is fungible, and borrowers hardly care where the money in a loan comes from. To understand how to compete in a world of commoditized products, author Henry Chesbrough recommends that companies turn their products into services on a platform.[13] In *Open Services Innovation*, companies should adopt a customer-centric business model where they can co-create with customers to build those experiences that customers really want. By practicing open services innovation, companies accelerate and deepen innovation and growth, and they provide more choice for customers. It is easy to see that banks and marketplace lenders could apply this model with success.

For open services innovation to be effective, new business models are necessary. It requires business models that take advantage of external innovation that adds value to existing services. This sounds similar to some of the FinTech innovation labs banks already run. However, because such labs often have rigid guidelines, banks set the frame for innovation too narrow. As a result, they mainly attract sustaining innovation and pass up the more promising ideas with the potential to shape the future. If banks opened up their innovation funnel for more radical ideas, these ideas might help them escape the financial services commodity trap. They might shift the focus away from product-focused innovation towards services that incorporate useful ideas, no matter where they originate.

Granted, banks mostly offer services to their customers already. However, their innovation model would profit from more openness. While they may be in touch with new companies in the marketplace lending and FinTech space, they prefer to keep them at arm's length instead of incorporating those services into their own business. This is not all the banks fault. Regulatory hurdles are also to blame. However, the way banks underwrite credit still rests on conservative principles that have changed little in decades. Banks could benefit from experimenting with ideas that originated in marketplace lending.

Open innovation comes with several requirements: banks need to be able to source ideas that might help them in the future; they will need processes to assimilate those ideas and co-develop them with the innovators; and they need to have enough fertile ground on which new ideas can flourish. It is easy to forget that FinTech companies need to do exactly the same. Without a thorough understanding of what banks actually do, they will be guilty of closed innovation, even though they may be a hip startup. This is why we have gone to great lengths to describe the inner workings of banks when it comes to underwriting and managing credit. Open innovation works when companies understand the business models of their competitors in detail.

15.7 THE ROLE OF LEADERSHIP IN DRIVING EMERGENT STRATEGY

There is, of course, no easy recipe for banks to face impending disruption. How marketplace lenders can successfully compete with banks in the long run is equally difficult to answer. One thing is certain: banking and credit are in flux, and the way customers will borrow in the future will be different to the way it is today. Instead of charting a digital roadmap for companies to adhere to over several years, doing business in a fast-changing environment needs a strategy that emerges as the road unfolds. Strategy formation in a company revolves around the interplay of the ever-changing environment, the organizational bureaucracy that seeks to stabilize the impact of the environment, and leadership, which mediates between the two forces.[14]

Options for strategy emerge from anticipated and unanticipated opportunities, and the real challenge is to find the right balance.[15] With a strong leader who understands how to strike that balance, companies will find it easier to cope with a disruptive environment. Instead of dismissing ideas and innovations as immaterial or unproven, managers should keep an open mind. This will help them see the opportunities and dangers in their market and react to them as they see fit. When emerging competitors launch innovations in the market, open-minded managers will have a better chance to recognize whether they have the potential to serve their own customers. Dealing with the opportunities and threats that present themselves in uncharted territory will demand an emergent strategy. When leaders have found a way that works, they can then switch to a deliberate roadmap—one that will please more traditional stakeholders and shareholders.

The transition to the credit sector of the future will hardly be plain sailing, and we are still in the early stages of the journey. Leaders who can successfully guide companies in rapidly changing global environments are hard to find, but the opportunities are immense. When established banks and marketplace lenders have found a winning combination that works, they will revolutionize the way credit works, both in established and newly developing markets.

What the credit sector of the future looks like is unclear, but it will be safer, more convenient, and more profitable than our current system. For this to happen, platforms and banks should look farther ahead, and entrepreneurs and bankers should make efforts to build the hybrid financial sector of the future together. Instead of cannibalizing each other, competitors should put value creation for customers before their pursuit of market share. They should find ways to innovate collaboratively, without trying to impose their rules of the game on each other. What exactly banks and marketplace lenders can learn from each other is the topic of the next chapter.

15.8 CONCLUDING REMARKS

In this chapter, we have discussed strategies to deal with the digital dilemmas that banks and marketplace lenders face. The first step in formulating digital strategy is taking into account the way in which innovations unfold in a digital market. Traditional frameworks to assess innovation are Rogers' Diffusion of Innovations, and Gartner's Hype Cycle. Both techniques fail to take into account the exponential growth of digital technologies. An alternative approach, Downes and Nunes' Big Bang Disruption, points out that innovation in the digital age no longer follows growth patterns that incumbent companies can simply observe while tweaking their response to new entrants. Instead, early signs of disruption—singularities—foreshadow a big bang that will change the pecking order in a market rapidly. Yesterday's market leaders can cope with digital disruption by becoming suppliers to newly emerging companies. The entrants themselves also need to be aware of the fleeting nature of their newly found hegemony because disrupting the disruptor is the credo of digital markets.

    The biggest challenge for banks is to overcome their inability to cultivate disruptive innovation on their own, and in their own midst. To stay relevant, banks need to overcome the innovator's dilemma—with strategies such as separating innovation companies from their main operations, planning to fail cheaply, relieving innovators from corporate rules and processes, and finding and cultivating new markets. Finally, open innovation can furnish banks with ideas to stay relevant to customers. Banks becoming more attractive for collaborations with innovators is one of the first important steps in crafting the hybrid financial sector of the future.

NOTES

1. Rogers, Everett (2003) *Diffusion of Innovations*, 5th Edition (New York: Free Press, a Division of Simon & Schuster).
2. Gartner (2015a) "Gartner Hype Cycle." http://www.gartner.com/technology/research/methodologies/hype-cycle.jsp.
3. Gilette, Felix (2011) "The Rise and Inglorious Fall of Myspace," *Bloomberg Business*, 22 June 2011, http://www.bloomberg.com/bw/magazine/content/11_27/b4235053917570.htm, date accessed 22 May 2015.
4. Dominic Rushe (2011) "Myspace sold for $35m in spectacular fall from $12bn heyday" (the *Guardian*, 30 June 2011), http://www.theguardian.com/technology/2011/jun/30/myspace-sold-35-million-news, date accessed 22 May 2015.
5. Millward Brown Digital (2015a) Compete, https://siteanalytics.compete.com/facebook.com/, date accessed 22 May 2015.
6. Bloomberg (8 September 2014) "Facebook Valuation Tops $200 Billion," http://www.bloomberg.com/infographics/2014-09-08/facebook-valuation-tops-200-billion.html, date accessed 22 May 2015.
7. Downes, Larry and Nunes, Paul (2014) *Big Bang Disruption: Strategy in the Age of Devastating Innovation* (New York: Penguin).
8. Christensen, Clayton (1997) *The Innovator's Dilemma: When New Technologies Cause Great Firms to Fail* (Harvard: Harvard Business School Press).

9. Ismail, Salim (2015) *Exponential Organizations: Why new organizations are ten times better, faster, and cheaper than yours (and what to do about it)* (New York: Diversion Books).

10. Diamandis, Peter and Kotler, Stephen (2015) *Bold: How to Go Big, Achieve Success, and Impact the World* (New York: Simon & Schuster).

11. Downes, Larry and Nunes, Paul (2014) *Big Bang Disruption: Strategy in the Age of Devastating Innovation* (New York: Penguin).

12. Chesbrough, Henry (2003) *Open Innovation: The New Imperative for Creating and Profiting from Technology* (Harvard: Harvard Business Review Press).

13. Chesbrough, Henry (2011) *Open Services Innovation: Rethinking Your Business to Grow and Compete in a New Era* (San Francisco: Jossey-Bass).

14. Mintzberg, Henry (1978) "Patterns in Strategy Formation" (*Management Science*, Vol. 24, No. 9 (May, 1978), pp. 934-948), http://www.jstor.org/stable/2630633.

15. Ibid.

CHAPTER 16

The Hybrid Financial Sector

Instead of exclusively focusing on either the established banking sector or emerging lending platforms, when advocating a strategy to move into the future, we propose taking a different approach. The future is hardly an either/or proposition, but a collaborative effort. It will be a question of which ideas in combination win, more so than which company will have the best ideas. Credit institutions and FinTech startups should join forces to accelerate the learning curve and exchange knowledge as they go. In the hybrid financial sector, the best of both worlds happily co-exist and co-create together with each other and their customers. The question is: what should banks and marketplace lending platforms do to learn from each? And what should they avoid to maximize their learning?

16.1 FORCES OF COMPETITION IN THE DIGITAL AGE

Several forces are at work when companies compete in the digital age.[1] They can help frame the discussion about the rivalry between marketplace lenders and banks. Among these forces are:

1. New pressure on prices and margins
2. Competitors emerging from unexpected places
3. Winner-takes-all dynamics
4. Plug-and-play business models
5. Growing talent mismatches
6. Converging global supply and demands
7. Relentlessly evolving business models—at higher velocity

Let's look at the forces in this list for a minute. Most of them are in effect in combination when marketplace lending platforms and banks compete.

16.1.1 New pressure on prices and margins

For instance, several trends exert pressure on prices and margins in the credit sector: technology brings down search costs, transactions costs, and labor costs, and it makes incomplete information more complete. When products and services go digital, they often become commodities. Customers can easily compare them, and when their features closely resemble each other, they will often choose those products or services that are the least expensive.

16.1.2 Competitors emerging from unexpected places

Competitors in the digital age often come from unexpected places because technology has lowered the barrier to entry. It is no surprise that many entrepreneurs in the FinTech space have good ideas but little background in finance. New entrants without a track record have a big advantage: they can drive a puppy dog strategy. Because of their unthreatening demeanor, incumbents tend to leave them alone until they have grown so strong that they are here to stay.[2] Of course, the puppy dog strategy makes sense for any kind of startup. However, in technology-enabled sectors, those competitors who come out of leftfield are even more dangerous because they can achieve critical mass at short notice when network effects and zero marginal cost play in their favor.

16.1.3 Winner-takes-all dynamics

The existence of winner-takes-all dynamics in marketplace lending is up for debate. A number of platforms are peacefully coexisting with established lending institutions, and there seems to be room for more than one marketplace lending platform. At the same time, new companies can concentrate on single niches in the absence of legacy products and an established identity. Additionally, when a niche turns out to be unprofitable, they can quickly rebrand and concentrate on another demographic until they become the winner in one particular niche. Even though marketplace lending may hardly usurp the entire credit market any time soon, banks should be aware of the danger that they may lose customers in specific niche markets rapidly and unexpectedly. At the same time, FinTech startups need to take scalability into account from the very beginning. They should prepare themselves for surges in transaction volume before they cross a tipping point.

16.1.4 Plug-and-play business models

Plug-and-play business models emerge when technology disintegrates traditional value chains. For some companies, it may not be economical to build certain parts of their value chain from scratch, so they simply integrate them into their operations. Banks and insurance companies sponsor FinTech accelerators for a reason: this keeps potential competitors close and lets them absorb innovation into their operations as it happens. At the same time, FinTech companies can benefit from the experience of banks and other financial institutions. Do they really need to rebuild the capacity for analytics and data handling from scratch, when banks have decades of experience in these fields?

16.1.5 Growing talent mismatches

As software replaces physical personnel, the workforce inevitably shrinks. Hirt and Willmott estimate that of the about 700 end-to-end processes in banks, algorithms could automate about half of them. But while banks cut positions, they also add new employees in their digital operations. The challenge is finding the right employees to keep in areas that are still hard to automate away.

16.1.6 Converging global supply and demands

Digital services easily transcend markets. While most marketplace lending platforms still focus on a single home market—most of them in the United States, the UK, and China—international collaborations are already emerging. For example, e-commerce platform Alibaba and the marketplace lending platform Lending Club have announced a planned partnership that will allow the marketplace lender to provide business loans for American customers of the Chinese ecommerce giant.[3] While this deal still centers on the United States, the leap for some marketplace lending platforms from the West into China may already be on the horizon. In addition to the global reach of software platforms over the internet, FinTech also profits from the fact that capital has no nationality. Digitally enabled financial services therefore leverage global supply and demand to the maximum.

16.1.7 Relentlessly evolving business models—at higher velocity

When business models go digital, their evolution never stops. Innovation in one sector will create upheaval in another in a shorter time than most incumbents of yesteryear have adapted to. For companies that started out with strong bricks-and-mortar operations, this transition might be difficult. On the other hand, game-changing tech companies can also become lethargic when they feel they have arrived at an unchallenged leadership position. Layers of middle management, bureaucracy, and lazy thinking are symptoms of market leaders in any domain. Companies must reinvent themselves and adapt their business models without mercy to stay competitive. If their business model is digital, this is even more the case.

16.2 THE DANGERS OF KNIFE FIGHTS

Unless existing incumbents and new entrants collaborate, a knife fight and attrition war may ensue that can have more damaging effects than a healthy cleansing of the financial sector. Any of the seven forces we just described might be the subject of a knife fight. For example, competition on margins could shrink the available pie by establishing a sense of entitlement with customers for low or no cost for services. For instance, in digital telephony, the advent of marketplace VoIP service Skype severely rattled the industry. Even though more people than ever before have gotten to use their computers and smartphones to connect around the globe for free, it has become incredibly hard to monetize VoIP calls. Skype's grab of 30 percent of the international market for phone calls came with less than 30 percent of its revenues. The technology company made phone calls less expensive for customers and shrunk the total revenue pool, while still turning a profit.[4] It is hard to beat something that is free. Without a doubt, the emergence of Skype has been a boon for many SMEs and individuals who are more connected for a lower cost than ever before. On balance, the contribution of VoIP technology has definitely had a positive impact on the world economy. However, the freemium business model of Skype has cannibalized an existing industry and put in place a limit to revenue growth for itself.

Competition on margin is already happening in financial services even without new competition in marketplace lending. Working at a bank has become increasingly unattractive in recent years while tech companies are paying record sums for the same talent. In the long-run, outspending the competition to gain access to talent, while fighting a war of attrition, is an unsustainable strategy. Sooner or later, FinTech companies need to turn a profit, too. If they build in barriers to raise margins with freemium business models they might sabotage their own future.

16.3 GOOD IDEAS IN MARKETPLACE LENDING THAT MIGHT BE HERE TO STAY

It is always difficult to look into the crystal ball, and we have no claims to special insight into the future. At the same time, some ideas we came across in our research of marketplace lending strike us as stronger than others, and we briefly outline the most important ones. If the hybrid financial sector takes these ideas seriously, and looks for ways to integrate them, win–win situations might emerge between existing players and new entrants. None of the ideas are fully developed as of yet, and we need all the brainpower available to make them stronger in the future. These ideas in marketplace lending that might be here to stay include credit scoring with fringe alternative data, the responsive bank, lending as a service (LaaS), the ability to invest in fragments of loans, unbundled financial services, and industrial-strength analytics for retail investors. Figure 16.1 summarizes them.

Let's look at some of the ideas with a high likelihood of staying relevant in the hybrid financial sector. We will discuss each of them in more detail now.

16.3.1 Credit scoring with fringe alternative data

These *alternative data* can make or break a deal, especially for consumers outside of the credit system. In the United States, credit bureaus now gather *mainstream alternative data*—for example, monthly bill payments. Such payments are similar in kind to monthly credit payments that are already a part of consumers' credit files. At the same time, some companies use so-called *fringe alternative data* to underwrite loans when no full credit report is available or as a complement to existing credit scores. These data include activity on social networks, shopping habits, location data, and web tracking, among others. Big Data and social network

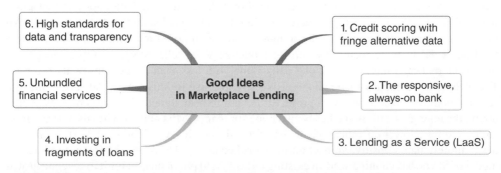

FIGURE 16.1 Good ideas in marketplace lending that might be here to stay

analysis (SNA) are a big part of marketplace lending platforms. Every online interaction generates droves of data, and they can help to determine who gets access to credit and on what terms. Whether fringe alternative data can accurately predict credit events is unproven. The fairness of credit scoring with fringe alternative data is also up for debate.[5]

Some FinTech founders believe new types of data have improved assessing counterparties, and they see the new approach to credit scoring as clearly superior to what banks are doing. Banks still largely rely on the financial history of borrowers and their credit ratings. However, it is far from clear if a rating approach that involves Big Data is superior. Some alternative rating algorithms, for example, take into account whether a borrower uses correct capitalization when filling out the loan application, along with the amount of time they spend online reading terms and conditions. Max Levchin, co-founder of PayPal, believes "The long game is to use data and software to chew up and revolutionize the financial ecosystem." Unfortunately, things are a little more complicated, and there is a risk of putting too much trust in data and software. Few venture capitalists who are funding FinTech startups are experts in the lending processes of banks and associated risk analytics.

While Big Data holds much promise, it still remains to be seen how the new models of borrower rating hold up. Fringe alternative data sources are still unproven in their efficacy and fairness when it comes to underwriting loans. Nevertheless, it is quite clear that internet-enabled devices will produce large amounts of data that will drive business in the future. The number of people online in the world will increase from 1.2 billion in 2010 to around 5 billion by 2020.[6] Each of the additional 3.8 billion people will generate data in each second of their waking lives. Where they go, what they do, and who they interact with will leave a trail of information that will inform business decisions.

Despite the shortcomings of alternative data, it is obvious that more than the credit score alone will indicate a borrower's willingness and ability to repay a loan. Robinson and Yu recommend that traditional credit bureaus seriously consider the inclusion of mainstream alternative data into credit files. Nevertheless, they should be careful with credit scoring models that rely on fringe alternative data. On the flipside, regulators should also scrutinize online marketing practices that rely upon credit data, as it is difficult for outside observers to understand the impact of online marketing on financially underserved individuals.[7]

16.3.2 Responsive, always-on banking and near-real-time credit

Over time, the expectations of customers of their financial service providers have changed and, in the digital age, the rate of change is increasing ever faster. As author Brett King points out, customers now expect to be in control and to have a choice about the services their bank offers them. By voting with their mouse clicks, customers will penalize those banks that fail to offer them flexibility and a level of empowerment.[8]

In Chapter 3 of this book, we discussed the technological and social factors that enabled online lending. Clearly, customers want financial services that are always on and ready when they are. They want their financial services to be comparable among the offerings of competitors, and they demand a customer experience that matches that of using a social network. The tolerance for tedious compliance, onerous documentation requirements, and unavailable representatives is wearing ever thinner. It just takes one company to introduce a more convenient way of doing banking and customers are certain to abandon those services that fall short without blinking.

Even though marketplace lending is still serving only a small fraction of the credit sector, it has introduced a new way of what getting a loan could feel like. This applies to consumer loans, but it might also work for larger ticket sizes, including large credit lines and home mortgages. More and more people will become accustomed to a cleaner and more pleasant user experience over time. Credit decisions still take several days, but some innovators have already set their sights on real-time credit provision. When this is a reality, a shopper would receive financing offers from marketplace lenders right on checkout at her favorite store: instead of a credit card company giving the option to "pay no money down for 90 days," a private investor would now lend money to the shopper in real-time. When marketplace loans become real-time or near-real-time, the glacially slow way of provisioning credit with a signature in the branch will fossilize overnight.

Is there a reason that these innovations and user experience factors should remain the exclusive domain of marketplace lenders? Hardly. Banks are free to act on those ideas just as anyone else. The emergence of innovations in mobile payments and wallets, such as PayPal and ApplePay should have been a wake-up call for banks. As soon as they become innovators themselves, banks could offer a more responsive service and up-to-date banking experience natively. To be fair, many banks already try their best in this respect. At the same time, some of their legacy and compliance processes prevent them from fully stepping up to the plate and moving their operations into the 21st century. Banks need to undo their shackles and leave their comfort zone. Why do customers need to step into a branch to complete security checks? Is there any reason that customers can only reach certain core functions of the bank Monday to Friday between 9 am and 5 pm? One gets the feeling that all such requests are more in favor of the bank than its customers. If nothing else, banks should at least learn a thing or two about the streamlined customer service that some FinTech companies have brought into the consciousness of consumers. For a bank, joining forces with a marketplace lending platform might be worthwhile for this reason alone.

16.3.3 Lending as a Service (LaaS)

According to author Frank Rotman,[9] there exist more than 13,000 small banks in the U.S. alone with difficulty generating high-quality loan portfolios. While small banks are excellent at deposit gathering, they often lack the skills to manage a lending business. Lending platforms with a streamlined origination process could offer loan origination as a service to banks— hence the term Lending as a Service (LaaS). Next to being an important service that small financial institutions may benefit from, LaaS could turn out to be the unifying glue that ties the emerging originations platforms to more established banking.

There exist several benefits in the segmentation of services between lending platforms and banks. For instance, banks can market products to their customers but retain only the assets they want. If banks wish to keep loans of a certain rating, the LaaS platforms can clear the other loans with capital from institutional and retail investors. In addition, LaaS provides non-banks with a convenient service to create loan products that serve their customers without having to build the systems and skills themselves. Banks can also profit from the experience and insight that some marketplace lenders have gained in years of collecting performance data. Being relatively nimble and unfettered operations, LaaS platforms can hire talent and invest in innovation, which has been notoriously difficult for traditional banks. In terms of user experience, banks that outsource their lending to LaaS platforms will have a strong competitive advantage over the traditional incumbents, especially in opening new digital channels that speak to younger customers.

As we pointed out in Chapter 13, when we discussed the analysis of a portfolio of marketplace loans, it seems the business model for marketplace loans could still become stronger with the better use of analytics and risk management. However, when platforms have collected additional information, experienced market stress, and have improved their models in the process, the time for Lending as a Service could be just around the corner for marketplace lenders. Instead of imagining what it would be like if a bank acquired a marketplace lending platform, it makes more sense to think of them as service providers. The same could be the case for those platforms that already partner with banks. Even though banks have always outsourced their lending operations and have a long history of buying loan portfolios from other partners, the innovation in LaaS is that technology-enabled platforms could now play the parts of credit scorer, loan originator, and loan servicer at the same time.

What would this new synergy between platforms and banks look like? Lending as a Service might take a similar form to the credit card program in a bank. Even though credit cards look like they are a native service of the bank, credit card companies are mostly separate entities from banks. It is also common that separate companies service different card programs in a bank. For instance, one company might operate the Platinum Card and another one the Gold Card of the same bank. The customer is often blissfully unaware of this fragmentation. In a similar approach, Lending as a Service might live under the brand of the bank, but a marketplace lending platform would provide the entire front-end experience and backend operations of the loan origination and servicing process.

16.3.4 The ability to invest in fragments of loans

Never before have retail investors had access to credit as an asset class. Sure, banks have always offered certificates of deposit (CDs), which are time deposits that pay interest that the bank receives by lending out the funds for a certain time. However, structuring their own credit portfolios across several loan grades or even directly investing in loans on a larger scale has only become possible with the advent of marketplace lending. Investors can browse the different loans, filter them by criteria, and finally select the ones they like to fund with as little as $25. Platforms present their loans like items in a store, where an investor simply adds loans to a shopping cart and pays for them on checkout. Alternatively, investors can let the system allocate their capital automatically to hundreds of loans according to certain criteria. Micro investments in consumer credit, auto loans, startups, student loans, and—eventually—corporate bonds, are an innovation that marketplace lending has pioneered. Just as online discount brokers have made investing in equities a mainstream phenomenon, marketplace lending platforms might eventually do the same for investments in loans to consumers and SMEs.

Again, before investment in marketplace loans can reach the mainstream, the asset class should mature and prove itself over a longer period of time. Secondary market liquidity would definitely help to make the asset class more attractive to those investors who might wish to trade in and out of loans before the duration is up. Variable-interest loans with a more flexible duration could also help tailor the asset class to even more investor tastes. In the end, credit exposure has been the missing asset class in retail portfolios that marketplace lenders could pioneer. If platforms partner with banks, offering crowd-sourced CDs might become a standard feature in our savings accounts of the future. Unified Analytics, which we will encounter in Chapter 17, could strongly support this approach. It would allow retail investors to understand their exposure and would make different contracts and portfolios comparable across all platforms.

16.3.5 Unbundled, streamlined financial services

When you step into the branch of a bank to renew your mortgage, the value you bring to the bank is much more than just the interest you will pay over the ensuing decades. The bank's sales representatives routinely use your data to cross-sell you additional banking services. The point of sale and the personal touch are one way for banks to maximize the value of their customers. At the same time, most people dread these meetings with their banker. Often lasting several hours, more than one of the people we interviewed in the course of writing this book likened the appointment with the bank's mortgage specialist with a trip to the dentist. At the end of the day, most of us care little about the coffee that the banker might serve you and the chit-chat about your job or your family. We prefer just to get the loan and then on with our lives.

Marketplace lenders have shown that they can meet KYC regulations over the internet without personal interaction. The screening and approval process for a loan is also much faster, and because we do everything online, the cost of origination is much lower. Getting a loan online is much more convenient for the customer. Because all interactions are digital, all documents exist on a server and have little risk of going missing. This ultimately also plays in the favor of banks. The Mortgage Bankers Association (MBA) reports the total loan production expense—commissions, compensation, occupancy, equipment and other production expenses and corporate allocations—increased to a whopping $7,000 per loan in Q1 2015.[10] The net cost to originate, which includes all production operating expenses and commissions minus fee income, secondary marketing gains, capitalized servicing, servicing released premiums, and warehouse interest spread, rose to $5,238 per loan.[11] Keeping staff occupied may still be a priority for banks, but their high origination costs will make it hard for banks to compete with online lenders in the future. Just as with Lending as a Service, providing an unbundled and streamlined user experience can help banks gain and retain customers. At the same time, they can rein in and manage their overhead, both in time and outlays.

Instead of driving down costs, most banks insist they graduate their services to a more premium experience. This may work on paper, because premium services have a bigger ticket size and fatter commissions. But is this what the customer wants? Most customers want simpler banking services rather than more complex ones. Instead of pushing toward the higher end of the market, banks should focus more on the long tail of no-frills services that most of their customers want. Banks should take a page from FinTech companies and rethink their push toward expensive premium services. At the end of the day, customers will wake up and realize it is them who pay for the glitter and the gold. With simpler financial services just mouse clicks away, customers are already opting for less complexity in their financial lives. This trend is bound to continue, and banks can profit from it just as much as FinTech companies.

16.3.6 High standards for data and transparency

Banks excel at gathering data about their borrowers. They organize and analyze data about market conditions and use it to drive decisions. Market data are relatively easy to access and well organized; yet personal information about individuals is often spotty and unreliable. Banks have long-standing experience when it comes to asking potential borrowers for documentation about their assets, income, and collateral—anything that is even remotely connected with the risk of a loan. Finally, banks leverage corporate ratings and credit scores to arrive at the decision whether to lend or not. When there is any doubt about a borrower's ability or willingness to repay, they will play it safe and decline the loan or mitigate counterparty risk to the market. This is why banks put so much effort in collateralizing their exposure.

Even though banks are good at corroborating a financial snapshot of their borrowers with traditional data, they have missed the boat on new data sources. As we just learned, credit bureaus already collect *alternative data*, such as bill payments, but banks rarely consider these data when underwriting loans. One level deeper is the universe of *fringe alternative data*—activity on social networks, shopping habits, location data, and web tracking. While marketplace lenders make frequent use of such data in their scoring algorithms, only a few banks do. They mostly outsource the task to collect and analyze fringe alternative data to third parties, and such data only play a limited role in lending decisions. This practice excludes borrowers without a credit history from becoming potential banking clients.

Finding appropriate data sources for a decision to lend is only half the story of underwriting profitable loans. A more pressing issue is data quality: personal data are often domain specific, spotty, and out of date, and are often unfit for use across different divisions of an organization, let alone different organizations or an entire sector. Each business unit in the financial industry uses different labels to describe the same thing. One unit might talk about sales and another about revenues when describing the same thing. Different financial professionals may call the amount of money given to the borrower capital, principal amount, or notional principal amount. Different business units are storing the same information using different attributes, which can lead to unnecessary confusion. The fact that labeling of data with identifiers is still far from standardized requires additional effort when conducting analysis and reporting with information. Some banks have literally hundreds of databases in their organization, each organized differently, and many with incomplete and outdated datasets. It often takes months—sometimes years—to untangle this mess. For banks, disorganization has been less of a problem. Whenever there are regulatory inquiries, they often request additional time to dive into their data to extract information, only to revise it later to the upside or downside, whichever is more convenient at the time.

When it comes to clean data, most online lenders have a leg up on banks. Because their operations are relatively nimble and have been fully digital from the start, online lenders collect large amounts of transaction data and organize them relatively well. In terms of transparency, banks are clearly making a hobbling entrance into a race where marketplace lenders are already circling the track in a blur. For example, market leader Lending Club is offering its entire loan books online for download, which would be unthinkable for banks.[12] Banks hardly have access to standardized and clean datasets themselves even if they wanted to. In any event, disclosure of client data would be against the *modus operandi* of banks. Deliberately clouding their operations is more the style of banks.

Marketplace lenders are also transparent to their borrowers about the cost of loans. Because their products are relatively Spartan—in essence a simple fixed annuity for all their contracts—platforms are at an advantage when it comes to explaining the product to borrowers and lenders. Banks, on the other hand, offer hundreds of different types of loans, some of which have hidden information that is hard to untangle. For borrowers, comparing loans across different marketplace lending platforms is therefore relatively straightforward. Nevertheless, the experience is different for lenders who would like to analyze and compare different platforms as potential investments. Even though marketplace lenders might make data and analytics available on their sites, each again has different data collection standards, nomenclature, and conventions about which data to collect and how to organize it. Objectively comparing the risk of such loans is almost impossible for the layperson but relatively easy for a professional investor.

16.4 THE ALTERNATIVE TO THE HYBRID FINANCIAL SECTOR: A DOOMSDAY SCENARIO FOR ESTABLISHED BANKS?

The hybrid financial sector is far from a foregone conclusion. It might well be possible that banks and FinTech companies continue on their separate trajectories; with each slowly eroding the other's market share by competing on margin, and fragmenting the market more and more. As we mentioned earlier, one danger with FinTech startups is that hardly any new entrants gain market share on the small business lending operations of established banks. Several market leaders providing unbundled digital financial services, joining forces on a new kind of banking platform, and offering services to customers identical to those they receive from banks— only much more transparent and affordable—would be a real game changer. Imagine online lenders, digital payment providers and wallets, online wealth managers, online brokers and trading platforms, crowd funding platforms, and digital currencies converging on one single platform where a customer could mix and match her own bank as if the different services were Lego bricks.

Banks should be part of such a modular banking platform as well—in fact, they could play a major part in it. The only antidote against irrelevance for banks is to become a part of the new hybrid financial system, both as an organizer of the platform and as a service provider in their own right. By opening their services and financial networks for new players in a fair and transparent way, banks would bring their strongest assets to the table. They would shape the future of the financial system together with new players. It is by no means a secret that to do this, a bank would have to think more like a startup itself. We discussed how banks can do this at length in Chapter 15. In Chapter 17, we will now look at Unified Analytics, which could be one starting point for banks to become part of the hybrid financial sector.

16.5 CONCLUDING REMARKS

In this chapter, we have looked at several forces of competition in the digital age, most importantly, competitors from unexpected places, winner-takes-all dynamics, plug-and-play business models, and relentlessly evolving business models. FinTech companies have advantages in many of these domains because they are digital natives without offline legacy assets. Banks need to be aware that these forces are at play when they compete with FinTech companies, and the forces are squarely in favor of the new entrants.

It would be a pity if a knife fight broke out between banks and FinTech companies. This might severely cannibalize the energy of the financial sector that could serve much better purposes for innovation and co-creation. Marketplace lending has introduced several good ideas that might be worth integrating for banks. Among them are credit scoring with fringe alternative data, lending as a service (LaaS), and real-time credit decision. Finally, the high standards for data quality and storage and transparency that marketplace lending has brought to the fore of credit pave the way for unified analytics, which we will now discuss.

NOTES

1. Hirt, Martin and Willmott, Paul (2014) "Strategic principles for competing in the digital age" (McKinsey & Company).
2. Fudenberg, Drew and Tirole, Jean (1984) "The Fat-Cat Effect, the Puppy-Dog Ploy, and the Lean and Hungry Look," *The American Economic Review*, Vol. 74, No. 2, May 1984.
3. Alloway, Tracy (2015) "Lending Club forms partnership with Alibaba" (*Financial Times*, 3 February 2015).
4. Kaminska, Izabella (2015) "How to eat a banker's lunch," (*Financial Times*, 17 March 2015) http://ftalphaville.ft.com/2015/03/17/2121994/how-to-eat-a-bankers-lunch/, date accessed 18 March 2015.
5. Robinson + Yu (2014) "Knowing the Score: New Data, Underwriting, and Marketing in the Consumer Credit Marketplace. A Guide for Financial Inclusion Stakeholders," http://www.robinsonyu.com/pdfs/Knowing_the_Score_Oct_2014_v1_1.pdf.
6. Ismail, Salim (2015) *Exponential Organizations: Why new organizations are ten times better, faster, and cheaper than yours (and what to do about it)* (New York: Diversion Books).
7. Robinson and Yu (2014) "Knowing the Score: New Data, Underwriting, and Marketing in the Consumer Credit Marketplace. A Guide for Financial Inclusion Stakeholders," http://www.robinsonyu.com/pdfs/Knowing_the_Score_Oct_2014_v1_1.pdf.
8. King, Brett (2013) *Bank 3.0* (Hoboken: Wiley).
9. Rotman, Frank (2015) "The Hourglass Effect: A Decade of Displacement," http://qedinvestors.com/frank-rotman-releases-the-hourglass-effect-a-decade-of-displacement/, date accessed 23 May 2015.
10. Swanson, Jann (2015) "Net Cost to Originate the Average Loan Rises to $5,238," (Mortgage News Daily, 2 April 2015), http://www.mortgagenewsdaily.com/04022015_mba_mortgage_profits.asp, date accessed 22 May 2015.
11. Ibid.
12. Lending Club (2015a) https://www.lendingclub.com/info/demand-and-credit-profile.action.

CHAPTER 17

Unified Analytics

Throughout this book, we have collected several puzzle pieces that describe the emerging FinTech sector, with a focus on marketplace lending. We have also examined how banks and the formal financial sector "do" lending. We have mapped a vision for the Hybrid Financial Sector and outlined the winning ideas it can champion and build upon. We feel that the lowest hanging fruit for collaboration between banks and marketplace lending platforms is providing better analytics to investors in marketplace loans. Platforms clearly need this, and banks have all the experience necessary to provide it. Such a collaboration could mark the starting point for the future of credit, which is the reason we discuss it in more detail in its own chapter.

First a note of caution: what we describe in this chapter is by no means supposed to be a prescription for marketplace lenders on how to run their businesses. They may have different goals for their companies, and they may have a different opinion about analytics and risk management. However, if their aim is to take a bigger bite of the credit sector and reinvent lending on a larger scale, platforms gain a lot from focusing on analytics for their investors. When they do this, they will have to integrate some of the banking analytics we examined in Part Two of this book. Adopting a banking risk-management approach to marketplace lending may sound simpler than it actually is. This is hardly about advocating FinTech companies to be more like banks, which will be impossible for a number of reasons. The power of FinTech is that it has little in common with the established practices of banks, which gives it the freedom from legacy processes and regulation to forge ahead into uncharted financial territory. Nevertheless, the main product—loans—of marketplace lenders and banks is very similar. Therefore, they should apply the same analytics.

At the same time, it makes sense to point out that the business cycle of established banks may be on the decline, as it has always been for large monopolists who have had their run for several centuries. Throughout history, business constantly changes, and it would be preposterous to believe that banking is immune to the passage of time. Individual brands may hardly survive another hundred years. On the other hand, credit as a product has had amazing staying power through the ages: it is easily thousands of years old. Since the dawn of credit, analytics and derivative instruments have constantly evolved. Banks' trading books, powered by derivatives trades, are to blame for the great losses of recent years. Nevertheless, dismissing banks as dinosaurs on the way out would be throwing out the baby with the bath water. Banks have much experience that comes from being in business for hundreds of years. FinTech startups can profit greatly from using the banks' distribution channels, their brands, and their existing customer networks to speed up innovation in the financial sector. If FinTech companies want to be true game changers, it will be in their interest to find ways of using the existing infrastructure in a smarter way, instead of trying to reinvent the wheel while fighting a war of attrition. The result will be a hybrid financial sector, in which FinTech companies and banks complement each other. The first step towards this will be finding the common ground between the two and bridging gaps between them. Analytics could be this bridge.

There are many ways to do analytics, and we can hardly claim that we have found the cure-all for the ills of the financial sector. In this chapter, we propose one approach for marketplace lenders to improve their services, take the sector to the next step, and lay the foundation of the hybrid financial sector. At the same time, banks should be excited to participate in this initiative. Sharing their knowledge and experience will align them organically with the FinTech sector, and it will allow them to define the future of credit, just as a mentor may shape the direction of a talented and promising but inexperienced student.

17.1 WHY DO MARKETPLACE LENDING PLATFORMS NEED UNIFIED FINANCIAL ANALYTICS?

Marketplace lending platforms are still in the process of earning their keep against the formal credit institutions and other alternative sources of credit. The emerging players in the sector are all lagging in terms of the quality of their risk analytics, so it is easy to understand why their focus is other than on unifying analytics across the sector. Online lenders are strong at using algorithms and Big Data to score borrowers and make credit decisions within minutes. Consistently, in interviews we conducted in the course of writing this book, entrepreneurs in marketplace lending pointed out the strength of their credit scoring algorithms over FICO scores and other "old-fashioned" metrics that banks use to assess borrowers. Whenever we asked about their risk management practices, platforms mentioned credit scoring as their only risk management practice. We explained that how, by doing this, marketplace lenders are measuring counterparty risk, and counterparty risk only. There are at least three grave issues with this single-minded approach to risk.

First, predicting future behavior by looking at past actions is like driving by looking in the rearview mirror. If there are any bumps in the road—such as unforeseen market turmoil—predictions based on historical data go out the window. Second, using Big Data algorithms to score borrowers is hardly an exercise in risk *management*; it is risk *measurement* at best, and then again, it only focuses on counterparty risk. Third, marketplace lenders seem to forget about the other risks that might lead to losses for their investors. Platforms are hardly measuring credit risk at the same level of detail as banks. They apply no portfolio analysis and stress testing, and they fail to measure credit exposure on the level of portfolios, counterparty and contract levels. Because the loans are uncollateralized, lenders have net exposure only. There is no analysis of market risk in credit exposure and losses, no expected loss analysis on the level of the counterparty and the portfolio, and no identification of seniorities. Meaningful and professional analytics for investors are missing in marketplace lending. Lenders are flying blind in terms of market risk, credit risk, and concentration risk. The latter is notoriously difficult to measure and manage, and it goes undetected even though platforms have the data that would allow them to identify concentration risk.

As we pointed out, in Chapters 11 and 12 on banking risk management, there is much more work necessary than simply scoring borrowers for their ability to repay a loan. A borrower's online activity and history with paying bills may be spotless, but his ability and willingness to pay has a lot to do with the strength of the market. What will happen to the loan book of a platform when market conditions change? What will happen when inflation speeds up, and when market interest rates rise? Predictive models for borrower behavior fail to forecast market behavior. We have investigated some stress scenarios in Chapter 13 with the analysis of a portfolio of marketplace loans, and we have seen that returns suffer even under light stress. Unfortunately, marketplace lenders are unprepared to deal with market risk.

It seems that by the term "risk management," platforms often understand managing their own risk only, such as legal risk from lenders who have lost capital by investing in marketplace loans. Sure, platforms can always point to the fine print in their terms of service and claim they did all they could to score borrowers properly. Some marketplace lenders go farther and claim that borrowers are indifferent about defaults because by the time defaults happen, borrowers will have made most of their money back thanks to the high interest rates. The hands-off approach of marketplace lenders works when the economy is doing well, there are few defaults, and interest rates outpace inflation. But when the economy tanks, when borrowers are underwater and defaulting *en masse*, lenders may demand that platforms do a little more work. Marketplace platforms should at least be on the same level as the formal credit sector when it comes to analyzing the risk of their loans. In fact, because the data of online lenders is cleaner and more centralized, they could easily surpass banks in the quality of their analytics. To cut a long story short, they need to up their game when it comes to analytics for their investors.

Retail investors have no other option than to rely on the relatively simple analytics that marketplace platforms provide on their websites. Several third-party services exist that allow lenders to analyze the loan books of some platforms in a little more detail. Third-party services range from professional offerings for institutional investors to labors of love of peer-to-peer lending enthusiasts. Unfortunately, they hardly take into account all the risk factors we described in Part Two of this book, and they give investors just half the picture about risk in their portfolios. To be fair, many credit institutions are in the same position. However, bank loans are less risky because they require collateral as a security they can liquidate if defaults occur.

If a marketplace lender or third-party analytics platform has an engine that takes into account the factors we have pointed out in our excursion into credit risk management in Chapters 9–12, they could deliver an accurate assessment of the potential risk for marketplace loans. Platforms might use this information to optimize their loans, and they might want to make it available as a competitive advantage to their investors.

It is difficult to understand why marketplace lending platforms feel they have no need for better risk analytics. Perhaps they see themselves as a service provider only, and less as a credit institution. Still, improving their approach to risk management on behalf of their investors is in the best interest of marketplace lending platforms themselves. Most platforms believe they have barely scratched the surface of what is possible in terms of market share. They have aggressive plans to take a bigger bite of the multi-trillion-dollar credit market in the U.S. with plans to branch out into car loans, student loans, and mortgages.[1] Nevertheless, originating collateralized loans is quite a different ballgame from unsecured consumer credit. Having physical or financial collateral in the mix requires more complex models to assess risk. Stricter regulation will inevitably follow when online lenders become bigger and more systemic, and marketplace loans will have to become more secure. Regulators and the market will need to understand better the impact of alternative lending on the financial sector in general.

So far, investors in marketplace loans are left to their own devices as far as risk analysis is concerned. Some platforms make their loan book available, but investors will still need to program their own risk model to extract some knowledge from the available data. Stressing a loan portfolio is a job that quickly exceeds the average retail investor's Excel skills, no matter how VBA-savvy he may be. Sure, if someone is knowledgeable and patient enough to program a financial model in MATLAB, C, or Java, they can simulate the expected performance of a marketplace loan portfolio with the publicly available data, in similar ways that banks do. We proved this in Chapter 13. It helped in the analysis that one of us (Akkizidis) holds a PhD in applied mathematics and programs financial risk models for a living. Still, to get the entire picture, we would need additional data not only about borrowers, but also about individual lenders, as well as data from other marketplace lenders. Platforms are sitting on these data, and it would make a lot of sense for them to pool data to understand better the risk in their asset class. This starts with standardizing the formats in which they collect and store data. If they aim to reinvent the future of credit, then why should they have an interest in keeping their investors in the dark?

Another argument for unified analytics is the aspect of pooling individual services that are expensive for platforms to develop and maintain on their own. Running a marketplace lending platform is expensive, which forces the platform operator to underwrite as many loans as possible. However, what if a community, such as a town with 5,000 residents, would like to run its own lending platform? Residents already know each other and might already extend credit to one another. Bringing this informal exchange of credit into the digital age with a marketplace lending platform makes a lot of sense. At the same time, running a small platform would be too expensive at the current time. However, if the individual marketplace lending services were available for rent, such as in software as a service (SaaS), scale would matter less. Once it has become affordable, a community, such as a company, club, church, or other special interest group may set up their own lending platform on which members could extend credit to each other. For example, a town might set up its own lending platform that a community bank may operate. Existing networks could also have proprietary lending platforms: a phone company, for instance, already has lots of data about its users, and they are already processing payments. It would be a small step for a phone company to allow its subscribers to extend credit to each other, especially when it can build a marketplace lending platform in a modular way. An add-on analytics module might be useful for such community platforms, should they emerge.

We will discuss in this chapter how exactly we could develop and implement a system for unified analysis. Because marketplace loans are still relatively simple uncollateralized annuities, we recommend lending platforms already think ahead to a time when their loans might have more moving parts, such as physical and financial collateral or several currencies when lending abroad. The benefits of such a system go beyond advantages to lenders—borrowers, platforms, and third parties who might partake in marketplace loans will gain as well. On top of that, unified analytics in marketplace lending would be a boon for banks also. Did we manage to spark your curiosity? Let's focus in more detail on these advantages.

17.1.1   Advantages for lenders

Marketplace lenders are the most obvious group to profit from more transparency of the risk of the loans they invest in. When they gain a more accurate picture of their exposure—regardless of whether they like to pile on more risk or try to avoid it—they can make a more educated decision in their asset allocation and improve the performance of their investment. Professional money managers already do this, and retail investors should have access to the same tools that let them perform credit risk analysis by themselves. Being able to provide lenders with stronger analytics would certainly be nice to have for platforms, the only obstacle being the high cost of developing industrial-strength tools in-house. How could marketplace lending platforms offer strong analytics without breaking the bank?

A framework for better analytics should enable investors with the following insights:

- Lenders should gain a clear idea about all financial risks including risk factors they have exposure to—such as interest rates, currencies, inflation, and asset prices. Expected and unexpected losses that may arise from exposure to market risk should also be clear.
- Unified analytics would allow comparison of marketplace loans across different platforms in the entire sector when it comes to risk exposure and expected returns. Investors then have a clear view of the entire market.
- Robust analytics should measure all risks based on real-world stressed market conditions, stressed default probabilities, in addition to behavior expectations. Identifying these risks next to counterparty credit risk would be another powerful enabler for lenders.
- Calculating unexpected losses from all potential risks is also a must. This would trump the current median expected rate of return that most platforms content themselves with.
- When we know the links and potential correlations between lenders and other peers (i.e., systemic and concentration risk) and between peers and guarantors that might provide credit enhancements (i.e., wrong way risk), we will have the full picture of the risk inherent in the entire marketplace lending sector. In the long run, this can set the foundations for establishing an integrated platform that is linked to other online lending platforms, similar to clearing houses.

Even though marketplace lending has undergone a name change from its earlier moniker peer-to-peer lending, individual persons lending to others is the endearing idea that keeps the sector in the limelight. We have already discussed the fact that retail investors gaining wider access to credit is a vital empowering feature of marketplace lending. Clarity about the actual risk and return of the loans they invest in, the corresponding income, and the future cash flows discounted to the present time will raise the confidence of the investing public. If investors have certainty about a positive income and potential expected losses during the lifetime of the contract, their financial literacy improves. What could be a better starting point for marketplace lenders to grow market share and launch additional products?

With unified analytics, investors gain more than a better understanding of their own exposure to loans from an individual platform. When they can compare their investments in credit across different originators and platforms, both in the alternative space and traditional financial institutions, they can structure their investment portfolios to make them more robust, with better performance and fewer losses. Lenders will also benefit from unbiased and meaningful reports of the performance of their credit portfolios.

17.1.2 Advantages for borrowers

The current consensus among marketplace lending platforms is that they will have to increase interest rates if they are to invest more in their analytics capability. This may ultimately lead to higher rates for borrowers and lower profits for investors. However, this reasoning is similar to complaining about the cost of a tune up for a car that will ensure the engine's integrity in the long term. With unified analytics across the sector, marketplace lending has a better chance of achieving escape velocity, to penetrate its current market deeper and branch out into other credit segments. If this is the case, borrowers are likely to benefit. They will gain the confidence that deals are fair for both sides, especially when collateral is involved. When individual borrowers and SMEs know that the terms of a loan are fair—considering risk-free probabilities and real world future assumptions—they are more likely to pay, which is ultimately in their own best interest. Of course, borrowers also have a stronger tool to shop for the best loans across several platforms.

Better analytics can also help foster more responsible borrowing behavior when borrowers have better information about their own exposure—or over-exposure—to credit risk. A lower default rate in the sector will ensure that even longer-term loans have the lowest possible interest in the future.

A unified analytics framework that is useful for borrowers should offer the following insights:

- It should clearly identify market risks that come with loans, such as fixed and variable interest rates, currency risk, prices of assets that borrowers could pledge as collateral.
- Borrowers should be aware of the consequences of defaulting on their obligations. These include possible fees and other penalties; the exercise of collateral and other credit enhancements; losses to other peers and the portfolio of the platform that result from the default of an individual borrower, via concentration and systemic analysis; and the impact of a default on the credit rating and other credibility scores.
- Borrowers should also have full transparency about possible options, such as prepayment. They should know whether prepayments are a good strategy, for instance, to roll over loans. Of course, risk-free probabilities and real-world assumptions about the future should inform fair value calculations of loans.

17.1.3 Advantages for marketplace lending platforms

By their own account, most marketplace lending platforms believe their risk management is superb, despite being extremely limited in reality. Platforms offload financial risk management of their loans to lenders; yet, to expect retail investors to run their own stress tests borders on cynicism. It is unclear what will happen when borrowers are under stress, and platforms should be aware of the negative consequences of widespread losses if they occur. Marketplace lenders gain much from offering more robust analytics to lenders and borrowers. When they are transparent about their product, all involved parties benefit.

In the run-up to the financial crisis of 2007/8, banks sold fuzzy products to investors who only cared about yield on paper. At the end of the day, it was the investors who shouldered the losses, and banks suffered reputational damage that still reverberates. Conversely, in post-crisis conditions, increased transparency will stimulate competition. If marketplace lending platforms have a serious interest in reinventing the way credit works, they should set an industry standard that centers on transparency. In the end, this stands to increase the reach of individual lending platforms and the size of the market in general.

Until regulators require platforms to calculate analytics with the same granularity as banks is just a matter of time. If platforms invest in this capability now, they are taking proactive steps to shape the dialogue about regulations and to be ready when compliance requirements ramp up. They should be in a position where they can prove they are providing stable and safe financial products. This is important for regulators and other financial partners, such as banks.

As an added bonus, platforms will also understand better the financial health of their platform in regards to risks and profitability.

Eventually, when lenders can compare marketplace loans with each other, a unified analytics engine can become best practice for all financial events, for all lending platforms and credit institutions, online and offline. At that point, marketplace lending has truly arrived on a level playing field with the established credit sector. Online lending platforms can then become ringleaders in the Hybrid Financial Sector. In the long term, platforms will standardize their analytics. Banks, of course, are also mostly running proprietary analytics, but the trend points toward a more unified system. In such a system, investors, markets and regulators have a common framework to assess risk. If platforms spearhead the approach and surpass banks on transparency, comparability, and regulatory compliance, they will have a leg up in the future.

Another reason points towards the need for unified analytics for marketplace lenders: when they re-bundle their offerings with a plug-and-play architecture, they can actually create a new kind of financial services company that banks will have a very hard time competing with. Instead of continuing on the path towards greater and greater fragmentation, where platforms serve one small niche demographic, they could go the other way. This would tip the scales in favor of the new entrants, and they might find themselves in a position of strength when bargaining with banks and other lending institutions for partnerships.

What are the first steps marketplace lenders can take towards unified analytics? Consistency of data with unified definitions and terminology of events, data formats, and time frames are a good starting point. Data lie at the core of understanding risks and rewards. Some marketplace lending platforms already have APIs in place for investors to execute transactions and keep track of their portfolios. However, they should also make data about their loan books available in real time.

17.1.4   Advantages for guarantors and protection sellers

For the time being, guarantors and protection sellers have little to do with marketplace lending. However, when online lenders offer collateralized loans, guarantors and protection sellers will enter the fold. Why do guarantors and protection sellers need unified analytics? Obviously, they would want to know the exact contractual payment obligations in case of a risk event and the associated pricing premiums. Guarantors need to know the real income and the potential claims so they can calculate the nominal value of the insured exposure. Market risk, counterparty risk, and concentration risk should build on real-world probabilities and stress conditions, instead of borrower analysis alone. With this information, guarantors and protection sellers can structure derivatives that insure them against financial risk. With derivatives, guarantors can hedge their exposure. They could also offer standardized insurance products, similar to credit default swaps, which platforms could then offer as a subscription to lenders.

17.1.5   Advantages for banks

Several FinTech services rebundling on a single platform would be a double whammy for banks: first, customers would learn that they can easily replace their banking services with add-ons that work in a plug-and-play architecture. Second, because those individual FinTech services operate on a single platform, regulators would have the opportunity to examine all of them via a single API. Regulators would have the full scope of operations on the platform. A FinTech platform standard for unified data would set an uneasy precedent for banks who benefit from complicating their operations with tangled data that take weeks and months to decrypt. If regulators have gotten used to clean digital records with immediate access from FinTech companies, there is just a small step to asking banks to provide the same convenience. Regulators will then be able to perform their own analysis and stress tests to identify financial risks and check for compliance in real time.

What is initially uncomfortable for banks would be a boon for consumers. Unified analytics would narrow the gap between the established financial sector and new entrants significantly. In the long run, it would also save banks and FinTech companies enormous time and effort needed for providing the results of analysis to comply with regulatory demands. Compliance has been one of the most expensive, unpleasant and risky operations in established financial institutions in recent years.[2]

The current leadership position of banks puts them in an ideal place to spearhead a unified analytics platform themselves. Banks have been slow to make their know-how available for a fee for the emerging FinTech sector, and marketplace lending in particular. If they jumped at the chance to actively lead the development of unified credit analytics and data standards, they might assure themselves pole position in the sector in the future. A possible point of entry into providing unified analytics for banks is to seclude a financial laboratory far from the mother ship, comprised of data scientists, financial mathematicians and statisticians ("geeks"). They could get to work on data collection standards, reporting standards, open APIs and robust interactive analytics that online lenders could use. A bank could launch such a venture with a relatively modest investment to the tune of what it costs to sponsor a yacht competing in the America's Cup. Banks have every reason to do this. When a new financial sector has formed without banks as members, it will be too late forever for them to regain their footing. If banks miss the boat, they will join the club of other companies that learned their services were no longer in demand after the digital revolution had disrupted their business model. Certainly, hindsight is 20/20, but banks will have no excuse to say that they didn't see the writing on the wall.

17.2   AN OVERVIEW OF A UNIFIED ANALYTICS PLATFORM

Unified analytics would make the marketplace lending sector safer and more transparent. However, analytics come with a high price tag. Banks spend millions of dollars annually to keep their analytics current and to push the envelope on making their algorithms smarter. The reason we point out that analytics should be unified is that it will then also be platform-independent. A third party could offer robust and transparent analytics for the entire sector as a service instead of every single platform reinventing the wheel with a proprietary analytics package. Many service providers already specialize in analytics software for banks, but they customize their solutions for each customer, running independently from the rest of the market. Third-party analytics solutions in the banking sector still have a long way to go towards unified analytics. Yet, with marketplace lending, a unified approach is doable because the market is still nascent and relatively small in size.

Individual marketplace lending platforms can pipe their data into a central analytics engine with an API. In return, they will receive the output of the analytics, in the form of data or charts. They can then use this output internally for their underwriting and risk management, or they can let borrowers and lenders use the engine to analyze their portfolios of loans. Figure 17.1 shows what a unified analytics engine might look like.

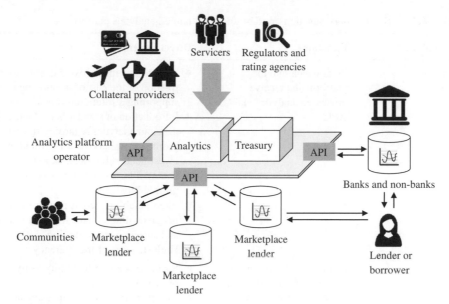

FIGURE 17.1 Unified analytics platform for marketplace lending with different stakeholders
Figure icons designed by Freepik

Let's now zoom in on the individual stakeholders of a unified analytics platform, their functions and direct benefits. We have already discussed some of these benefits in the previous paragraphs. Table 17.1 summarizes them and adds a few additional benefits.

Part Two of the book introduced most of the functions of the computational engine underlying a unified analytics platform. Repeating them here at length would therefore be redundant. The list below summarizes the most important functions of the analytics engine.

- Capability to securely plug in to multidimensional marketplace lending systems and platforms
- Get all information in regarding
  - Financial risk factors (market, counterparty, behavior) linked to individual contracts
  - Peers (counterparties)
- Map all contract agreements
- Structuring portfolios
- Calculate the value of all contracts, e.g., loans
- Identify and estimate all expected in and out cash-flows of all contracts to identify the
  - Market liquidity
  - Funding liquidity
- Calculate the value and liquidity at risk based on real world probabilities
- Calculate the income (i.e., P&L)
- Calculate the concentration risk in the level of
  - Counterparties, i.e., all types of Peers
  - Exposures
- Know the Systemic Risk in regards to

TABLE 17.1   Stakeholders, functions, and benefits of a unified analytics platform

Stakeholders	Functions	Direct benefits
Marketplace lenders	Stream data into the platform and receive processed analytics via APIs	■ World-class interactive analytics for a fraction of the cost of developing and supporting a solution in-house ■ Introduction of standards for financial data and analytics regarding risk and profitability analysis. This would make investments robust against risk and potential losses and ensure optimal profitability ■ Interoperability across platforms helps understanding of hard-to-quantify risks and systemic concentration ■ High standard of transparency
Lenders	Adjust variables on a customizable interface on the marketplace lender's website	■ Strong risk and profitability analysis portfolios and loans ■ Compare and combine investments across platforms and investment products from formal sector
Borrowers	Analyze existing contracts and exposure	■ Clarity about their ability to service loans and borrow under stress ■ Clarity about available options to prepay and the consequences of executing these options on borrowers, correlated counterparties, and the entire platform or the wider credit system
Communities operating a closed lending platform	Stream data into the platform and receive processed analytics via APIs	■ Low overhead with on-demand add-ons, such as analytics
Operator of the unified analytics platform	Develop, operate, and support the unified analytics platform	■ Revenues from platforms, banks, governments (regulators)
Collateral providers and servicers	Stream data into the platform and receive processed analytics via APIs	■ Real-time feedback for changes in collateral ■ Digitization of operations: central record keeping, central data standard
Regulators and rating agencies	Adjust variables on a customizable interface	■ Real-time stress testing ■ Real-time compliance checks ■ Digitization of operations, central record keeping, central data standard

TABLE 17.1 *(Continued)*

Stakeholders	Functions	Direct benefits
Banks and non-banks	Stream data into the platform and receive processed analytics via APIs or Banks could develop a unified analytics platform for marketplace lenders and other online lenders	■ Banks could spearhead a unified analytics platform with their existing experience and talent ■ Provide and use world-class interactive analytics for a fraction of the cost of developing and supporting a solution in-house ■ Introduction of data and analytics standards ■ Stewardship of best practices in the industry ■ Promoting transparency in the credit asset class ■ Interoperability across platforms helps understand hard-to-quantify risks (concentration) ■ High standard of transparency ■ Integration of the formal and informal financial sector

- ■ Correlated (linked) counterparties, i.e., all types of peers
- ■ Correlated exposures
- ■ Capability to restructure a portfolio to
  - ■ Increase (real) profitability
  - ■ Optimize the exposure to different financial risks
  - ■ Minimize losses
  - ■ Manage the exposure to risks
  - ■ Mitigate risk (by structuring credit enhancements)

17.2.1 Standardizing financial data and analytics

A big step forward—and a feasible one in the short-term—would be uniform data standards for marketplace lenders. A data standard needs agreement on conventions to meta tag the data they collect and report on counterparties and loans on their system. It may be difficult for individual platforms to agree on standards at the current time when they are still driving a fragmentation strategy, hoping to capture market share from each other. Therefore, introducing data standards and analytics opens up a huge market opportunity for third parties who can provide this service. If a company focuses exclusively on providing risk analytics and financial reporting for loans, and manages to get the dominant marketplace lending platforms on board, its services will be very useful for all stakeholders.

Some platforms already offer services and analytics for institutional investors to invest across several platforms in the U.S. They might just as well go the other way and perform the same service in the other direction, where they offer a data standard into which all underwriters of marketplace loans plug in. Unified analytics would be available by platforms via an API. The platform would standardize and process the data and return outputs that marketplace lenders could then make available interactively on their sites. Unified analytics that let investors compare loans in the entire asset class would be a boon and a huge step forward. By the same token, unified standards for data reporting and analytics need hardly stop at marketplace lenders. Other alternative lenders with online operations could also benefit from this service, and so could banks, eventually. Imagine investors objectively comparing the risk of loans, originated on different online platforms, with more traditional investments from banks or non-banks. What a quantum leap forward this would be from the opacity and guesswork that the current investment process in some financial products entails.

However, wrangling financial data from reluctant institutions and reporting financial analytics can be an expensive endeavor for a startup or online lending platform. This is a specialist domain within the financial services industry, with the available talent firmly concentrated in established financial institutions. Because banks have the experience and talent and in fact wrote the book about industrial-strength analytics and data collection, this invites them to jump in and provide unified analytics for newly emerging marketplace lenders. Next to offering a useful service, positioning themselves at the helm of unified analytics for online lenders is an excellent opportunity for banks to hedge their bets on financial technology innovation and stay relevant with the new players in the future.

17.2.1.1 Data and analytics standards Regulators, investors, and other stakeholders are urging financial institutions across different markets to provide standardized reports that are homogenous and comparative. This increases the confidence of markets in the profitability and stability of financial institutions. It also enhances the infrastructure for reporting key information to identify, monitor, and manage risks. Data standards serve the decision-making process by increasing the speed at which information is available and decisions can be made. They also improve an organization's quality of strategic planning and the ability to manage the risk of new products and services.

Unfortunately, financial reports are often incongruent, even though we assume that we have clean and homogenous information. This is happening because every analytics system may use similar—but not identical—algorithms and methods. Therefore, even when we use the same data for calculating financial events, the result and reports for liquidity, value, profit and loss, risk exposures and measurements may vary more than we would expect. Again, standardizing data across a relatively small segment of the credit sector, such as the marketplace lending niche, is a doable first step towards harmonization. Figure 17.2 shows the different categories of data that platforms would have to collect.

Unified analytics in the financial sector has been a dream of the analytics community for a while. The shopping list for data in unified analytics is relatively modest, yet getting the financial system to report these data accurately and on time is difficult. Without pointing the finger, it is clear that financial institutions can use their regulatory overhead to delay publishing accurate results and obfuscating relevant information in their numbers. Banks then pass the mess to regulators with the ungrateful task of untangling it. A much more elegant solution is the unified analytics platform from Figure 17.1. To force thousands of banks onto such a platform is impossible today. However, marketplace lending would be a feasible test case. Dealing with a few hundred small platforms, and their loan books with about 200,000 contracts each, is doable today.

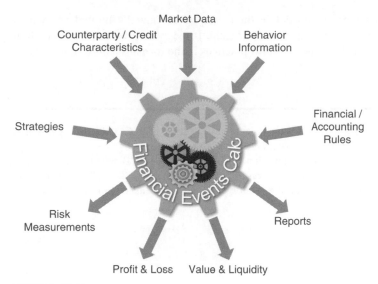

FIGURE 17.2 One engine providing consistent results, e.g., credit, liquidity value and their risk measurements

17.2.1.2 Who should push for unified analytics? Who should drive the strategy for unified data and analytics? Even though banks are ideally positioned to create an analytics platform, they might be blind to its benefits. Therefore, marketplace lending platforms themselves should take the lead and get to work on unified analytics. Instead of the sector anxiously waiting for the regulatory hammer to drop, marketplace lenders can take matters into their own hands and propose a solution. This could take a similar form to the payment networks that several large banks own collectively. At the same time, the young marketplace lending industry can prove that it truly cares about transparency and playing by the rules.

Honesty is the best policy, especially for those in credit provision. What a powerful signal self-imposed standards on data, analytics, and transparency would send to all players in a market that thrives on opaque information. Certainly, such an aggressive strategy comes with risks attached. At the same time, the marketplace lending sector is in a position where it can afford to take bold steps forward.

17.3 CONCLUDING REMARKS

The hybrid financial sector will happen; it is just a matter of time. However, the leadership position in the hybrid financial sector is still up for grabs. Throughout this book, we have explored how banks actually have the most to gain from disrupting themselves. They can set standards for the financial sector of the future by leading it forward. Unified analytics is a relatively low hanging fruit with immediate benefits for all stakeholders in the credit sector. It is the ideal point of entry for banks to assure their relevance in years to come.

Marketplace lenders might as well be the leaders of the hybrid financial sector by taking ownership as its architects. The newcomers in the credit sector can rewrite the rule book and define how regulators will interact with them in the future. If they preempt mandatory standards for data and analytics and define their own by introducing unified analytics, marketplace lenders have little to lose and much to gain. If the system works, there is a high probability that regulators will expand it as best practices in the formal credit sector as well.

NOTES

1. Su, Jean Baptiste (2015) "Exclusive Interview: Lending Club CEO Plans Expansion Into Car Loans, Mortgages," Forbes, 1 April 2015, http://onforb.es/1CxLItj.
2. Center for the Study of Financial Innovation (CSFI) (2014) "Banking Banana Skins 2014: Inching towards recovery," http://www.csfi.org/files/Banking_Banana_Skins_2014.pdf, date accessed 28 May 2015. According to the report, "regulatory risk" has been ranked No 1 in 2005, 2006, 2007 and 2014, No 3 in 2009 and 2012.

Bibliography

Accenture (2014) "The Rise of Fintech: New York's Opportunity for Tech Leadership," http://www.accenture.com/us-en/Pages/insight-rise-fintech-new-york.aspx.

Agar, Jon (2013) *Constant Touch: A Global History of the Mobile Phone* (London: Icon Books).

Berger, Allen; Molyneux, Philip and Wilson, John (2010) "Banking, an Overview" in *The Oxford Handbook of Banking* (Oxford: Oxford University Press).

Brammertz, Willi; Akkizidis, Ioannis; Breymann, Wolfgang; Entin, Rami and Rustmann, Marco (2009) *Unified Financial Analysis, The Missing Links of Finance* (Hoboken: Wiley).

Brito, Jerry and Castilo, Andrea (2013) "Bitcoin, a Primer for Policy Makers" (George Mason University, 2013), mercatus.org/sites/default/files/Brito_BitcoinPrimer.pdf.

Broeders, Henk and Khanna, Somesh (2015) Strategic choices for banks in the digital age (McKinsey and Company), http://www.mckinsey.com/insights/financial_services/Strategic_choices_for_banks_in_the_digital_age.

Buford, John; Yu, Heather and Lua, Eng Keong (2009) *P2P Networking and Applications* (Burlington: Elsevier).

Center for the Study of Financial Innovation (CSFI) (2014) "Banking Banana Skins 2014: Inching towards recovery," http://www.csfi.org/files/Banking_Banana_Skins_2014.pdf.

Chao, Georgia T. (2012) "Organizational Socialization: Background, Basics, and a Blueprint for Adjustment at Work," in Kozlowski, Steve (editor) *The Oxford Handbook of Organizational Psychology*, Volume 1 (Oxford: Oxford University Press).

Chesbrough, Henry (2003) *Open Innovation: The New Imperative for Creating and Profiting from Technology* (Harvard: Harvard Business Review Press).

Chesbrough, Henry (2011) *Open Services Innovation: Rethinking Your Business to Grow and Compete in a New Era* (San Francisco: Jossey-Bass).

Choudhry, Moorad (2004) *An Introduction to Credit Derivatives* (Elsevier, 2004).

Christensen, Clayton (1997) *The Innovator's Dilemma: When New Technologies Cause Great Firms to Fail* (Harvard: Harvard Business School Press).

Christensen, Clayton; Allworth, James and Dillon, Karen (2012) *How Will You Measure Your Life?* (New York: Harper Business)

Chu, Catherine and Smithson, Steve (2007) "E-business and organizational change: a structurational approach" (*Information Systems Journal*, 10/2007), http://onlinelibrary.wiley.com/doi/10.1111/j.1365-2575.2007.00258.x/abstract.

Croxford, Hugh; Abramson, Frank and Jalbonowski, Alex (2005) *The Art of Better Retail Banking* (Hoboken: Wiley).

Dang, Tri Vi; Gorton, Gary; Holstroem, Bengt and Ordonez, Guillermo (2014) "Banks as Secret Keepers," National Bureau of Economic Research (NBER), www.nber.org/papers/w20255.

Demirguc-Kunt, Asli and Klapper, Leora (2012) "Measuring Financial Inclusion" (World Bank, Policy Research Working Paper 6025, April 2012).

Devasabai, Kris (2014) "Hedge funds, securitisation and leverage change P2P game," Risk.net 12 October 2014, www.risk.net/risk-magazine/feature/2372612/hedge-funds-securitisation-and-leverage-change-p2p-game.

Diamandis, Peter and Kotler, Stephen (2015) *Bold: How to Go Big, Achieve Success, and Impact the World* (New York: Simon & Schuster).

Downes, Larry and Nunes, Paul (2014) *Big Bang Disruption: Strategy in the Age of Devastating Innovation* (New York: Penguin).

Evans, Philip and Wurster, Thomas (2000) *Blown to Bits: How the New Economics of Information Transforms Strategy* (Harvard: Harvard Business School Press).

Federal Reserve Bank of New York (2014) "Key Findings of the Small Business Credit Survey, Q4/2013," http://www.newyorkfed.org/smallbusiness/Fall2013/pdf/summary-of-key-findings-2014.pdf.

Fudenberg, Drew and Tirole, Jean (1984) "The Fat-Cat Effect, the Puppy-Dog Ploy, and the Lean and Hungry Look," *The American Economic Review*, Vol. 74, No. 2, May 1984.

Gallo, Carmine (2010) *The Innovation Secrets of Steve Jobs: Insanely Different Principles for Breakthrough Success* (New York: McGraw-Hill).

Gordon Mills, Karen and McCarthy, Brayden (2014) "The State of Small Business Lending: Credit Access during the Recovery and How Technology May Change the Game" (Harvard Business School Working Paper, 22 July 2014), http://www.hbs.edu/faculty/Publication%20Files/15-004_09b1bf8b-eb2a-4e63-9c4e-0374f770856f.pdf.

Gregory, Jon (2012) *Counterparty Credit Risk and Credit Value Adjustment: A Continuing Challenge for Global Financial Markets* (Chichester: Wiley).

Hagel, John III and Rayport, Jeffrey (1997) "The Coming Battle for Customer Information" (*Harvard Business Review*, January 1997 Issue), https://hbr.org/1997/01/the-coming-battle-for-customer-information.

Hirt, Martin and Willmott, Paul (2014) *Strategic Principles for Competing in the Digital Age* (McKinsey&Company).

Ismail, Salim (2015) *Exponential Organizations: Why new organizations are ten times better, faster, and cheaper than yours (and what to do about it)* (New York: Diversion Books).

King, Brett (2010) *Bank 2.0* (Singapore: Marshall Cavendish International).

King, Brett (2013) *Bank 3.0: Why Banking is No Longer Somewhere You Go, But Something You Do* (Hoboken: Wiley).

King, Brett (2014) *Breaking Banks: The Innovators, Rogues, and Strategists Rebooting Banking* (New York: Wiley).

Kurzweil, Ray (2005) *The Singularity Is Near: When Humans Transcend Biology* (London: Duckworth Overlook).

Levitt, Theodore (1960) "Marketing Myopia," *Harvard Business Review* 2004 Jul-Aug;82(7-8):138-49, https://hbr.org/2004/07/marketing-myopia.

Manbeck, Peter and Hu, Samuel (2014) "The Regulation of Marketplace Lending: A Summary of the Principal Issues" (Chapman and Cutler LLP White Paper, April 2014), http://www.aba.com/Tools/Offers/Documents/Chapman_Regulation_of_Marketplace_Lending_0414.pdf.

Markoff, John (2005) *What the Dormouse Said: How the Sixties Counterculture Shaped the Personal Computer Industry* (New York: Penguin).

McGrath, Rita and MacMillan, Ian (1995) "Discovery-Driven Planning" (*Harvard Business Review*, July 1995 Issue), https://hbr.org/1995/07/discovery-driven-planning/ar/1.

Mintzberg, Henry (1978) "Patterns in Strategy Formation" (*Management Science*, Vol. 24, No. 9 (May, 1978), pp. 934-948), http://www.jstor.org/stable/2630633.

Moldow, Charles (2014) "A Trillion Dollar Market By the People, For the People" (Foundation Capital, 2014), http://www.foundationcapital.com/downloads/FoundationCap_MarketplaceLendingWhitepaper.pdf.

Nash, Ryan, and Eric Beardsley (2015) "The Future of Finance: The Rise of the New Shadow Bank, Part 1," Goldman Sachs Equity Research.

Peter, Laurence and Hull, Raymond (1969) *The Peter Principle: Why Things Always Go Wrong* (New York: William Morrow and Company).

Prahalad, C K and Hamel, Gary (1990) "The Core Competence of the Corporation" (*Harvard Business Review* May–June 1990).

Robinson + Yu (2014) "Knowing the Score: New Data, Underwriting, and Marketing in the Consumer Credit Marketplace. A Guide for Financial Inclusion Stakeholders," http://www.robinsonyu.com/pdfs/Knowing_the_Score_Oct_2014_v1_1.pdf.

Rogers, Everett (2003) *Diffusion of Innovations, 5th Edition* (New York: Free Press, a Division of Simon & Schuster).

Rotman, Frank (2015) "The Hourglass Effect: A Decade of Displacement", 13 April 2015, http://qedinvestors.com/frank-rotman-releases-the-hourglass-effect-a-decade-of-displacement/.

Schiinbucher, Philipp J. (2003) *Credit Derivatives Pricing Models* (Hoboken: Wiley).

Shapiro, Carl and Varian, Hal (1999) *Information Rules* (Harvard: Harvard Business School Press).

Skinner, Chris (2014) *Digital Bank: Strategies to launch or become a digital bank* (Singapore: Marshall Cavendish Business).

Sviokla, John and Cohen, Mitch (2014) *The Self-Made Billionaire Effect: How Extreme Producers Create Massive Value* (New York: Penguin).

Thiel, Peter and Masters, Blake (2014) *Zero to One: Notes on Startups or How to Build the Future* (New York: Crown Business).

Turkle, Sherry (2011) *Alone Together: Why We Expect More from Technology and Less from Each Other* (New York: Basic Books).

World Economic Forum (2011) "Personal Data: The Emergence of a New Asset Class," http://www3.weforum.org/docs/WEF_ITTC_PersonalDataNewAsset_Report_2011.pdf.

Index

2007/8 financial crisis, 1, 5, 64

accrual interest patterns, contracts, 101–102
aircraft development, 270–271
alternative borrowers, 47
alternative data, 280–281, 285
Amazon, 62
analytics, 57–58, 117–118, 252–255
  standardization, 299–301
  unified analytics, 289–302
API *see* Application Programming Interface
Apple Pay, 69
Application Programming Interface (API), 118
Asia, 7, 9–10, 85, 279
asset-based credit enhancements, 162–165
ATMs (automated teller machines), 84
Australia, credit outstanding to households/ NPISHs, 8–9

back testing, 191
balance sheet lenders, 33, 34–35
banks
  always-on banking, 281–282
  analytics, 252–255, 295–296
  antipathy towards, 63
  ATMs, 84
  Barclays Bank, 26
  buying vs. selling portfolio businesses, 259–260
  challenges to, 1, 11, 26, 66
  collaboration, 75, 271–272
  cooperation vs. competition, 256–258
  core competencies, 77, 78–79
  credit access, customers', 64–65
  credit sector disruptions, 267–268
  customer service, 64–65, 282, 284
  data mining/selling, 26
  data standards, 284–286
  digital competencies, 252–255
  digital dilemmas, 255–260
  digital separation vs. integration, 259
  digital strategies, 69, 216, 263–275
  disruptions in credit sector, 267–268
  disruptive innovation, 72
  disruptive vs. defensive strategies, 255–256
  diversification vs. concentration, 258–259
  economic role of, 83
  expected loss calculation, 45
  financial laboratories, 296
  future of, 81, 85, 286
  guarantors, 121, 122
  HSBC, 64
  'imprisoned' resources, 77
  innovation
    adoption of, 57, 84, 215
    approach to, 72–73, 215–216
    by-passing banking sector, 69–82
    difficulties with, 76–79, 269–271
    Innovator's Dilemma, 269–271
  interest rates, 65
  as intermediators, 253
  know-your-customer process, 63
  lending process, 30–31
  Lending as a Service, 282–283
  licenses, 25
  loan characteristics, 117
  loan investments, 283–284
  loss calculations, 45
  low-margin products, 72–73
  marginal thinking trap, 80

banks (*Continued*)
  marketplace lending comparison, 45
  mobile banking, 19, 21, 84–85
  mudslide hypothesis, 71
  and online lending, 30–31, 45, 51–52
  premium services, 284
  privacy concerns, 26
  producer to supplier switch, 271–272
  protection sellers, 121, 122
  regulation, 64
  resource 'imprisonment', 77
  role of, 83, 251
  Santander, 75
  straight-through processing, 252
  streamlining of financial services, 284
  technology mudslide hypothesis, 71
  threats to, 1, 11, 26, 66
  transformation of, 83–84
  treasury, 206, 209, 212
  unexpected loss calculation, 45
  U.S. Federal Reserve Bank, 144
  Wells Fargo Bank, 45, 64
Barclays Bank, 26
behavior
  borrowers, 153
  elements of, 140, 148
  financial contracts, 103–104
behavior risk, 107–108, 139–149, 224
  defaults, 144–145
  downgrading, 144–145
  draw-downs, 141–142
  facilities/credit lines, 142
  prepayments, 140–141
  recoveries, 146–147
  sale of assets, 143–144
  withdrawals, 143
Big Bang Disruption, 266–267
Big Data, 23, 49, 57–58, 252, 280–281, 290
Bitcoin network, 18
Blockbuster, 80
bond markets, 40–41
book trade, 38
borrowers
  alternative borrowers, 47
  analytics, 293–294
  behavior of, 153
  credit scores, 242

defaults, 122, 179
fees, 34
market allocation, 134–135, 136
onboarding, 41–43
quality overestimation, 240–245
risk allocation, 133
business models, 15–28, 33, 40–41, 278, 279
business units, strategic, 77
businesses, buying/shedding dilemma,
    259–260

cash flows
  contracts, 94–99
  defaults, 161, 162
  discounted cash flows, 116
CD *see* certificates of deposit
CDS *see* credit default swaps
cell phones, 51–52, 172–173
centralized systems, 36–37, 40
certificates of deposit (CD), 283
China
  collaborations, 279
  credit outstanding to households/NPISHs,
      7, 9–10
Christensen, Clayton, 70–71, 72, 80, 269
close-out netting, 163
coin-flipping analogy, 108
collaboration, 75, 217, 271–272, 279
collateral, 163–164, 246
collections accounts, 33
community lending, 292
companies, tree model, 76
comparability of services, 60
competition, 256–258, 277–280
computers, 57–58, 60–62
concentration risk, 184–188, 290
  counterparties, 185–186
  credit exposure, 184–185
contracts, 89–106
  see also counterparties
  accrual interest patterns, 101–102
  behavior patterns, 103–104
  cash flow patterns, 94–99
    fixed principal amounts at fixed PIT and
        TTC, 95, 96
    fixed principal cash-flows paid within
        variable PIT and TTC, 95, 97

variable principal amounts at fixed PIT and TTC, 97–98
variable principal amounts at variable PIT and TTC, 99
counterparty evaluation, 90
credit enhancements, 102–103, 170, 171
credit exposures, 154
defaults, 161
derivative contract agreements, 166–167
elements of, 89–90
financial events, 91, 92–106
  example, 104–106
interest patterns, 99–101
  fixed interest at fixed PIT and/or within fixed TTC, 100
  variable interest at fixed PIT and/or within fixed TTC, 100–101
interest rates, 99–101
liquidity, 191
mechanisms, 92–106
mobile phone contracts, 172–173
parameters, 93
phone contracts, 172–173
point in time events, 91, 93–106
rules, 93
cooperation vs. competition, 256–258
core competencies, 77, 78–81
corporate bond markets, 40–41
corporations, tree model, 76
correlations analysis, 180–181
counterparties, 121–138
behavior risk, 139–149
characteristics of, 123–124
concentration risk, 185–186
correlations analysis, 180–181
credit enhancements, 165–167, 170, 171
credit exposures, 157–158
credit ratings, 129–130
credit risk, 124–130, 223–224
credit spreads, 130–131
credit status, 153
default probability, 124–130, 144–145
descriptive characteristics, 123–124
evaluation of, 90
market linkage, 131–136
  obligor market allocation, 134–135, 136
  obligor risk allocation, 133

prepayments, 140–141
probability of default, 124–130, 144–145
real-world probabilities, 130–131
risk elements, 122, 137
roles of, 121–123
systemic risk, 180–183
types of, 121–123
use at default, 145–146
withdrawals, 143
counterparty-based credit enhancements, 165–167, 170, 171
credit access, 64–65
credit cards, 23, 46–47
credit default swaps (CDS), 166
credit derivatives, 166–167
credit discount spreads, 114–115
credit downgrading, 180, 181
credit enhancements, 161–176
asset-based, 162–165
collateral allocation to credit exposures, 163–164
contracts, 102–103, 170, 171
counterparty-based, 165–167, 170, 171
default credit events, 178, 179
double default, 168–169
guarantor systems, 174–175
life insurance, 174
loyalty points, 173–174
marketplace lending, 167, 170–175
maturity mismatch, 170
payment times, 170
phone contracts, 172–173
real estate titles, 172
structure, 162
types, 162
wrong way risk, 169–170
credit exposures, 151–159
chain reactions after default credit event, 178–180
collateral allocation, 163–164
concentration risk, 184–185
counterparties linkage, 157–158
credit losses, 156–157
distribution of, 155–156
evolution of, 152–155
gross exposure, 151, 152–155
guarantee allocation, 165–166

credit exposures (*Continued*)
  net exposure, 152–155
  portfolios, 225–226, 227, 243, 244, 246
  systemic risk, 177–180, 183–184
credit lines behavior, 142, 145–146
credit losses, 156–157
credit outstanding to households/
    non-financial companies, 5–10
credit ratings, 129–130
credit risk
  behavior, 139–149
  counterparties, 124–130
  intensity models, 127–128
  measurement, 290
  real-world default probabilities, 128–129
  risk-neutral default probabilities, 128–129
  structural models, 125–126
credit scores/scoring, 47, 48–49, 242,
    280–281
credit sector disruptions, 267–268
credit spreads, 234
credit status, 153
crime, 59
crowdfunding, 17
cryptocurrencies, 18
currencies, virtual, 18
customer needs/service, 64–65, 78–79, 282,
    284
cybercrime, 59

data
  alternative data, 280–281, 285
  analytics standards, 300–301
  Big Data, 23, 49, 57–58, 252, 280–281,
    290
  data science, 22
  fringe alternative data, 280–281, 285
  mining of, 26
  mobile user tracking, 61
  online lending, 29–30
  selling of, 26
  standards, 284–286, 295, 299–301
  transparency, 66
default credit events, 178–180, 181, 182
default probability, 124–130
  counterparties, 144–145
  credit ratings, 129–130

impacts of default and non-default
    statuses, 125
  intensity models, 127–128
  real-world default probabilities, 128–129
  risk-neutral default probabilities, 128–129
  structural models, 125–126
defaults
  behavior risk, 144–145
  counterparties, 122
  double default, 168–169
  time factor, 234, 235, 236
  use at default, 145–146
defensive strategies, 255–256
derivative contract agreements, 166–167
diffusion of innovation, 264–265
digital competencies, 252–255
digital currencies, 18
digital dilemmas, 255–260
  cooperation vs. competition, 256–258
  digital separation vs. integration, 259
  disruptive vs. defensive strategies,
    255–256
  diversification vs. concentration, 258–259
digital integration, 21
digital strategies, 69, 216, 263–275
  leadership, 273–274
  purpose of, 263–264
disclosure, online lending, 50
discount brokerage industry, 22
discount rate curves, 110–111
discounted cash flows, 116
discovery-driven planning, 73
disintermediation, peer-to-peer networks,
    38–39
disruptive innovation, 20–22, 70–73, 74,
    269–270
disruptive strategies, 255–256
diversification vs. concentration, 258–259
double default, 168–169
draw-downs, behavior risk, 141–142
DVD rental business, 80

e-business, 216, 279
ECOA *see* Equal Credit Opportunity Act
economic capital allocation, 202–203
economic scenarios, 109–110
economic shocks, 231–233

Equal Credit Opportunity Act (ECOA), 49
equity-based crowdfunding, 17
ExOs *see* Exponential Organizations
expected loss, banks, 45
Exponential Organizations (ExOs), 270
exposures *see* credit exposures

Facebook, 62
facilities/credit lines behavior, 142
failures, 74–75, 270
fair lending laws, 49
farms, loans to, 64, 65
file sharing, 37
financial advisors, 18–19, 24
financial analysis of portfolio model,
      219–249
financial collateral, 163
financial contracts *see* contracts
financial crisis (2007/8), 1, 5, 64
financial events, contracts, 91, 92–106
financial innovation, FinTech contrast, 3–4
FinTech (financial technology innovation)
   advantages of, 1
   banking licenses, 25
   Big Data overestimation, 23
   business models, 15–28
   challenges for companies, 24–26
   core competencies, 79–81
   crowdfunding, 17
   cryptocurrencies, 18
   data science overestimation, 22
   definition, 2–3
   digital currencies, 18
   digital dilemmas, 255–260
   digital integration, 21
   disruptive innovation, 20–22, 73, 74
   dynamic/fragmented nature of, 19
   existing infrastructure use, 21, 215, 278,
      289–290
   financial advisors, 18–19, 24
   financial innovation contrast, 3–4
   human interface deficiency, 24–25
   importance of, 23–24
   industry standards, 21
   innovation
      breakthroughs, 73–76
      disruptive potential, 20–22, 73, 74

   outside banking sector, 69–82
   themes, 15–20
   long-term focus, 26–27
   mobile-first banks, 19
   mobile point of sale, 18
   online lending, 15–17
   payment processing, 17
   Personal Financial Management, 17–18
   pitfalls, 22–23
   potential of, 20–22
   privacy concerns, 26
   regulation, 23
   roadblocks for companies, 24–26
   robo-advisors, 18–19, 24
   service unbundling, 21–22
   startup areas, 4
   streamlining user experience, 21
   sustaining innovation, 73
   transactions, 17
   virtual currencies, 18
forward rates, 111–113
fringe alternative data, 280–281, 285
FTP *see* funds transfer pricing
funding accounts, 33, 34
Funding Circle, 75
funds transfer pricing (FTP), 205–210
   profit centers, 207, 208
   transfer rates, 207–209

GAP reports, liquidity, 195, 231, 232, 241,
      242
Germany, credit outstanding to households/
      NPISHs, 7–8
global credit, peer-to-peer loan comparison,
      51
Google, "p2p lending" searches, 10
gross credit exposure, 151, 152–155
guarantees, 165–166, 174–175
guarantors, 121, 122, 295

haircuts, 184
hedge funds, 48
hedging exposure, 246
historical model scenarios, 110
households, credit extension, 5–10
HSBC, 64
human interface, 24–25

hybrid financial sector, 5–10, 75, 277–287
  alternative data, 280–281
  always-on banking, 281–282
  collaboration, 217
  competition, 277–280
  credit scoring, 280–281
  data standards, 284–286
  fringe alternative data, 280–281
  future prospects, 286
  Lending as a Service, 282–283
  near-real-time credit, 281–282
  new ideas, 280–286
  service unbundling, 284
  streamlining of financial services, 284
  transparency, 284–286
hype cycle, 265–266

incentive systems, 74–75
income, 197–203
  economic capital allocation, 202–203
  elements of, 197, 211
  estimation of, 198–199
  portfolio performance, 226–229
  profit and loss analysis, 199
  risk, 199, 202–203
  stochastic process, 201–202
  stress testing, 200–201
infomediaries, 39–40, 61–62
information value chain, 39–40
innovation
  analysis of, 264–267
  autonomy of innovators, 270–271
  banks, 57, 72–73, 76–79, 84, 215–216
  Big Bang Disruption, 266–267
  buying innovation, 75–76
  centers of, 3, 12
  challenges of, 76–79
  diffusion of, 264–265
  disruptive innovation, 20–22, 70–73, 74, 269–270
  FinTech breakthroughs, 73–76
  frameworks, 264–267
  hype cycle, 265–266
  in-house vs. buying-in, 75–76
  Innovator's Dilemma, 71, 72, 269–271
  marginal thinking trap, 80
  new markets, 271

  open services, 272–273
  overview, 15–20
  performers vs. producers, 78
  sustaining innovation vs. disruptive innovation, 70–73
  technology catch-up dangers, 216
  themes, 15–20
Innovator's Dilemma, 71, 72, 269–271
institutional investors, 48
insurance, 174
intangible assets, 163
intensity-based credit risk models, 127–128
interest rates
  cash flows, 116
  contracts, 99–101
  drivers of, 116
  forward rates, 111–113
  low rate environment, 65
  pricing models, 107
  risk-free interest rates, 116
  saver behavior, 108
  stress scenarios, 200
intermediary-oriented marketplaces, 39–40
intermediators, 253
internet, 58–60, 279
investors, 48

know-your-customer process (KYC), 63

LaaS see Lending as a Service
leadership, 273–274
legislation, 49
lender-agnostic marketplaces, 33, 35
lenders
  balance sheet lenders, 33, 34–35
  expectations of, 121–122
  onboarding, 43–44
Lending Club (online lender), 29, 45, 46, 48, 49, 124, 279
  portfolio model analysis, 219–249
Lending as a Service (LaaS), 282–283
licenses, banking, 25
life insurance, 174
liquidity, 190–196
  analysis types, 191–192
  contracts, 191
  elements of, 190, 211

measurement, 195
portfolio performance, 227–228, 230, 231
reporting, 195
risk, 192–195, 210, 211
spreads, 115
time factor, 191–192
loans, characteristics of, 117
Lockheed, 270–271
Long-Term Capital Management (LTCM), 183
losses
profit and loss analysis, 199
systemic risk, 183–184
low-margin products, 72–73
loyalty points, 173–174
LTCM *see* Long-Term Capital Management

M-Pesa (money transfer service), 17, 173
marginal thinking trap, 80
margins, 209, 277–278
mark-to-market, 164
market risk, 192–195, 222–223, 290
marketplace lending, 31–34
see also peer-to-peer...
analytics, 292–295
bank credit comparison, 45
bond markets, 40–41
borrower onboarding, 41–43
business model, 40–41
challenges, 42
collections accounts, 33
credit card debt comparison, 46–47
credit enhancements, 167, 170–175
credit scores, 47, 48–49
funding accounts, 33, 34
investors, 48
lender onboarding, 43–44
new ideas, 280–286
onboarding process, 41–44
origination process, 33
platform notes, 34
profitability, 219–249
regulation, 49–50
risk, 219–249
underwriting, 48–49
unified analytics, 292–295

markets, 107–119
coin-flipping analogy, 108
counterparties, 131–136
credit discount spreads, 114–115
discount rate curves, 110–111
discounted cash flows, 116
economic scenarios, 109–110
elements of, 108, 119
evolution of, 153
forward rates, 111–113
liquidity spreads, 115
low-margin products, 72–73
new markets, 271
peer-to-peer lending, 117–118
prices, 111–113
real-world expectations/probabilities, 108–110
risk factors, 107
risk-neutral default probabilities, 114–115
risk-neutral expectations, 108–113
spreads, 114–116
yield curves, 110–111
maturity mismatch, 170
Metcalfe's law, 59
micro investments, 283
minimills, 72
mobile banking, 19, 21, 84–85
mobile devices, 60–62
mobile payments, 17, 18, 173
mobile phones, 51–52, 172–173
mobile point of sale (mPOS), overview, 18
modeling of portfolio performance, 226–244
see also business models
money transfer services, 17, 173
monitoring practices, 50
monopolies, 38, 61–62
Monte Carlo approach, 201
Motorola, 52
mPOS *see* mobile point of sale
mudslide hypothesis, 70–73
music business, 38

Napster, 37
net credit exposure, 152–155
net present value (NPV), 164
Netflix, 80

network effects, 40, 58–60
new production, 203–205
non-default status, 161
non-profit institutions serving households (NPISHs), credit extension, 5–10
NPV *see* net present value

obligors *see* borrowers
onboarding process, 41–44
online balance sheet lenders, 33, 34–35
online financial advisors, 18–19, 24
online lending
   actions, 32
   alternative lending, 47
   analytics, 57–58
   balance sheet lenders, 33, 34–35
   and banks, 30–31, 45, 51–52, 75
   Big Data, 49, 57–58
   business models, 33
   challenges, 32, 33
   characteristics, 32
   collaboration with banks, 75
   data reliance, 29–30
   definition, 11
   disclosure, 50
   disruptive potential of, 4–5
   lender types, 31–35
   lender-agnostic marketplaces, 33, 35
   marketplace lending platforms, 31–34
   monitoring practices, 50
   online balance sheet lenders, 33, 34–35
   oversight, 50
   overview, 15–17, 29–55
   peer-to-peer networks, 36–40
   regulation, 49–50
   reporting requirements, 50
   security, 59
   social factors, 58, 62–63
   structural factors, 58, 63–65
   technology, 29–30, 57–62
   terminology use, 3
   transparency, 50
   trends, 66–67
   types of lender, 31–35
open innovation, 272–273
operational risk, 239–240
oversight standardization, 50

P2P *see* peer-to-peer
partnerships, 279
payments
   credit enhancements, 170
   mobile payments, 17, 173
   processing, 23
PayPal, 17
PCs (personal computers), 57–58, 60–62
PD (probability of default) *see* default probability
peer-to-peer (P2P) lending
   global credit comparison, 51
   Google searches for, 10
   markets, 117–118
   terminology use, 2
   treasury, 209–210
   uses of loans, 47
peer-to-peer (P2P) networks, 36–40
   bilateral linkage, 38
   central directories, 40
   direct and indirect connections, 36
   disintermediation, 38–39
   infomediaries, 39–40
   information value chain, 39–40
   intermediary-oriented marketplaces, 39–40
   re-intermediation, 38–39
personal computers (PCs), 57–58, 60–62
Personal Financial Management (PFM), 17–18
physical collateral, 163
PIT *see* point in time
planning
   discovery-driven planning, 73
   new production, 203–205
platform notes, 34
plug-and-play business models, 278
point in time (PIT) events
   contracts, 91, 93–106
   prepayments, 140
portfolios
   borrower quality, 240–245
   buying vs. selling businesses, 259–260
   collateral, 246
   construction of, 224–226, 227
   diversification of, 187
   exposure, 225–226, 227, 243, 244, 246

hedging exposure, 246
income performance, 226–229
liquidity performance, 227–228, 230, 231
maturity mismatch, 170
model analysis, 219–249
  assumptions, 220–222
  construction of portfolio, 224–226, 227
  layout, 221
  modeling, 226–244
  returns performance, 234–236, 239–244
  risk, 222–224, 236–246
operational risk, 239–240
optimization, 245
performance modeling, 226–244
restructuring of, 245
risk, 187, 222–224, 236–246, 291
selling vs. buying businesses, 259–260
stress testing, 228–244
systemic risk, 187
premium services, 284
prepayments, 140–141, 234
prices, 111–113, 277–278
privacy concerns, 26
probability of default (PD) *see* default probability
profit centers, 207, 208
profit and loss analysis, 199
profitability, marketplace lending, 219–249
Prosper (online lender), 29, 49
protection sellers, 121, 122, 295

railroads, 71
re-intermediation, peer-to-peer networks, 38–39
real estate titles, 172
real-world expectations, 108–109
real-world probabilities
  counterparties, 130–131
  defaults, 128–129
  economic scenarios, 109–110
recovery behavior, 146–147
regulation, 23, 49–50, 64
reporting, 50, 195
resource 'imprisonment', 77, 78
retail investors, 48, 293
reward-based crowdfunding, 17

risk
  see also risk management
  analysis of, 291–292
  behavior risk, 107–108, 139–149, 224
  concentration risk, 184–188, 290
  counterparties, 122, 223–224
  credit risk, 290
  credit spreads, 234
  default probability, 124–130
  definition, 107
  income, 199, 202–203
  liquidity, 192–195, 210
  market risk, 192–195, 222–223, 290
  marketplace lending, 219–249
  measurement, 290
  portfolio performance, 222–224, 291
  systemic risk, 177–184, 187–188
  value, 199, 202–203
  wrong way risk, 169–170
risk-free interest rates, 116
risk management
  key points, 203
  liquidity, 211
  portfolio performance, 236–246
  understanding of, 291
risk-neutral default probabilities, 114–115, 128–129
risk-neutral expectations, 108–109, 110–113
robo-advisors (online financial advisors), 18–19, 24

sale of assets, behavior risk, 143–144
Santander, 75
SBUs *see* strategic business units
scenarios
  credit exposures, 155, 158
  stress testing, 200, 231–244
Securities and Exchange Commission (SEC), 50
security, online, 59
services
  comparability, 60
  customer service, 64–65, 282, 284
  open services, 272–273
  premium services, 284
  streamlining, 284
  unbundling, 21–22, 66, 284

shadow banking sector, 39, 183
Simple (mobile bank), 19
simulation, stress testing scenarios, 234
SIVs *see* Structured Investment Vehicles
Skunk Works program (Lockheed), 270–271
Skype, 37–38, 279
small and medium enterprises (SMEs),
    64–65, 294
smartphones, 58, 60–62
SMEs *see* small and medium enterprises
social factors, online lending, 58, 62–63
social networking, 62–63
spreads
   credit discount spreads, 114–115
   credit spreads, 130–131
   liquidity spreads, 115
   markets, 114–116
static analysis, 191–192
statistics, behavior risk, 139
steel mills, 72
stochastic process, 201–202
stochastic scenarios, 110
straight-through processing (STP), 252
strategic business units (SBUs), 77
strategies
   buying vs. selling portfolio businesses,
     259–260
   cooperation vs. competition, 256–258
   digital separation vs. integration, 259
   digital strategies, 263–275
   disruptive vs. defensive strategies,
     255–256
   diversification vs. concentration, 258–259
streamlining
   financial services, 284
   user experience, 21
stress testing
   canonical conditions in ideal world,
     231–233
   income and value, 200–201
   portfolios, 228–244
   scenarios, 231–244
   simulation of scenarios, 234
structural models, credit risk, 125–126
Structured Investment Vehicles (SIVs), 84
supplier-oriented marketplaces, 39
switching costs, 4

systemic risk, 177–184, 187–188
   counterparties, 180–183
   credit exposures, 177–180, 183–184
   losses, 183–184
   portfolio diversification, 187

TBS *see* Time Bucket System
technology, 57–62
   adoption rates, 58
   computers, 57–58, 60–62
   mobile devices, 60–62
   mudslide hypothesis, 70–73
   network effects, 58–60
   online lending, 29–30
   security, 59
   trust, 59
telephony, 51–52, 172–173, 279
testing, 191
through the cycle (TTC), contracts, 91,
     93–106
Time Bucket System (TBS), 92
time factor
   contracts, 90–92, 93
   credit enhancements, 170
   default scenarios, 234, 235, 236
   liquidity, 191–192
transactions, overview, 17
transfer rates, 207–209
transparency, 50, 60, 284–286
treasury, 205–210
tree model of corporations, 76
trust, 23, 26, 59
TTC *see* through the cycle

Uber, 40
underwriting, 48–49, 242
unexpected loss, 45
unified analytics, 289–302
   bank advantages, 295–296
   benefits of, 298–299
   borrower advantages, 293–294
   drivers of, 301
   functions, 298–299
   guarantor advantages, 295
   lender advantages, 292–293
   marketplace lending, 292–295
   need for, 290–296

overview of, 296–301
protection seller advantages, 295
stakeholders, 297, 298–299
United Kingdom (UK), credit outstanding to
  households/NPISHs, 6–7
United States (US)
  credit outstanding to households/NPISHs,
    5–6
  Federal Reserve Bank, 144
  FinTech investment, 12
  loans to SMEs and farms, 64, 65
  venture capital, 12, 13
use at default, 145–146
user experience (UX) streamlining, 21

value, 197–203
  economic capital allocation, 202–203
  elements of, 197, 211
  estimation of, 197–198
  principles of valuation, 199
  risk, 199, 202–203

stochastic process, 201–202
stress testing, 200–201
valuation principles, 199
Value at Risk (VaR), 201
venture capital, 4, 11–12, 13
video rental business, 80
virtual currencies, 18
Vodafone, 17, 173
voice over P2P (VoP2P), 37–38
VoIP (Voice over Internet Protocol), 279
VoP2P *see* voice over P2P

Wells Fargo Bank, 45, 64
what-if scenarios, 110
winner-takes-all dynamics, 278
withdrawals, behavior risk, 143
wrong way risk, 169–170

yield curves, 110–111

Zopa, 29

Compiled by INDEXING SPECIALISTS (UK) Ltd., Indexing House, 306A Portland Road, Hove, East Sussex BN3 5LP United Kingdom.